INTERVENTIONS: NEW STUDIES IN MEDIEVAL CULTURE
ETHAN KNAPP, SERIES EDITOR

CHAUCER'S (ANTI-)EROTICISMS
AND THE QUEER MIDDLE AGES

Tison Pugh

THE OHIO STATE UNIVERSITY PRESS · COLUMBUS

Copyright © 2014 by The Ohio State University.
All rights reserved.

Library of Congress Cataloging-in-Publication Data
Pugh, Tison.
  Chaucer's (anti-) eroticisms and the queer Middle Ages / Tison Pugh.
    pages cm. — (New studies in Medieval culture)
  Includes bibliographical references and index.
  ISBN 978-0-8142-1264-6 (cloth : alk. paper) — ISBN 978-0-8142-9368-3 (cd)
  1. Chaucer, Geoffrey, -1400—Criticism and interpretation. 2. Homosexuality in literature. 3. Eroticism in literature. 4. Sex in literature. I. Title.
  PR1933.H66P84 2014
  821'.1—dc23

                              2014005341

Cover design by AuthorSupport.com
Text design by Juliet Williams
Type set in Goudy Old Style

∞ The paper used in this publication meets the minimum requirements of the American National Standard for Information Sciences—Permanence of Paper for Printed Library Materials. ANSI Z39.48–1992.

9 8 7 6 5 4 3 2 1

To my husband, David Dean

CONTENTS

Acknowledgments   ix

CHAPTER ONE   Introduction: Chaucer's (Anti-)Eroticisms and the
                 Queer Middle Ages   1

CHAPTER TWO   Mutual Masochism and the Hermaphroditic Courtly
                 Lady in Chaucer's *Franklin's Tale*   30

CHAPTER THREE   "For to be sworne bretheren til they deye":
                 Satirizing Queer Brotherhood in the Chaucerian Corpus   65

CHAPTER FOUR   Necrotic Erotics in Chaucerian Romance: Loving
                 Women, Loving Death, and Destroying Civilization
                 in the *Knight's Tale* and *Troilus and Criseyde* 98

CHAPTER FIVE   Queer Families in the *Canterbury Tales*: Fathers,
                 Children, and Abusive Erotics   127

CHAPTER SIX   Chaucer's (Anti-)Erotic God   169

CHAPTER SEVEN   Epilogue: Chaucer's Avian Amorousness   204

Works Cited   217

Index   237

ACKNOWLEDGMENTS

I thank Dean José Fernandez and the University of Central Florida College of Arts and Humanities for a sabbatical release that greatly facilitated the completion of this monograph. Also, two chapters of this monograph have been previously published: "'For to be sworne bretheren til they deye': Satirizing Queer Brotherhood in the Chaucerian Corpus" originally appeared in *Chaucer Review* 43.3 (2009): 282–310, and "Mutual Masochism and the Hermaphroditic Courtly Lady in Chaucer's *Franklin's Tale*" originally appeared in *Studies in the Age of Chaucer* 33 (2011): 149–81. I very much appreciate the editorial guidance of David Raybin, Susanna Fein, and David Matthews during the preparation of these essays, as well as their generosity in allowing them to be reprinted here.

CHAPTER ONE

INTRODUCTION

Chaucer's (Anti-)Eroticisms and the Queer Middle Ages

> *Who shal yeve a lovere any lawe?*
> —The Knight's Tale

Courtly knights and horny clerks, chaste young virgins and lecherous old wives, randy chickens and amorous planets: eroticism circulates throughout Geoffrey Chaucer's corpus, and as his characters pursue the fruition of their desires, they demonstrate through a mix of emotions—hope and despair, anticipation and fear, lust and longing—the ways in which pursuing one's affections exalts and debases those caught in love's throes. Norman Eliason proclaims Chaucer to be "the first [love poet] of any consequence in English and one of the finest who ever wrote,"[1] and a wide body of scholarship plumbs the influence of various amatory traditions on Chaucer's literature, particularly regarding his debt to Ovid as the premier classical poet of amatory satire, such that he is frequently dubbed the "medieval Ovid."[2] Virtually all of Chaucer's

---

1. Norman Eliason, "Chaucer the Love Poet," in *Chaucer the Love Poet*, ed. Jerome Mitchell and William Provost (Athens: University of Georgia Press, 1973), 9–26, at 9.
2. On the epithet "medieval Ovid," see, for example, Michael Calabrese, *Chaucer's Ovidian Arts of Love* (Gainesville: University Press of Florida, 1994), 1; and Daniel Sylvia et al., "Thwarted Sexuality in Chaucer's Works," *Florilegium* 3 (1981): 239–67, at 239. On Chaucer's debts to Ovid, John Fyler summarizes: "Chaucer and Ovid . . . are poets who speak for the comic pathos of human frailty and human pretensions, including those of the poet himself—emphatically human, emphatically limited, unable to rest assured in any earthly truth he discovers" (*Chaucer and Ovid* [New Haven, CT: Yale University Press, 1979], 163). The Ovidian influence on Chaucer is the subject of an important subfield of Chaucerian studies, including such additional works as Robert Hanning, *Serious Play: Desire and Au-*

major works, including the *Canterbury Tales, Troilus and Criseyde, Legend of Good Women, Book of the Duchess, House of Fame,* and *Parliament of Fowls,* address love, sexuality, and eroticism to some degree, in scenes ranging from the zealous pursuit of intercourse in his fabliaux to the complex negotiations of love and *maistrye* in his marriage tales. From a narratological perspective, love's frustrations, rather than its succors, lay the foundation for the plots of Chaucer's tales, including genres as disparate as romance, fabliau, dream vision, hagiography, and exemplum. The quest for sexual fulfillment, even if achieved by a story's end, exposes the desperate lengths to which ordinary humans will pursue erotic union, whether in momentary coupling or lifelong marriage. Furthermore, the potential continually arises for erotic pursuits to camouflage, or to be camouflaged by, the anti-erotic desires that serve as their latent counterpart, thus calling into question the very meanings of desire in Chaucer's corpus—as well as in numerous other literary, religious, and social paradigms of the Middle Ages.

(ANTI-)EROTICISMS IN THE QUEER MIDDLE AGES

Amatory pursuits at times necessitate amatory transgressions, and this simple observation resonates throughout medieval literature, much of which is predicated on the striking collision of courtly love (with its premise of adulterous—or at least nonmarital—attraction) and a Christian faith that expressly forbids such attachments. Within Chaucer's *Canterbury Tales* and other works, such transgressions of social codes of sexuality evoke analyses based on queer theoretical perspectives, those attuned to disjunctions between individual desires and social practices as articulated in multiple and contradictory discourses of the Western Middle Ages. As Arcite inquires in the *Knight's Tale* when he prepares to pursue Emily despite

---

thority in the Poetry of Ovid, Chaucer, and Ariosto (New York: Columbia University Press, 2010); Gregory Heyworth, *Desiring Bodies: Ovidian Romance and the Cult of Form* (Notre Dame, IN: University of Notre Dame Press, 2009), esp. 103–76; Robert Edwards, *The Flight from Desire: Augustine and Ovid to Chaucer* (New York: Palgrave Macmillan, 2006); Marilyn Desmond, *Ovid's Art and the Wife of Bath: The Ethics of Erotic Violence* (Ithaca, NY: Cornell University Press, 2006); Gregory Sadlek, *Idleness Working: The Discourse of Love's Labor from Ovid through Chaucer and Gower* (Washington, DC: Catholic University of America Press, 2004); and James Paxson and Cynthia Gravlee, eds., *Desiring Discourse: The Literature of Love, Ovid through Chaucer* (Selinsgrove, PA: Susquehanna University Press, 1998). For an excellent resource detailing the extent of Ovidian allusions in the *Canterbury Tales*, see Richard Hoffman, *Ovid and the* Canterbury Tales (Philadelphia: University of Pennsylvania Press, 1966).

Palamon's claims for her affections, "Who shal yeve a lovere any lawe?" (1.1164), with his words succinctly capturing the fracturing of the social order always potential when a lover pursues erotic satisfaction.[3] When love becomes divorced from the social and religious codes that ostensibly regulate it, queerness disrupts the communal order upon which love itself is founded. Gregory Hutcheson and Josiah Blackmore consider queerness in medieval culture to be "that which normativity—in this case a cultural normativity—must reject or conceal in order to exist. Its presence is always palpable in the incongruities, excesses, or anxieties of normative discourse, but it is only exceptionally given expression, and this only at the margins."[4] *Queer* need not imply homosexuality as much as a divergent stance vis-à-vis ideological normativity in matters of gender and sexuality; it is not a synonym for *homosexual* but rather a term that captures the disorienting effect of nonnormative sexual identities and their frequent clash with ideological power—of which anti-eroticisms may well be a part. Homosexuality and queerness are not intrinsically interrelated, yet they are often mutually implicated by ideological systems that link same-sex eroticism (homosexuality) with cultural disenfranchisement arising from sexuality (queerness).

Queer theory allows a broad view into the nexus of eroticism and anti-eroticism, for it showcases the ways in which either of these oppositional amatory valences can be rendered nonnormative within disparate discourses. As Jeffrey Jerome Cohen observes, "queer theory's tremendous strength is in its insistence upon the historical instability of epistemological categories, especially those involving sexuality," and he calls queer theory "the most radical challenge yet posed to the immutability of sexual identities."[5] In this light, queer theory interrogates not only homosexualities but heterosexualities as well, and extends further to consider the ways in which anti-eroticisms such as virginity and chastity alternately reinforce and subvert cultural normativity. Calvin Thomas posits that "one possible goal, then, of a straight negotiation with queer theory is ... neither to appropriate the signifier *queer* nor to

---

3. All quotations of Chaucer throughout this monograph are taken from *The Riverside Chaucer*, ed. Larry D. Benson, 3rd ed. (Boston: Houghton Mifflin, 1987).

4. Gregory Hutcheson and Josiah Blackmore, introduction to *Queer Iberia: Sexualities, Cultures, and Crossings from the Middle Ages to the Renaissance*, ed. Gregory Hutcheson and Josiah Blackmore (Durham, NC: Duke University Press, 1999), 1–19, at 3.

5. Jeffrey Jerome Cohen, *Medieval Identity Machines* (Minneapolis: University of Minnesota Press, 2003), 38, 40. Cohen offers a deft analysis of the utility of queer theory for medieval literature, 40–42.

arrogate or confiscate queer theory but rather to proliferate the findings of queer theory in unexpected ways, or at least from unexpected points of enunciation."⁶ In deploying queer theory on Chaucer's predominantly "straight" texts, ones that, for the most part, do not engage with issues of same-sex desire, *Chaucer's (Anti-)Eroticisms and the Queer Middle Ages* participates in the process of untangling the privileges and privations of heterosexual desire in medieval culture. The advantages of normative sexuality in the Middle Ages are hidden under a web of innate and internalized contradictions such that, while heteroerotic passion is lionized in much medieval thought, it is also criticized in favor of the anti-eroticism inherent in chastity and virginity. Chaucer's fictions, far removed chronologically and ideologically from a sense of homosexuality as an act that confers social and individual identity, nonetheless foreground the queer potential of human sexuality and eroticism in the various circumstances against which his various characters must react. Primarily, by investigating the ways in which (anti-)eroticisms intercede in and dismantle narratives of otherwise normative desires, this monograph advances analyses of Chaucerian sexuality to include the queer potential in desires on the border between the erotic and the anti-erotic.

As historians of medieval sexuality and theorists of ideology have amply demonstrated, an individual's erotic and sexual desires often clash with the mores and prohibitions of the social order, rendering the erotic a troubled site of conflicting desires. "Sexuality *is* culture: it is representative of a culture's religion, attitudes, taboos, and experience," argue April Harper and Caroline Proctor, and such regulations of sexual acts in no small manner define the social positions of various individuals.[7] Caution is particularly warranted in analyses of medieval sexuality because, as Pierre Payer acknowledges, "Sexuality is decidedly not [a] medieval categor[y]."[8] From this perspective, homosexuality and other modern constructions of sexuality, whether queer or not, are historically inappropriate hermeneutics for assessing medieval gender and sexuality. Despite the potentially anachronistic examinations of the Middle Ages that these categories create, it is no less illuminating—and often more so—to examine the past

---

6. Calvin Thomas, "Straight with a Twist: Queer Theory and the Subject of Heterosexuality," in *Straight with a Twist: Queer Theory and the Subject of Heterosexuality*, ed. Calvin Thomas (Urbana: University of Illinois Press, 2000), 11–44, at 30.

7. April Harper and Caroline Proctor, eds., *Medieval Sexuality: A Casebook* (New York: Routledge, 2008), 2; italics in original.

8. Pierre Payer, *The Bridling of Desire: Views of Sex in the Later Middle Ages* (Toronto: University of Toronto Press, 1993), 15.

through interpretive frameworks alien to it. Michel Foucault's excurses on the relationship between ideology and desire have alerted scholars of medieval culture to the ways in which sexuality is a conflicted category, and thus the need for the protean constructions of sexuality within a given society to be analyzed within their own historical conditions.[9] The Western medieval world lacked a hermeneutic sense of homosexuality *contra* heterosexuality as a defining feature of an individual's identity, yet this predominantly Christian culture faced continuous struggles in defining the proper role of love and eroticism for its people.[10]

---

9. See Michel Foucault, *The History of Sexuality*, trans. Robert Hurley, composed of three volumes: *An Introduction* (1978; New York: Vintage, 1990); *The Use of Pleasure* (1985; New York: Vintage, 1990); and *The Care of the Self* (New York: Vintage, 1988). See also Thomas Laqueur, *Making Sex: Body and Gender from the Greeks to Freud* (Cambridge, MA: Harvard University Press, 1990), for his study of various historical constructions of sex and sexuality, particularly regarding the distinction between the one-sex and two-sex models. For medieval constructions of sexuality, see Karma Lochrie, Peggy McCracken, and James A. Schultz, eds., *Constructing Medieval Sexuality* (Minneapolis: University of Minnesota Press, 1997); and Jacqueline Murray and Konrad Eisenbichler, eds., *Desire and Discipline: Sex and Sexuality in the Premodern West* (Toronto: University of Toronto Press), 1996.

10. For the foundational study of medieval homosexuality, see John Boswell's *Christianity, Social Tolerance, and Homosexuality: Gay People in Western Europe from the Beginning of the Christian Era to the Fourteenth Century* (Chicago: University of Chicago Press, 1981). Boswell's monumental work on classical and medieval homosexuality has drawn numerous criticisms, notably for his use of modern terminology to describe classical and medieval sexualities; see, for example, the essayists in Matthew Kuefler, ed., *The Boswell Thesis: Essays on Christianity, Social Tolerance, and Homosexuality* (Chicago: University of Chicago Press, 2006). Nonetheless, the breadth of his analysis amply proves his central thesis concerning the relatively unremarkable reactions to homoeroticism in various discourses of these periods. Additional relevant studies of medieval sexuality and same-sex desire include Michael Goodich, *The Unmentionable Vice: Homosexuality in the Later Medieval Period* (Santa Barbara, CA: ABC-Clio, 1979); Mark Jordan, *The Invention of Sodomy in Christian Theology* (Chicago: University of Chicago Press, 1997); Allen Frantzen, *Before the Closet: Same-Sex Love from Beowulf to Angels in America* (Chicago: University of Chicago Press, 1998); Carolyn Dinshaw, *Getting Medieval: Sexualities and Communities, Pre- and Postmodern* (Durham, NC: Duke University Press, 1999); Glenn Burger and Steven Kruger, eds., *Queering the Middle Ages* (Minneapolis: University of Minnesota Press, 2001); William Burgwinkle, *Sodomy, Masculinity, and Law in Medieval Literature: France and England, 1050–1230* (Cambridge: Cambridge University Press, 2004); Anna Klosowska, *Queer Love in the Middle Ages* (New York: Palgrave Macmillan, 2005); Karma Lochrie, *Heterosyncrasies: Female Sexuality When Normal Wasn't* (Minneapolis: University of Minnesota Press, 2005); James A. Schultz, *Courtly Love, the Love of Courtliness, and the History of Sexuality* (Chicago: University of Chicago Press, 2006); David Clark, *Between Medieval Men: Male Friendship and Desire in Early Medieval English Literature* (Oxford: Oxford University Press, 2009); and Glenn W. Olsen, *Of Sodomites, Effeminates, Hermaphrodites, and Androgynes: Sodomy in the Age of Peter Damian* (Toronto: Pontifical Institute of Mediaeval Studies, 2011).

The difficulty of identifying medieval sexual normativity arises from the traditions that condemned apparently normative sexualities in favor of a range of behaviors that can be conjointly termed anti-erotic. Karma Lochrie points out the inherent contradictions between modern and medieval conceptions of sexual normativity:

> Desire for someone of the opposite sex in modern norm-speak is natural or normal because it is the most widespread sexual practice and, secondarily, because of religious ideology that is likewise dependent on the concept of norms. Desire for someone of the opposite sex in medieval nature-speak is natural in the corrupted sense of resulting from the Fall, but it is not in any sense legitimated by its widespread practice or idealized as a personal or cultural goal.[11]

Within medieval traditions of love and eroticism, the Christian Church encouraged the faithful to adopt the anti-eroticism of chastity in accordance with Paul's injunctions: "dico autem non nuptis et viduis bonum est illis si sic maneant sicut et ego. quod si non se continent nubant melius est enim nubere quam uri" (1 Corinthians 7:8–9; "But I say to the unmarried, and to the widows: It is good for them if they so continue, even as I. But if they do not contain themselves, let them marry. For it is better to marry than to be burnt").[12] He also declares, in a similar vein, "volo autem vos sine sollicitudine esse qui sine uxore est sollicitus est quae Domini sunt quomodo placeat Deo. Qui autem cum uxore est sollicitus est quae sunt mundi quomodo placeat uxori et divisus est" (1 Corinthians 7:32–33; "But I would have you to be without solicitude. He that is without a wife, is solicitous for the things that belong to the Lord, how he may please God. But he that is with a wife, is solicitous for the things of the world, how he may please his wife: and he is divided"). Within Pauline thought, anti-erotic identities (virgins, bachelors) marked by chastity and sexual temperance are preferred over those identities (husbands, wives) defined partially by the erotic activities expected in marriage. Paul's words on anti-eroticism reverberated throughout the Middle Ages such that, in the late eleventh century, Pope Gregory VII categorized all Christians according to their erotic status: "Preterea uniuersus catholice ecclesie cetus aut uirgines sunt aut continentes aut coniuges. Quicumque ergo extra hos tres ordines reperitur, inter filios ecclesie siue intra christiane religionis limites non

---

11. Karma Lochrie, *Heterosyncrasies*, xxiii.

12. Biblical quotations are taken from *Biblia sacra iuxta vulgatam versionem* (Stuttgart: Deutsche Bibelgesellschaft, 1994); translations are from *Holy Bible: Douay-Rheims Version* (Charlotte, NC: Tan, 2009).

numeratur" ("Moreover the whole company of the catholic church are either virgins or chaste or married. Whoever stands outside these three orders is not numbered amongst the sons of the church or within the bounds of the Christian religion").[13] In this simplistic yet universal assessment of the sex lives of the faithful, only three identities are licit, and only married people are permitted to act on their sexual drives.

The lines between licit and illicit sexualities shift in varying theological discourses, however, for as much as abstinence and virginity stood as medieval cultural ideals within the Christian church, the propagation of humanity, quite obviously, depends on intercourse (within the bounds of marriage from this cultural perspective). As Chaucer's Wife of Bath tartly attests in her argument against virginity: "For hadde God comanded maydenhede, / Thanne hadde he dampned weddyng with the dede" (3.69–70). Due to the necessity of intercourse, marital eroticism was accommodated within religious worldviews, and, as Payer notes, medieval theologians justified intercourse on four primary grounds—"to have children, to pay the marriage debt, to avoid fornication, [and] to satisfy lust or for the sake of pleasure."[14] Their ambivalence on the subject of human sexuality is recorded as well, such as in Augustine's ruminations over marriage, in which he accords a place for intercourse while condemning the "evil of lust":

> Marriage has also this good, that carnal or youthful incontinence, even if it is bad, is turned to the honorable task of begetting children, so that marital intercourse makes something good out of the evil of lust. . . . There is the added fact that, in the very debt which married persons owe each other, even if they demand its payment somewhat intemperately and incontinently, they owe fidelity equally to each other.[15]

Expressing his disapproval of eroticism, Augustine imagines couples engaging in intercourse "intemperately and incontinently," yet he can justify such sexual exuberance if it cements the fidelity the couple pledges in marriage.

---

13. Pope Gregory VII, "To Bishop Otto of Constance," in *The Epistolae Vagantes of Pope Gregory VII*, ed. and trans. H. E. J. Cowdrey (Oxford: Clarendon, 1972), 18–23, at 20–21.

14. Pierre Payer, *The Bridling of Desire*, 62. For studies of the necessity of accommodating sexuality into the medieval worldview, see Joan Cadden, *Meanings of Sex Difference in the Middle Ages* (Cambridge: Cambridge University Press, 1993), esp. "Is Sex Necessary? The Problem of Sexual Abstinence," 259–77; and Ruth Karras, *Sexuality in Medieval Europe: Doing unto Others* (New York: Routledge, 2005), esp. "The Sexuality of Chastity," 28–58.

15. Augustine, *St. Augustine on Marriage and Sexuality*, ed. Elizabeth Clark (Washington, DC: Catholic University of America Press, 1996), 46.

Numerous medieval writers echo Augustine's cautions against eroticism, abjuring their readers to abstain from its pleasures while acknowledging its necessity, as well as its likelihood. For instance, Thomas Aquinas concedes that "the marriage act that is done out of sensuous pleasure is a lesser sin,"[16] yet the pleasures of eroticism implicate even marital lovemaking as a transgression.

These strands of anti-eroticism in Christian thought and medieval social practice denigrated love and its enactments, rendering the erotic a vexed sphere of activity and of inactivity, of pleasure and its disavowal, all the while circulating around the concept of love. Chaucer's Parson echoes the views of Paul, Augustine, and Aquinas in his "Remedium contra peccatum Luxurie":

> Thanne shal men understonde that for thre thynges a man and his wyf flesshly mowen assemble. The firste is in entente of engendrure of children to the service of God, for certes that is the cause final of matrimoyne. Another cause is to yelden everyich of hem to oother the dette of hire bodies, for neither of hem hath power of his owene body. The thridde is for to eschewe leccherye and vileynye. The ferthe is for sothe deedly synne. (10.939–40)

Sufficiently versed in clerical injunctions to voice them through his Parson, Chaucer recognized his religion's long history of strictures against eroticism, as much as he surely recognized that their narrative reper-

---

16. Thomas Aquinas, *The Summa Theologica of St. Thomas Aquinas, Second Part of the Second Part, QQ. CXLI–CLXX*, trans. Fathers of the English Dominican Province (New York: Benziger Brothers, 1921), 138. In addition to the studies of Payer, Cadden, and Karras cited previously, studies of medieval love and eroticism pertinent to the theoretical foundations of this monograph include C. Stephen Jaeger, *Ennobling Love: In Search of a Lost Sensibility* (Philadelphia: University of Pennsylvania Press, 1999); Lara Farina, *Erotic Discourse and Early English Religious Writing* (New York: Palgrave Macmillan, 2006); and Cary Howie, *Claustrophilia: The Erotics of Enclosure in Medieval Literature* (New York: Palgrave Macmillan, 2007). See also such classics in the field as C. S. Lewis, *The Allegory of Love: A Study in Medieval Tradition* (Oxford: Oxford University Press, 1936), and Denis de Rougemont, *Love in the Western World*, trans. Montgomery Belgion (1940; New York: Pantheon, 1956). The field of medieval sexuality studies owes much to the foundational work of Vern Bullough and James Brundage, including their *Sexual Practices and the Medieval Church* (Buffalo, NY: Prometheus, 1982) and *Handbook of Medieval Sexuality* (New York: Garland, 1996), as well as Brundage's *Law, Sex, and Christian Society in Medieval Europe* (Chicago: University of Chicago Press, 1990). Martha Brozyna's *Gender and Sexuality in the Middle Ages: A Medieval Source Documents Reader* (Jefferson, NC: McFarland, 2005) provides an excellent overview of primary sources.

cussions would be stifling. Narrative theory posits that some type of transgression is a likely starting point for much literature, and many of Chaucer's tales counterbalance the anti-eroticism endorsed in much medieval thought through pursuits of desire fracturing the already tenuous borderlines between approved and disapproved eroticisms. While Chaucer would not have labeled such narrative strategies as queer, as neither would the classical and contemporary poets from whom he drew inspiration for style and subject matter, queer theory illuminates the disjunction between licit and illicit portrayals of desire within his fictions. The dialogic relationships between eroticism and anti-eroticism undermine the very discourses that proclaim their respective merits, rendering literary treatments of the erotic as queer sites of conflicting desires.

Despite the many clerical and scholastic injunctions discouraging eroticism, the people of the Middle Ages glorified love and its expression as the most ennobling of passions in a variety of venues, yet even here the complementary force of anti-eroticism often arises. For example, Dante's praise of love, "dicimus illud esse maxime delectabile quod per pretiosissimum obiectum appetitus delectate: hoc autem venus est" ("here I say that what is most pleasurable is what is the most highly valued object of our desires; and this is love"), appears, with its focus on pleasure, to endorse eroticism unabashedly.[17] Building from this foundation, his portrayals of Beatrice in *La Vita Nuova* and *Divina Commedia* illustrate the power of erotic attraction to guide one's soul. Nonetheless, in most instances in which medieval poets address love, the lines between the amatory, the erotic, and the anti-erotic can be fine ones indeed, and Robert Edwards explicates how, for Dante, amatory pursuits flirt with transgressions, in that "love . . . offers a framework of conventions for expression and reception, for coding and uncoding, within which desire speaks obliquely, as by definition it must."[18] Erotic attractions frequently carry with them a frisson of transgression, and because so many medieval discourses castigate eroticism and extol anti-eroticism, voices such as Dante's that celebrate love must often address their subject through codes, obfuscations, and apologies.

Many medieval treatments of eroticism, extolling desire in heartfelt tones yet muddling its expression, evince affinities with the precepts of courtly love promulgated by Andreas Capellanus in his *De Amore*. This

---

17. Dante Alighieri, *De vulgari eloquentia*, ed. and trans. Steven Botterill (Cambridge: Cambridge University Press, 1996), 2.2.7, at 52–53.

18. Robert Edwards, *The Flight from Desire*, 2.

text, which continually teeters between irony and instruction, exalts love as the necessary suffering that catalyzes desire:

> Amor est passio quaedam innata procedens ex visione et immoderata cogitatione formae alterius sexus, ob quam aliquis super omnia cupit alterius potiri amplexibus et omnia de utriusque voluntate in ipsius amplexu amoris praecepta compleri.[19]

> Love is a certain inborn suffering derived from the sight of and excessive meditation upon the beauty of the opposite sex, which causes each one to wish above all things the embraces of the other and by common desire to carry out all of love's precepts in the other's embrace.[20]

Andreas rejects his celebration of love in his excursus's third book to praise anti-erotic asceticism instead, but his theories of love nonetheless play out in numerous medieval narratives, particularly in the romance tradition. As C. Stephen Jaeger demonstrates, many medieval conceptions of love distilled—or attempted to distill—the erotic from the amatory in a like manner. In his interpretation of medieval amatory writings, he concludes, "The dilemma of romantic love is created by the tensions between sexuality and an ideal of virtuous love. In order to ennoble, love had to be a subject of virtue; it had to derive from virtue and in some sense also to be its source."[21] Ruth Karras likewise urges caution in assessing medieval depictions of eroticism and carnality from a modern perspective: "While for us the erotic equates with the carnal, for many medieval thinkers the erotic, to the extent it overlapped with the spiritual, was opposed to the carnal."[22] The flimsy borders between the erotic and the carnal allow anti-eroticism to seep into discourses of eroticism, and it is this juncture where eroticisms and anti-eroticisms converge that I focus on as a primary location of queerness in the Middle Ages. Who, indeed, can give a lover any law, when anti-eroticisms stand as preferred enactments of human sexuality in much of the Middle Ages? By the very

---

19. Andreas Capellanus, *De Amore*, ed. E. Trojel (Havniae: In Libraria Gadiana, 1892), 3.

20. Andreas Capellanus, *The Art of Courtly Love*, trans. John Jay Parry (New York: Columbia University Press, 1960), 28.

21. C. Stephen Jaeger, *Ennobling Love*, 7.

22. Ruth Karras, *Sexuality in Medieval Europe*, 57. See also Caroline Walker Bynum, *Fragmentation and Redemption: Essays on Gender and the Human Body in Medieval Religion* (New York: Zone, 1991), esp. 79–117, for her argument against interpreting medieval sexuality and eroticism through modern expectations.

nature of being a lover in the Middle Ages, particularly if one is unmarried, one transgresses numerous religious doctrines, and so the possibility of love without transgression is rendered an ever more elusive goal.

A further interpretive difficulty in examining medieval eroticism arises in the disjunction between the obvious physical markers of the subject—the human body in or in pursuit of sexual congress—and the obfuscating discourses that couch texts addressing love and sexuality in allegorical, elliptical, ironic, satiric, or otherwise hazily anti-erotic frameworks. The conclusion of Boccaccio's *Decameron* illustrates the ways in which eroticism, if not carnality, may be resignified at a narrative's end, imposing an anti-erotic theme on a text boundlessly exploring the pleasures of eros. After Dioneo tells the collection's final story, the king appends a moral that reinterprets the meaning of the many erotic and ribald tales: "For, as far as I have been able to observe, albeit the tales related here have been amusing, perhaps of a sort to stimulate carnal desire, . . . neither in word nor in deed nor in any other respect have I known either you or ourselves to be worthy of censure."[23] Boccaccio revels in narrative carnality throughout his fictions, only to curtail this frisson of pleasure by rejecting his numerous erotic plots and themes as he draws the collection to a close: the audience of the tales, both textually and metatextually, is preserved from the contaminating influence of their sexually charged narrative play. As mentioned previously, so too does Andreas Capellanus recant the erotic lessons of *De Amore* when he appeals to his friend Walter to dismiss the pursuit of sexual satisfaction:

> Taliter igitur praesentem lege libellum, non quasi per ipsum quaerens amantium tibi assumere vitam, sed ut eius doctrina refectus et mulierum edoctus ad amandum animos provocare a tali provocatione abstinendo praemium consequaris aeternum et maiori ex hoc apud Deum merearis munere gloriari.[24]

> Read this little book, then, not as one seeking to take up the life of a lover, but that, invigorated by the theory and trained to excite the minds of women to love, you may, by refraining from so doing, win an eternal recompense and thereby deserve a greater reward from God.[25]

---

23. Giovanni Boccaccio, *The Decameron*, trans. G. H. McWilliam (Harmondsworth, UK: Penguin, 1972), 825.
24. Andreas Capellanus, *De Amore*, 314.
25. Andreas Capellanus, *The Art of Courtly Love*, 187.

Following this convoluted logic, learning seductive and erotic techniques enhances one's holiness, but only when one recants the pleasures arising from such amatory instruction. From a queer theoretical perspective, such rhetorical posturing disrupts the social construction of sexual normativity, for Boccaccio's and Andreas's texts revel in transgression only then to recode such transgressions as appropriate within the very discourses that would castigate them.

Within this medieval world of sexual injunctions and literary play, in which eroticisms and anti-eroticisms confront each other at a loggerheads of desire rendered queer through their mutual unintelligibility, and echoing Boccaccio's and Andreas's apologies for their narratives' investments in carnality, Chaucer famously exonerates those "tales of Caunterbury . . . that sownen into synne" in his retraction (10.1085). The most likely candidates that fit this description are Chaucer's fabliaux, but it would be unwise to circumscribe his apology solely to these tales of erotic immoderation. In this passage concluding the *Canterbury Tales*, Chaucer makes clear his realization that his narratives transgressing Christian teachings might offend certain readers, as he also makes the dubious claim that he merely follows biblical injunctions: "For oure book seith, 'Al that is writen is writen for oure doctrine,' and that is myn entente" (10.1082). Echoing and blatantly misappropriating Paul's statement "quaecumque enim scripta sunt ad nostrum doctrinam scripta sunt" (Romans 15:4; "For what things soever were written, were written for our learning"), Chaucer proposes the moral value of his tales, whether ribald or devout, yet provides readers with strikingly little evidence to suspect that any such morality is indeed located within the bawdier narratives.[26] Interpreting the moral lessons afforded by such tales as the Miller's, Reeve's, Merchant's, and Shipman's in line with Christian teachings on sexual morality would tax even the most creative of exegetes, and thus, through their very presence in the *Canterbury Tales*, Chaucer's narratives that "sownen into synne" map out the queer narrative tensions between eroticism and anti-eroticism, with the former providing the necessary humor, allure, and excitement to generate literary pleasure, and the latter redirecting this play to moral ends, yet ultimately in an equally pleasurable manner. The erotic politics percolating throughout Chaucer's fictions proves the unlikelihood of quarantining sexuality from his non-fabliau tales as well,

---

26. On the difficulties readers have faced in uniting Chaucer's literary achievements with his bawdy fictions, see Donald Green, "Chaucer as Nuditarian: The Erotic as a Critical Problem," *Pacific Coast Philology* 18.1–2 (1983): 59–69.

yet the spiritual and narrative pleasure of such anti-eroticism can never be divorced from the full scope of Chaucer's literary play.

CHAUCER'S (ANTI-)EROTICISMS, OR, WAS CHAUCER QUEER?

If taken literally, the above subheading is silly, for one cannot know the intimate desires of a man dead for over six hundred years, and neither would this information affect in any measurable manner contemporary readers' pleasure in his texts.[27] In light of the commingling of sex, desire, and anti-eroticism in his fictions, it is nonetheless intriguing to consider Chaucer's own relationship to love and its disappointments, yet the scant evidence from Chaucer's sexual biography does little to illuminate the treatment of eroticism in his literature.[28] The historical record notes his marriage to Philippa de Roet in 1366, but the extant documents cannot enlighten our understanding of its tenor, which, as Donald Howard muses, "may have been anything from a tender idyll to an open war."[29] Longstanding rumors allege that Philippa was John of Gaunt's mistress, and thus that Chaucer was, perhaps knowingly, cuckolded, but evidence for these claims is tenuous.[30] Surviving records also indicate that Geoffrey and Philippa produced at least four children—Thomas, Lewis, Elizabeth, and Agnes—but the fact that the marriage was consummated and generated offspring provides little insight into its dynamics. The vexed question of Cecilia

---

27. Numerous postmodern theorists have proclaimed the "death of the author" as a topic for literary analysis, but, despite the hoary edges to biographical criticism, Seán Burke calls for critics to investigate texts in relation to their "situated authorship" and to explore the author for the fact that she or he is *"the principle of specificity in a world of texts."* Burke proceeds to argue, "far from consolidating the notion of a universal or unitary subject, the retracing of the work to its author is a working-back to historical, cultural and political embeddedness" (*The Death and Return of the Author: Criticism and Subjectivity in Barthes, Foucault, and Derrida*, 2nd ed. [Edinburgh: Edinburgh University Press, 1998], 202).

28. The definitive biography of Chaucer is Donald Howard, *Chaucer: His Life, His Works, His World* (New York: Dutton, 1987); see also John Gardner, *The Life and Times of Chaucer* (New York: Vintage, 1978); Richard West, *Chaucer, 1340–1400: The Life and Times of the First English Poet* (New York: Carroll & Graf, 2000); and D. S. Brewer, *The World of Chaucer* (Cambridge: Brewer, 2000).

29. Donald Howard, *Chaucer*, 95.

30. On Philippa's relationship with Gaunt, see Donald Howard, *Chaucer*, 342–44, and John Gardner, *The Life and Times of Chaucer*, 160–62. Howard dismisses allegations of Philippa's adultery, tersely advising his readers, "You can believe [these allegations], if you want" (342).

Chaumpaigne's accusation of *raptus* against Chaucer, a charge indicative either of rape or of kidnapping but a charge from which she later exonerated Chaucer from all responsibility, further complicates any coherent vision of his erotic life.[31]

The historical record cannot be distilled for more than the barest insights into Chaucer's views of marital and extramarital erotics, nor do his fictions illuminate his amatory experiences beyond shadowy outlines. Readers see hints of Chaucer's desires in his poetry, such as in "Lenvoy de Chaucer a Scogan," in which he sighs over the unfulfilled desires of aging men:

> Now, certes, frend, I dreed of thyn unhap,
> Lest for thy gilt the wreche of Love procede
> On alle hem that been hoor and rounde of shap,
> That ben so lykly folk in love to spede. (29–33)

One can read these lines in numerous ways: a humorous wink to desires long past but warmly remembered; a piquant and ironic jab at aging men who fail to act in accordance with the wisdom ostensibly congruent with their age; or even a rueful lament adumbrating erotic despair. Much as Chaucer's recurrent hints at his immoderate girth do not give us a clear picture of his physical appearance,[32] these lines in "Lenvoy de Chaucer a Scogan" do little to illuminate Chaucer's views of the erotic and its disappointments. The poems "To Rosemounde" and "Womanly Noblesse" respectively register Chaucer's regret that Rosemounde offers him no dalliance (8, 16, 24)

---

31. For the historical account of this event, see Martin Crow and Clair Olson, eds., *Chaucer Life Records* (Austin: University of Texas Press, 1966), 343. For discussions of rape and its repercussions on Chaucer's life and literature, see Christopher Cannon, "*Raptus* in the Chaumpaigne Release and a Newly Discovered Document Concerning the Life of Geoffrey Chaucer," *Speculum* 68 (1993): 79–94, as well as his "Chaucer and Rape: Uncertainty's Certainties," *Studies in the Age of Chaucer* 22 (2000): 67–92. Additional studies include Carolyn Dinshaw, "Rivalry, Rape, and Manhood: Gower and Chaucer," in *Violence against Women in Medieval Texts*, ed. Anna Roberts (Gainesville: University Press of Florida, 1998), 137–60; Christine Rose, "Reading Chaucer, Reading Rape," in *Representing Rape in Medieval and Early Modern Literature*, ed. Elizabeth Robertson and Christine Rose (New York: Palgrave, 2001), 21–60; Suzanne Edwards, "The Rhetoric of Rape and the Politics of Gender in the *Wife of Bath's Tale* and the 1382 Statute of Rapes," *Exemplaria* 23.1 (2011): 3–26; and Richard Firth Green, "Cecily Champain v. Geoffrey Chaucer: A New Look at an Old Dispute," in *Law and Sovereignty in the Middle Ages and Renaissance*, ed. Robert Sturges (Turnhout: Brepols, 2011), 261–85.

32. For Chaucer's references to his girth, see *Sir Thopas* 7.700–701 and *House of Fame* 574.

and that his beloved will not alleviate his amatory suffering (22–23), but these poems' deployments of the standard tropes of love-longing fail to enlighten his personal sense of the erotic. Neither have scholars yet ascertained to whom, if to any actual woman, they were addressed, especially given their formulaic adherence to the expected tropes of amatory verse. In a similar vein, Craig Davis observes the structural similarities between Chaucer's marriage to Philippa and Arveragus's marriage to Dorigen in the *Franklin's Tale,* in which "a socially inferior husband marries up in the world: above his own *rank* in the case of the knight Arveragus, above his own *estate* or *class* in the case of Geoffrey Chaucer," and hypothesizes that the tale "shows us that perfect marriages can be just as fraught emotionally as any other kind."[33] These fictive glimpses into Chaucer's desires pique more than sate one's curiosity, and we are left with an erotic biography that can only remain conjectural beyond the skeletal outline of a man who married a woman and fathered children but who wrote continually of love's vagaries in his fictions.

If the preceding thumbnail portrait of Chaucer's erotic life sketches him as a medieval male with heteronormative sexual desires presumably sated in marriage, his narrative stances vis-à-vis his fictions nonetheless allow for, if not encourage, queer readings of sex, eroticism, and sexuality.[34]

---

33. Craig Davis, "A Perfect Marriage on the Rocks: Geoffrey and Philippa Chaucer, and the *Franklin's Tale,*" *Chaucer Review* 37.2 (2002): 129–44, at 129 and 142; italics in original.

34. Studies of Chaucer, sexuality, and gender that inform this study include Carolyn Dinshaw, *Chaucer's Sexual Poetics* (Madison: University of Wisconsin Press, 1989); Elaine Tuttle Hansen, *Chaucer and the Fictions of Gender* (Berkeley: University of California Press, 1992); Susan Crane, *Gender and Romance in Chaucer's* Canterbury Tales (Princeton, NJ: Princeton University Press, 1994); Angela Jane Weisl, *Conquering the Reign of Femeny: Gender and Genre in Chaucer's Romance* (Cambridge: Brewer, 1995); Anne Laskaya, *Chaucer's Approach to Gender in the* Canterbury Tales (Cambridge: Brewer, 1995); Jane Chance, *The Mythographic Chaucer: The Fabulation of Sexual Politics* (Minneapolis: University of Minnesota Press, 1995); Catherine Cox, *Gender and Language in Chaucer* (Gainesville: University Press of Florida, 1997); Peter Beidler, ed., *Men and Masculinities in Chaucer: Approaches to Maleness in the* Canterbury Tales *and* Troilus and Criseyde (Cambridge: Brewer, 1998); Robert Sturges, *Chaucer's Pardoner and Gender Theory: Bodies of Discourse* (New York: St. Martin's, 2000); Jill Mann, *Feminizing Chaucer* (Cambridge: Brewer, 2002); Glenn Burger, *Chaucer's Queer Nation* (Minneapolis: University of Minnesota Press, 2003); Richard Zeikowitz, *Homoeroticism and Chivalry: Discourses of Male Same-Sex Desire in the Fourteenth Century* (New York: Palgrave Macmillan, 2003); Mark Miller, *Philosophical Chaucer: Love, Sex, and Agency in the* Canterbury Tales (Cambridge: Cambridge University Press, 2004); Susan Schibanoff, *Chaucer's Queer Poetics: Rereading the Dream Trio* (Toronto: University of Toronto Press, 2006); Alcuin Blamires, *Chaucer, Ethics, and Gender* (Oxford: Oxford University Press, 2006); Holly Crocker, *Chaucer's Visions of Manhood* (New York: Palgrave Macmillan, 2007); and John Pitcher, *Chaucer's Feminine Subjects: Figures of Desire in the* Canterbury Tales

Modeling the subversive erotic potential in his fictions, Chaucer embodies for his readers the disorienting effects of narrative desire through his assumption of queer stances in and toward his tales. In their landmark queer-theory studies of Chaucer's literature, Susan Schibanoff describes Chaucer's relationship to his fictions as "the queer artist who wears passivity over his agency, who claims outsider status even as he stands at the centre of his work,"35 and Glenn Burger reads "Chaucer within his queer nation" to find "the perverse dynamic at work within the *Canterbury Tales.*"36 As Schibanoff and Burger astutely demonstrate throughout their readings, Chaucer assumes such a willfully conflicted position to his narration throughout his fictions, notably when he refutes responsibility for his own literature in the *General Prologue*:

> Whoso shal telle a tale after a man,
> He moot reherce as ny as evere he kan
> Everich a word, if it be in his charge,
> Al speke he never so rudeliche and large,
> Or ellis he moot telle his tale untrewe,
> Or feyne thyng, or fynde wordes newe. (1.731–36)

Chaucer does not address sexuality or eroticism in these lines, yet they license him to speak of any taboo topic he might desire. As Laura Kendrick explains, "What enabled [Chaucer's] rebellious and revitalizing discovery of forbidden desires, his undoing of the censoring artifices of the authoritative, ritualized text, were these metatextual, contextual denials of reality or seriousness: festive time, laughter, and the foolish persona that was patently *not himself*."37 In a similar vein, Geoffrey Gust observes the

---

(New York: Palgrave Macmillan, 2012). It should be noted as well that this monograph continues my efforts to think through the queer ramifications of Chaucer's fictions, as evident in chapters of my previous monographs: "Chaucer's Queering Fabliaux" and "Queer Desires and Queering Genres in Chaucer's *Troilus and Criseyde*," in *Queering Medieval Genres* (New York: Palgrave Macmillan, 2004), 45–106, and "Queering Harry Bailly: Gendered Carnival, Social Ideologies, and Masculinity under Duress in the *Canterbury Tales*" and "'He nedes moot unto the pley assente': Queer Fidelities and Contractual Hermaphroditism in Chaucer's *Clerk's Tale*," in *Sexuality and Its Queer Discontents in Middle English Literature* (New York: Palgrave Macmillan, 2008), 49–99.

 35. Susan Schibanoff, *Chaucer's Queer Poetics*, 308.
 36. Glenn Burger, *Chaucer's Queer Nation*, xvii.
 37. Laura Kendrick, *Chaucerian Play: Comedy and Control in the* Canterbury Tales (Berkeley: University of California Press, 1988), 32–33; italics in original. On Chaucerian game and play, see also Carl Lindahl, *Earnest Games: Folkloric Patterns in the* Canterbury Tales (Bloomington: Indiana University Press, 1987).

ways in which Chaucer's "seeming presence" within his literature "is a kind of narrative mirage, inconsistent and unreliable."[38] Through his multiple performances of author, narrator, fabulist, and pilgrim, Chaucer liberates himself to address sexuality as both game and as earnest, as both erotic and anti-erotic, in which play spreads truths to medieval society while these truths are safely preserved from opprobrium under a ludic guise. Here then arises the potential for Chaucer's narrative queerness, in that the multiple and converging layers of discourse—with Chaucer as narrator and as observer, with the text as game and as play—destabilize hermeneutic stability and, indeed, authorial culpability, as he addresses the border between erotic desires and their willful abandonment.

Beyond this authorial posturing that preserves him from any cultural repercussions arising from his own works, as if he did not control precisely the unfolding of his fictions, Chaucer metaphorically queers himself as author while further encoding himself in them in a humorous scene in the *House of Fame*. When he queries the eagle sent to snatch him to the heavens, "Wher Joves wol me stellyfye, / Or what thing may this sygnifye?" (2.586–87), Chaucer aligns himself with the homoerotic archetype Ganymede while simultaneously refusing to acknowledge their parallels. John Boswell affirms that Ganymede was used virtually "as a synonym for 'gay'" in medieval literature, noting the prevalence of Jove's cupbearer in homoerotic literature in the classical era as well.[39] Chaucer, however, denies any affiliation between Ganymede's erotic service to Jupiter and his own divine conscription:

"I neyther am Ennok, ne Elye,
Ne Romulus, ne Ganymede,
That was ybore up, as men rede,
To hevene with daun Jupiter,
And mad the goddys botiller." (2.588–92)

The multiple denials—that Chaucer in this moment of divine rapture does not represent Enoch, Elijah, Romulus, or Ganymede—stretch the bounds of the reader's credulity, for Chaucer addresses his place in the literary tradition in the *House of Fame*, only here to deny any kinship with these four figures from the Hebrew Bible and classical mythology.[40]

---

38. Geoffrey Gust, *Constructing Chaucer: Author and Autofiction in the Critical Tradition* (New York: Palgrave Macmillan, 2009), 1.

39. John Boswell, *Christianity, Social Tolerance, and Homosexuality*, 245.

40. For excellent studies of Chaucer's treatment of the literary tradition in *House of*

Chaucer's denial is all the more unconvincing in that he lists four such figures elevated to the heavens, yet elaborates only on Ganymede's journey (and duties) in any detail. In reading the myth of Ganymede, Jane Chance suggests that "Ganymede's rape by Jove's eagle implies anagogically transcendent ravishment,"[41] and Chaucer envisions himself undergoing such a rapturous metamorphosis, one that simultaneously allegorizes his poetic mission to Dante's. Schibanoff observes of this scene, "Regardless of Jove's intentions, Geffrey's thoughts of stellification clearly project his own imagined ravishment. . . . Geffrey is associated with the Dante who dreamed himself Ganymede on the border between Inferno and Purgatory."[42] The queer figure of Ganymede allows Chaucer (and Dante before him) to comment on his place in the poetic tradition: he is ravished by divine insight to utter the wonders of the ineffable, but he must conquer this impossible task through his transcendent yet queer vision of himself and his fictions that both sets him apart from and ensconces himself within the literary tradition. In this light, Chaucer's deployment of the Ganymede legend registers as both erotic and anti-erotic, for he calls upon this literary tradition of divinely homoerotic concupiscence while denying its sexual relevance to himself. Seeking to enjoy the privileges both of divine rapture and of literary kinship with Dante, Chaucer relies on a homoerotic tradition while resignifying its sexual valence as anti-erotic. Authors cannot strip their allusions of all registers, and the traces of eroticism and desire left behind in Chaucer's allusion to Ganymede inflect him with their queer edges, no matter his denials.

And such is the crux of erotic, narrative, and all other desires: to desire is always to desire again, to confront the anti-erotic counterbalanc-

---

Fame, see Glenn Steinberg, "Chaucer in the Field of Cultural Production: Humanism, Dante, and the *House of Fame*," *Chaucer Review* 35.2 (2000): 182–203; Ivan Cañadas, "The Shadow of Virgil and Augustus on Chaucer's *House of Fame*," *Medieval and Early Modern English Studies* 18.1 (2010): 57–79; and John Kerr, "The Underworld of Chaucer's *House of Fame*: Virgil, Claudian, and Dante," in *Medieval and Renaissance Humanism: Rhetoric, Representation, and Form*, ed. Stephen Gersh and Bert Roest (Leiden: Brill, 2003), 185–202.

41. Jane Chance, *The Mythographic Chaucer*, 123–24.

42. Susan Schibanoff, *Chaucer's Queer Poetics*, 158–59. For a detailed analysis of eagle symbolism in medieval literature, see John Steadman, "Chaucer's Eagle: A Contemplative Symbol," *PMLA* 75.3 (1960): 153–59; for Dante's use of eagle symbolism, see Warren Ginsberg, "Dante's Dream of the Eagle and Jacob's Ladder," *Dante Studies* 100 (1982): 41–69. As Steadman and Ginsberg demonstrate, eagles connote a wide range of meanings in medieval literature, including contemplation, thought, and transcendence. In this instance, by linking the eagle to the legend of Ganymede and Jove, Chaucer imbues the scene with a rapturous subtext he denies but cannot efface.

ing of eroticism, for when desires cease, so too does the lover, and often the narrative as well. Even if an initial desire can be fulfilled, desire is itself always a reconstruction of other emotional and cultural forces, as Gilles Deleuze and Félix Guattari posit: "Desire has nothing to do with a natural or spontaneous determination; there is no desire but assembling, assembled, desire."[43] These fragments of hypothetical desires are patched together to form an empty whole that consistently founders at the moment of its construction. In a similar vein, Judith Butler sketches the complex circularity of desire: "the desire to desire is a willingness to desire precisely that which would foreclose desire, if only for the possibility of continuing to desire."[44] Thus, one of the sustaining threads of this volume is that, due to their inherent flux and interweaving, all desires bear the potential to be queering and anti-erotic ones, even ostensibly normative desires, for their pulsating circuitry continually pushes lovers in pursuit of they know not what, even to the ultimate anti-erotic consummation of their very selves in death. As Robert Rouse observes, "Often that which is viewed as erotic is somewhat transgressive of the norms of conventional sexuality, positioning the erotic at the margins of accepted behavior."[45] Erotic desires pique lovers to pursue their affections, but doing so necessitates that they breach cultural codes regulating social and communal relations, for the communal order imposes its authority by disciplining the individual in the very moment of his or her most personal acts.

Such queer dynamics of Chaucerian desire are strikingly evident in "The Complaint of Chaucer to His Purse," a poem that, on its surface, focuses on financial needs rather than eroticism but simultaneously showcases how these ostensibly disparate desires merge in Chaucer's poetry. In this poetic plea, Chaucer requests pecuniary assistance from King Henry IV while apostrophizing his purse as "my lady dere" (2). In lamenting its emptiness—"I am so sory, now that ye been lyght" (3)—Chaucer metaphorically constructs his purse as a vagina in need of filling, and he extends the metaphor by linking the yellow of gold to the yellow of his lady's hair, which "of yelownesse hadde never pere" (11). In this poem, Chaucer is powerless to effect the happy ending he seeks

---

43. Gilles Deleuze and Félix Guattari, A Thousand Plateaus: Capitalism and Schizophrenia, trans. Brian Massumi (Minneapolis: University of Minnesota Press, 1987), 399.

44. Judith Butler, The Psychic Life of Power: Theories in Subjection (Stanford, CA: Stanford University Press, 1997), 61.

45. Robert Rouse, "The Medieval Eroticism of Heat," in The Erotic in the Literature of Medieval Britain, ed. Cory Rushton and Amanda Hopkins (Cambridge: Brewer, 2007), 71–81, at 79.

and exhorts Henry IV to answer his petition. Because only the king, not Chaucer, can fill the purse, the poet depicts himself as emasculated in the complaint's erotic register. Furthermore, the poem's conclusion reveals Chaucer's homosocial desire of ingratiating himself to the king, whose rocky road to the throne likely necessitated the murder of his predecessor Richard II.[46] These homosocial desires are camouflaged under financial distress for much-needed funds and under heteroerotic longing for sexual consummation with a woman, yet such obfuscation ironically exposes Chaucer's greater interest in his king than in his beloved. It is worth remembering that the poem's female beloved does not exist other than as a metonymic representation of Chaucer's lack—a lack, however, not of sexual but of financial fulfillment. As Robert Sturges argues of the power dynamics of this short poem, "the patron-poet relationship can be deconstructed as a relation that is . . . both gendered and eroticized: like any discourse of desire or lack, the economic discourses has its gendered aspect."[47] In a time of political flux, Chaucer speaks to his purse as if it were a lady so that he may win the patronage—the affections—of his new ruler, which queers Chaucer and relegates heteroerotic desire to a secondary position within the masculine environs of the newly established court.

Within this framework of amatory longing and pecuniary need, mediated through a purse so that he may speak to his king, the apparent anti-eroticism of a simple homosocial request for funds is coupled with frequent allusions to death. The three stanzas of the poem end, "Beth hevy ageyn, or elles moot I dye" (7, 14, 21), as Chaucer also admonishes the purse, "For certes but yf ye make my hevy chere, / Me were as leef be layd upon my bere" (4–5).[48] With such lines, Chaucer enhances the tensions among heteroerotic longing for a phantom beloved, homosocial desire for financial assistance, and a latent revelation of the death drive, which can be seen as the ultimate incarnation of anti-eroticism. Within this heady mixture of desires acknowledged, repressed, and redirected, it is unclear whether the king will grant the poem's petitions, as it is also unclear whether Chaucer will succeed in the sexual pursuit that likens his purse

---

46. For Henry IV's possible role in Richard II's death, see Nigel Saul, *Richard II* (New Haven, CT: Yale University Press, 1997), 366–404, as well as Paul Strohm, *England's Empty Throne: Usurpation and the Language of Legitimation, 1399–1422* (New Haven, CT: Yale University Press, 1998), for the rhetorical crises arising from Henry's accession.

47. Robert Sturges, *Chaucer's Pardoner and Gender Theory*, 17.

48. On the potential crux of the phrase "make me hevy chere," see John Burrow, "Chaucer as Petitioner: Three Poems," *Chaucer Review* 45.3 (2011): 349–56, at 350–51.

to his "Quene of comfort and of good companye" (13). The reference to Henry IV as "conquerour of Brutes Albyon, / Which that by lyne and free eleccion / Been verray kyng" (22–24) also introduces political anxieties into the poem. Paul Strohm's meticulous reading of Chaucer's rhetorical situation at this moment—requesting money from a newly installed king, whose rise to the throne took place under questionable circumstances—highlights the author's strategic phrasings to win his monarch's favor: "With his reference to Henry as conqueror, Chaucer cuts through more frequent and authorized reference to 'recovery' with a starker formulation, but then mitigates against any severity by displacing the conquest to the legendary Britain of the chronicles."[49] Appealing to Britain's mythic past, Chaucer aggrandizes his king as he diminishes himself in stature before him. One need not agree with the thesis of Terry Jones's provocative *Who Murdered Chaucer?*—that Chaucer found himself out of favor in Henry IV's court and died, or was executed, soon after—to grant that the currents at court were changing swiftly, and that Chaucer's poem to his purse may have failed in its effort to ingratiate the petitioner to his king.[50] Nonetheless, in Chaucer's positioning himself as an avatar of chastity—"For I am shave as nye as any frere" (19)—it is clear that now, as when he took flight as an allegorical reenactment of Ganymede while refusing to acknowledge the implications of this allusion, he situates himself in a sexualized position ostensibly divorced from eroticism while nonetheless embroiled in it, seeking the succor of his king to relieve the emptiness of his finances, so that he may escape the metaphorical comparison to a chaste friar that reveals both his relative poverty and his emasculation in service to his king.

To answer the question with which this section of the chapter began—"Was Chaucer queer?"—the example of "The Complaint of Chaucer to

---

49. Paul Strohm, "Saving the Appearances: Chaucer's *Purse* and the Fabrication of the Lancastrian Claim," in *Chaucer's England: Literature in Historical Context*, ed. Barbara Hanawalt (Minneapolis: University of Minnesota Press, 1992), 21–40, at 32.

50. It is unclear whether Chaucer was successful in winning Henry IV's favor. In *Who Murdered Chaucer? A Medieval Mystery* (New York: St. Martin's, 2003), Terry Jones, Robert Yeager, Alan Fletcher, Juliette Dor, and Terry Dolan intriguingly conjecture that Chaucer was likely executed due to the court's suspicions of his continued loyalty to Richard II; they cite the lack of documentation concerning Chaucer's death to ground this hypothesis, but it is, of course, difficult to build a convincing argument upon a dearth of evidence. See also R. F. Yeager, "Chaucer's 'To His Purse': Begging, or Begging Off?" *Viator* 36 (2005): 373–414; and B. W. Lindeboom, "Chaucer's 'Complaint to His Purse': Sounding a Subversive Note?" *Neophilologus* 92 (2008): 745–51.

His Purse" demonstrates that Chaucer realized the necessity of queering himself before his new king by performing his subservience within the bounds of homosocial patronage networks, by reimagining and implicitly denigrating heteroerotic desires, and by embodying the anti-erotic chastity of a friar to underscore his king's puissance. Under the authority of a king, virtually all men, whether their sexual desires are heteroerotic or homoerotic, encounter what can be termed situational queerness, for they face disenfranchisement from the pursuit of their desires, should their rulers so determine. As Chaucer's poem illustrates, the rhetorical predicaments in which such queered men find themselves necessitate articulating a vast range of desires, erotic and otherwise, to advance their goals within such a hierarchical paradigm. The question then becomes not whether Chaucer was sexually normative, anti-erotic, or otherwise queer in his desires but how he understood the political, religious, and other social conditions that challenged one's ability to voice one's desires, and how strategies that we today might label queerly anti-erotic illuminate these contradictions.

CHAUCER'S (ANTI-)EROTICISMS AND THE QUEER MIDDLE AGES

Following the lines of inquiry sketched in miniature in the preceding analysis of "The Complaint of Chaucer to His Purse," *Chaucer's (Anti-) Eroticisms and the Queer Middle Ages* investigates the author's contradictory stances toward (anti-)eroticism, outlining the nexus of the self and society in his fictions as it is conjointly negotiated in the vexed sphere of amatory affairs. For Chaucer, erotic pursuits establish the thrust and tenor of many of his narratives, as they also expose the frustrations inherent in pursuing erotic desires, whether encouraged or frowned upon by the religious foundations of Western medieval culture. Paul Taylor believes that "Chaucer is a love poet [who] conceives of love as the philosophic principle behind the ontological fact of creation,"[51] yet it should not be overlooked that Chaucer frequently couples such a bounteous view of eroticism with violence. Cory Rushton and Amanda Hopkins propose that "Chaucer often presents male sexuality as inherently but not necessarily problematically violent,"[52] and W. W. Allman and Thomas Hanks, in their analysis

---

51. Paul Taylor, *Chaucer's Chain of Love* (Madison, NJ: Fairleigh Dickinson University Press, 1996), 13.

52. Cory Rushton and Amanda Hopkins, "Introduction: The Revel, the Melodye, and

of erotics in the *Canterbury Tales*, conclude that "Chaucer's characters, male and female alike, unite to refer to erotic experience in terms of a man's stabbing or cutting a woman."[53] As their study persuasively demonstrates, Chaucer's portrayals of desire and copulation elicit rhetorical flourishes of bloody penetration: from Theseus's triumphant victory over "al the regne of Femenye" (1.866) that wins him Hippolyta's hand in marriage in the *Knight's Tale* to Phoebus Apollo's murder of his adulterous wife in the *Manciple's Tale*, sex, love, and violence unite in Chaucer's fictions, exposing the ways in which erotic desires fracture concepts of self, beloved, and community that they ostensibly uphold. One cannot love freely within an ideological framework that polices sexuality, yet loving queerly creates escapes from social structures inimical to eroticism and its at times violent expressions. Normativity depends on the queer for its privileged cultural position, as the fatigued binary logic of ideology builds power through opposition to and denigration of the abjected Other, yet the queer then builds a radical means of reassessing the cultural codes that demand its subjected status. Furthermore, anti-eroticisms open outlets of unexpected desires in these texts, confounding the maintenance of erotic identities and codes as normative when the rejection of any type of erotic activity would be preferable to its expression.

The following chapter, "Mutual Masochism and the Hermaphroditic Courtly Lady in Chaucer's *Franklin's Tale*," analyzes the queer challenges to heteroeroticism in its most culturally idealized locus: a loving marriage between man and wife. This tale, heralded by many readers as the successful resolution of the marriage debate undertaken by various Canterbury pilgrims, appears to celebrate the erotic ideal of marriage without *maistrye*, yet Dorigen and Arveragus's mutually satisfying union is achieved only after heart-rending suffering both for the lovers and for Dorigen's suitor, Aurelius. Conjoined pain makes possible the anti-erotic sacrifices at the heart of the tale, in that both Dorigen and Arveragus suffer in their courtship and marriage, with their mutually masochistic relationship stripping them of the pretense of gender as each inhabits the role of the imperious courtly lady who demands her lover's obsequious service and painful sacrifice. If the eroticism at the heart of this tale triumphs in its conclusion, it

---

the Bisynesse of Solas," in *The Erotic in the Literature of Medieval Britain*, 1–17, at 13.

53. W. W. Allman and Thomas Hanks, "Rough Love: Notes toward an Erotics of the *Canterbury Tales*," *Chaucer Review* 38.1 (2003): 36–65, at 53. On Chaucer's depiction of erotic violence in the *Wife of Bath's Prologue*, see Marilyn Desmond, *Ovid's Art and the Wife of Bath: The Ethics of Erotic Violence*, and Michael Calabrese, *Chaucer's Ovidian Arts of Love*, 81–111.

can only do so by fracturing the contours of gender within the patriarchal structures of medieval romance and reimagining them as fundamentally dependent on masochistic rituals stripped of gender stability. The masochistic play at the heart of this romance mirrors the Franklin's play of modesty for his fellow pilgrims, as his creation of a tale lacking a climax forces his auditors to reconceive their perception of narrative pleasure. In both the tale and its narration, an erotic façade masks its deeper investment in the anti-erotic pleasures of a masochistic disavowal of desire.

Whereas chapter 2 explores the vagaries of heteroerotic desire in marriage, chapter 3, "'For to be sworne bretheren til they deye': Satirizing Queer Brotherhood in the Chaucerian Corpus," addresses the sublimated eroticism of sworn brotherhood in Chaucer's fictions. In the *Knight's Tale*, *Friar's Tale*, *Pardoner's Tale*, *Shipman's Tale*, and *House of Fame*, Chaucer portrays men who have sworn oaths of brotherhood to each other, yet the potential homoeroticism in such close male bonds undermines the likelihood of depicting these deep friendships in a positive light. On the contrary, the quick rejections of these oaths satirize the men who pledge them, often emphasizing their failure to successfully enact aristocratic fraternal codes due to their inferior social positions. In these instances, subsumed eroticism elicits Chaucer's debased treatment of male homosociality, for the potential homosexuality lurking beneath a veneer of homosocial respectability threatens to infiltrate the courtly cultures where these oaths are sworn. Such a perspective illuminates Chaucer's conflicted treatment of disruptive erotics because his fictions, in this instance, police desires deemed subversively queer to medieval society despite their overarching normativity. The irony, therefore, is that, although one may expect to find queer desires between men in homosocial relationships, the mere fact that two men bond themselves together through an oath should be insufficient to undermine its status as normative; at the same time, the anti-erotic valence to the relationship cannot dispel the specter of queerness lurking in the background of any such homosocial friendship.

Many medieval romances celebrate the codes of eros as a knight quests to win his lady's love and then her hand in marriage, but Chaucer rejects the potential fecundity of this storyline by concentrating on the intersection of necrotic and erotic desires in his *Knight's Tale* and *Troilus and Criseyde*. This monograph's fourth chapter, "Necrotic Erotics in Chaucerian Romance: Loving Women, Loving Death, and Destroying Civilization in the *Knight's Tale* and *Troilus and Criseyde*," analyzes the ways in which Emily and Criseyde are figured as objects of desire who reject the cultural imperative to reproduce through their avowed anti-eroticism.

Respectively a virgin and a childless widow, Emily and Criseyde desire to refrain from amatory pursuits with men, yet their narrative positions as the beloved and idealized lady of romance constrain their ability to negotiate the erotic landscapes in which they are ensnared. Only by exposing the necrotic underbelly of male heterosexual desires can they resist their construction as the beloved in amatory affairs that they reject, at least initially. In complementary fashion, Arcite and Troilus continually stress their willingness to die for love at the hand of their "sweet foes," and in this manner, Chaucer illustrates the ways in which the union of erotic and necrotic desires corrupts the pleasurable fantasies of romance. When loving a woman entails loving death, the queer workings of desires are made manifest, for the love of death is revealed to be the preeminent desire of the narratives. Assuming the ostensibly anti-erotic roles of virgin and widow, Emily and Criseyde destabilize the meaning of male sexuality by negotiating the pitfalls of unsolicited love, as they also expose the frailty of civilizations erected against the desires of women.

"Queer Families in the *Canterbury Tales*: Fathers, Children, and Abusive Erotics," the fifth chapter, studies the eroticized violence frequently accompanying depictions of children in Chaucer's corpus. In their assumed cultural positions as avatars of asexuality, rendered anti-erotic through a cultural fantasy of their sexual ignorance, children are nonetheless drafted into amatory rivalries centered on their fathers' attenuated masculinities. For Maline in the *Reeve's Tale*, Thomas's dead child in the *Summoner's Tale*, Walter and Griselda's unnamed children in the *Clerk's Tale*, and Virginia in the *Physician's Tale*, paternal authority entails not merely the assumed control of the child but subsuming the child's erotic agency in service of the father's desires. The father's erotic drives are implicated with a vision of his child(ren) as his property and as representative of his erotic puissance, and thus these children become pawns in aggressive contests between men. Within this perverse system in which a man's offspring measures his sexuality, the children depicted in these narratives tacitly resist their construction as sexual surrogates in homosocial conflicts, demonstrating their passive ability to reconstitute the erotic terrain of these tales. The queer vision of the desired child, rendered a sexual object of predatory and rapacious adults, proves the undesirability of adult sexuality when unmoored from social structures of conjugality.

The sixth chapter, "Chaucer's (Anti-)Erotic God," addresses Chaucer's depictions of God's sensuality, his sexual desires, and his queer interactions with his female beloveds, including Dido of the *Legend of Good Women* and Cecilia of the *Second Nun's Tale*. In a startling passage in her legend, Dido's stunning beauty excites God's passion, and the virginal Cecilia renounces earthly eroticism with her husband Valerian in light of the promises of heavenly rapture with the Divine. Visions of an erotic God also build Chaucer's fabliau humor, most notably in the digressions concerning God's *pryvetee* in the *Miller's Tale* and Jesus's facilitating of sexual congress in the *Wife of Bath's Prologue*. At key points in these narratives, Chaucer imagines God in terms of a very human eroticism, and these texts enlighten Chaucer's exegesis on human reason and sensuality in his *Parson's Tale*, in which God fails to regulate human sexuality and thus becomes implicated with the erotic transgressions at the heart of religious experience. Chaucer's God establishes the Law only to ignore it, casting anti-eroticism as a site of religious discipline that seeks its own destruction, and thus, contradictorily, the reinstantiation of its perpetual authority. From this perspective, medieval culture's policing of human sexuality is founded on the misapprehension of God's own desires, which queerly extend to the earthly realm in terms of a strikingly human, yet insistently divine, love.

The brief epilogue of *Chaucer's (Anti-)Eroticisms and the Queer Middle Ages*, "Chaucer's Avian Amorousness," leaves the realm of the human to examine the amorousness of chickens and thereby to postulate the possibilities and inherent problems of the rooster Chauntecleer serving as an erotic role model for the Canterbury pilgrims. No character in Chaucer's corpus—not even the randy protagonists of his fabliaux—succeed in their erotic desires as frequently, energetically, and unabashedly as Chauntecleer. "He fethered Pertelote twenty tyme, / And trad hire eke as ofte, er it was pryme" (7.3177–78), the Nun's Priest narrates in a candid observation of animal sensuality unmoored from human restraints, with Chauntecleer also fulfilling the role of courtly lover for his beloved Pertelote in a comic performance of courtly masculinity. When read through Gilles Deleuze and Félix Guattari's theories of becoming-animal, Chauntecleer models the potential to transcend the pitfalls of marital sexuality, if only through the sheer erotic humor of a horny yet virtually human rooster. Notwithstanding Chauntecleer's erotic virtuosity, sexual discontents undermine the tale's celebration of intercourse in its repeated reminders of avian incest. The incest taboo circulates throughout individual sexual desires and the structures of civilization to keep untamed sexuality in check, yet Chauntecleer's breaching of this prohibition showcases the excess of desire necessary to achieve erotic autonomy, while also pointing to the precarious nature of societies without sexual taboos and thus the concomitant need for anti-eroticism.

Taken together, the chapters of *Chaucer's (Anti-)Eroticisms and the Queer Middle Ages* chart amorous territories from heterosexual love in marriage to homosocial friendship in bachelorhood, from death in the midst of heteroerotic courtship to the dire situations faced by children ostensibly produced from the joys of matrimony, from the heavenly longings of the Divine to the animal lust of chickens. Along the way, these investigations expand the scope of queer theory's utility for medieval literary studies through a conjoined, but not deferential, interest in psychoanalytic perspectives. Freud and Lacan's foundational theorizations of consciousness underpin much of the ensuing analysis, as do Julia Kristeva's, Gilles Deleuze and Félix Guattari's, and Slavoj Žižek's reformulations of the field. Queer theory and psychoanalytic theory ponder the meaning of desire in the formation of culture and the individual, and this overlap testifies to the productivity of their union, for desire, in destabilizing identities, bears the potential to jar, to discombobulate, and to queer one's foundational sense of self and psyche as mediated through the amatory field. Queer theoreticians including Lee Edelman, Tim Dean, and Simon Gaunt have unpacked the convoluted workings of heterosexual desire by arguing for queer theory's necessity in interrogating social norms and their incoherencies. Edelman posits that "queerness attains its ethical value precisely insofar as it . . . accept[s] its figural status as resistance to the viability of the social while insisting on the inextricability of such resistance from every social structure."[54] Within this realm of inquiry, the aims of queer theory overlap with those of Lacanian examinations of desire. Tim Dean posits the unique conjunctions of analysis available by uniting queer theory with Lacanian thought, suggesting that "Lacanian psychoanalysis may provide handy ammunition for queer theory's critique of . . . heteronormativity"; certainly, as Dean points out, "by theorizing subjectivity in terms of language and culture, Lacan also denaturalizes sex."[55] In *Beyond Sexuality*, Dean further observes, "Lacan's response to normativity is not to produce alternative imaginaries, but to elaborate an alternative of a different order—that of the real, a conceptual category intended to designate everything that *resists* adaptation."[56]

---

54. Lee Edelman, *No Future: Queer Theory and the Death Drive* (Durham, NC: Duke University Press, 2004), 3. See also Edelman's *Homographesis* (New York: Routledge, 1994), for his earlier efforts to align queer theory with Lacanian psychoanalysis.

55. Tim Dean, "Lacan and Queer Theory," in *The Cambridge Companion to Lacan*, ed. Jean-Michel Rabaté (Cambridge: Cambridge University Press, 2003), 238–52, at 238, 243.

56. Tim Dean, *Beyond Sexuality* (Chicago: University of Chicago Press, 2000), 230; italics in original.

Moreover, both psychoanalysis and queer theory frequently return to the question of love and its effects. As Simon Gaunt summarizes, "Love, for Lacan, encourages the belief in a perfect and symmetrical union between a man and a woman . . . [b]ut this perfect union is a discursive lure, a myth, fantasy (in the strictly Lacanian sense of that which structures the symbolic order)." The utility of this myth for queer analysis, as Gaunt details, is that a "Lacanian framework may help us to understand . . . how courtly literature can be *both* profoundly homosocial *and yet* apparently attracted to the idea of a perfect union between a man and a woman."[57] From both psychoanalytic and queer perspectives, sex must be divorced from naturalistic discourses that establish it as a sacrosanct ideal of normativity; it must be exposed to show the contradictions of consciousness and culture that surface as inherent conditions in pursuing an erotic attraction to another person.

Furthermore, so that readers may appreciate the full and contradictory vistas of Chaucerian eroticism, this volume traces connections among disparate tales and narratives, many of which are infrequently examined together in Chaucerian scholarship: *Knight's Tale, Friar's Tale, Pardoner's Tale, Shipman's Tale,* and *House of Fame* in the chapter on homosocial brotherhood; *Reeve's Tale, Summoner's Tale, Clerk's Tale,* and *Physician's Tale* in the chapter on the eroticized suffering of children; and *Miller's Tale, Wife of Bath's Prologue, Second Nun's Tale, Parson's Tale,* and *Legend of Good Women* in the chapter on God's eroticism in Chaucer's literature. Despite their many similarities in tone, theme, and genre, *Knight's Tale* and *Troilus and Criseyde* are seldom addressed in tandem, most likely due to the abundance of textual riches each puts forth for the pleasure and analysis of readers and scholars. Only the *Franklin's Tale* merits its own chapter in this study, for this narrative showcases the Herculean task necessary to build a heteroerotic attachment based on mutuality and affection.

In Chaucer's literature, erotic attachments might elevate and ennoble his various characters, or eroticism might denigrate and degrade them, but in virtually every instance, eroticism and its counterpart of anti-eroticism reveal the potential queerness ubiquitous in the quest for human contact. Chaucer's thematic return to shared issues of eroticism and anti-eroticism in such disparate texts allows wider insights into how love and desire function beyond the contours of a given genre, which, I hope, will

---

57. Simon Gaunt, *Love and Death in Medieval French and Occitan Courtly Literature: Martyrs to Love* (Oxford: Oxford University Press, 2006), 170–71; italics in original.

open new perspectives on these endlessly entertaining works. As Holly Crocker suggests in her study of Chaucer's masculinities, "Thinking about our emotive investments in the historical reception of Chaucer allows us to confront the ways in which we continue to naturalize masculinity's claim to universality by maintaining its privileged invisibility."[58] So too does thinking through the possibilities of queerness and anti-eroticism in Chaucer's fictions enable us to reconsider the foundations of the English literary tradition, as we see anew the queer paternalism that this originary fantasy engenders and camouflages.

---

58. Holly Crocker, *Chaucer's Visions of Manhood*, 13.

CHAPTER TWO

MUTUAL MASOCHISM AND THE HERMAPHRODITIC COURTLY LADY IN CHAUCER'S *FRANKLIN'S TALE*

"The best part of married life is the fights. The rest is merely so-so," writes Thornton Wilder in *The Matchmaker*,[1] with his words capturing a simple truth of narrative pleasure: in many instances, readers prefer depictions of conflict over companionship, of aggression over amour, and such is certainly the case throughout Chaucer's *Canterbury Tales*. Marriage recurs frequently as a subject during the Canterbury pilgrimage, but, as is readily apparent, often in problematic or unsettling ways. Cuckoldry and sexual aggression cloud the portrayals of marriage in the *Miller's Tale*, *Reeve's Tale*, *Merchant's Tale*, and *Shipman's Tale* (and even when cuckoldry is not surely depicted in Chaucer's fabliaux, its specter lingers, as in the flirtatious behavior between Thomas's wife and the friar of the *Summoner's Tale*). Domestic violence, both physical and emotional, disrupts marital harmony in the *Wife of Bath's Prologue*, *Clerk's Tale*, and *Manciple's Tale*, and marriage catalyzes religious conflict in *Man of Law's Tale* (in which Custance's mothers-in-law embark on their murderous and duplicitous acts in response to their sons' unions) and *Second Nun's Tale* (in which Cecilia threatens Valerian with his imminent demise should he seek satisfaction for the marital debt). Due to the antagonism, pain, and humiliation associated with marriage

---

1. Thornton Wilder, *Three Plays: Our Town, The Skin of Our Teeth, and The Matchmaker* (New York: Harper Perennial, 1985), Act II, 299.

in so many of the *Canterbury Tales*, the *Franklin's Tale*, with the apparently egalitarian relationship between Dorigen and Arveragus, stands as the strongest antidote to Chaucer's matrimonial satire.[2]

But if Wilder is correct that the "best part of married life is the fights," then where is the pleasure of the *Franklin's Tale*, a narrative that, at least on the surface, doggedly refuses to depict marital disharmony? Numerous critics have analyzed the *Franklin's Tale* and its depiction of marital tribulations, pointing to subtle gradations of power and authority enacted in Dorigen and Arveragus's union. Notable voices in these discussions include Cathy Hume, who argues, "having established an egalitarian marriage ideal at the beginning of the *Tale*, Chaucer goes on to explore how such an ideal would be tested by real world circumstances";[3] Craig Davis similarly observes, "Chaucer's *Franklin's Tale* shows us that perfect marriages can be just as fraught emotionally as any other kind, even when they are contracted with deliberate consideration of advantage and liability in social status, wealth, or political alliance."[4] These nuanced assessments of the marital dynamics depicted in the *Franklin's Tale*, along with those of Emma Lipton, Elizabeth Robertson, Conor McCarthy, David Raybin, Angela Lucas, and many others, enhance readers' understanding of a union that appears outwardly harmonious yet also hints at its inherent discontents.[5]

---

2. It should be noted that additional companionate marriages appear in the *Canterbury Tales*: Melibee and Prudence's marriage in Chaucer's *Tale of Melibee* exemplifies mutuality, yet their rich discussion of forgiveness is set within the context of the horrific violence against their family. Chauntecleer and Pertelote's union in *Nun's Priest's Tale*, despite Chauntecleer's polygamous tendencies, surprisingly models for human readers the possibility of a healthy, if excessively animalistic, eroticism, as discussed in the monograph's Epilogue.

3. Cathy Hume, *Chaucer and the Cultures of Love and Marriage* (Cambridge: Brewer, 2012), 33.

4. Craig Davis, "A Perfect Marriage on the Rocks: Geoffrey and Philippa Chaucer, and the *Franklin's Tale*," *Chaucer Review* 37.2 (2002): 129–44, at 142.

5. Emma Lipton, "Married Friendship: An Ideology for the Franklin," in *Affections of the Mind: The Politics of Marriage in Late Medieval English Literature* (Notre Dame, IN: University of Notre Dame Press, 2007), 21–50; Elizabeth Robertson, "Marriage, Mutual Consent, and the Affirmation of the Female Subject in the *Knight's Tale*, the *Wife of Bath's Tale*, and the *Franklin's Tale*," in *Drama, Narrative, and Poetry in the* Canterbury Tales, ed. Wendy Harding (Toulouse: Presses Universitaires du Mirail, 2003), 175–93; Conor McCarthy, "Love, Marriage, and Law: Three *Canterbury Tales*," *English Studies* 83.6 (2002): 504–18; David Raybin, "'Wommen, of kynde, desiren libertee': Rereading Dorigen, Rereading Marriage," *Chaucer Review* 27.1 (1992): 65–86; and Angela Lucas, "The Presentation of Marriage and Love in Chaucer's *Franklin's Tale*," *English Studies* 72.6 (1991): 501–12. Kathryn Jacobs, in *Marriage Contracts from Chaucer to the Renaissance Stage* (Gainesville: University Press of

The marital mutuality that stands at the core of the *Franklin's Tale* is not achieved easily, and Arveragus and Dorigen's mutual masochism enables their sharing of authority and submission in marriage. As a disavowal of sexual desire, with such desire sublimated through pain and denial, masochism registers the anti-eroticism latent in relationships predicated upon hierarchy, for particularly in the Middle Ages, marriage can be stripped of its gendered hierarchy only through concentrated effort. Numerous theoretical accounts of courtly love posit a sadistic/masochistic valence between the suffering suitor and his female beloved, but the *Franklin's Tale* subverts this binary relationship and invites readers to contemplate the possibility of a relationship founded upon oscillating positions of masochistic subservience, as well as the fruits of such a refiguring of romance. Concomitant with the mutually masochistic potential in courtly romance is the refiguring of gender roles within this archetypal dyad: the Courtly Lady need not be a lady when a relationship is defined through mutual masochism, and thus, when Arveragus assumes the mantle of this presumably feminine role, he models the latent hermaphroditism of ostensibly rigid gender hierarchies. The Franklin's mutually masochistic tale undermines standard structures of narrative as well, with the tale's focus on masochism paralleling that of the Franklin's performance of modesty for his fellow pilgrims, through which he likewise compels them to confront the fictions of gender.[6]

MUTUAL MASOCHISM AND THE HERMAPHRODITIC COURTLY LADY, OR WHY CAN'T THE COURTLY LADY BE MORE LIKE A MAN?

The logic of courtly love: such a phrase should be paradoxical, for under which epistemology (except perhaps its own) should its mores be considered logical? Slavoj Žižek ponders the intransigence of courtly love in modern society, questioning its enduring legacy, its continued appeal despite its outmoded forms, and its persistently gendered tropes, all of which ostensibly assume an internal logic:

Florida, 2001), analyzes the contractual language spoken by Dorigen, Arveragus, and Aurelius in their many conflicting promises to one another (24–27 and 53–57).

6. In her *Chaucer and the Fictions of Gender* (Berkeley: University of California Press, 1992), Elaine Tuttle Hansen explores the intersection of "the mutability of gender . . . and the instability of meaning" in Chaucer's canon, a pithy yet illuminating encapsulation of his play with gender, literary form, and social structure (60).

Why talk about courtly love [*l'amour courtois*] today, in an age of permissiveness when the sexual encounter is often nothing more than a "quickie" in some dark corner of an office? The impression that courtly love is out of date, long superseded by modern manners, is a lure blinding us to how the logic of courtly love still defines the parameters within which the two sexes relate to each other.[7]

The archetypal genders of courtly love—evident in the troubadour tradition of the male poet pleading mercy for his fair beloved—endure in modern culture, but often these archetypes more obscure than reflect the gendered dynamics of the medieval texts, particularly lyrics and romance, from which they arise.[8] Foremost among these paradigms is the vision of the Courtly Lady, whose cruel and imperious command over her lover accords her absolute and arbitrary power over him. Jacques Lacan's excurses on the Courtly Lady have reified her standard characteristics into a static entity, one who not only is eternal but is dehumanized as a reflection of unknown and untapped desires. For Lacan, courtly love in its entirety is a fantasy, a structure of imbuing meaning through elaborate images divorced from reality. His sense of *fin' amors* is of a complex poetic game, one with certain gendered tropes that are insistently uniform: "courtly love was, in brief, a poetic exercise, a way of playing with a number of conventional, idealizing themes, which couldn't have any real concrete equivalent. Nevertheless, these ideals, first among which is that of the Lady, are to be found in subsequent periods, down to our own."[9] For Lacan, the Lady is ideal in her abstract yet recurrent features and persistent through time: she survives the Middle Ages and courtly literature to flourish in the present day, yet she never existed other than as an imaginary formulation of desire's impossibility.[10]

---

7. Slavoj Žižek, *Metastases of Enjoyment: Six Essays on Women and Causality* (London: Verso, 1994), 89.

8. For a representative sampling of such troubadour verse, see Robert Kehew, ed., *The Lark in the Morning: The Verses of the Troubadours* (Chicago: University of Chicago Press, 2005), including such lyrics as Jaufre Rudel's "Lanquan li jorn," Guillem de Cabestanh's "Lo jorn qu'ie-us vi, dompna, primeiramen," and Arnaut de Marueill's "Si•m destreignetz, dompna, vos et Amors," among many others.

9. Jacques Lacan, *The Ethics of Psychoanalysis, 1959–1960. The Seminar of Jacques Lacan, Book 7.* Ed. Jacques-Alain Miller. Trans. Dennis Porter (1986; New York: Norton, 1992), 148.

10. Recent scholarship explores modern theorists' debts to medieval literature, in such studies as Andrew Cole and Vance Smith, eds., *The Legitimacy of the Middle Ages: On the Unwritten History of Theory* (Durham, NC: Duke University Press, 2010), Erin Felicia Labbie, *Lacan's Medievalisms* (Minneapolis: University of Minnesota Press, 2006), and Bruce Hols-

Of course, the Lady need never have existed in order to function because her existence, in this instance, does not accord with her power. She is a psychological construct, one revealing the narcissistic desire of her suitor to assert his masculinity within the realm of a primarily homosocial grouping. Žižek discerns the Otherness that the Lady must embody and posits her as a reflection in which the knightly lover views himself narcissistically in response to her imperious commands:

> This coincidence of absolute, inscrutable Otherness and pure machine is what confers on the Lady her uncanny, monstrous character—the Lady is the Other which is not our "fellow-creature"; that is to say, she is someone with whom no relationship of empathy is possible. . . . Deprived of every real substance, the Lady functions as a mirror on to which the subject projects his narcissistic ideal.[11]

Stripped of her humanity in Žižek's formulation, the Lady is rendered inhuman and inhumane, serving merely to mirror masculine desire. In this paradigm male narcissism transforms a woman into monstrosity: in needing and thus creating the cruel Lady as a means of ideal self-definition, the knight must metamorphose a woman into the Lady, must define himself through his relationship with her despite the fact that she has been rendered monstrous due to her presumed lack of humanity. In so doing, the knight's play with narcissistic desires reveals the inherent queerness of performing heterosexuality, for the narcissistic yearning to be desired by a woman reveals the intransigence but ultimate superfluousness of the woman's role in the process. (As Narcissus himself showed, any mirror will serve this purpose.) The Courtly Lady becomes a mirror reflecting male desire for desirability who thus queerly reflects the knight's image: she highlights his failure to attain the standards of masculinity she is coded to represent.

In this light, the Courtly Lady embodies a queer torquing of the knight's desires, despite his apparent sexual normativity, for the homosocial valence of his performance of heterosexuality cannot be stripped from his courtship. At its core, *being* entails *being without*, and for Lacan,

---

inger, *The Premodern Condition: Medievalism and the Making of Theory* (Chicago: University of Chicago Press, 2005). In Labbie's words, these investigations reveal "how the medieval is still dominant in our contemporary epistemological investigations" (34). Along these lines, this chapter ponders how modern theory distorts the dynamics of medieval texts while nonetheless, in a cross-parallax of vision and insight, illuminating them.

11. Slavoj Žižek, *Metastases of Enjoyment*, 90.

the Lady signifies a lack, an absence that the knight seeks to fill through her position as the inscrutable Other: "The object involved, the feminine object, is introduced oddly enough through the door of privation or of inaccessibility."[12] The Lady can only be accessed through the knight's lack and thus becomes a cipher for the knight to decode, albeit an ultimately indecipherable code, one whose actions reflect not her desires but his refracted desires to project his identity through her. Lacan explains the ways in which the Lady must embody cruelty at its most arbitrary so that she represents both the knight's desire and the impossibility of comprehending desire:

> By means of a form of sublimation specific to art, poetic creation consists in positing an object I can only describe as terrifying, an inhuman partner.
>
> The Lady is never characterized for any of her real, concrete virtues, for her wisdom, her prudence, or even her competence. If she is described as wise, it is not because she embodies an immaterial wisdom or because she represents its functions more than she exercises them. On the contrary, she is as arbitrary as possible in the tests she imposes on her servant.
>
> The Lady is basically what was later to be called, with a childish echo of the original ideology, "cruel as the tigers of Ircania."[13]

Because of this cruelty, many readers see the courtly lady as the sadist to the knightly masochist, and Lacan cites Chrétien de Troyes's literature as a prime example of this dynamic (despite the paucity of evidence to support his claims).[14] Jeffrey Jerome Cohen memorably refers to Guinevere, in his Deleuzian reading of Chrétien's *Lancelot, ou Le Chevalier de la charrete*, as "Guinevere in Furs," a mordant yet apropos assessment of her arbitrary

---

12. Jacques Lacan, *The Ethics of Psychoanalysis*, 149.
13. Ibid., 150–51.
14. Ibid., 151. For a reading of the Lacanian dynamics of *Lancelot, ou Le Chevalier de la charrete*, see Robert Sturges, "La(can)ncelot," *Arthurian Interpretations* 4.2 (1990): 12–23. Other than Guinevere in *Lancelot*, one might well wonder to which of Chrétien's female characters Lacan refers. As I discuss briefly at the end of this section, Enide in *Erec et Enide* more fits the role of the suffering suitor than the cruel Courtly Lady, and *Cliges* focuses more on the mutuality of suffering, first between Alexander and Soredamors and then between Cliges and Fenice, than on these women's supposed cruelties. Laudine's request that Yvain return to her after a year of knightly homosocial pastimes seems quite reasonable in its demands upon him, and Perceval's relationship with Blancheflor gives her little opportunity to dispense arbitrary or cruel tests of his knightly abilities.

power over an often hapless and suffering Lancelot.¹⁵ Because the knight fails to prove his constant devotion by hesitating a mere two steps before debasing himself in the cart while attempting to rescue her, Guinevere asserts her amatory authority over him and unleashes much physical pain to punish him, notably in the tournament scenes in which she bids him to do his worst and thus to suffer mightily and physically. While Chrétien imbues these scenes with a sly and ironic humor, as frequently accompanies such depictions of courtly love, the power dynamics remain in force, with Guinevere staging Lancelot's actions.

It is nonetheless unclear in such scenes whether the Lady acts on her own volition or whether she is acted through in service of the knight's masochistic desires. Continuing his discussion of the Courtly Lady, Lacan describes her not as an agent but as a catalyst, one conscripted into her service as the Thing:

> The idealized woman, the Lady, who is in the position of the Other and of the object, finds herself suddenly and brutally positing, in a place knowingly constructed out of the most refined of signifiers, the emptiness of a thing in all its crudity, a thing that reveals itself in its nudity to be the thing, her thing, the one that is to be found at her very heart in its cruel emptiness. That Thing . . . is in a way unveiled with a cruel and insistent power.¹⁶

Lacan's passive descriptions of the Lady, who "finds herself" in the position of "brutally positing . . . the emptiness of a thing," establish her cruelty as incidental to her character (if she is granted any sense of character at all). If, for Lacan, *das Ding* is that which represents "the beyond-of-the-signified," whose function is that the subject is thereby "constituted in a kind of relationship characterized by primary affect, prior to any repression,"¹⁷ the Lady's gender is ultimately unnecessary because, as she metamorphoses into *das Ding*, whose purpose is freed from her body, the knight grapples not with her corporeality but with his own interiority and his desires vis-à-vis his homosocial milieu. The Courtly Lady is thus also a Queer Thing, one by which the knight must confront the potential

---

15. Cohen's rich reading of Guinevere and Lancelot's relationship pays particular attention to its inherently unstable dynamics and oscillating gendered inflections; see his "Masoch/Lancelotism," in *Medieval Identity Machines* (Minneapolis: University of Minnesota Press, 2003), 78–115.

16. Jacques Lacan, *The Ethics of Psychoanalysis*, 163.

17. Ibid., 54.

homoerotic desire inherent in the narcissistic mirroring that she performs for him. Furthermore, if the Lady is acted through rather than acting, she inhabits not a sadistic but a powerless and ultimately anti-erotic position, one paradoxically staged by the knight through his own masochistic performance of subservience to and for her. Gilles Deleuze suggests that sadomasochism is primarily an illusion, positing instead that "the concurrence of sadism and masochism is fundamentally one of analogy only" and that the male masochist must "fashion the woman into a despot . . . persuade her to cooperate and get her to 'sign.'"[18] Stripping away the façade of sadomasochism in medieval romance reveals the mutual masochism at its heart and the queer tensions inherent in a man defining and refining both his desire and his desirability through a woman acting as a Queer Thing, one who latently reflects the potential desirability of the knight among his homosocial affiliations rather than one who simply exists as a woman (if this possibility is available to her at all).

Accessing the power that the Courtly Lady purportedly wields, the knight seeks his narcissistic ideal by relying on the play of masochism, for masochism is often a performance. Žižek explains:

> The next crucial feature of courtly love is that it is thoroughly a matter of courtesy and etiquette; it has nothing to do with some elementary passion overflowing all barriers, immune to all social rules. We are dealing with a strict fictional formula, with a social game of "as if," where a man pretends that his sweetheart is the inaccessible Lady.[19]

The knight engages in an elaborate theatrical ritual in which he shields his agency in service to his lady, but this subservience only masks his real power that is queerly designed to emasculate him. For in the patriarchal environs of the Middle Ages, when men wielded authority in virtually all realms of life, such performances are almost laughable in their farce-like enactments of male submission yet nonetheless transformatively effective in altering the gendered landscape of courtly society. One need only think of the rapist knight in Chaucer's *Wife of Bath's Tale* to see the severe penalties for forgoing the masochistic play of courtly love in favor of the violent sadism inherent in rape, yet these transgressions paradoxically

---

18. Gilles Deleuze, *Masochism* (New York: Zone, 1991), 46 and 21. Deleuze dismisses the hypothetical union embodied in sadomasochism with such memorable turns of phrase as "pseudomasochism" (124) and as a "semiological howler" (134).

19. Slavoj Žižek, *Metastases of Enjoyment*, 91.

encode further the pleasures of masochistic ritual at the heart of knightly identity: the female victim of Chaucer's rapist knight is forgotten by the tale's end, but he atones for his crime by embracing the passive queerness of submission to his wife. In this disturbing reversal, in which a rapist finds himself rewarded sexually for his earlier crime against a woman, his masochistic performance of servility then redounds to his pleasure when she metamorphoses into a young, beautiful, and faithful wife. Normative heterosexuality in marital bliss triumphs at this tale's conclusion, yet it is nonetheless a queered enactment of heterosexuality in which intercourse must be resignified into a pleasure so that it no longer signifies the violence or abjection that made it possible, either in his rape of the maiden or in his new wife's sly taunting of his sexual puissance: "Fareth every knyght thus with his wyf as ye? / Is this the lawe of kyng Arthures hous?" (3.1088–89). The knight who sadistically raped a woman undergoes a moment of teasing that threatens to resignify sexual pleasure into a degrading experience with an unattractive woman, but this ruse merely delays the pleasures due him when he accepts the performance of masochism he has for too long denied.

If the masochist stages the encounter with his cruel lady (or at the very least finds himself rewarded for accepting the role), then sadism itself is a ruse within the masochistic ritual, and the Courtly Lady may herself partake of the masochistic posturings frequent in the play of courtly love. Žižek investigates the tension between the masochist and his female partner, stressing the performative nature of their play:

> Masochism . . . is made to the measure of the victim: it is the victim (the servant in the masochistic relationship) who initiates a contract with the Master (woman), authorizing her to humiliate him in any way she considers appropriate (within the terms defined by the contract) and binding himself to act "according to the whims of the sovereign lady." . . . It is the servant, therefore, who writes the screenplay—that is, who actually pulls the strings and dictates the activity of the woman [*dominatrix*]: he stages his own servitude. One further differential feature is that masochism, in contrast to sadism, is inherently theatrical: violence is for the most part feigned, and even when it is "real," it functions as a component of a scene, as part of a theatrical performance. Furthermore, violence is never carried out, brought to its conclusion; it always remains suspended, as the endless repeating of an interrupted gesture.[20]

---

20. Ibid., 91–92.

Again the Courtly Lady wields little power: in Žižek's formulation, she follows the will of her masochistic lover, who "pulls the strings and dictates the activity of the woman." Feigning his lack of authority as he "stages his own servitude," the knight also stages the servitude of the Courtly Lady by directing her cruel behavior toward him so that he will be queered and so that the narrative will thus unfold on the expectation that he will somehow rehabilitate himself from this queering. Freedom from the gendered roles of male masochist and female sadist potentially emerges in this theatricality, for if the Courtly Lady is not a sadist because she responds to her suitor's masochistic contract, it is furthermore possible that she can stage her own complementary masochistic ritual in tandem with and in response to her suitor's, to define herself narcissistically through him by likewise employing him as a Queer Thing.

For why must the Courtly Lady be a woman? If her function is to allow the knight to confront the impossibility of his subjectivity against the void of signification, to see the emptiness of himself as a signifier as he narcissistically attempts to assert just such an identity, could not a man fulfill this role? If one is guided by the logic of the phallus, the answer must be no, since the phallus's role in signification adheres to a man's body, signifying the potential for signification even when such signifying is rendered incoherent. As Judith Butler argues in her deconstruction of phallologocentric "logic" and its insistent gendering of bodies, "The psychoanalytic critique succeeds in giving an account of the construction of 'the subject'—and perhaps also the illusion of substance—within the matrix of normative gender relations,"[21] and here the "logic" of courtly love sutures over Lacan's and Žižek's critiques of Freud in terms of their own gendered arguments. Because the Lady is coded in and of absence, at least in Freudian terms, she better symbolizes the privations of identity and signification that stand at the heart of the encounter between her and her beloved. As Žižek also observes, relying on the body to distinguish the sexes obscures the symbolic processes at the heart of sexual identity: "It thus seems more productive to posit as the central enigma that of sexual difference—*not*

---

21. Judith Butler, *Gender Trouble: Feminism and the Subversion of Identity* (New York: Routledge, 1990), 28–29. Butler's provocative troublings of psychoanalytic theories are relevant to the masochistic play of desire as well, as in her perceptive observation "Desire will aim at unraveling the subject, but be thwarted by precisely the subject in whose name it operates. A vexation of desire, one that proves crucial to subjection, implies that for the subject to persist, the subject must thwart its own desire. And for desire to triumph, the subject must be threatened with dissolution" (*The Psychic Life of Power: Theories in Subjection* [Stanford, CA: Stanford University Press, 1997], 9).

as the already established symbolic difference (heterosexual normativity) but, precisely, as that which forever eludes the grasp of normative symbolization."[22] Affirming the gender of the Courtly Lady as female, however, succumbs to the logic of "established symbolic difference," whereas according the potential for the Courtly Lady to be a man, or to be a hermaphroditic figure capable of inhabiting masculine and feminine genders simultaneously, allows readers the freedom of "elud[ing] the grasp of normative symbolization."

In the queer play of man and woman when heterosexuality falters at the point of desire, hermaphroditism emerges as a key tactic in ongoing power struggles in courtship and marriage. As a hermeneutic theorizing the breakdown and reassemblage of gender, hermaphroditism captures the insistent possibility of surpassing the gender binary through new models of bodies and desires, and this modern conception of hermaphroditism's potential strikingly aligns with classical conceptions of gender stripped of rigorous distinctions between male and female. The Ovidian sense of hermaphroditism is detailed in his etiological account of Salmacis and Hermaphroditus, in which the naiad's attempted rape of Mercury and Aphrodite's son ends as the two merge into one body following her invocation to the gods:

"pugnes licet, inprobe," dixit
"non tamen effugies. ita di iubeatis, et istum
nulla dies a me nec me deducat ab isto."
vota suos habuere deos: nam mixta duorum
corpora iunguntur faciesque inducitur illis
una.

"However hard
you try, you won't escape, you wayward one!
O gods, do grant my plea: may no day dawn
that sunders him from me, or me from him."
Her plea is heard; the gods consent: they merge
the twining bodies: the two become
one body with a single face and form.[23]

---

22. Slavoj Žižek, *The Ticklish Subject: The Absent Centre of Political Ontology* (London: Verso, 1999), 324.

23. William Anderson, ed., *Ovid's Metamorphoses: Books 1–5* (Norman: University of Oklahoma Press, 1997), 4.370–75; the translation is from Allen Mandelbaum, *The Metamorphosis of Ovid* (San Diego, CA: Harvest, 1993), 124. For the figure of the hermaphrodite

Twining and then united, their bodies register as one, but what is the gender of this newly sexed body? Conflicting models of hermaphroditism coexist, which entail both the erasure of the male/female binary in the depiction of a single body and envisioning it as a battleground of conflicting genders forced to share the same body.[24] Ovid's story in its entirety illustrates both these models, in the descriptions of the gender switching evident in Hermaphroditus's femininity (despite his male body) and Salmacis's masculinity (despite her female body) prior to their union in one form. Given the inherent flux of hermaphroditic identities, their potential to signify in contradictory and complementary fashions disrupts gendered binaries by negating gender as a stable referent.

If readers grant the variability of the sexed body in relation to the identity of the Courtly Lady in medieval romances and courtly lyrics, numerous texts showcase her ultimately hermaphroditic cast. For example, Jane Burns notes the gender play inherent in courtly love, pointing out the "cross-gendered conundrum that lies at the very heart of courtly lyrics where a man's role (that of the feudal lord) is played by a woman who, while retaining the highly fetishized and desired female body, wields masculine abilities and male prerogative in love."[25] Such a polyvalent and hermaphroditic Courtly Lady is strikingly evident in Chrétien de Troyes's *Erec et Enide*, his account of the legend of "Gereint and Enid" as told in the *Mabinogion*. In brief, are not Erec/Gereint's stern commands to Enide/Enid reminiscent of Guinevere's callous treatment of Lancelot in their virtually inexplicable cruelty, in their insistent punishments of trivial transgressions, in the ways in which the sadism apparently on display ultimately returns the masochistic suffering of Lancelot and Enide to prove their virtue and desirability? Indeed, Gereint's motivations—why must he treat her so cruelly?—are so obscured in the texts of Chrétien and the *Mabinogion* that Alfred, Lord Tennyson, provides a more credible explanation for this protagonist's inscrutable actions in *Idylls of the King*, positing Gereint's fear that Guinevere's adultery has tainted Enid:

. . . and there fell
A horror on him, lest his gentle wife,

in medieval literature, see David Rollo, *Kiss My Relics: Hermaphroditic Fictions of the Middle Ages* (Chicago: University of Chicago Press, 2011).

24. Tison Pugh, *Sexuality and Its Queer Discontents in Middle English Literature* (New York: Palgrave Macmillan, 2008), 80–81.

25. Jane Burns, "Courtly Love: Who Needs It? Recent Feminist Work in the Medieval French Tradition," *Signs* 27.1 (2001): 23–57, at 27. Burns provides an excellent accounting of feminist readings of the courtly love tradition.

> Thro' that great tenderness for Guinevere,
> Had suffer'd, or should suffer any taint
> In nature.[26]

Without this hint of credible motivation, Erec/Gereint's actions appear merely arbitrary, designed to punish Enide/Enid and to force her to revel in masochistic abjection so that she may eventually triumph through her own masochistic ritual. In the *Mabinogion*, Enid merely declares, "Woe is me, if on my account these arms and chest are losing the fame and fighting ability they once possessed"[27]; in Chrétien's *Erec et Enide*, she states, "Con mar i fus,"[28] a remarkably ambiguous phrase translated as divergently as "How disastrous for you"[29] and "Beloved, / How you've been wronged."[30] This obscure yet innocuous statement instigates Erec's incessant testing of his wife in the medieval tradition, yet Tennyson's Enid, in contrast, states more clearly, "O me, I fear that I am no true wife,"[31] a phrase misinterpreted within the context of the story yet more damaging in terms of its apparent denotation. Tennyson frees his retelling of Gereint and Enid's relationship from the incoherency of desire frequent in medieval romance while maintaining the mutual masochism at its heart. Jeanne Nightingale argues of genders' mutability in this romance that Enid functions as Erec's mirror, positing that "her creative function in the narrative is to free the narcissistic paragon from the burdens of his inflated self-image . . . and redefine . . . Erec's proper role in chivalric society."[32] In a similar vein, Michel-André Bossy suggests, "this strategy enables Chrétien to splay male and female consciousness into discrete realms of discourse, even while keeping his two characters present to each other and engaging them in the same adventures."[33] With their gendered realms discrete yet

---

26. Alfred, Lord Tennyson, *Idylls of the King*, ed. J. M. Gray (London: Penguin, 1983), 76, lines 28–32.

27. *The Mabinogion*, trans. Jeffrey Gantz (London: Penguin, 1976), 278.

28. Chrétien de Troyes, *Erec et Enide*, ed. Jean-Marie Fritz (Livre de Poche, 1992), 206, line 2503.

29. Chrétien de Troyes, *Arthurian Romances*, trans. D. D. R. Owen (London: Everyman, 1993), 33.

30. Chrétien de Troyes, *Erec and Enide*, trans. Burton Raffel (New Haven, CT: Yale University Press, 1997), 80, lines 2506–7.

31. Alfred, Lord Tennyson, *Idylls of the King*, 78, line 108.

32. Jeanne Nightingale, "Erec in the Mirror: The Feminization of the Self and the Reinvention of the Chivalric Hero in Chrétien's First Romance," in *Arthurian Romance and Gender*, ed. Friedrich Wolfzettel (Amsterdam: Rodopi, 1995), 130–46, at 135.

33. Michel-André Bossy, "The Elaboration of Female Narrative Functions in *Erec et Enide*," in *Courtly Literature: Culture and Context*, ed. Keith Busby and Erik Kooper (Am-

unintelligible to each other except through the performance of masochism, Erec and Enide model the queer disavowal of eroticism that dismantles the genders so central to their performance.

Beyond this example from the genre of romance, many medieval lyrics play with such masochistic desires between the male suitor and his imperious beloved. As mentioned previously, the troubadour tradition foregrounds such constructions of desire, and so do many such Middle English poems, including "Love for a Beautiful Lady," "A Song in His Lady's Absence," "A Love Letter," and "To the One I Love Most."[34] The genders of these roles can be readily reversed or otherwise reimagined, however, such as in the figure who might be termed the Beautiful Monastic Boy, the object of desire in courtly love verses written by monastic authors who cast themselves as suffering masochistically when bereft of the ravishing boy's amorous attention.[35] Each of these texts and genres merit deeper investigation for their occluded hermaphroditic treatment of courtly identity, but I now turn to Chaucer's *Franklin's Tale*, in which these dynamics subvert the vision of companionate marriage by revealing the queer torsions of identity needed to achieve its peaceful resolution.

MUTUAL MASOCHISM AND THE HERMAPHRODITIC COURTLY LADY IN CHAUCER'S *FRANKLIN'S TALE*

The opening lines of the *Franklin's Tale* stress its key theme of courtly love's masochistic edge in a knight's willingness to suffer for his beloved. In introducing Arveragus to the Canterbury pilgrims, the Franklin emphasizes his protagonist's love through his ready acceptance of pain and thus codes this character as a masochistic suitor who eagerly serves his lady according to the precepts of the courtly love tradition: "In Armorik, that

---

sterdam: Benjamins, 1990), 23–38, at 28. See also Lynn Tarte Ramey, "Representations of Women in Chrétien's *Erec et Enide*: Courtly Literature or Misogyny?" *Romanic Review* 84.4 (1993): 377–86, for an assessment of misogynist tropes in Enide's portrayal.

34. For these poems and others of their ilk, see R. T. Davies, ed., *Medieval English Lyrics: A Critical Anthology* (Evansville, IL: Northwestern University Press, 1964).

35. For a study of this dynamic in monastic verse, see Thomas Stehling, "To Love a Medieval Boy" (*Journal of Homosexuality* 8 [1983]: 151–70), in which he describes how monastic lyrics idealizing male beauty express a "casual indifference to female/male distinctions" (152). See also Gerald Bond, "The Play of Desire: Baudri of Bourgueil and the Formation of the Ovidian Subculture," in *The Loving Subject: Desire, Eloquence, and Power in Romanesque France* (Philadelphia: University of Pennsylvania Press, 1995), 42–69, for his reading of amatory verse in monastic settings, where such desires would presumably be taboo.

called is Britayne, / Ther was a knyght that loved and dide his payne / To serve a lady in his beste wise" (5.729–31). The Franklin's ambiguous description of Arveragus's love muddies attempts to read the knight's motivations: particularly, the object of his affections appears not to be Dorigen herself, who is as yet unnamed in the story and thus as yet indistinguishable from any other Courtly Lady, as so too is Arveragus as yet indistinguishable from any other courtly lover.[36] Rather, the Franklin's words—that Arveragus "loved and did his payne"—affirm not the knight's love for his lady but his love for the pain of serving her. Surely this passage contextually implies that Arveragus loves Dorigen and "did his payne" to win her affections, but its grammatical construction establishes Arveragus's objective to be his painful service of Dorigen. It is a telling example of the conflicted play of *fin amours*, in which desire for a beloved favors the pain of amatory service rather than its solaces. The Franklin also soon comments, "Lerneth to suffre, or elles, so moot I goon, / Ye shul it lerne, wher so ye ye wole or noon" (5.777–78), thereby reaffirming his key theme of suffering's necessity throughout his depiction of an apparently ideal marriage.

The narrative moves quickly to Arveragus and Dorigen's marriage but not before gesturing strongly to the standard tropes of the long-suffering courtier and his imperious beloved, whom he perceives as unattainable due to her high social status:

> And many a labour, many a greet emprise,
> He for his lady wroghte er she were wonne.
> For she was oon the faireste under sonne,
> And eek therto comen of so heigh kynrede
> That wel unnethes dorste this knyght, for drede,
> Telle hire his wo, his peyne, and his distresse. (5.732–37)

Within the traditional tropes of romance courtship in which this scene is colored, to love a beautiful and high-born woman requires a knight to labor incessantly to break through her cold exterior to the love she hides underneath the surface. Arveragus's woe, pain, and distress are merely cat-

---

36. In her *Naming and Namelessness in Medieval Romance* (Cambridge: Brewer, 2008), Jane Bliss notes the "performative function of name" in medieval romance in regard to "what it can do to characters in the story and what effect it can have on an audience" (15). In the *Franklin's Tale*, the delay in revealing Arveragus's and Dorigen's names first accentuates their status as stock literary characters—the courtly lover and his imperious beloved—before individualizing them and then troubling their performances of these expected roles.

alogued in these opening lines, rather than recounted in precise detail, because they are tropes that signal extensive suffering through their superficial mentioning. The brevity of the account, however, does not lessen the pain that has constituted his life in courting (and thus in suffering for) Dorigen.

In response to Arveragus's masochistic posturings, Dorigen confronts the shifting potential of courtly love, in which the ostensibly sadistic Courtly Lady may find herself bereft of the authority she purportedly wields. Deleuze posits that masochism "is animated by a dialectical spirit, . . . resulting in a scene being enacted simultaneously on several levels with reversals and reduplications in the allocation of roles and discourse,"[37] and this dialectical spirit circulates in the erotic tensions of their relationship. As encoded in the hierarchical gender roles of courtship, the Lady is granted power in contrast to the man's submissiveness, yet the mutuality of masochism, which springs from its dialectical play, upsets typical expectations of feminine amatory authority. As she falls in love with Arveragus and accedes to her position as wife, Dorigen loses the power of the Courtly Lady while nonetheless maintaining the role:

> But atte laste she, for his worthynesse,
> And namely for his meke obeysaunce,
> Hath swich a pitee caught of his penaunce
> That pryvely she fil of his accord
> To take hym for hir housbonde and hir lord. (5.738–42)

Arveragus's worthiness and meek obedience define his character in this passage, but his agency emerges in these submissive performances, for it is through this play that Dorigen "fil of his accord." In accord with Žižek's theorization of masochism as a performance, Arveragus successfully enacts his painful subservience so that Dorigen renounces her amatory authority. Intriguingly, Chaucer mentions Arveragus's "penance" in this passage, but readers see no evidence of any amorous (or spiritual) transgression for which he need atone; the suffering courtly lover, however, need not actually transgress against the dictates of love, for such transgressions are always and already the precondition of his pursuit and the basis of his performance.[38] From viewing Arveragus's performance of masochism, Dorigen

---

37. Gilles Deleuze, *Masochism*, 22.
38. *Penance* conjures a range of denotations and connotations, which, as registered in the *Middle English Dictionary*, include: "the sacrament of penance or reconciliation"; "repentance, change of heart; compunction, contrition"; "penalty, punishment; a judicial

realigns her role from imperious Courtly Lady to wife, one that further shifts the gendered inflections of their relationship. Both Courtly Ladies and wives are women, of course, but the genders accorded to these feminine roles range widely, and thus the transience of gendered categories points to the hermaphroditic potential inherent in the Courtly Lady. If a woman can assume both the roles of Courtly Lady and of wife, so too may her suitor assume both the roles of husband and of Courtly Lady in an ultimate queering of gender.

After ceding her authority as Courtly Lady, Dorigen appears to be Arveragus's amatory equal, and the Franklin praises mutuality as love's key value. For courtly and marital relationships to prosper, the narrator argues, both a knight and his lady must embrace the mutuality inherent in their love:

> For o thyng, sires, saufly dar I seye,
> That freendes everych oother moot obeye,
> If they wol longe holden compaignye.
> Love wol nat been constreyned by maistrye. (5.761–64)

The narrator's call for mutual obeisance stands as the ideal virtue espoused in the narrative, and the Franklin's vision of a successful marriage relies upon the impossibility of sadism through the renunciation of *maistrye*. Long-standing interpretations of the *Franklin's Tale* as the resolution of the marriage debate posit that, by declaring "freendes everych oother moot obeye," the Franklin refutes the vision of husbandly sadism embodied by Walter in the *Clerk's Tale*.[39] Certainly, Arveragus's relationship with Dorigen evinces little of the cruelty evident in Walter's relationship with Griselda, but to view these marriages as opposite ends of a spectrum occludes their overlapping concern with the play of gender when hus-

---

sentence; also, divine chastisement"; "the practice of asceticism and self mortification as a penitential discipline"; and "pain, suffering; affliction, hardship; also, a distasteful task or duty." The glosses of *penance* in *The Riverside Chaucer* (178, 1276) focus on the word's meaning as pain and suffering, yet given the hazy confluence of spiritual and amatory discourses in the play of courtly love, it seems likely that Chaucer encodes numerous connotations of *penance*, including its religious valences, in his descriptions of Arveragus's suffering for love.

39. Over 100 years later, G. L. Kittredge's "Chaucer's Discussion of Marriage" (*Modern Philology* 9 [1912]: 435–67) remains relevant in exploring Chaucer's depiction of marriage. He concludes that the *Franklin's Tale* "ends an elaborate debate" and urges readers "to accept the solution which the Franklin offers" (467). Jill Mann, particularly in her chapter "The Surrender of *Maistrye*," offers a compelling evaluation of marriage and "maistrye" in the *Franklin's Tale*; see her *Feminizing Chaucer* (Cambridge: Brewer, 2002), 70–99.

bands and wives debate their respective authority and control over each other.

Within the masochistic play of courtly love, such a paradigm shift as evident in Arveragus and Dorigen's attempts to renounce *maistrye* would require not only for the Courtly Lady to relinquish the veneer of sadism attributed to her but also for her male suitor to relinquish the play of masochism through which he orchestrates his lady's actions. But such a simplistic resolution merely camouflages the intertwined play of desire initiated in mutual masochism, in which cruelty can never be fully renounced because the anti-erotic play of both knight and lady now requires that each beloved demand his/her partner to instigate masochistically cruel rituals to test each other. Complementing their renunciation of *maistrye*, Arveragus and Dorigen vow sufferance to each other so that they may live together in harmony:

> And therfore hath this wise, worthy knyght,
> To lyve in ese, suffrance hire bihight,
> And she to hym ful wisly gan to swere
> That nevere sholde ther be defaute in here. (5.787–90)

How, though, can one promise *sufferance* without subjecting oneself to another's *maistrye*? The *Middle English Dictionary* includes among the definitions of *sufferance* the "willingness to be acted upon by an agent," which underscores the passivity inherent in Arveragus and Dorigen's marriage through their joint adherence to this marital virtue.[40] As opposed to *maistrye*, mutual *sufferance* defines the parameters of conjugal harmony in this marriage, yet it is a virtue of masochistic passivity in which, paradoxically, Arveragus and Dorigen accept each other's *maistrye*, despite their purported rejection of it, through their mutual *sufferance*. Mutual masochism should not be envisioned as necessitating an on/off switch, in which one partner embraces the masochistic position of subservience to the other's Courtly Lady in rigid demarcations of performance and identity; on the contrary, these oscillating identities pulse erratically in Dorigen and Arveragus's relationship. Deleuze believes that masochism is characterized by its dialectical qualities, which, in this instance, emerge in the continuing return of *maistrye* to a marriage from which it has presumably been banished.

---

40. The *Middle English Dictionary* also defines *sufferance* as "the undergoing of hardship, affliction, punishment, etc."; "suffering"; "the capacity to endure or manner of bearing up under pain"; and "the patient endurance of hardship, affliction, etc."

The hermaphroditism inherent in the Courtly Lady comes to the surface of the narrative as the Franklin subverts and reimagines gender roles throughout his romance. Foremost, the Franklin exposes the contradictions at the heart of courtly love when he hints that women, who should enjoy the prerogatives of the Courtly Lady's authority, wield little real power: "Wommen, of kynde, desiren libertee, / And nat to been constreyned as a thral; / And so doon men, if I sooth seyen shal" (5.768–70). Both women and men desire liberty, but it is noteworthy that the Franklin emphasizes women's potential to be "constreyned as a thral" despite their supposedly superior positions in courtly love. The hazy relationship between courtly love and marriage, in that the two are often interrelated in medieval amatory discourse yet need not be so, could explain these lines in the latent suggestion that a woman cedes her power in courtship upon becoming a wife (which again underscores the variability in the gender roles of Courtly Lady and of wife). Within the overlapping traditions of courtship and marriage, sharp distinctions are often encoded, such as in Andreas Capellanus's foundational text *De Amore*, when, in a passage from the Eighth Dialogue between a man and woman of the higher nobility, the man declares:

> "Confiteor, me pulchram satis habere uxorem, et ego quidem ipsam totius mentis affectione diligo maritali. Sed quum sciam, inter virum et uxorem posse nullatenus esse amorem, et in hac vita nullum posse fieri bonum, nisi illud ex amore originis sumpserit incrementa, non immerito extra nuptialia mihi foedera postulare cogor amorem."[41]

> "I admit that I have a wife who is beautiful enough, and I do indeed feel such affection for her as a husband can. But since I know that there can be no love between husband and wife . . . and that there can be nothing good done in this life unless it grows out of love, I am naturally compelled to seek for love outside the bonds of wedlock."[42]

Mark Taylor reads the *Franklin's Tale* as an interrogation of such distinctions between marital and courtly love, in which Chaucer "adopt[s] the ideal of the anti-adultery tradition and defend[s] it against the tradition

---

41. Andreas Capellanus, *De Amore*, ed. E. Trojel (Havniae: In Libraria Gadiana, 1892), 172.

42. Andreas Capellanus, *The Art of Courtly Love*, trans. John Jay Parry (New York: Columbia University Press, 1960), 116.

of adulterous love."[43] Taylor's account of love's vagaries is persuasive, yet the ultimate impossibility of distinguishing between marital and courtly love once mutual masochism disrupts the expected parameters of this gendered paradigm muddies a dichotomous view either of Courtly Lady or of wife. For even when the *Franklin's Tale* most clearly endorses mutuality, the inherent imbalance of masochistic ritual remains in effect, as does the threat of serving "as a thral."

If a woman as Courtly Lady faces the possibility of losing her authority in love and thus of sliding into a subservient position of thralldom when married, the Franklin's concomitant observation regarding men's desire "nat to been constreyned as a thral" is clearly linked to courtship rather than to marriage. Given medieval culture's assumption of masculine authority in marriage, men should not be expected to face thralldom in marriage after their masochistic performances during courtship have ceased.[44] The Franklin notes the distinction between men's gender roles in courtship and in marriage:

Thus hath she take hir servant and hir lord—
Servant in love, and lord in mariage.
Thanne was he bothe in lordshipe and servage.
Servage? Nay, but in lordshipe above,
Sith he hath bothe his lady and his love. (5.792–96)

Similar to the ways in which the biological sex of the lady masks two complementary yet discrete gender roles of Courtly Lady and wife, the knight's biological sex obscures the competing yet complementary versions of masculinity open for his performance: suffering suitor, authoritarian husband, and even, as Arveragus soon demonstrates, Courtly Lady. Here the knight's play of masochistic subservience in courtship is revealed as a ruse to gain control of his beloved in marriage, and even the egalitarian ideal of mutuality is merely a patriarchal façade, one by which Arvera-

---

43. Mark Taylor, "Servant and Lord / Lady and Wife: The *Franklin's Tale* and Traditions of Courtly and Conjugal Love," *Chaucer Review* 32.1 (1997): 64–81, at 77.

44. As studies of medieval marriage and widowhood have shown, women often found greater freedoms after their husbands' deaths than during their marriages, which highlights the patriarchal gender dynamics of medieval matrimony. See Cindy Carlson and Angela Jane Weisl, eds., *Constructions of Widowhood and Virginity in the Middle Ages* (New York: St. Martin's, 1999); Louise Mirrer, ed, *Upon My Husband's Death: Widows in the Literature and Histories of Medieval Europe* (Ann Arbor: University of Michigan Press, 1992); and Sue Sheridan Walker, ed., *Wife and Widow in Medieval England* (Ann Arbor: University of Michigan Press, 1993).

gus is able to maintain lordship over Dorigen in marriage because he wins her both as the Courtly Lady of romance and as his love in marriage. Both Courtly Ladies and wives, in their performance of gendered femininity, must accede to male prerogatives, yet nonetheless the man's potential position as Courtly Lady will reveal his willingness to perform for her narcissistic desires when she stages her own masochistic rituals.

Once married, Dorigen experiences the keen pain of suffering while awaiting her husband's return from England, and in these scenes she mirrors Arveragus's masochistic torments during their courtship.[45] Similar to her husband, who performed "many a labour" to win her, she snares the amatory attention of a suitor through the masochistic and public ritual of suffering without him. Deleuze theorizes that waiting enhances the masochist's experience of suffering, that the "masochist is morose," and this "moroseness should be related to the experience of waiting and delay."[46] After Arveragus departs, pain dominates Dorigen's life: "She moorneth, waketh, wayleth, fasteth, pleyneth; / Desir of his presence hire so destreyneth / That al this wyde world she sette at noght" (5.819–21). Her desire for Arveragus empties her life of meaning, and she sees herself as bound to Fortune's cruel vagaries: "Allas . . . on thee, Fortune, I pleyne, / That unwar wrapped hast me in thy cheyne" (5.1355–56). Even the black rocks, emblematic of her emotional torment during Arveragus's absence, signify the performativity encoded in her suffering. On a surface level, they are concrete reminders of her loss and her fears for her husband's safety, yet Timothy Flake intriguingly suggests that Dorigen needs these rocks, that she "really does not want the rocks to be removed. The rocks' presence . . . is the foundation of her sense of certainty, for it is on this certainty that she bases her defense against Aurelius's advances and her declaration of faithfulness to Arveragus."[47]

---

45. Dorigen's status in a primarily masculine world has drawn the attention of numerous scholars, such as Alison Ganze, who sees her negotiating masculine values in her search for *trouthe* ("'My trouthe for to holde—allas, allas!': Dorigen and Honor in the *Franklin's Tale*," *Chaucer Review* 42.3 [2008]: 312–29); Andrea Rossi-Reder, who describes the ways in which the tale establishes that "masculine mobility is grounded in female fixity" ("Male Movement and Female Fixity in the *Franklin's Tale* and *Il Filocolo*," in *Masculinities in Chaucer: Approaches to Maleness in the* Canterbury Tales *and* Troilus and Criseyde, ed. Peter Beidler [Cambridge: Brewer, 1998], 106–16, at 115); and Mary Bowman, who describes Dorigen as a possession traded between men rather than as an individual ("'Half as she were mad': Dorigen in the Male World of the *Franklin's Tale*," *Chaucer Review* 27.3 [1993]: 239–51).

46. Gilles Deleuze, *Masochism*, 70–71.

47. Timothy Flake, "Love, *Trouthe*, and the Happy Ending of the *Franklin's Tale*," *English Studies* 77.3 (1996): 209–26, at 219. Concerning these rocks, see also John Friedman, "Dori-

The pain that readers witness in Arveragus's performance of masochism during courtship, which cracked when he could finally "tell hire his wo, his peyne, and his distresse," now envelops Dorigen in marriage, but through such apparent passivity, she defines her own narcissistic image. Aurelius's desire for her—which he has hidden "two yeer and moore" (5.940) but can hide no longer—indicates her success in this regard, for it is at the moment of her deepest pain that he can no longer hide his desire for her.

The cause of Dorigen's suffering is at least somewhat arbitrary, for why, except to allow his wife to stage her masochistic ritual, does Arveragus depart for England? The Franklin mentions the knight's journey without explaining his motivation beyond a cursory reference to his knightly duties, and so here Arveragus enacts the arbitrary callousness of the Courtly Lady, as he compels Dorigen to experience his former suffering:

> A yeer and moore lasted this blisful lyf,
> Til that the knyght of which I speke of thus,
> That of Kayrrud was cleped Arveragus,
> Shoop hym to goon and dwelle a yeer or tweyne
> In Engelond, that cleped was eek Briteyne,
> To seke in armes worshipe and honour—
> For al his lust he sette in swich labour—
> And dwelled there two yeer; the book seith thus. (5.806–13)

From a conventional perspective, Arveragus is a knight and knights must engage in battle and fight in tournaments; it is simply an occupational obligation, one that reflects negatively neither upon him nor upon his devotion to Dorigen. Yet such a rationalization is based on establishing an internal logic to the machinations of courtly love, an amatory system almost immune to logic in its oscillating play of gender and amatory authority. Similar moments in other romances when knights fail to prioritize their ladies over their homosocial responsibilities and pleasures—such as in Chrétien de Troyes's *Yvain, ou Le Chevalier au lion*, when Yvain departs from Laudine to join Gawain in knightly tournaments, and in Marie de France's *Lanval*, when Lanval fails to adhere to his Lady's demand for silence regarding their relationship—highlight these knights' propensity to sabotage their love in order to replay the mutual masoch-

---

gen's 'Grisly rokkes blake' Again," *Chaucer Review* 31.2 (1996): 133–44, who associates them with a "pre-Christian or actively anti-Christian point of view" (142).

ism that should no longer be necessary due to love's fruition. Such scenes privilege the knight's homosocial relationships with his peers over his love for his lady, thus further positioning her as a narcissistic mirror of his performances for other men's pleasure. These plotlines also suggest that once the knight's relationship with his beloved is so firmly established that he need no longer enact his masochistic ploys, he compels her to experience the painful effects of his newly returned sense of agency, even to his own detriment, for by refusing his initial position of masochistic subservience, the knight paradoxically ensures that both he and his beloved will suffer more than previously by undermining the foundations of their love. At the very least, the Franklin's declaration that Arveragus prefers the worship and honor of arms to the sexual bliss of marriage—"For al his lust he sette in swich labour"—denigrates the love he so desperately sought but from which he seeks to escape after merely "[a] yeer and moore." With the erotic pleasures of marriage forsworn in favor of the (assumedly) chaste pleasures of homosocial companionship in service to his lord and fellow men, Arveragus anticipates two years—approximately twice the length of the year or so he spent with Dorigen as husband and wife—without the sexual pleasures he so keenly pursued in the narrative's opening. The Franklin cites his textual source in this moment—"the book seith thus"—and this rhetorical flourish provides documentary evidence to a common trope of romance that makes little sense according to external logic but profoundly affects the contours of courtly love and its perverse traditions. Fracturing the bliss of their marriage through his actions, Arveragus provides Dorigen with the opportunity to stage her own masochistic ritual, one that ensnares both her husband and her suitor in a new round of suffering. As she served as Queer Thing / Courtly Lady for Arveragus as suitor, he will serve this role for her by encouraging her to abandon the sadism to which she ostensibly had access in her role as Courtly Lady and to undergo the suffering play of contractual masochism with both him and Aurelius.

Aurelius loves and fears Dorigen, and, like his rival Arveragus, he employs the standard tropes of masochistic disavowal in approaching her. "My righte lady . . . / Whom I moost drede and love as I best kan, / And lothest were of al this world displese" (5.1311–13), he declares, performing his trepidation before her, and he also accords her the imperious position of the Courtly Lady by referring to her as "my sovereyn lady" before humbly placing his fate in her hands (5.1325, cf. 5.1072). Readers learn that Aurelius has long loved Dorigen without seeking relief for his suffering: "But nevere dorste he tellen hire his grevaunce. / Withouten coppe he drank al his penaunce" (5.941–42). In these amatory posturings, complete with their tropes of suffering and penance, Aurelius mirrors Arveragus, and in this nascent conflict, it appears that the *Franklin's Tale* will address the vexed (and often queer) negotiations of aggression and affection inherent in triangulations of desire.[48] Arveragus, Dorigen, and Aurelius's relationship bears the structure of an erotic triangle, and readers might expect the narrative to end with Arveragus and Aurelius fighting in a tournament to ensure the winner's position as her beloved, in a manner similar to Palamon and Arcite's combat at the conclusion of the *Knight's Tale*. In terms of the erotic choice before Dorigen, little distinguishes Arveragus and Aurelius from each other in terms of personality, appearance, or profession: like Palamon and Arcite in the *Knight's Tale*, the two men are nearly interchangeable in their performance of amatory ritual, yet within the logic of this romance, Arveragus's position as Dorigen's first lover, and thus as her husband, cannot be stripped from him.[49] Nor should it be: despite surface similarities between Arveragus and Aurelius, Arveragus's role as Dorigen's husband is sacrosanct within the erotic logic of this tale. The *Franklin's Tale* focuses on the pains and pleasures of abstention first in courtship and then in marriage, not of action in adultery, and so this erotic triangle—unlike the violent enactment of triangulated desire in the *Knight's Tale*—concentrates on sharing masochistic ritual with Aurelius and thereby disciplining him into love's service. One does not need to defeat a masochist in an erotic rivalry that, by the tale's end, is rendered anti-erotic; one need only encourage him to continue his masochistic subservience and to alienate him, to queer him, from a vision of masculinity predicated upon amatory success with women. He must be taught not to transcend masochism as the primary seductive tactic in a man's erotic repertoire but to languish in its painful pleasures.

And so, rather than bolstering the aggression latent in triangulated desire, masochism infuses Arveragus and Aurelius's amatory competition with a mutually painful dynamic that strips away the aggression latent in

---

48. Eve Sedgwick's *Between Men: English Literature and Male Homosocial Desire* (New York: Columbia University Press, 1985) remains the theoretical foundation for analyzing the homoerotic cast of erotic triangles.

49. Palamon and Arcite resemble each other in numerous qualities, but Catherine Rock, in her "Forsworn and Fordone: Arcite as Oath-Breaker in the *Knight's Tale*" (*Chaucer Review* 40.4 [2006]: 416–32), explores how Arcite's actions after falling in love with Emily distinguish him morally from his sworn brother. In this instance Chaucer's refusal to distinguish between erotic rivals reflects the inscrutable vagaries of Fortune in amatory affairs.

love. Foremost, Arveragus remains unaware of Aurelius's desire for his wife throughout most of the narrative, in which several years pass with little to advance the narrative. Time passes quickly yet slowly in the *Franklin's Tale*, which heightens the Franklin's rhetorical flourishes regarding love's suffering. For example, Aurelius suffers "two yeer and moore" after confessing his love for Dorigen (5.1102), and this line regarding time's passage heightens the emotional pain of this scene, pointing to the long periods of suffering that the characters endure.[50] While pursuing another man's wife, Aurelius, rather than openly confronting his rival, publicly performs his masochistic suffering, and in this masterful enactment of desire he sings numerous songs of love purportedly to hide yet paradoxically to announce his amorous intentions:

> He was despeyred; no thyng dorste he seye,
> Save in his songes somwhat wolde he wreye
> His wo, as in a general compleynyng;
> He seyde he lovede and was biloved no thyng.
> Of swich matere made he manye layes,
> Songes, compleintes, roundels, virelayes,
> How that he dorste nat his sorwe telle,
> But langwissheth as a furye dooth in helle. (5.943–50)

Aurelius hides his amatory woe, but only to reveal it in song in no less than five separate genres, as it if were a "general compleyning," not his personal lament. Both revealing and cloaking his pain, Aurelius transforms his private suffering into a public performance, one that occludes his masochism while it is nonetheless on full display for his audience.

When Dorigen confronts Aurelius about the impropriety of his desires, she focuses on the painful pleasure of forbearance, encouraging him to accept the queer regenderings of masochism available to him by renouncing the possibility of consummating his desires. In her rhetorical question to him—"What deyntee sholde a man han in his lyf / For to go love another mannes wyf, / That hath hir body whan so that hym liketh?" (5.1003–5)—she emphasizes that he should disavow sexuality while simultaneously highlighting Arveragus's former enjoyment of sexual pleasure with her. Michael Calabrese rightly points out the provocative nature of Dorigen's words, seeing them as "an inflammation

---

50. Other such lines addressing time's passage in the tale include 806, 809, 813, 940, 1568, and 1582.

of the male rivalry that Aurelius is conducting. . . . By reminding him in sexually suggestive terms that her body *is* freely enjoyed, but not by him, she only encourages Aurelius to commit himself to achieving the 'impossible' and to have what his rival freely enjoys."[51] I would only qualify Calabrese's perceptive observation by changing its verb tense: her body is not *currently* being freely enjoyed by Arveragus, who is in England pursuing homosocial knightly pastimes rather than sating his amatory desires when she speaks these words; rather, erotic pleasure, at the moment of this confrontation, is unavailable to Dorigen, Arveragus, and Aurelius, which leaves only the specter of sexuality behind. By so publicly performing her suffering during Arveragus's absence and by reminding Aurelius of the sexual pleasure of which she herself cannot partake, Dorigen accentuates love's pains as a renouncing rather than as a fulfilling of desire. In this passage she is both the Courtly Lady who enhances Aurelius's suffering through her cruel rejoinder while also serving as the masochist subservient to Arveragus, who, in his own role as Courtly Lady, disciplines her by denying her the erotic pleasure available to her in marriage (and, it appears from these lines, keenly missed).

In his masochistic ritual with its polymorphous gender play, Aurelius enacts the theatrical ploys of masochism not merely for Dorigen but for the magician who supernaturally obscures the black rocks so central to Dorigen's heartfelt performance of erotic suffering. These structural similarities of masochistic ritual in Aurelius's appeal to the magician do not suggest a latent homoeroticism in this scene but instead point to the queer and masochistic underbelly of desires circulating both through men and women and throughout their relationships; regardless of Dorigen's or of the magician's biological sex, Aurelius's narcissistic strategies reveal the ubiquity of masochism throughout virtually all encounters in this tale. He assumes the masochist's obsequious position vis-à-vis his superior, even threatening the magician with his suicide should his amatory pains be left unresolved:

> Aurelius in al that evere he kan
> Dooth to this maister chiere and reverence,
> And preyeth hym to doon his diligence
> To bryngen hym out of his peynes smerte,
> Or with a swerd that he wolde slitte his herte.

---

51. Michael Calabrese, "Chaucer's Dorigen and Boccaccio's Female Voices," *Studies in the Age of Chaucer* 29 (2007): 259–92, at 264; italics in original.

> This subtil clerk swich routhe had of this man
> That nyght and day he spedde hym that he kan
> To wayten a tyme of his conclusioun. (5.1256–63)

Aurelius's relationship with the magician structurally mirrors that of his relationship with Dorigen, in which his masochism encourages these "masters" to act on his behalf, as Dorigen does in her rash promise to love him should he remove the black rocks. His ready embrace of death wins "swich routhe" from "this maister" that his plan to win Dorigen's affections proceed apace. Deleuze believes that death intertwines with eroticism in masochism, such that "destruction is always presented as the other side of a construction, as an instinctual drive which is necessarily combined with Eros,"[52] and in this manner Aurelius pursues erotic satisfaction through his declared readiness for death.

From her relationship with Arveragus, Dorigen learns that masochistic suitors do not act except through their contractual performance of suffering, and so she is duly shocked when Aurelius informs her that he has successfully moved the black rocks from the coast. In a tale that emphasizes forbearance and inaction, Aurelius's apparent rejection of passivity shocks Dorigen:

> "Allas," quod she, "that evere this sholde happe!
> For wende I nevere by possibilitee
> That swich a monstre or merveille myghte be!
> It is agayns the proces of nature." (5.1342–45)

Dorigen refers to a "monstre" in Aurelius's successful removal of the black rocks, and this "monstre" could signify either the magical event or Aurelius himself. In at long last rising from his melancholic torpor and momentarily refusing the masochistic suffering that the suitor should continually perform, he metaphorically transforms into a monster who abrogates the expected rituals of courtly love merely by acting. Surely the disappearance of the black rocks "is agayns the proces of nature," but so too is Aurelius, who disrupts the expected sexual roles of lover and beloved by disavowing the mutual masochism at the heart of their relationship in favor of activity rather than passivity. Like the Courtly Lady, he now acts as a Queer Thing in this passage, forcing Dorigen to confront the emptiness of her masochistic performances of forbearance and the possibility that the

---

52. Gilles Deleuze, *Masochism*, 116.

narcissistic image she created for herself is merely an anti-erotic veneer, one that defined her virtue while awaiting Arveragus's return, but that can no longer withstand the pressures of an eroticism unconstrained by masochism. The irony, however, of Aurelius's presumed activity is that he has, in fact, done little other than stage his suffering both for Dorigen and the magician; whatever illusion obscures the black rocks is the magician's work, not his, and the narrator reports the evanescence of this magical feat: "But thurgh his magik, for a wyke or tweye, / It semed that alle the rokkes were aweye" (5.1295–96). To compel Dorigen to abandon her façade as the impervious courtly lady, Aurelius relies on the appearance of action rather than on action itself, demonstrating yet again the ruse of masochistic passivity in a startling display of inactivity couched as his passionate pursuit of her.

The remainder of the *Franklin's Tale* must quell this disruption to its masochistic logic so that passivity will triumph as the defining feature of eroticism and its queer disruptions of gendered paradigms. When Dorigen contemplates suicide in a scene akin to Aurelius's threat of suicide to the magician, she again appears to be acting masochistically in pursuit of punishment, and Deleuze notes the "provocative fear" that sparks the masochist to "aggressively demand punishment since it resolves anxiety and allows him to enjoy the forbidden pleasure."[53] Due to Dorigen's multiple positions—as Courtly Lady, as Queer Thing, and as masochistic performer of her own suffering—gender can no longer guide her in her decisions, for gender is incapable of pinning down these oscillating roles to a singularly sexed body. When she catalogs virtuous wives and maidens who choose suicide over dishonor, she attempts to gird herself to act, to embrace the agency necessary to abrogate her suffering:

"And with my deth I may be quyt, ywis.
Hath ther nat many a noble wyf er this,
And many a mayde, yslayn hirself, allas,
Rather than with hir body doon trespas?" (5.1363–66)

Unlike the many heroines of Chaucer's *Legend of Good Women*, who prove their virtue by their willing deaths, Dorigen does not act; instead, she "pleyned . . . a day or tweye, / Purposynge evere that she wolde deye" (5.1457–58). As Warren Smith attests, "Dorigen's Lament reveals her struggling toward a resolution of her dilemma which will keep her from

---

53. Ibid., 75.

suicide and preserve both her 'trothe' and her fidelity to her husband."[54] This moral conundrum also allows her masochistic performances to continue, for ending them through suicide would abrogate the oscillations at the core of her romance that define her pursuit of pleasure. Although some might argue that suicide represents the logical end point of masochism in the disavowal of desire through death, suicide corrupts the performative nature of suffering and substitutes irrevocable action for momentary posturings designed to perpetuate the lovers' anti-erotic play.

In his capricious and arbitrary reaction to Dorigen's amatory suffering, Arveragus again assumes the position of the hermaphroditic Courtly Lady, one whose actions deflect internal logic yet compel Dorigen as masochist to embrace ever more suffering. Strangely, he initially seems pleased with Dorigen's plight: in response to her tears, he replies "with glad chiere, in freendly wyse" (5.1467), and his words to her, "Is ther oght elles, Dorigen, but this?" (5.1469), imply that the matter of her incipient unfaithfulness is a trifling concern, of little relevance to their continued happiness. Alcuin Blamires perceives in Arveragus's reaction "the Stoic ideal of the compassionate person, who relieves those who are in tears, but without weeping *with* them,"[55] and this image of reacting by not reacting captures the rigidity of the Courtly Lady's stance, in which the suitor must prove his devotion by acting against his own self-interest and privileging the beloved's inscrutable desires. In a swift reversal of his initial nonchalance, Arveragus then threatens Dorigen with her imminent death: "I yow forbede, up peyne of deeth, / That nevere, whil thee lasteth lyf ne breeth, / To no wight telle thou of this aventure" (5.1481–83). Raymond Tripp observes an "irony . . . emerg[ing] in the fact that Arveragus, in his attempt to escape his masculine role (and all of its attendant trials and complications), finds himself assuming an *absolute maistrye* over Dorigen, even to the point of threatening her with the 'peyne of deeth.'"[56] Whether the imperious Courtly Lady or the masochistic suitor, Arveragus acts through his inaction and thus paradoxically circulates masochistic desire throughout the triangulated affair. For in compelling Dorigen to degrade herself sexually in response to his

---

54. Warren Smith, "Dorigen's Lament and the Resolution of the *Franklin's Tale*," *Chaucer Review* 36.4 (2002): 374–90, at 389.

55. Alcuin Blamires, *Chaucer, Ethics, and Gender* (Oxford: Oxford University Press, 2006), 154–55; italics in original.

56. Raymond Tripp, "The Franklin's Solution to the Marriage Debate," in *New Views on Chaucer: Essays in Generative Criticism*, ed. William Johnson and Loren Gruber (Denver: Society for New Language Study, 1973), 35–41, at 39.

arbitrary rulings as Courtly Lady / Queer Thing, Arveragus showcases his impervious self-control by preparing himself for the pain of her cuckolding him, thereby reconfiguring himself into yet another masochistic position, once again defined by anti-eroticism. Deleuze observes the masochist's propensity to pander his wife: "the masochist persuades his wife, in her capacity as good mother, to give herself to other men."[57] The male masochist's ultimate humiliation in cuckoldry is thus the fullest pleasure available to him, but one to which he must coerce his wife to submit so that the queer pleasure of abjection will surface through the circulation of a woman among a male homosocial milieu.

The ending of the *Franklin's Tale* details the perfect stasis of masochism, in which the four primary characters cannot sate their desires other than through the continued play of forbearance. The Franklin records Arveragus and Dorigen's "happily ever after" ending and then dismisses them from the narrative: "Of thise two folk ye gete of me namoore" (5.1556). It is intriguing to contemplate Arveragus's masochistic disappointment in his wife's failure to cuckold him, and readers see little evidence to suggest that the purportedly "happily ever after" ending concludes the mutually masochistic maneuverings that define their courtship and marriage. At the very least, the tale continues after its ostensible protagonists' departure from the narrative, which highlights that this husband and wife's marital adventures cannot circumscribe its thematic concerns, and instead posits masochism as a generative force within various human relationships. In light of Arveragus and Dorigen's mutual masochism, Aurelius purges himself of desire:

> And in his herte he caughte of this greet routhe,
> Considerynge the beste on every syde,
> That fro his lust yet were hym levere abyde
> Than doon so heigh a cherlyssh wrecchednesse
> Agayns franchise and alle gentillesse. (5.1520–24)

Furthermore, Aurelius is prepared to abase himself perpetually for their love: "I have wel levere evere to suffre wo / Than I departe the love bitwix yow two" (5.1531–32). Choosing perpetual pain, Aurelius emerges as an avatar of masochism, one rid of any desire other than to suffer for others so that he may be celebrated for such suffering. In a final scene of recu-

---

57. Gilles Deleuze, *Masochism*, 63.

perating and reframing desire, the magician sacrifices monetary gain and forgives Aurelius his debt. From the mutually masochistic play of courtly love and marriage, Dorigen, Arveragus, Aurelius, and the magician embody the emptiness of gender and the intransigence of the queer Courtly Lady, a hermaphroditic position that guides them to renounce desire for the sake of the anti-erotic pleasure at the heart of this renunciation and the narcissistic refashioning of desirability through the suffering and depredations incurred.

EPILOGUE: THE MODEST FRANKLIN

I do not argue in this chapter's concluding section that the Franklin engages in a mutually masochistic relationship with Harry Bailly and his fellow pilgrims by telling his tale. The relatively scant descriptions of the Franklin—his *General Prologue* portrait (1.331–60), his words with the Squire at the close of the *Squire's Tale* (5.673–708), and his *Prologue* (5.709–28)—do not offer sufficient evidence to warrant such an interpretation. The masochistic performances of amatory submission in the Franklin's tale and his performance of modesty in tale-telling are nonetheless analogous in their deployment of submission as an obfuscatory tool that camouflages desires circulating throughout interpersonal relationships. Power and gender dynamics resonate throughout the Canterbury pilgrimage, and the Franklin's modesty emerges as yet another tactic in the ongoing squabbling among the pilgrims, couched as it is under the guise of play and game.

The Franklin's relationship with his fellow pilgrims showcases the subtle power of modesty and etiquette, in which social pleasantries and his amiable disposition cloak his authority. In describing the Franklin in the *General Prologue*, Chaucer stresses this character's largesse and hospitality. He is compared to St. Julian, patron saint of hospitality (1.340), and the abundance of food in his house establishes the character's ample generosity: "It snewed in his hous of mete and drynke" (1.345). Likewise, when the Franklin joins the narrative action of the pilgrimage by interrupting the Squire's rambling tale, readers witness the latent authority accessible to those who understand social ritual. "As to my doom, ther is noon that is heere / Of eloquence that shal be thy peere, / . . . / For of thy speche I have greet deyntee" (5.677–78, 81), the Franklin graciously declares to the Squire, but, of course, his deeper purpose is not to praise the young man but to silence him. Similarly, after Harry Bailly rudely interrupts the

Franklin—"Straw for youre gentillesse!" (5.695)—the Franklin employs his eloquence to silence Harry while promising to submit to him:

> "Gladly, sire Hoost," quod he, "I wole obeye
> Unto your wyl; now herkneth what I seye.
> I wol yow nat contrarien in no wyse
> As fer as that my wittes wol suffyse.
> I prey to God that it may plesen yow." (5.703–7)

Much like the Clerk, who earlier pledged his obedience to Harry's will but then immediately qualified this submission—"And therfore wol I do yow obeisance, / As fer as resoun axeth, hardily" (4.24–25)—the Franklin promises fidelity to Harry's rule while simultaneously excluding his full adherence to this authority. Like the masochist who performs subservience for his imperious beloved, the Franklin plays his role in submission to Harry's authority, but this performance only highlights the potential emptiness of such playacting.

Chaucer continues his description of the Franklin's submissiveness when, in the *Franklin's Prologue*, the Franklin introduces his tale through his modesty topos and dissembles his rhetorical skills:

> "I lerned nevere rethorik, certeyn;
> Thyng that I speke, it moot be bare and pleyn.
> I sleep nevere on the Mount of Pernaso,
> Ne lerned Marcus Tullius Scithero." (5.719–22)

Such proclamations of rhetorical modesty appear in other Chaucerian narratives, and Donald Fritz posits that these instances of modesty reveal that Chaucer's characters "wrestl[e] with the problem of artistic communication of deep and abiding truths."[58] In this instance, the Franklin cannot openly criticize the social structure of the Canterbury pilgrimage, but he can employ his story to reimagine the gendered dynamics of the pilgrimage that the blustering Harry Bailly controls. Tale-telling involves rhetorical choices that at times camouflage violent desires, as Sandra McEntire provocatively explains of the *Franklin's Tale:* "In taking old stories, remaking them and interpreting them, Chaucer is in effect acting like Aurelius with the body of narrative. He takes a texts and breaks it apart, rapes

---

58. Donald Fritz, "The Prioress's Avowal of Ineptitude," *Chaucer Review* 9.2 (1974): 166–81, at 179.

and dismembers it as it were, and puts it back together—remembers it—with his own insights, subtexts, interpretations."[59] McEntire's startling metaphors of rape and dismemberment for retelling narratives capture the aggressive dynamics latent throughout the Canterbury pilgrimage and points to the ways in which the Franklin engages in such aggression through rhetorical choices rather than through direct insults or bawdily allegorical narratives.

In regendering narrative through his mutually masochistic tale, the Franklin forecloses masculine pleasure in climax, and, in so doing, queers the meaning of normative gender for his fellow pilgrims. Numerous narratological theories posit that plotlines emulate the physiological pleasures of male orgasm, such as in Robert Scholes's (in)famous formulation:

> The archetype of all fiction is the sexual act. In saying this I do not mean merely to remind the reader of the connection between all art and the erotic in human nature. . . . For what connects fiction—and music—with sex is the fundamental orgiastic rhythm of tumescence and detumescence, of tension and resolution, of intensification to the point of climax and consummation. In the sophisticated forms of fiction, as in the sophisticated practice of sex, much of the art consists of delaying climax within the framework of desire in order to prolong the pleasurable act itself.[60]

But what of narratives without climaxes? Where is the narrative pleasure of orgasm in an ultimately anti-erotic tale that refuses its reader the pleasure of climax? One would be hard-pressed to locate a climax in the *Franklin's Tale:* is it Dorigen's decision to commit suicide (which she then ignores), her confession to Arveragus of her commitment to Aurelius (which he then forgives), her meeting with Aurelius in which she is prepared to fulfill her obligations (of which he then absolves her)? One could argue that the tale's climax and its inconclusive conclusion unite in its closing *demande d'amour*, as the Franklin queries: "Which was the mooste

---

59. Sandra McEntire, "Illusions and Interpretation in the *Franklin's Tale*," *Chaucer Review* 31 (1996): 145–63, at 160.

60. Robert Scholes, *Fabulation and Metafiction* (Urbana: University of Illinois Press, 1979), 26. See also Peter Brooks, "Freud's Masterplot: A Model for Narrative," in his *Reading for the Plot* (New York: Vintage, 1984), 90–112. For critiques of such narratological theories, see Theresa de Lauretis, *Alice Doesn't: Feminism, Semiotics, Cinema* (Bloomington: Indiana University Press, 1984), esp. 103–57; and Susan Winnett, "Coming Unstrung: Women, Men, Narrative, and Principles of Pleasure," *PMLA* 105.3 (1990): 505–18.

fre, as thynketh yow? / Now telleth me, er that ye ferther wende. / I kan namoore; my tale is at an ende" (5.1622–24). To end a narrative with a *demande d'amour*, however, encodes a fundamentally different structure into its plotline, for in Chaucer's other narratives containing *demandes d'amour*—the *Knight's Tale* and the *Wife of Bath's Tale*—these amatory rhetorical questions occur early in the plot and are at least implicitly resolved. The *Knight's Tale* queries, "Who hath the worse, Arcite or Palamoun?" (1.1348), and although the debate of whether the imprisoned lover who can see his beloved fares better or worse than the emancipated lover who cannot see her is not definitively answered, the narrative concludes in favor of Palamon as he wins Emily in marriage and thus settles any unresolved aspects of the lovers' fates. The provocative query at the heart of the *Wife of Bath's Tale*—"What thyng is it that wommen moost desiren" (3.905)—is conclusively answered: "Wommen desiren to have sovereynetee / As wel over hir housbond as hir love, / And for to been in maistrie hym above" (3.1038–40). The Franklin, in contrast, ends his tale with a question that refuses a pat answer and thus rejects the narrative rhythms of male desire and masculinist plotlines. As his play of modesty invites his fellow pilgrims to dismiss him as an inept storyteller before he commences his narrative, the Franklin reveals his sophisticated technique throughout his tale, which culminates without a climax or definitive conclusion. In so doing, he asks his fellow pilgrims to consider the possibility of a form of narrative pleasure distinct from those that have come before, one in which recalcitrant inaction trumps action.

The Franklin's refusal to end his story conclusively encodes an absence in his narrative, and as Elizabeth Scala argues, such absences, in many instances, constitute a narrative's core: "In these complex medieval stories themselves, and through their indications of what is *not* the subject of the story, the absent narrative is revealed as an unconscious subject of narrative."[61] Because Chaucer did not depict the pilgrims' reactions to the *Franklin's Tale*, it is impossible to gauge their responses to it and its narrative ploys. Nonetheless, in reconfiguring the narratological expectations of pleasure in climax, the Franklin effectively asks his audience to experience female narrative pleasure. The Franklin does not address narratology when he declares, "Pacience is an heigh vertu, certeyn / For it venquysseth, as thise clerkes seyn, / Thynges that rigour sholde nevere atteyne" (5.773–75), but these words are intriguing in their dismissal of

---

61. Elizabeth Scala, *Absent Narratives, Manuscript Textuality, and Literary Structure in Late Medieval England* (New York: Palgrave Macmillan, 2002), 12; italics in original.

masculine rigor in favor of endless patience and suffering and in their rewriting of mutually masochistic forbearance into the rules of courtly love and of narrative. As Dorigen, Arveragus, and Aurelius queer the foundations of gender and reveal the inherently convoluted play of masochistic desire in the *Franklin's Tale*, so too does the Franklin coerce his fellow pilgrims to embrace such patience, even if this narrative strategy refuses them the pleasure of climax in favor of patiently waiting for an ending that will never arrive.

CHAPTER THREE

"FOR TO BE SWORNE BRETHEREN TIL THEY DEYE"

Satirizing Queer Brotherhood in the Chaucerian Corpus

In Chaucer's canon, when a man swears an oath of brotherhood to another man, the vow is soon repudiated, rejected, or otherwise rendered problematic.[1] No exceptions to this rule appear. Fraternal promises in Chaucer's literature evoke homosocial tensions and aggressions, and this dynamic hints that, for Chaucer, these particular bonds of brotherhood carried with them the likely possibility of erotic queerness. By characterizing such homosocial relationships as intrinsically susceptible to betrayal and ridicule, Chaucer hints that male friendships, as incarnated through brotherhood oaths, were often viewed suspiciously in courtly and aristocratic contexts of fourteenth-century

---

1. Studies of oaths in Chaucer's literature include Lois Roney, "Chaucer Subjectivizes the Oath: Depicting the Fall from Feudalism into Individualism in the *Canterbury Tales*," in *The Rusted Hauberk: Feudal Ideals of Order and Their Decline*, ed. Liam Purdon and Cindy Vitto (Gainesville: University of Florida Press, 1994), 269–98; Daniel Kline, "'Myne by right': Oath Making and Intent in the *Friar's Tale*," *Philological Quarterly* 77 (1998): 271–93; and William Keen, "Chaucer's Imaginable Audience and the Oaths of the *Shipman's Tale*," *Topic* 50 (2000): 91–103. Richard Firth Green addresses many of Chaucer's works in his *A Crisis of Truth: Literature and Law in Ricardian England* (Philadelphia: University of Pennsylvania Press, 1999); the chapters "From Troth to Truth" (1–40) and "Trothplight" (41–77) are particularly relevant for their analysis of the social discourses surrounding truths and oaths and the ways in which oaths reflect character. This chapter analyzes the particular subset of Chaucerian oaths pledged between two or more men in which they guarantee to act as brothers for their common good.

England, despite the normative and chaste valence accorded such relationships in these same social settings. The discrepancies between Chaucer's depiction of homosocial oaths and those of his contemporaries point to the inherent difficulty of locating queerness in the Middle Ages, as we see in this instance that the same social phenomenon can reflect both queerness and normativity, both submerged eroticism and presumed antieroticism, depending upon the circumstances of its enactment. In their potential to spark either suspicions of latent homoeroticism or approval of ennobling social ritual, brotherhood oaths straddle the lines of sexually illicit and asexually licit.

Chaucer deploys brotherhood oaths satirically in each of the five narratives in which they appear—*House of Fame, Knight's Tale, Friar's Tale, Pardoner's Tale,* and *Shipman's Tale*. The narrator of the *House of Fame* describes a plenitude of brotherhood oaths at the narrative's close, and this scene, which mocks the allegorical figures who engage in such relationships, imbues the poem with a comic dismissal of homosocial friendships that teasingly undermines its conclusion. The *Knight's Tale* features Palamon and Arcite's oaths of brotherhood, which are subverted in their decision to forgo sworn homosocial union in pursuit of heteroerotic courtship and marriage with Emily; in this instance, fraternal oaths structure the narrative's deconstruction of romance values. In the *Friar's Tale, Pardoner's Tale,* and *Shipman's Tale,* Chaucer mocks the pretensions of noncourtly men—including summoners, devils, rioters, merchants, and monks—who enact courtly rituals, thereby highlighting the fractious issues of social class, mercantilism, and religion inherent in the Canterbury pilgrimage. Through these examples, both individually and collectively, it becomes apparent that Chaucer found great satiric potential in male brotherhood oaths, with which he causes narrative constructions of fraternal masculinity to founder, because the chaste foundations of these pairings bear the potential, slight though it may be, for homoeroticism to blossom.

Chaucer's satire, by highlighting the failure of homosocial oaths to direct proper masculine conduct, strips male brotherhood of its gravitas. In other literary and historic texts of the fourteenth century, however, such oaths are depicted as ennobling the men who swear fidelity to each other. As C. Stephen Jaeger describes the social phenomenon of ennobling love, as practiced in medieval courtly and ecclesiastical cultures, "It is a form of aristocratic self-representation. Its social function is to show forth virtue in lovers, to raise their inner worth, to increase their honor and enhance their reputation."[2] This possibility of positive homosociality through sworn bonds of brotherhood, which is dependent upon the presumed absence of eroticism between the men, is repeatedly frustrated in Chaucer's literature. Certainly, Chaucer depicts numerous other incarnations of brotherhood, including fraternal relationships based on blood and/or friendship, in a positive light. For example, the Parson and the Plowman in the *General Prologue* apparently embody a mutually beneficial example of brotherhood, but their brotherhood is predicated upon blood and spirituality rather than courtly and chivalric oaths.[3] In contrast, brotherhood as enacted through sworn oaths consistently merits narrative ridicule and satire due to its latent erotic potential.

In describing medieval brotherhood oaths as potentially queer, my goal is not to locate a submerged homosexuality within the fictions of the Chaucerian corpus but to expose the ways in which the latent possibility of eroticism in male friendships bleeds into narrative circumstances addressing other social phenomena. *Queer* alludes to sexual acts and gendered identities that stray from constructions of cultural normativity, yet it is critical to realize that medieval brotherhood oaths participated within the range of normative behavior while simultaneously bearing the potential to subvert normativity. These pledges constituted a recognized part of knightly culture in the Middle Ages, yet the normativity of such oaths could never fully eclipse their queer potential. As Richard Zeikowitz documents in his study of courtly discourse, "Chivalric treatises also illustrate how ideal chivalric conduct promotes male–male intimacy."[4] The barest potential for normative homosocial intimacy, which is predicated upon anti-erotic assumptions of friendship rather than of homosexual desire, can elicit fear of nonnormative eroticism under certain circumstances. In this

---

2. C. Stephen Jaeger, *Ennobling Love: In Search of a Lost Sensibility* (Philadelphia: University of Pennsylvania Press, 1999), 6.

3. Although the Parson and Plowman are typically viewed as role models for their fellow pilgrims, avatars of proper Christian fellowship and humility, recent scholarship has begun to question this position. See Katherine Little, "Chaucer's Parson and the Specter of Wycliffism," *Studies in the Age of Chaucer* 23 (2001): 225–53; Derrick Pitard, "Sowing Difficulty: The *Parson's Tale*, Vernacular Commentary, and the Nature of Chaucerian Dissent," *Studies in the Age of Chaucer* 26 (2004): 299–330; and Frances McCormack, *Chaucer and the Culture of Dissent: The Lollard Context and Subtext of the* Parson's Tale (Dublin: Four Courts, 2007).

4. Richard Zeikowitz, *Homoeroticism and Chivalry: Discourses of Male Same-Sex Desire in the Fourteenth Century* (New York: Palgrave Macmillan, 2003), 23; see also his discussion of "Sodomy as a Discursive Weapon," 102–29.

manner, perceptions of sodomy could construe men who swear fraternal oaths as meriting cultural opprobrium, despite the absence of homoeroticism in their relationships.

As Paul Strohm observes of sworn brotherhood within the Chaucerian corpus, "Chaucer's poetry not only presents a society in which vassalage has been replaced by an array of more casual relations epitomized by sworn brotherhood, but includes a critique of those relations."[5] In the *House of Fame*, *Knight's Tale*, *Friar's Tale*, *Pardoner's Tale*, and *Shipman's Tale*, Chaucer deploys the satiric potential of brotherhood oaths to criticize social values. According to Paul Miller, medieval satire adheres to the following characteristics: "its proper form is verse; dialogue is often included; the style ranges between humour (as in Horace) and severity (as in Lucilius); the tone is moderate; the language is 'low' (*humilis*), which befits both the subject-matter and the audience; irony is frequently employed; and allegory is eschewed."[6] The two great Roman satirists, Horace and Juvenal, established contrasting models for satiric voices: the Horatian satire invites the reader to laugh at the target of criticism, whereas the Juvenalian satire encourages the audience to feel anger and contempt toward the object of the invective. For the most part, Chaucer's satire of brotherhood appears Horatian in spirit: the failure of the brotherhood oaths contributes to the humor of the tales, even if the tales themselves—such as the *Knight's Tale* and *Pardoner's Tale*—are not particularly comic in content. The sharp irony that accompanies Chaucer's portraits of brotherhood oaths—men pledging fidelity in one breath and breaking their pledges in the next—establishes a Horatian valence to these texts that builds humor while criticizing a persistent social phenomenon within Ricardian England.

Chaucer's congruency in satiric aim in these five narratives does not accordingly construct them as satires. Defining a narrative's genre inevitably elicits a critical debate, and, with an appreciation of the benefits and liabilities of deeming these polyvalent texts as representative of singular genres, I consider the *House of Fame* primarily to be a dream vision, the

---

5. Paul Strohm, *Social Chaucer* (Cambridge, MA: Harvard University Press, 1989), 96. In his analysis of "Opportunistic Brotherhood," Strohm addresses the oaths of the *Friar's Tale*, *Summoner's Tale*, *Pardoner's Tale*, and *Shipman's Tale*. Although brotherhood is mentioned in the *Summoner's Tale*, the friar and Thomas are not depicted as united through a brotherhood oath to each other; therefore, I do not address this instance of brotherhood in this chapter, but instead consider their relationship in regard to its homosocial and latently eroticized wrangling in chapter 5, pp. 145–51.

6. Paul Miller, "John Gower, Satiric Poet," in *Gower's Confessio Amantis: Responses and Reassessments*, ed. Alastair Minnis (Cambridge: Brewer, 1983), 79–105, at 81.

Knight's Tale a romance, the *Friar's Tale* an exemplum, the *Pardoner's Tale* a sermon, and the *Shipman's Tale* a fabliau.[7] My objective in this chapter is not to argue for the generic identification of these texts as satires but to explore how their satiric moments allow insight into Chaucer's view of brotherhood oaths and their convoluted status in relation to eroticism. Indeed, it becomes apparent that Chaucer's satiric depiction of brotherhood oaths crosses many borders among the diverse genres within his corpus. One might expect the romance of the *Knight's Tale* to have little in common with the fabliau of the *Shipman's Tale*, but brotherhood oaths unite these disparate texts through their shared skepticism regarding fraternal union.

Chaucer's satiric touch in his treatment of this theme is nonetheless somewhat surprising, given that the cultural record documents the gravity and respect ideologically accorded to such fraternal relationships in numerous circumstances. Recent studies of sworn homosocial friendships and brotherhood oaths attest to the prevalence of such relationships in the Middle Ages. Such pledges were known throughout the medieval era, but the cultural response to such relationships is difficult to ascertain. John Boswell concludes his controversial *Same-Sex Unions in Premodern Europe* with an entreaty to acknowledge the hitherto unacknowledged: "Recognizing that many—probably most—earlier Western societies institutionalized some form of romantic same-sex union gives us a much more accurate view of the immense variety of human romantic relationships and social responses to them than does the prudish pretense that such 'unmentionable' things never happened."[8] In response to

---

7. For introductory discussions of the genres of these tales, see Helen Cooper, *Oxford Guides to Chaucer: The Canterbury Tales* (Oxford: Oxford University Press, 1989). On identifying *House of Fame* as a satire, see Alfred David, "Literary Satire in *The House of Fame*," *PMLA* 75 (1960): 333–39.

8. John Boswell, *Same-Sex Unions in Premodern Europe* (New York: Villard, 1994), 282. Studies of historical homosocial relationships and friendships have developed into a subspecialty of queer studies, and key texts in this burgeoning field include David Clark, *Between Medieval Men: Male Friendship and Desire in Early Medieval English Literature* (Oxford: Oxford University Press, 2009); Alan Bray, *The Friend* (Chicago: University of Chicago Press, 2003); Michael Rocke, *Forbidden Friendships: Homosexuality and Male Culture in Renaissance Florence* (New York: Oxford University Press, 1996); and "The Work of Friendship," a special issue of *GLQ: A Journal of Lesbian and Gay Studies* (10.3 [2004]: 319–541). Additional studies of love and friendship include Reginald Hyatte, *The Arts of Friendship: The Idealization of Friendship in Medieval and Early Renaissance Literature* (Leiden; New York: Brill, 1994); Ronald Weissman, *Ritual Brotherhood in Renaissance Florence* (New York: Academic, 1982); and Laurens Mills, *One Soul in Bodies Twain: Friendship in Tudor and Stuart Drama* (Bloomington, IN: Principia, 1937).

Boswell's claims, many scholars questioned his argument that same-sex unions were considered analogous to heterosexual marriage throughout the classical and medieval eras.[9] Although scholars do not agree on the precise cultural meaning of these homosocial oaths, the extant records of their performance document a form of homosocial union between men, even if such relationships were ideologically constructed as wholly asexual and normatively masculine. Such brotherhood oaths, as enacted through civil and social ritual, were a familiar part of the medieval social fabric, and thus it is difficult to imagine that these relationships gave free rein for men to indulge in queer eroticism. Leaving aside the question of whether homosocial oaths were viewed as analogous to heterosexual marriage oaths, James A. Schultz argues that the ambiguity of homosocial relationships stems from their cultural particularity and uniqueness, and that scholars need a new model for studying homosocial attachment, "one that does not assimilate male couples of the Middle Ages to modern homosexuality but that also does not refuse them the possibility of erotic involvement."[10]

Despite the social approbation accorded to brotherhood oaths in certain circumstances, it is also likely that they could mask queer affinities under a veneer of normativity. Although disagreeing with much of Boswell's hypothesis, Constance Woods concurs that such strong ties between two men might spark the "suspicion that such exclusive friendships could lead to homosexual activity."[11] Brotherhood oaths potentially incarnate both normativity and queerness, as these ideologically sanctioned homosocial pacts allow two men to join in a courtly relationship in which their primary allegiance is to each other, even to the extent of marginalizing both the women whom they should serve as courtly lovers and the lords whom they should serve as vassals. Describing such relationships as marriages may be overstating the case, but as the ensuing examples document, the bonds enacted through homosocial oaths were powerful indeed.

Such homosocial covenants can be traced throughout their long literary history. In the Judeo-Christian Bible, the friendship between David

---

9. See, for example, Camille Paglia, "Plighting Their Troth," review of John Boswell, *Same-Sex Unions in Premodern Europe* (*Washington Post*, 17 July 1994, p. wkb1); and Constance Woods, "Same-Sex Unions or Semantic Illusions?" *Communio* 22 (1995): 316–42, at 321.

10. James A. Schultz, *Courtly Love, the Love of Courtliness, and the History of Sexuality* (Chicago: University of Chicago Press, 2006), 95.

11. Constance Woods, "Same-Sex Unions," 320.

and Jonathan is described in terms that stress both the depth of their friendship and the covenant that binds them together:

> et factum est cum conplesset loqui ad Saul, anima Ionathan conligata est animae David, et dilexit eum Ionathan quasi animam suam . . . inierunt autem Ionathan et David foedus diligebat enim eum quasi animam suam. nam expoliavit se Ionathan tunicam qua erat vestitus et dedit eam David et reliqua vestimenta sua usque ad gladium et arcum suum et usque ad balteum. (1 Samuel 18:1, 3–4)

> And it came to pass, when he had made an end of speaking to Saul, the soul of Jonathan was knit with the soul of David, and Jonathan loved him as his own soul. . . . And David and Jonathan made a covenant, for he loved him as his own soul. And Jonathan stripped himself of the coat with which he was clothed, and gave it to David, and the rest of his garments, even to his sword, and to his bow, and to his girdle.

Indeed, the relationship between David and Jonathan achieves such an emotional pitch that it is explicitly compared to heteroerotic love, and heteroerotic love is found lacking: "doleo super te frater mi Ionathan, decore nimis et amabilis super amorem mulierum" (2 Samuel 1:26; "I grieve for thee, my brother Jonathan: exceeding beautiful, and amiable to me above the love of women"), David sings in his lament over Jonathan's death.[12] Such a close homosocial relationship, which surpasses man's love for woman, is not necessarily homosexual, especially in that the relationship then assumes a maternal cast as David compares himself to Jonathan's mother. Furthermore, extensive evidence testifies to David's heteroerotic love interests, especially his lust for Bathsheba that results in Uriah's murder. The interpretive crux that this friendship poses demands that modern readers accord a place for homosocial covenants of love coexisting with heterosocial relationships. The homosocial beauty of David and

---

12. For analysis of this passage, see Boswell, *Same-Sex Unions*, 135–37. For additional biblical passages describing the covenant and love between David and Jonathan, see 1 Samuel 20:8, 20:16–17, and 23:18. For a recent study of David and Jonathan's relationship, see Susan Ackerman, *When Heroes Love: The Ambiguity of Eros in the Stories of Gilgamesh and David* (New York: Columbia University Press, 2005); she concludes of this arresting passage, "David's words in 2 Samuel 1:26 [mean] that David perceived Jonathan to have loved him in a way analogous to the sexual-emotional way in which a woman (Michal, say) would love a man and to imply that David returned that love, finding it to be something 'wonderful,' indeed, more wonderful than the love David received from the women with whom he had been sexually involved" (192).

Jonathan's relationship resonated throughout the Middle Ages, as it is referred to in numerous texts as a model for male–male relationships.[13] Chaucer's own reference to Jonathan and David's friendship in *Legend of Good Women*—"Hyd, Jonathas, al thy frendly manere" (F 251)—is elliptical, but it seems to point to the moment in 1 Samuel 19:2 when Jonathan protects David from Saul's murderous intentions.

The concept of homosocial sworn brotherhood persisted throughout the Middle Ages, and evidence of such relationships survives in medieval literature. Romances such as *Amis and Amiloun* and *Eger and Grime* describe the deep friendships between the eponymous protagonists and the oaths that link them together.[14] *Amis and Amiloun* survives in the Auchinleck manuscript, and scholars have long accepted that Chaucer read this compilation.[15] In this passage from *Amis and Amiloun*, the narrator recounts the homosocial oath of brotherhood the two young men pledge to each other:

> On a day the childer, war & wight,
> Trewethes to-gider thai gun plight,
> While thai might live & stond
> That bothe bi day & bi night,
> In wele & wo, in wrong & right,
> That thai schuld frely fond
> To hold to-gider at everi nede,
> In word, in werk, in wille, in dede,
> Where that thai were in lond,

---

13. Medieval references to David and Jonathan's friendship can be found in such varied sources as the writings of Dhuoda (Jaeger, *Ennobling Love*, 43), Abelard (John Boswell, *Christianity, Social Tolerance, and Homosexuality: Gay People in Western Europe from the Beginning of the Christian Era to the Fourteenth Century* [Chicago: University of Chicago Press, 1980], 238–39), and the Cambridge Songs (Jaeger, *Ennobling Love*, 55).

14. I address these romances in greater detail in *Sexuality and Its Queer Discontents in Middle English Literature* (New York: Palgrave Macmillan, 2008) in the following chapters: "From Boys to Men to Hermaphrodites to Eunuchs: Queer Formations of Romance Masculinity and the Hagiographic Death Drive in *Amis and Amiloun*," 101–21, and "Queer Castration, Patriarchal Privilege, and the Comic Phallus in *Eger and Grime*," 123–44.

15. Studies that argue for Chaucer's familiarity with the Auchinleck manuscript include Laura Hibbard Loomis, "Chaucer and the Breton Lays of the Auchinleck Manuscript," *Studies in Philology* 38 (1941): 14–33, and her "Chaucer and the Auchinleck Manuscript: *Thopas* and *Guy of Warwick*," in *Essays and Studies in Honor of Carleton Brown* (1940; Freeport, NY: Books for Libraries, 1969), 111–28. Ralph Hanna establishes that the Auchinleck romances were widely known in metropolitan circles of the fourteenth century (*London Literature, 1300–1380* [Cambridge: Cambridge University Press, 2005], 104–47).

Fro that day forward never mo
Failen other for wele no wo:
Ther-to thai held up her hond. (145–56)¹⁶

Amis and Amiloun's oath to maintain fidelity to each other "In wele and wo" is reminiscent of the vow of "for bettere for wors" in heterosexual marriage rites.¹⁷ Regardless of any semantic similarities in the phrasing of the oath with marriage vows, their pledge establishes them as united in pursuit of each other's common good.

Within the romance world of *Amis and Amiloun*, this oath takes precedence over all other social and familial obligations, including those to the knights' lords, wives, and children. Indeed, Amiloun soon repeats their oath and reminds Amis to be true to him in all circumstances:

"Brother, as we er trewthe-plight
Bothe with word & dede,
Fro this day forward never mo
To faily other for wele no wo,
To help him at his nede,
Brother, be now trewe to me,
& y schal ben as trewe to the,
Also god me spede!" (293–300)

The repetition of the vow establishes its narrative significance, as more attention is paid to this oath of fraternal union than to the vows solemnized at the knights' respective weddings. For instance, to save his beloved brother Amiloun from leprosy, Amis sacrifices his two children. Homosocial union directs Amis and Amiloun's every action as they live and fight together until they die; they then share a grave for all eternity: "Both on oo day were they dede / And in oo grave were they leide, / The knyghtes both twoo" (2503–5). Despite that their heterosexual love interests are

---

16. MacEdward Leach, ed., *Amis and Amiloun* (London: Early English Text Society, 1937); line numbers are cited parenthetically.

17. For medieval marriage vows and the "for bettere for wors" phrasing, see Barbara Hanawalt, *The Ties That Bound: Peasant Families in Medieval England* (New York: Oxford University Press, 1986), 203; and Kenneth Stevenson, *Nuptial Blessing: A Study of Christian Marriage Rites* (New York: Oxford University Press, 1983), 75. Additional studies of medieval marriage include D. L. D'Avray, *Medieval Marriage: Symbolism and Society* (Oxford: Oxford University Press, 2005); Conor McCarthy, *Marriage in Medieval England: Law, Literature, and Practice* (Cambridge: Boydell, 2004); and Christopher Brooke, *The Medieval Idea of Marriage* (Oxford: Oxford University Press, 1989).

nowhere to be seen at the romance's conclusion, Amis and Amiloun epitomize the overarching normativity of male homosociality and sworn brotherhood in the Middle Ages.[18]

Likewise, the eponymous protagonists of *Eger and Grime* share an oath of brotherhood that directs their every action, as in this scene in which Grime explains the primacy of their relationship to Eger:

> "Egar," he said, "thou & I are brethren sworne,
> I loued neuer better brother borne;
>   betwixt vs tow let vs make some cast,
> & find to make our formen fast,
> for of our enemies wee stand in dread,
>   & wee Lye sleeping in our bedd." (489–94)[19]

In the illustration of Eger and Grime sharing a bed together, readers see that homosocial—but not necessarily homosexual—intimacy deeply colors their relationship.[20] Brotherhood oaths so powerfully define these knights that forming other amatory and familial relationships becomes difficult, because brotherhood means more to them than any other social connection. Eger and Grime conclude the narrative by marrying women, yet the

---

18. Studies of gender and genre in regard to *Amis and Amiloun* include Richard Zeikowitz, *Homoeroticism and Chivalry*, 51–54; Sheila Delany, "A, A, and B: Coding Same-Sex Union in *Amis and Amiloun*," in *Pulp Fictions of Medieval England: Essays in Popular Romance*, ed. Nicola McDonald (Manchester: Manchester University Press, 2004), 63–81; John Ford, "Contrasting the Identical: Differentiation of the 'Indistinguishable' Characters of *Amis and Amiloun*," *Neophilologus* 86 (2002): 311–23; and Ojars Kratins, "The Middle English *Amis and Amiloun*: Chivalric Romance or Secular Hagiography?" *PMLA* 81 (1966): 347–54.

19. James Ralston Caldwell, ed., *Eger and Grime: A Parallel-Text Edition of the Percy and the Huntington-Laing Versions of the Romance* (Cambridge, MA: Harvard University Press, 1933). Since the manuscripts of *Eger and Grime* date to the fifteenth century, it is difficult to ascertain whether Chaucer would have known this romance; however, given the oral nature of literary performance in the Middle Ages, it likely circulated orally prior to being written down. Whether or not Chaucer knew this particular narrative, its existence points both to the longevity of sworn brotherhoods throughout the Middle Ages and to their practice throughout the British Isles. For a detailed study of *Eger and Grime* and its treatment of friendship, see Mabel Van Duzee, *A Medieval Romance of Friendship: Eger and Grime* (New York: Franklin, 1963).

20. See Alan Bray, *The Friend*, 153–54 and 167–68, for the social import of men sharing beds. Bray's analysis ranges beyond the Middle Ages, but his admonition that "the shared bed and the embraces of masculine friendship suggested the sodomitical no more than the conventions of the familiar letter" (167) is surely applicable to the circumstances depicted in *Eger and Grime*.

romance focuses more on their struggle to maintain their vows to each other than on the pleasures of wooing their respective ladies.[21] Their mutual (and presumably chaste) affection for each other takes precedence over the erotic pursuits of their wives until the narrative ends with a tremendous display of fecundity through the births of their many children.

In romances such as *Amis and Amiloun* and *Eger and Grime*, homosocial oaths reflect the characters' deep similarity to each other, such that their shared biological sex and preternatural physical resemblance render them more similar to each other than to their wives. Amis and Amiloun are virtually twins, and Eger and Grime share a similar unexplained yet unbreakable bond. These friendships thus parallel Cicero's belief that "Verum etiam amicum qui intuetur, tamquam exemplar aliquod intuetur sui" ("Again, he who looks upon a true friend, looks, as it were, upon a sort of image of himself").[22] From this classical perspective on friendship, which endured throughout the Middle Ages, homosocial relationships allow a man to find his mirror image not through heterosexual contact with a woman but through homosocial union with a man whose body reflects his own. From this perspective, eroticism is transcended through homosociality, yet its specter lingers in many narratives focused on such brotherhoods, latently querying the role of the erotic in texts from which it has been, at least on the surface, erased.

Beyond the literature of the Middle Ages, brotherhood oaths appear in historical records as well. Boswell and Bray uncover numerous homosocial relationships in their scholarship, and the ones likely most relevant to Chaucer's understanding of such oaths would include the relationships of Edward II and Piers Gaveston and of John Clanvowe and William

---

21. Additional romances, such as *Guy of Warwick*, *Athelston*, and *King Horn*, depict a homosocial world of deep male friendships, yet their eponymous protagonists do not share the stage equally with their male friends. Another subset of homosocial romances includes narratives such as "The Tale of Balyn and Balan" in Malory's *Morte D'Arthur*, in which the brothers are indeed blood brothers. The variety of romances in which brotherhood appears testifies to the popularity of this theme, as well as to the diverse incarnations of friendships that might appear within such texts.

22. Cicero, *De Senectute, De Amicitia, De Divinatione*, ed. and trans. William Falconer (Cambridge, MA: Harvard University Press, 1979), 132–33. See also Cicero, "Laelius: On Friendship," in *On the Good Life*, trans. Michael Grant (London, 1971), in which the translation reads, "When a man thinks of a true friend, he is looking at himself in the mirror" (189). I thank Robert Sturges for directing me to Cicero's work in his *Dialogue and Deviance: Male–Male Desire in the Dialogue Genre* (New York: Palgrave Macmillan, 2005). For a brief review of Cicero's status in the Middle Ages and the legacy of his ideas on friendship, see M. J. Ailes, "The Medieval Male Couple and the Language of Homosociality," in *Masculinity in Medieval Europe*, ed. D. M. Hadley (London: Longman, 1999), 214–37, esp. 215–16.

Neville. The relationship between Edward and Piers is memorialized in their shared covenant of brotherhood: "quem filius regis intuens, in eum tantum protinus amorem iniecit quod cum eo fraternitatis fedus iniit, et pre ceteris mortalibus indissolubile dileccionis vinculum secum elegit et firmiter disposuit innodare" ("the king's son felt so much love for him that he entered into a compact of brotherhood with him and chose and decided to tie himself to him, against all mortals, in an unbreakable bond of affection").[23] Another such fraternal union was formalized between two of Chaucer's contemporaries, John Clanvowe and William Neville; similar to the fictions of *Amis and Amiloun*, these two men were buried together in the same grave.[24] Timothy O'Brien suggests that "Chaucer's connections with such knights as John Clanvowe and William Neville . . . make it likely that he knew well the language and conventions of sworn brotherhood."[25] From the biblical, literary, and historical record, as well as within the courtly circles in which Chaucer circulated, homosocial oaths of brotherhood were an accepted ritual of solidarity between two men. Given the normative valence of such fraternal relationships in these circumstances, why might Chaucer satirize them as potentially erotic and thus latently queer, rather than depicting them in their more culturally sanctioned role as chaste and anti-erotic partnerships?

When social ideologies conflict, normativities often collapse, and such appears to be the case with fraternal oaths. As vows of brotherhood served as an accepted rite of chivalric honor and mutual respect between

---

23. Pierre Chaplais, *Piers Gaveston: Edward II's Adoptive Brother* (Oxford: Clarendon, 1994), 12–13. The quoted passage is from the "Chronicle of the Civil Wars of Edward II" (BL MS Cotton Cleopatra D ix, fos. 86r–88r); the translation is Chaplais's. For Edward II's sexual orientation and possible homosexuality, see Roy Haines, *King Edward II* (Montreal: McGill-Queen's University Press, 2003), 42–43. For a study of Piers and Edward II's brotherhood in relation to Chaucer's literature, see John Bowers, "Queering the Summoner: Same-Sex Union in Chaucer's *Canterbury Tales*," in *Speaking Images: Essays in Honor of V. A. Kolve*, ed. Robert Yeager and Charlotte Morse (Asheville, NC: Pegasus, 2001), 301–24, esp. 315–18; and Seymour Phillips, *Edward II* (New Haven, CT: Yale University Press, 2010), 100–103.

24. S. Dull, A. Luttrell, and M. Keen, "Faithful unto Death: The Tombe Slab of Sir William Neville and Sir John Clanvowe," *Antiquaries Journal* 71 (1991): 183–84; cited in Timothy O'Brien, "Brother as Problem in the *Troilus*," *Philological Quarterly* 82 (2003): 125–48, at 128.

25. Timothy O'Brien, "Brother as Problem," 128. See also John Bowers, "Three Readings of the *Knight's Tale*: Sir John Clanvowe, Geoffrey Chaucer, and James I of Scotland," *Journal of Medieval and Early Modern Studies* 34 (2004): 279–307, for his study of how Clanvowe's reading of Chaucer's *Knight's Tale* demonstrates the ways in which "this text's meanings coalesce with shifting ideologies of chivalric performance and male erotic attraction to expose significant cultural transitions within the Ricardian period" (279).

men, such relationships could nonetheless mask queerness (and possibly eroticism), leaving onlookers perplexed as to the true nature of the friendship. (As I soon discuss, such confusion appears to have surrounded Edward II's relationship with Piers Gaveston, which provides another cultural context for Chaucer's satiric depiction of sworn brotherhoods.) Reflecting this occluded possibility, Chaucer's satires of homosocial oaths entail his likely perception that some of these relationships might be not latently but rather blatantly queer. Ostensibly a simple relationship of blood or of mutual honor, brotherhood refuses to signify clearly about the meaning of the relationship described. Chaucer depicts brotherhood in various ways in his tales, and Jean Jost taxonomizes his varying illustrations of fraternal relationships into seven primary divisions:

> (1) literal brothers of the same mother such as Placebo and Justinus in the *Merchant's Tale*; (2) closely related kin such as the cousins Palamon and Arcite in the *Knight's Tale*; (3) the putative "cousins," the monk and the merchant, in the *Shipman's Tale*; (4) the three comrades who pledge sworn brotherhood in the *Pardoner's Tale*; (5) men connected in some affectionate or emotional bond such as the philosopher and his "leve brother" in the *Franklin's Tale* (V 1607); (6) those bound together in a religious confraternity such as the Franciscans in the *Summoner's Tale*; and (7) simple acquaintances who acknowledge the other's friendship, as does Harry advising the Miller, "Robyn, my leeve brother."[26]

Brotherhoods as enacted through oaths muddy the borders of Jost's taxonomy, as her second, third, and fourth categories—referring respectively to the brotherhoods illustrated in the *Knight's Tale*, *Shipman's Tale*, and *Pardoner's Tale*—are united through their thematic focus on men swearing oaths to each other. Nonetheless, these many categories of friendship point to the multiplicity of ways in which Chaucer uses brotherhood to develop the themes and characters of his fictions.

Chaucer's satiric depiction of brotherhood oaths does not extend uniformly throughout his treatment of brotherhood, which is rich and multivalent in its portrayal, including negative and positive depictions. Of course, brotherhoods, including brotherhoods not depicted as consummated through fraternal rituals, are often illustrated in a problematic light in the Chaucerian corpus. For example, Chaucer frequently uses "brother"

---

26. Jean Jost, "Ambiguous Brotherhood in the *Friar's Tale* and the *Summoner's Tale*," in *Masculinities in Chaucer: Approaches to Maleness in the* Canterbury Tales *and* Troilus and Criseyde, ed. Peter Beidler (Cambridge: Brewer, 1998), 77–90, at 78.

as an ironic term, such as when the Miller refers to the Reeve with dripping sarcasm as "Leve brother Osewold" (1.3151), and his male characters also use it as an ingratiating term to win their superior's approval, as when Placebo sycophantically refers to January as his brother: "Myn owene deere brother and my lorde, / So wysly God my soule brynge at reste, / I holde youre owene conseil is the beste" (4.1488–90). Timothy O'Brien demonstrates that, in *Troilus and Criseyde*, the theme of brotherhood "get[s] exploited—by the poem's characters and even to a lesser extent by the narrator,"[27] and this narrative offers Chaucer's most extensive consideration of male–male friendship, to such an exaggerated extent that Pandarus declares to Troilus, "For the have I bigonne a gamen pleye / Which that I nevere do shal eft for other, / Although he were a thousand fold my brother" (3.250–52).[28] Despite the importance of their friendship to each other, however, Troilus and Pandarus never formalize their relationship through an oath of brotherhood.[29]

For Chaucer, however, brotherhood is not intrinsically a subject of satire and ridicule, and the positive depictions of brotherhood in such narratives as the *Franklin's Tale* and the *Second Nun's Tale* highlight the good that arises from brothers caring for each other and tending to each other's needs. Aurelius's brother helps him to overcome his melancholic torpor over Dorigen in the *Franklin's Tale*, and Valerian encourages Tiburce to convert to Christianity for his spiritual salvation in the

---

27. Timothy O'Brien, "Brother as Problem," 125.

28. Key studies of Pandarus and Troilus's friendship include Timothy O'Brien, "Brother as Problem"; John Hill, "Aristocratic Friendship in *Troilus and Criseyde*: Pandarus, Courtly Love, and Ciceronian Brotherhood in Troy," in *New Readings of Chaucer's Poetry*, ed. Robert Benson and Susan Ridyard (Cambridge: Brewer, 2003), 165–82; Gretchen Mieszkowski, *Medieval Go-Betweens and Chaucer's Pandarus* (New York: Palgrave Macmillan, 2006), esp. 139–42; Richard Zeikowitz, *Homoeroticism and Chivalry*, esp. 131–50; and Alan Gaylord, "Friendship in Chaucer's *Troilus*," *Chaucer Review* 3 (1969): 239–64.

29. Why might Chaucer avoid describing Troilus and Pandarus's brotherhood as enacted through a chivalric oath? In *Amis and Amiloun*, *Eger and Grime*, and the *Knight's Tale*, the many physical similarities between the two male characters underscore the appropriateness of their vows. Troilus and Pandarus, however, are never depicted as resembling each other, and readers have long wondered about their respective ages. Although Chaucer never answers this question, it appears that Pandarus is somewhat older than Troilus: Sally Slocum posits that Pandarus, while "perhaps older than the lovers, is nevertheless close to them in age" ("How Old Is Chaucer's Pandarus?" *Philological Quarterly* 58 [1979]: 16–25, at 23). The following idea can only remain a conjecture, but it seems likely that Chaucer did not see Troilus and Pandarus as sufficiently similar to each other in terms of physical appearance and age to undertake such a vow. Certainly, their friendship is not predicated upon any detailed likenesses to each other, as is explicitly the case in *Amis and Amiloun*, *Eger and Grime*, and the *Knight's Tale*.

Second Nun's Tale. These positive depictions of male relationships contrast directly with Chaucer's satiric depiction of brotherhood and brotherhood oaths in the *House of Fame, Knight's Tale, Friar's Tale, Pardoner's Tale,* and *Shipman's Tale*. In the conflicting visions of brotherhood as ironic in some instances and as sincere in others, Chaucer allows himself a wide artistic license with which to depict brotherhood; such an ecumenical perspective contracts to a singular disparaging view when brotherhood is enacted through ritual oaths.

In the *House of Fame*, Chaucer depicts fraternal oaths at the end of the narrative and immediately dismisses them as representative of the most vain and empty chatter. Allegorical figures representing truth and falsehood, who reside in the House of Rumor, undertake such promises in a willy-nilly fashion, and Chaucer as narrator notes that these oaths of truth metamorphose into falsehoods:

> And somtyme saugh I thoo at ones
> A lesyng and a sad soth sawe,
> That gonne of aventure drawe
> Out at a wyndowe for to pace;
> And, when they metten in that place,
> They were achekked bothe two,
> And neyther of hem moste out goo
> For other, so they gonne crowde,
> Til ech of hem gan crien lowde,
> "Lat me go first!" "Nay, but let me!
> And here I wol ensuren the,
> Wyth the nones that thou wolt do so,
> That I shal never fro the go,
> But be thyn owne sworen brother!
> We wil medle us ech with other,
> That no man, be they never so wrothe,
> Shal han on [of us] two, but bothe
> At ones, al besyde his leve,
> Come we a-morwe or on eve,
> Be we cried or stille yrouned."
> Thus saugh I fals and soth compouned
> Togeder fle for oo tydynge. (2088-109)

Chaucer's sources for this passage—Ovid's *Metamorphoses* and Dante's *Il Convivio*—similarly treat the mixture of truth and lies and the spread of rumor, yet with no mention of sworn brotherhood in their respective passages.[30] This passage parodies oaths of brotherhood through the haphazard fashion in which allegorical representations of truth and falsehood pledge them, and Chaucer as narrator declares that the promises communicate only falsehoods. How could it be otherwise, since a lie uniting with a truth can only result in truth being besmirched by falsehood, rather than falsehood being elevated to truth, as they compound into "oo tydynge"?

Queerness permeates this scene, as the allegorical figures pledge fidelity to one another, yet the fulfillment of this oath would ironically destroy any truth at the basis of the relationship. Truth—both literal and allegorical—can only be lost in this particular instance of oath-making. Moreover, the promise that truth and falsehood "wil medle us ech with other" peripherally connotes erotic activity and the debasement of the oath through carnal practice: according to the *Middle English Dictionary*, *medlen* primarily means "to blend, mix," but the word carries sexual connotations as well in its secondary meaning of "to join sexually, to have sexual intercourse." Chaucer uses the word "medlen" in *Romaunt of the Rose* to connote sexuality several times, which indicates the word's utility for addressing amatory affairs.[31] As the many truths and falsehoods in the *House of Fame* so promiscuously promise to enjoy brotherhood and to "meddle" together with one another, the satiric scene exaggeratedly debases fraternal oaths as potentially queering all discourse through a perverse orgy of "inter-meddling."

Most scholars concur that, in the *House of Fame*, Chaucer tackles the meaning of poetry and his place in the poetic tradition,[32] but it seems unlikely that scholars will ever definitively identify the "man of gret auctorite" (2158) who abruptly concludes this poem. Indeed, as A. J. Minnis notes of the *House of Fame*, the "man of gret auctorite" threatens

---

30. In *Metamorphoses*, Ovid writes: "Atria turba tenet: veniunt, leve vulgus, euntque / mixtaque cum veris passim commenta vagantur / milia rumorum confusaque verba volutant" (*Le Metamorfosi*, ed. Ferruccio Bernini [Bologna: Zanichelli, 1974], vol. 2, 12.53–55). Allen Mandelbaum translates this passage as: "A crowd— / forever coming, going—fills the halls; / and mingling with the true, the false reports— / in thousands—babble, wandering about" (*The Metamorphoses of Ovid* [San Diego: Harvest, 1993], 399). For the relevant passage in Dante, see *Il Convivio (The Banquet)*, trans. Richard Lansing (New York: Garland, 1990), 1.3, at 8–10, in which he builds upon and alludes to Vergil in the fourth book of the *Aeneid*: "Fame thrives on movement and acquires greatness by going about" (10).

31. For Chaucer's use of "medlen" in *Romaunt of the Rose*, see lines 3788, 4545, 6036, and 6050.

32. See Glenn Steinberg, "Chaucer in the Field of Cultural Production: Humanism, Dante, and the *House of Fame*," *Chaucer Review* 35 (2000): 182–203, for an overview of Chaucer's relationship to his poetic forebears.

the poem on a narrative level, foreclosing the sense of play unleashed throughout the dream vision: "there is no place for 'the reasoned, authoritative, single voice.' The 'man of grete auctorite' should not be admitted; he would only spoil the party."[33] Chaucer's suggestive depiction of truths and falsehoods vowing homosocial oaths to one another so promiscuously could also explain the poem's terse ending. Is this the moment when the joke goes too far, when a real and powerful man might find himself insulted by Chaucer's play with homosociality, if not homosexuality, as well as with the slippage between truth and lies that might sully this unidentified man's reputation? As with any conjectures about the "man of gret auctorite," this point cannot be conclusively proved, yet the pieces of evidence unite in a compelling fashion to indicate that, in this instance, Chaucer realized the potential limits of his penchant for satirizing male brotherhood and homosociality.

For example, one "man of gret auctorite" during Chaucer's lifetime was Richard II, whose potentially erotic relationship with Robert de Vere piqued queer suspicions among the English court. As Michael Hanrahan documents,

> Thomas Walsingham unmistakably establishes the sexual threat posed by Richard's favorites. During his account of Robert de Vere's royal appointment to the Duke of Ireland in 1386, Walsingham describes Richard and de Vere, the king's closest friend and confidante, as sharing "obscene intimacies" ("*familiaritatis obscoenae*"), an attack that implies that unmentionable vice, sodomy. Adam of Usk will later record a more overt reference to Richard's sodomy, when he includes the king's "sodomies" ("*sodomica*") among the causes of Richard's deposition. The charge of sodomy was never officially brought against Richard, but its occurrence in these Lancastrian chronicles betray[s] the political agenda behind the allegations, namely, Richard's unfitness for rule.[34]

The Evesham chronicler also hints at sinful sexual behavior in his account, recording that "totam noctem in potacionibus et aliis non dicendis in sompnem duceret" ("he would spend all night in drinking and other things that ought not be mentioned until passing out").[35] If Chaucer

---

33. A. J. Minnis, with V. J. Scattergood and J. J. Smith, *Oxford Guides to Chaucer: The Shorter Poems* (Oxford: Oxford University Press, 1995), 226.

34. Michael Hanrahan, "Seduction and Betrayal: Treason in the Prologue to the *Legend of Good Women*," *Chaucer Review* 30 (1996): 229–40, at 235.

35. George Stow Jr., ed., *Historia Vitae et Regni Ricardi Secundi* (Philadelphia: University

intended to depict Richard II as the "man of gret auctorite," perhaps he then realized he was taking his joke too far by presenting his king so soon after illustrating a roomful of sexually licentious and homosocially sworn allegorical figures breeding falsehoods among themselves. Given the historical record's suggestive accounts of Richard's relationship with de Vere, it seems unlikely that the monarch would appreciate any queerly homosocial relationships being obliquely hinted at in such an outrageous manner, even within the covert space of allegorical representation. Typically the *House of Fame* is dated to 1379–80, and it has been hypothesized that the poem, had Chaucer completed it, was intended to celebrate Richard's anticipated marriage to Anne of Bohemia; if these theories are correct, the satiric inclusion of denigrated brotherhood oaths would ostensibly be corrected in the announcement of the marriage. It should be reiterated that any allegorical and contextual identifications of the "man of gret auctorite," including this one, are highly speculative, but the latent queer dynamics of the scene color the poem's inconclusive conclusion, rendering a definitive ending increasingly difficult to imagine.

In the *Knight's Tale* Palamon and Arcite are precisely the type of aristocratic protagonists who might be expected to pledge and maintain brotherhood oaths to each other.[36] Indeed, before the *Knight's Tale* was given its place of prominence in the *Canterbury Tales*, Chaucer refers to it as "the love of Palamon and Arcite" in the Prologue of the *Legend of Good Women* (F 420), a title that identifies love as the narrative's theme but ambiguously allows the possibility for love between its eponymous protagonists as well as for their love of the as-yet-unnamed Emily.[37] The reader first sees them in a reverse image of Amis and Amiloun's final resting place in a shared grave, in that Palamon and Arcite are buried but still alive:

And so bifel that in the taas they founde,
Thurgh-girt with many a grevous blody wounde,
Two yonge knyghtes liggynge by and by,
Bothe in oon armes, wroght ful richely. (1.1009–12)

---

of Pennsylvania Press, 1977), 166.

36. For analysis of brotherhood oaths in *Knight's Tale*, see Catherine Rock, "Forsworn and Fordone: Arcite as Oath-Breaker in the *Knight's Tale*," *Chaucer Review* 40 (2006): 416–32; and Robert Stretter, "Rewriting Perfect Friendship in Chaucer's *Knight's Tale* and Lydgate's *Fabula duorum mercatorum*," *Chaucer Review* 37 (2003): 234–52.

37. For Chaucer's revising of "the love of Palamon and Arcite," see John Bowers, "Three Readings of the *Knight's Tale*," 287–91.

The iconography of their shared arms stresses their similarity to each other, which the narrator iterates in mentioning that they "weren of the blood roial / Of Thebes, and of sustren two yborn" (1.1018–19). In these early scenes Chaucer prepares the reader to learn of their brotherhood oaths; ironically, these oaths are broken before readers realize that the cousins undertook such pledges. Only after their shared sighting of Emily threatens the foundations of their relationship does Palamon remind Arcite of the promises that should unite them under all circumstances:

> "It nere," quod he, "to thee no greet honour
> For to be fals, ne for to be traitour
> To me, that am thy cosyn and thy brother
> Ysworn ful depe, and ech of us til oother,
> That nevere, for to dyen in the peyne,
> Til that the deeth departe shal us tweyne,
> Neither of us in love to hyndre oother,
> Ne in noon oother cas, my leeve brother,
> But that thou sholdest trewely forthren me
> In every cas, as I shal forthren thee—
> This was thyn ooth, and myn also, certeyn." (1.1129–39)

This oath should guide Palamon and Arcite's every action, but because they continually fail to act in a manner to "trewely forthren" each other's needs, the oath registers their ready sacrifice of each other's desires in pursuit of their own. In subsequent moments Palamon reminds Arcite that he is "to my conseil and my brother sworn" (1.1147), and Arcite similarly acknowledges that Palamon is "to my cosyn and my brother sworn" (1.1161). Despite the repeated allusions to their oath, the bulk of the narrative concentrates on its dissolution after the two men see Emily. Palamon also foreshadows the tale's conclusion; his words "Til that the deeth departe shal us tweyne" bespeak not the fulfillment of a life lived together, but the failure of the vow to unite them until death. Also, the phrase "Til that the deeth departe shal us tweyne" echoes marriage rites, which points both to the gravity of the vows and to the preeminence this homosocial bond should hold over subsequent heterosocial unions.[38] Furthermore, such an emphasis on brotherhood and brotherhood oaths, as well as Palamon and Arcite's quick and aggressive bickering, does not appear in

---

38. Kenneth Stevenson, *Nuptial Blessing*, 79.

Boccaccio's *Teseida*, in which the young men initially comfort each other over love's wounds.[39]

Palamon and Arcite break their brotherhood oath after they espy Emily and begin competing for her affections, but Chaucer reinforces its thematic meaning at key points in the narrative. When the two knights prepare to fight to the death, Palamon threatens Arcite with his imminent demise: "I drede noght that outher thow shalt dye, / Or thow ne shalt nat loven Emelye. / Chees which thou wolt, or thou shalt nat asterte!" (1.1593–95). Arcite soon returns with the necessary battle gear, and the narrator underscores the similarity between the two foes by detailing their shared thoughts. Here the men are literally of one mind, with the narrator recounting their identical reaction to each other and their shared predicament:

> ... "Heere cometh my mortal enemy!
> Withoute faille, he moot be deed, or I,
> For outher I moot sleen hym at the gappe,
> Or he moot sleen me, if that me myshappe."
> So ferden they in chaungyng of hir hewe,
> As fer as everich of hem oother knewe. (1.1643–48)

Although it may appear paradoxical to argue that their shared minatory musings reestablish the theme of brotherhood, these lines underscore the singular like-mindedness of the two men. In a manner consistent with Cicero's description of brotherhood as a man looking at an image of himself or into a mirror, the narrator evokes the deep connection that continues to unite Palamon and Arcite, despite their outward antagonism. Furthermore, the narrator then somewhat surprisingly remarks, "Everich of hem heelp for to armen oother / As freendly as he were his owene brother" (1.1651–52). The irony of these lines, in that congenial brotherhood is now represented when the two men arm each other for the purpose of their mutual destruction, reminds the reader of the brotherhood oath while highlighting their inability to adhere to its basic tenets.

Sworn brotherhood fails to foster Palamon and Arcite's goodwill toward each other, and there is little to suggest that Chaucer sees such chivalric brotherhood in a positive light in the remainder of the narrative. After

---

39. For the relevant passages in Boccaccio's *Teseida* depicting Palamon and Arcite's initial sighting of Emily and their kind responses to each other's suffering, see N. R. Havely, ed. and trans., *Chaucer's Boccaccio: Sources of* Troilus *and the* Knight's *and* Franklin's Tales (Cambridge: Brewer, 1980), 113–15.

Arcite's fatal accident (but before he dies), Theseus consolidates civic and martial order by calling for brotherhood between the two men's opposing factions:

> For which anon duc Theseus leet crye,
> To stynten alle rancour and envye,
> The gree as wel of o syde as of oother,
> And eyther side ylik as ootheres brother;
> And yaf hem yiftes after hir degree,
> And fully heeld a feeste dayes three. (1.2731–36)

After brotherhood oaths have fomented fraternal battles rather than fraternal peace, these words ring with irony. If Theseus succeeds in restoring order at this moment, the peace is likely to be short-lived, as readers see little evidence that men treating each other like sworn brothers quells any tendencies toward male–male aggressions or competition.[40] Male brotherhood has foundered due to the allure of heteroeroticism, and one sees little reason to believe that Theseus's call for brotherhood will vanquish the erotic rivalries that inevitably arise and disrupt presumably chaste brotherhoods.

Critical analysis of Palamon and Arcite's brotherhood highlights the ways in which fraternal union stands in conflict with heterosexual courtship and marriage. Robert Stretter argues that Chaucer deploys "brotherhood as shorthand for a (theoretically) indestructible male relationship in order to highlight the power of an even stronger force that destroys it—love between the sexes,"[41] and Patricia Clare Ingham likewise notes that "the tale's denouement displays state-sponsored heterosexual union as a compensation for the losses to chivalric fraternity."[42] The satiric potential engendered by Palamon and Arcite's oath is thus multivalently formulated to celebrate heterosexuality and to debase homosociality. If heterosexuality is to trump homosociality in this romance, if Palamon

---

40. Homosocial competition is one of the defining features of the *Canterbury Tales*, especially the narratives of Fragment A. See Anne Laskaya, "Men in Love and Competition: The *Miller's Tale* and the *Merchant's Tale*," in her *Chaucer's Approach to Gender in the Canterbury Tales* (Cambridge: Brewer, 1995), 78–98; Emily Jensen, "Male Competition as a Unifying Motif in Fragment A of the *Canterbury Tales*," *Chaucer Review* 24 (1990): 320–28; and Carl Lindahl, "Conventions of a Narrative War," in *Earnest Games: Folkloric Patterns in the* Canterbury Tales (Bloomington: Indiana University Press, 1987), 73–155.

41. Robert Stretter, "Rewriting Perfect Friendship," 237–38.

42. Patricia Clare Ingham, "Homosociality and Creative Masculinity in the *Knight's Tale*," in Biedler, *Masculinities in Chaucer* 23–35, at 27.

is to win Emily's hand in marriage, the oath must be sacrificed. The potential queerness incarnated through the oath, in that two men united themselves to each other and then cohabitated in a prison where their only sexual releases could have been masturbatory or homoerotic, is then vehemently denied by their determined pursuit of Emily. As John Bowers asserts, "Chivalric brotherhood of the sort idealized by the Knight came freighted with an unspoken and unspeakable anxiety that a same-sex pair might lapse into a homosexual bond, as Palamon and Arcite might have done during life-long imprisonment in their single cell."[43] The satire of this narrative arises in that the brotherhood oath cannot escape the threat of queerness, no matter whether it is upheld or cast aside: maintaining the oath leaves Palamon and Arcite united in homosocial union and thus alienated from the heterosexual pursuits of courtly love, but breaking the oath detracts from their chivalric status as knights of honor. Interpretations of the *Knight's Tale* frequently address the Knight's ambiguous relationship to his tale, and this failed oath of brotherhood provides another example that Chaucer encodes a critique of chivalric values within this romance.[44]

The Miller certainly sees queer potential in the Knight's romance, as he debases and transforms it into his own fabliau, in which the rarefied homosocial brotherhood of knights metamorphoses into a sordid sexual competition between clerks. At the conclusion of his tale, the hot iron with which Absolon penetrates Nicholas bears a historical forebear in the implement responsible for the demise of Edward II and Piers Gaveston, as the uneasiness that surrounded their homosocial relationship spurred accounts of Edward's execution by means of a hot iron inserted in his anus.[45] Historians disagree whether the story is true or apocryphal, but the factuality of the incident, in this instance, is secondary to its ideological import, in its lurid depiction of an anal punishment for a man united in brotherhood with another man. Absolon's branding of Nicholas's buttocks with a hot coulter in the *Miller's Tale* ironically and violently indicts sodomy, as the Miller satirizes the Knight's romance of

---

43. John Bowers, "Queering the Summoner," 305.

44. The most famous critique of the Knight, his tale, and its implied debasement of courtly values remains Terry Jones, *Chaucer's Knight: The Portrait of a Medieval Mercenary* (Baton Rouge: Louisiana State University Press, 1980). See also David Aers, *Chaucer* (Atlantic Highlands, NJ: Humanities Press, 1986), 24–32; and Charles Muscatine, *Chaucer and the French Tradition: A Study in Style and Meaning* (Berkeley: University of California Press, 1957), who finds that the plot does "not sustain very close scrutiny" (175).

45. For a discussion of Edward's demise due to the insertion of a hot iron poker, see John Boswell, *Christianity, Social Tolerance, and Homosexuality*, 300.

homosocial brotherhood and courtly love by inverting its narrative status and meaning. As Chaucer transforms the Knight's romance populated with courtly lovers into a fabliau of debased and predatory sexuality, the hot iron makes explicit the possibility of anal intercourse between Palamon and Arcite latent in the *Knight's Tale* and thus deepens the satiric potential of both the Knight's and the Miller's narratives. Within the *Knight's Tale*, and within the Miller's reconstruction of its amatory politics, homosocial union provokes Chaucer's satire of men whose erotic pursuits are entangled with those of other men, even when such pursuits are entirely heterosexual in nature. The heterosexuality of these relationships cannot preserve men united in a brotherhood oath from the tinge of queerness that their friendship carries, no matter the greater likelihood of the heteroerotic orientation of their desires.

The men who swear fraternal oaths in the *Friar's Tale*, *Pardoner's Tale*, and *Shipman's Tale* likewise break their promises almost immediately upon enunciating them, and in these tales Chaucer satirizes the aristocratic pretensions of noncourtly men who perform chivalrous acts without the requisite social status to imbue the acts with appropriate meaning. When oaths of male brotherhood appear in these tales, they build humor through their merciless ridiculing of aristocratic pretension as enacted by characters of other, and predominantly lower, social classes.[46] In the *Friar's Tale* the summoner's erotic venality, as evidenced by his work as a pimp (3.1355–62), encourages readers to view his actions suspiciously, and this vocational pursuit locates him on the fringes of society in regard to his sexually inflected identity. When he then pledges a fraternal oath with his new friend, readers should realize that it will soon be broken:

> "*Depardieux*," quod this yeman, "deere broother,
> Thou are a bailly, and I am another.
> I am unknowen as in this contree;
> Of thyn aqueyntance I wolde praye thee,
> And eek of bretherhede, if that yow leste.
> I have gold and silver in my cheste."
> . . . .

---

46. Studies of social class in the Chaucerian canon include David Wallace, *Chaucerian Polity: Absolutist Lineages and Associational Forms in England and Italy* (Stanford, CA: Stanford University Press, 1997); Britton Harwood and Gillian Overing, eds., *Class and Gender in Early English Literature* (Bloomington: Indiana University Press, 1994); Paul Olson, *The Canterbury Tales and the Good Society* (Princeton, NJ: Princeton University Press, 1986); and Jill Mann, *Chaucer and Medieval Estates Satire: The Literature of Social Classes and the General Prologue to the Canterbury Tales* (Cambridge: Cambridge University Press, 1973).

> "Grant mercy," quod this somonour, "by my feith!"
> Everych in ootheres hand his trouthe leith,
> For to be sworne bretheren til they deye.
> In daliance they ryden forth and pleye. (3.1395–1400, 1403–6)

The repetition of "broother," "bretherhede," and "bretheren" in this passage ridicules the morally corrupt summoner, who engages in this oath with a man whom he has only recently met and about whom he knows little (other than that he carries gold and silver). Indeed, the word *brother* occurs more frequently in the *Friar's Tale* than in any other Chaucerian work except *Troilus and Criseyde*, a work approximately twenty times longer.[47] The relationship is based more on the desire for pecuniary gain than on fraternal affection, and Chaucer ironically mocks their romance pretensions of male–male bonding, as this oath is enacted by the most morally unscrupulous of men. Certainly, the summoner is not known for his courtly treatment of women, as evidenced by his cruelty to the old woman whom he plans to cheat of her twelve pence and pan.

Queer edges to the *Friar's Tale* satirically suggest that this summoner and his new friend engage in a homoerotic relationship. The two men engage in "daliance" (3.1406), a word that carries a sexual undertone.[48] Linking "daliance" to "pleye," Chaucer also hints at a muted sexual tension in this scene because this word likewise carries sexual connotations. According to the *Middle English Dictionary*, *pleye* can refer to "sexual play, sexual intercourse," as well as the "copulating of animals." Furthermore, the Friar depicts the devil as somewhat of a medieval dandy, as he is described as

> A gay yeman, under a forest syde.
> A bowe he bar, and arwes brighte and kene;
> He hadde upon a courtepy of grene,
> An hat upon his heed with frenges blake. (3.1380–83)

The "brighte and kene" arrows indicate that this apparent yeomen does not use his equipment, as they register no telltale signs of wear and tear.

---

47. John Tatlock and Arthur Kennedy document that "brother" appears nineteen times in *Friar's Tale*, in comparison to its forty appearances in *Troilus and Criseyde*. The other works in which the word "brother" most appears include *Second Nun's Tale* (ten times) and *Knight's Tale* (nine times). See Tatlock and Kennedy, *A Concordance to the Complete Works of Geoffrey Chaucer and to the* Romaunt of the Rose (Gloucester, MA: Peter Smith, 1963).

48. Tison Pugh, *Queering Medieval Genres* (New York: Palgrave Macmillan, 2004), 57–58.

The green "courtepy" (jacket) most obviously serves as part of the devil's disguise as a woodsman, as this color also appears in the depiction of the Yeoman in the *General Prologue* ("And he was clad in cote and hood of grene" [1.103]). In addition to green's connotations of woodsmen and forestry, the green jacket also bears numerous unsavory and sexual registers, as Laura Hodges elucidates in her explication of medieval color symbolism: "[green] was the color of love; it was a color 'particularly suitable for the clothing of newly-weds'; it was the most commonly worn color of church vestments. In addition, green carried negative meanings such as inconstancy."[49] Each of these qualities of green debases the character of the devil/yeoman and, by extension, the summoner: the greenness of the coat satirically casts the two as lovers; it positions them as "newlyweds" recently joined in bonds of brotherhood; and it calls to mind the vestments of the clergy and thereby satirizes the summoner's failure to maintain the ideals of his church office. Chaucer's use of green to connote inconstancy, in addition to this instance, is evident in "Against Women Unconstant," which ends every stanza with the lament, "In stede of blew, thus may ye were al grene" (7, 14, 21). Such inconstancy in the *Friar's Tale* foreshadows the climactic demise of their brotherhood when the devil leads the summoner to hell, adhering to the old woman's curse rather than to his oath with the summoner. In this remarkably detailed picture, the depiction of homosocial union as enacted through a brotherhood oath sets the stage for the exemplum's satiric message condemning religious hypocrisy and greed, and the implied homoeroticism between the summoner and the devil magnifies the enormity of their transgressions.

Beyond the submerged eroticism of this brotherhood, such a relationship also corrupts the social class borders of Ricardian England in its intermingling of marginal men from ecclesiastical and courtly milieus. Summoners and yeomen serve in subservient positions to men of greater authority and prestige in distinct realms of spiritual and secular authority, and these two men thus violate the associative positions tied to their vocational identities by forming their friendship. David Wallace notes that the bond "is undermined from the start by bad faith: rather than the sharing of professional secrets (as encouraged in the guilds) we find a disguising of professional identities";[50] this bastardized commingling fractures the basic tenets of sworn brotherhood, in that such relationships

---

49. Laura Hodges, *Chaucer and Clothing: Clerical and Academic Costume in the* General Prologue *to the* Canterbury Tales (Cambridge: Brewer, 2005), 102. See also D. W. Robertson, "Why the Devil Wears Green," *Modern Language Notes* 69 (1954): 470–72.

50. David Wallace, *Chaucerian Polity*, 143.

should be based on friendship and social similitude. The devil warns the summoner that he assumes a pleasing form to expedite his nefarious intentions ("For we . . . wol us swiche formes make / As moost able is oure preyes for to take" [3.1471–72]), and, according to this logic, the similitude of their male bodies serves a seductive purpose. The summoner of the *Friar's Tale* thus appears especially susceptible to the advances of a devil assuming the form of a male yeoman, with the lure of homosocial union proving more effective in seducing him than the enticements of heterosexual passion. The summoner's temptation is thus intrinsically different from the temptations offered to medieval saints such as Antony, who withstood the seductive blandishments of the devil in female form.[51] Furthermore, the most frequently cited analogues of the *Friar's Tale*—including "De Injustitia," "Narracio de quodam senescallo sceleroso," and Robert Rypon's "A Greedy Bailiff"—make no such mention of brotherhood or the seductive tactics of the devil figure, suggesting that Chaucer's attention to sworn brotherhood and submerged eroticism is his unique contribution to this tale.[52] Finally, it should be noted that the Friar is insulting his enemy the Summoner with this tale, and thus the queer edges to the friendship between the summoner and the devil within his narrative comment metatextually on the Summoner and Pardoner's queer friendship, as evident when these men sing "Come hider, love, to me!" to each other in the *General Prologue* (1.672).

The Friar's exemplum teaches a lesson to the pilgrims about religious hypocrisy, as it also alerts them to the dangers of rashly swearing brotherhood oaths. In a similar manner, the Pardoner's sermon instructs his audience of the moral turpitude associated with homosocial union and its potentially erotic valence. The morally bankrupt Pardoner recounts an instructive sermon during the Canterbury pilgrimage, and he structures his lesson by depicting three riotous, dangerous, and stupid criminals. Numerous studies explore the satiric potential of Chaucer's depiction of the Pardoner and his sexual ambiguity, primarily in regard to his interactions with the other pilgrims.[53] By including a homosocial oath of broth-

---

51. For the story of Antony of Egypt, see Robert Meyer, *St. Athanasius: The Life of St. Antony* (New York: Newman, 1978).

52. For "De Injustitia," "Narracio de quodam senescallo sceleroso," and Robert Rypon's "A Greedy Bailiff," see Robert Correale and Mary Hamel, eds., *Sources and Analogues of the Canterbury Tales* (Cambridge: Brewer, 2002), 1.87–99.

53. The Pardoner and his ambiguous gender attract a great deal of scholarly interest, including Monica McAlpine, "The Pardoner's Homosexuality and How It Matters," *PMLA* 95 (1980): 8–22; Glenn Burger, "Kissing the Pardoner," *PMLA* 107 (1992): 1143–56; Richard

erhood within the tale, Chaucer links the frame narrative's concern with the Pardoner's sexual indeterminacy—evidenced in descriptions of both his appearance and his enigmatic friendship with the Summoner—to his depiction of the rioters within the tale. The Pardoner is introduced through his connection to the Summoner: "With [the Summoner] ther rood a gentil PARDONER / Of Rouncivale, his freend and his compeer" (1.669–70). Although this friendship is not presented within the context of a sworn brotherhood, it sets the stage for the inclusion of a brotherhood oath in the *Pardoner's Tale*, which exposes the corruption of brotherhood as enacted by textual rioters and metatextual religious men. Chaucer's description of the Pardoner's sexual ambiguity makes manifest the erotic suspicions that the men's friendship sparks:

A voys he hadde as smal as hath a goot.
No berd hadde he, ne nevere sholde have;
As smothe it was as it were late shave.
I trowe he were a geldyng or a mare. (1.688–91)

Given the questionable nature of the Pardoner's gender, sexuality, and his friendship with the Summoner, it is initially perplexing that he criticizes brotherhood oaths in his tale. Nonetheless, he lambastes numerous sins in his sermon that he confesses to in his prologue, and so readers witness yet another example of this character exposing his stunning hypocrisy.

After determining to kill Death (and thus laying the groundwork for their imminent demise), the three rioters in the *Pardoner's Tale* undertake a fraternal vow to one another. The lead rioter exhorts his fellows:

"Herkneth, felawes, we thre been al ones;
Lat ech of us holde up his hand til oother,
And ech of us bicomen otheres brother,
And we wol sleen this false traytour Deeth.

Firth Green, "The Pardoner's Pants (and Why They Matter)," *Studies in the Age of Chaucer* 15 (1993): 131–45, as well as his "Further Evidence for Chaucer's Representation of the Pardoner as a Womanizer," *Medium Ævum* 71 (2002): 307–9; Steven Kruger, "Claiming the Pardoner: Toward a Gay Reading of Chaucer's *Pardoner's Tale*," *Exemplaria* 6 (1994): 115–39; Robert Sturges, *Chaucer's Pardoner and Gender Theory: Bodies of Discourse* (New York: St. Martin's, 2000); Lee Patterson, "Chaucer's Pardoner on the Couch: Psyche and Clio in Medieval Literary Studies," *Speculum* 76 (2001): 638–80; Richard Zeikowitz, "Silenced but Not Stifled: The Disruptive Queer Power of Chaucer's Pardoner," *Dalhousie Review* 82 (2002): 55–73; and Will Stockton, "Cynicism and the Anal Erotics of Chaucer's Pardoner," *Exemplaria* 20.2 (2008): 143–64.

> He shal be slayn, he that so manye sleeth,
> By Goddes dignitee, er it be nyght!"
>   Togidres han thise thre hir trouthes plight
> To lyve and dyen ech of hem for oother,
> As though he were his owene ybore brother. (6.696–704)

Approximating consanguinity through their vow, the three rioters affirm their fraternal union and their joint mission to conquer Death. Once again, such a brotherhood oath represents Chaucer's elaboration of his source materials—including such exempla and folk tales as "De tribus sociis, qui thesaurum invenerunt" ("Of three companions who found a treasure"), "De Contemptu mundi" ("Of contempt for the world"), and an exemplum based on the life of St. Bartholomew—that depict these rioters simply as friends or even as Christ's disciples.[54]

Of course, the vow is then broken both when two of the three men decide to kill the third and when the third man likewise determines to poison the other two; however, in Chaucer's telling of the tale, even at the moment when the two rioters decide to betray their brother, the vow is not forgotten. Rather, the rioter who advocates fratricide ironically reminds his friend of their communal oath when pressuring him to conspire against their momentarily departed companion: "Thow knowest wel thou art my sworen brother; / Thy profit wol I telle thee anon. / Thou woost wel that oure felawe is agon" (6.808–10). The exquisite irony of these lines, with the rioter reminding his "brother" of their fraternal vow while simultaneously cajoling him to murder their sworn brother, punctures any value accorded to homosocial oaths. The murder itself carries latent queer potential as well, as Steven Kruger observes: "At the heart of the Pardoner's exemplum, we find a physical penetration, a violent parody of sexual intercourse, that leads not to renewed life . . . but rather to a stark

---

54. For Chaucer's sources for the story of the three rioters and their untimely deaths, see Robert Correale and Mary Hamel, eds., *Sources and Analogues of the* Canterbury Tales, 1.287–313. In the folktale "De tribus sociis, qui thesaurum invenerunt" ("Of three companions who found a treasure"), the men are described as "tres socii mercatores" ("three friends, traders") who try to steal gold from a hermit. In another exemplum (from British Library, MS Add. 27336, fol. 40, #187), the story is cast in the form of a parable from the life of St. Bartholomew, in which Jesus appends the moral to the tale after some disciples have died as a result of their avariciousness: "Sic dixi vobis: quod propter aurum et argentum multa mala fiunt, sic ut videtis; modo accidit hic" ("Thus I said to you: that for the sake of gold and silver many evils come about. As you see, it has just happened here" [290–91]). The exemplum "De contemptu mundi" is quite similar to this exemplum from the life of St. Bartholomew, except that the figure of Jesus is played by the generic figure of a "quidam philosophus" ("certain philosopher").

and sterile death."⁵⁵ In a world where oaths are uttered so promiscuously, they indicate little other than the depravity of the men who speak them. By including this scene in the *Pardoner's Tale*, Chaucer adds yet another level of queerness to the Pardoner's morally complex and sexually perplexing character.

The end of the *Pardoner's Tale* features the Pardoner's hypocrisy yet again, as he attempts to sell his relics to the pilgrims, and Harry Bailly's indignant and crude anger in response. Harry re-symbolizes male eroticism into male aggression with his graphic rejoinder:

> "I wolde I hadde thy coillons in myn hond
> In stide of relikes or of seintuarie.
> Lat kutte hem of, I wol thee helpe hem carie;
> They shul be shryned in an hogges toord!" (6.952–55)

In his description of handling a man's testicles, Harry reimagines homosexual fondling as castration, a sharp reinterpretation of the submerged homoerotic dynamics ubiquitously potential in sworn brotherhoods. Furthermore, his imagery of male genitalia "shryned in an hogges toord" tacitly points to anal intercourse as yet another potential outcome of male homosociality. The Knight's call for Harry and the Pardoner to kiss and reconcile in some ways ironically establishes a "brotherhood" between these two men who detest each other:

> "I prey yow that ye kisse the Pardoner.
> And Pardoner, I prey thee, drawe thee neer,
> And, as we diden, lat us laughe and pleye."
> Anon they kiste, and ryden forth hir weye. (6.965–68)

As the clearest representative of aristocratic and courtly values, the Knight demands a kiss to soothe over the fractured social harmony of the pilgrimage. The final irony of the *Pardoner's Tale*, then, is the reinstitution of a homosocial bond that can never withstand the animosity that it cloaks. Any sort of friendship between Harry and the Pardoner carries a latent hint of forced queerness, in that they are compelled to reconcile due to the commands of a powerful and aristocratic man, not in response to their own sense of homosocial affection. From his tale of Palamon and Arcite, the Knight should understand the folly of enforcing male friendships, yet

---

55. Steven Kruger, "Claiming the Pardoner," 130–31.

he compels these men of the pilgrimage to unite in momentary affection that can in no manner quell their mutual antagonism.

The *Shipman's Tale* likewise deploys an oath of homosocial brotherhood to heighten the narrative's satiric effect and to undermine narrative masculinity. In the carnivalesque environment of the fabliau, normativity as a social and ideological construction often establishes the inversionary grounds of the narrative, which is readily apparent in the genre's thematic deployment of cuckoldry as a measure of masculinity. As Holly Crocker argues, "Throughout the fabliau corpus, structuring desire on a binarized lack reduces women as well as men to competitive, oppositional, and instrumental relations. . . . [I]t produces a form of masculinity that only gains authority through competitive, oppositional, and instrumental relations."[56] Chaucer's primary sources for the *Shipman's Tale* include the first two tales of the eighth day in Boccaccio's *Decameron*, but in neither of these tales do the men swear oaths of brotherhood to each other.[57] In Chaucer's adaptation of the story, the merchant wholly trusts his sworn brother, Daun John, because of their oaths of brotherhood, as well as this man's vocation as a monk:

> The monk hym claymeth as for cosynage,
> And he agayn; he seith nat ones nay,
> But was as glad therof as fowel of day,
> For to his herte it was a greet plesaunce.
> Thus been they knyt with eterne alliaunce,
> And ech of hem gan oother for t'assure
> Of bretherhede, whil that hir lyf may dure. (7.36–42)

The oath cements the merchant's trust in his friend the monk, as it thus establishes the foundation for this fabliau's satiric and humorous consideration of dishonest trade, religious hypocrisy, and adulterous marriage. As John Hermann notes, "The circulation of vows as defective signs in the tale takes place against the background of the marital vows of the couple and religious vows of the Monk."[58] No oath is sacred in this tale, which

---

56. Holly Crocker, "Disfiguring Gender: Masculine Desire in the Old French Fabliau," *Exemplaria* 23.4 (2011): 342–67, at 354.

57. For Boccaccio's tales and their influence on Chaucer's *Shipman's Tale*, see John Scattergood, "The Shipman's Tale," in Correale and Hamel, *Sources and Analogues of the* Canterbury Tales, 2.565–81.

58. John Hermann, "Dismemberment, Dissemination, Discourse: Sign and Symbol in the *Shipman's Tale*," *Chaucer Review* 19 (1985): 302–37.

points to the dissolute state of the fallen world that provides an appropriate setting for a fabliau.

Similar to the "brothers" of the *Friar's Tale* and the *Pardoner's Tale*, the merchant and the monk do not belong to the aristocratic social class deemed appropriate for such relationships, and thus readers are well prepared for Daun John's randy rejection of brotherhood so that he may enjoy lascivious delights with his brother's wife:

> "He is na moore cosyn unto me
> Than is this leef that hangeth on the tree!
> I clepe hym so, by Seint Denys of Fraunce,
> To have the moore cause of aqueyntaunce
> Of yow, which I have loved specially
> Aboven alle wommen, sikerly.
> This swere I yow on my professioun." (7.149–55)

According to John, the brotherhood oath with the merchant was merely a ruse so that he could approach the man's wife, but in a narrative heavy with irony, Chaucer adds an additional layer of comic betrayal in that the monk swears his love "on my professioun." His monastic vows are as meaningless as his brotherhood oaths, and both are used to seduce his friend's wife rather than to uphold his sense of fraternal union with the merchant or spiritual union with his order (or with God, for that matter).

The merchant's wife cuckolds him so that she may build her wardrobe, and this emasculation of husbandly authority accords ironically with the merchant's misprision of fraternal loyalty as a mutually constitutive relationship. The ending is consistent with the debasement of homosocial oaths enacted in Chaucer's other treatments of this theme, and, through the term "cosynage," the wife defends her duplicity by using the merchant's relationship with the Monk as a blind:

> "For, God it woot, I wende, withouten doute,
> That he hadde yeve it me bycause of yow
> To doon therwith myn honour and my prow,
> For cosynage, and eek for beele cheere
> That he hath had ful ofte tymes heere." (7.406–10)

Due to the close relationship between the two men, the wife argues, it would be perfectly reasonable for the monk to show his affection for him through her as an intermediary figure. Queer theory asks readers to look at the diverse sexual energies circulating in a text, and in the *Shipman's Tale*, readers see the familiar structure of the erotic triangle, in which two men pursue the same woman.[59] Adding an even queerer edge to this dynamic, however, is that the wife focuses her husband's attention on the source of his betrayal, which is his own relationship with another man. Moreover, the wife's erotic energies focus more on her clothes and debts than on either man, who serve as conduits to her sartorial rather than her sexual passions. Thus, at the end of the tale when the wife declares to the merchant, "Ye shal my joly body have to wedde; / By God, I wol nat paye yow but abedde!" (7.423–24), the man is promised sexual pleasure but at the price of his masculine worth as a lover. As Mary Leech avows in her reading of the Old French fabliaux *Le Chevalier a la robe vermeille* and *Les Braies au Cordelier*, which tackle similar sexual and social dynamics as the *Shipman's Tale*, "The male role of dominance is usurped, leaving the male authority deceived, chastised, and impotent to change or even understand the situation. In the end, although the appearance of social stability is maintained, the tale shows that masculine authority is an illusion that is as changeable as a suit of clothes."[60] In this light, the merchant need not confront his cuckoldry because he never learns of his wife's infidelity, and this moment raises a question of almost philosophical depth for a fabliau: if a man's wife cheats on him, but he and no one else realizes it, is he truly a cuckold, if cuckoldry is at least partially determined by a concomitant sexual humiliation? Regardless of the answers posed to this question, readers see the merchant's queered masculinity at the tale's conclusion, which showcases yet again the disruptive erotic energies sparked by an apparently anti-erotic brotherhood.

These examples of sworn brotherhood from Chaucer's diverse genres consistently proclaim the undesirability of such relationships. Different genres strive for various literary effects, whether entertainment (romance and fabliau), or spiritual enlightenment (exemplum and sermon), or a mixture of the two (dream vision). In Chaucer's fictions, however, the entertainments of romance and fabliau contain a corresponding didactic aspersion against homosocial brotherhoods, and the hortatory impulses of exemplum and sermon are accompanied by satiric and amusing depic-

---

59. For the theoretical framework of the erotic triangle, see Eve Sedgwick, *Between Men: English Literature and Male Homosocial Desire* (New York: Columbia University Press, 1985).

60. Mary Leech, "Dressing the Undressed: Clothing and Social Structure in Old French Fabliaux," in *Comic Provocations: Exposing the Corpus of Old French Fabliaux*, ed. Holly Crocker (New York: Palgrave Macmillan, 2006), 83–96, at 87.

tions of sworn brotherhood oaths failing to ennoble the non-aristocratic men who swear them. In Chaucer's polygeneric play, the consistency with which he treats this theme argues for an overarching distrust of such relationships despite the countervailing views promulgated in numerous contemporary texts. The historic and literary record documents that male oaths of friendship and brotherhood were often revered as enactments of the noblest virtues, but such was not the case for Chaucer. In each instance in his literature when men pledge brotherhood to each other, the subsequent betrayal of the oath satirizes and ridicules this social practice. Speculations regarding the reasons behind Chaucer's satiric disdain for such relationships aside, it is clear that he found no opportunity in his vast literary canon to depict such oaths and the men who swore them in a positive light. Such an absence of positive depictions, contrasted with a plenitude of negative ones, is queer indeed, and points to the ways in which apparently chaste social paradigms carry latent implications of an unwelcome eroticism destructive to their own conception and practice.

CHAPTER FOUR

NECROTIC EROTICS IN CHAUCERIAN ROMANCE

Loving Women, Loving Death, and Destroying Civilization in the *Knight's Tale* and *Troilus and Criseyde*

To distill the genre of medieval romance to its core, a knight defeats his enemy so that he may love his lady, thus laying the foundation for the perpetuation of his bloodline through procreation. In his classic study *Mimesis*, Erich Auerbach succinctly declares, "Except feats of arms and love, nothing can occur in the courtly world,"[1] for, as he explains, love and battle serve as the preeminent concerns of these tales. In his retellings of Boccaccio's *Teseida* and *Il Filostrato*, Chaucer degrades the amatory fecundity of the romance tradition into a death-driven and moribund genre in his *Knight's Tale* and *Troilus and Criseyde*: in these narratives, a knight's love for a woman is inextricably interconnected with images and fantasies of death and destruction, culminating in his death for love and, at least potentially, his love for death. Moreover, from this perspective of male narcissism in love, the *Knight's Tale* and *Troilus and Criseyde* rewrite female fertility into morbidity, underlining the nexus of love and death, eros and thanatos, in sexual relationships. With women reflecting the inherent emptiness of male narcissism rather than acting on their own amatory desires, these tales suggest the inherent fatality of male desire and the queer force of female antieroticism. A virgin and a widow, Emily and Criseyde, who are cast unwill-

---

1. Erich Auerbach, *Mimesis: The Representation of Reality in Western Literature*, trans. Willard Trask (1953; Princeton, NJ: Princeton University Press, 2003), 140.

ingly into the roles of the imperious beloveds of romance, paradoxically achieve signifying force by rechanneling male eroticism to its necrotic ends, thus threatening, if not achieving, the destruction of civilizations antithetical to female desire. In contrast to the amorous desires of Arcite, Palamon, and Troilus, Emily's and Criseyde's desires for freedom from eroticism arise in the spectral image of Athens and Troy destroyed, for these commonweals evince little concern for female agency, as evidenced by their conquest of and trade in women.

In exposing the death-dealing underbelly of heteroeroticism and its fantasies of self-destruction, Chaucer's tales counter affirmative conceptions of romantic love, especially in regard to its tacit promise to propagate the human species through childbirth. Sigmund Freud affirms that the erotic is the "prototype of all happiness," such that "genital erotism [should be] the central point of life";[2] he also argues that eroticism binds communities together, positing that "a group is clearly held together by a power of some kind: and to what power could this feat be better ascribed than Eros, which holds together everything in the world."[3] Indeed, Freud theorizes that civilization itself emerges from erotic drives: "civilization is a process in the service of Eros, whose purpose is to combine single human individuals, and after that families, then races, peoples, and nations, into one great unity, the unity of mankind."[4] In positing the relationship between eroticism and the death drive, which counters the organic unity of eros, Freud insists that erotic drives are the primary force in the daily pursuit of life and love: "the death instincts are by their nature mute and . . . the clamour of life proceeds for the most part from Eros."[5] The death drive, in subverting eros, impels one to destruction and dissolution, but Freud simultaneously sees eros and the death instinct as integrally fused, proposing that "Only by the concurrent or mutually opposing action of the two primal instincts—Eros and the death-instinct—, never by one or the other alone, can we explain the rich multiplicity of the phenomena of life."[6] He further declares, "From the concurrent and opposing action of [eros and thanatos] proceed the phenomena of life which are brought to

---

2. Sigmund Freud, *Civilization and Its Discontents*, ed. and trans. James Strachey (New York: Norton, 1961), 56.

3. Sigmund Freud, "Group Psychology and the Analysis of the Ego," in *The Standard Edition of the Complete Psychological Works of Sigmund Freud*, ed. and trans. James Strachey (London: Hogarth, 1953–74), 18.65–144, at 92.

4. Sigmund Freud, *Civilization and Its Discontents*, 81.

5. Sigmund Freud, "The Ego and the Id," in *Standard Edition*, 19.1–66, at 46.

6. Sigmund Freud, "Analysis Terminable and Interminable," in *Standard Edition*, 23.209–53, at 243.

an end by death."⁷ For Freud, the business of life is the desire for eroticism coupled with a muted but no less insistent desire for death, for death will come, whether desired or not.

Many medieval romances showcase the complementary yet conflicted interplay of eros and thanatos: such narratives are sites of converging erotic and necrotic desires, in which a knight's erotic desire to love his lady is frequently coupled with (and projected externally through) his necrotic desire to kill his enemy. As Northrop Frye observes, romances frequently incorporate depictions and fantasies of death only then to stage their transcendence: "romance is nearest of all literary forms to the wish-fulfillment dream. . . . [T]he romance expresses . . . the passage from struggle through a point of ritual death to a recognition scene that we discovered in comedy."⁸ Certainly, many romances, like comedies, feature generative resolutions, concluding with marriage and the birth of a child (or children). With an astonishing display of fertility, *Havelok the Dane* ends as Havelok and his queen Goldeboru "geten children hem bitwene / Sones and doughtres right fivetene."⁹ *Sir Tryamour* concludes by celebrating "Kyng Tryamowre and hys qwene" who share "mekyll joye" because "man chylder had they twoo,"¹⁰ and in *Eger and Grime*, Eger fathers fifteen children with his wife Winglaine, Grime fathers ten children with Loosepine, and their friend Pallyas fathers five children with Emyeas.¹¹ Such fecundity can be achieved only after the knights dispatch their enemies, and in this manner medieval romances encapsulate the struggle between eros and thanatos in the story of a knight's victory over death (as represented by his foe) and his subsequent enjoyment of erotic pleasure resulting in reproduction and the perpetuation of his bloodline. Similarly, many romances conclude with depictions or promises of marriage, thus ending with the expectation that the knightly protagonist will propagate his bloodline, even if the expected children of the union do not yet appear.

---

7. Sigmund Freud, "Anxiety and Instinctual Life," in *Standard Edition*, 22.81–111, at 107.

8. Northrop Frye, *Anatomy of Criticism* (Princeton, NJ: Princeton University Press, 1957), 186–87.

9. *Havelok the Dane*, ed. Donald Sands, in *Middle English Verse Romances* (Exeter: University of Exeter Press, 1986), 55–129, at lines 2978–79.

10. *Sir Tryamour*, ed. Harriet Hudson, in *Four Middle English Romances* (Kalamazoo, MI: Medieval Institute Publications, 1996), 173–232, at lines 1705–7.

11. James Ralston Caldwell, ed., *Eger and Grime: A Parallel-Text Edition of the Percy and the Huntington-Laing Version of the Romance, with an Introductory Study* (Cambridge, MA: Harvard University Press, 1933), lines 1453–64.

Whereas *Havelok the Dane*, *Sir Tryamour*, and *Eger and Grime* provide clean divisions between eros and thanatos, in which the punishment of death is inflicted outwardly so as to preserve the illusion of erotic desire purged of its necrotic taint, Chaucer's *Knight's Tale* and *Troilus and Criseyde* intertwine these desires, braiding them together into a dark mixture of ostensibly opposed impulses. In her reading of *Romeo and Juliet*, Julia Kristeva observes the necessity of death and its organic unity with erotic desire in the play's resolution: "Death, like a final orgasm, like a full night, waits for the end of the play."[12] Death is the final enactment of sexual desire in *Romeo and Juliet*, as it is also the penultimate register of desire in the *Knight's Tale* and the conclusive desire of *Troilus and Criseyde*. As Celia Lewis affirms of Chaucer's literature and its frequent emphasis on themes of death, "fiction's inadequacy rests not only on its ability to offer spiritual consolation, but in its impotence vis-à-vis the preservation of physical life."[13] If to love a woman is to embrace death, however, the male desires that drive these narratives must themselves bear a necrotic responsibility for the unhappy endings, more so than the women who find themselves objects of desires unsought and unimagined. In destabilizing the erotic foundations of these genres, Chaucer's narrators encode a queer power of resistance to Emily's and Criseyde's respective roles of virgin and widow: preferring the anti-heteroerotic freedom of life without men, these female characters allow an intriguing glimpse into alternate models of kinship and alliance. Coincident with female eroticism freed from men emerges the submerged narrative panic such a vision sparks, because it encodes the erasure of children, fertility, and propagation that might well portend the collapse of civilization.

CHAUCERIAN ROMANCE AND THE NECROTIC ALLURE OF WOMEN

As is well established in the critical tradition, Chaucer's treatment of romance throughout the *Canterbury Tales* suggests his ambivalence toward the genre.[14] The *Squire's Tale* and *Sir Thopas* are both interrupted

---

12. Julia Kristeva, *Tales of Love*, trans. Leon Roudiez (New York: Columbia University Press, 1987), 215.

13. Celia Lewis, "Framing Fiction with Death: Chaucer's *Canterbury Tales* and the Plague," in *New Readings of Chaucer's Poetry*, ed. Robert Benson and Susan Ridyard (Cambridge: Brewer, 2003), 139–64, at 141.

14. For studies of Chaucer and romance, see Susan Crane, *Gender and Romance in*

rather than allowed to conclude on their own terms, which implies Chaucer's amused impatience with the genre, and the *Nun's Priest's Tale* records the narrator's dismissal of the romance tradition, as he ironically compares the truthfulness of his tale of amorous chickens to that of Arthurian romance: "This storie is also trewe, I undertake, / As is the book of Launcelot de Lake, / That wommen holde in ful greet reverence" (7.3211–13). From the Nun's Priest's perspective, medieval romance is a woman's tradition, not a man's, but even when Chaucer puts a romance in a woman's voice in his *Wife of Bath's Tale*, this Arthurian romance only superficially endorses the protocols of the genre, particularly in casting a rapist in the role of its knightly protagonist. Furthermore, the conclusion of the *Wife of Bath's Tale* indicates that Alison, as she curses "olde and angry nygardes of dispence" and wishes that "God sende hem soone verray pestilence" (3.1263–64), perceives and indicts the hollow fantasies of romance.[15] Of course, *Squire's Tale*, *Tale of Sir Thopas*, *Wife of Bath's Tale*, along with *Knight's Tale* and *Troilus and Criseyde*, do not exhaust Chaucer's engagement with romance, and scholars have noted the interplay of romance with other genres, such as hagiography and exemplum, in his literature, discerning connections among these distinct genres in such works as the *Man of Law's Tale* and the *Clerk's Tale*. Furthermore, the *Franklin's Tale*'s genre of Breton lai depends primarily on the romance tradition. It is beyond the scope of this chapter to engage fully with these disparate treatments of romance, but this brief survey illustrates that Chaucer found the traditional parameters of romance to be confining and that he played with the form in numerous ways.

From this perspective, in counterbalancing necrotic drives with eroticism in the *Knight's Tale* and *Troilus and Criseyde*, Chaucer tacitly acknowledges the uncomfortable fit between narratives of the classical past and medieval idealizations of courtly love in romance, as did Boccaccio before him in *Teseida* and *Il Filostrato*.[16] As Winthrop Wether-

---

Chaucer's Canterbury Tales (Princeton, NJ: Princeton University Press, 1994); and Angela Jane Weisl, *Conquering the Reign of Femeny: Gender and Genre in Chaucer's Romance* (Cambridge: Brewer, 1995). For an especially strong overview, see Corinne Saunders, "Chaucer's Romances," in *A Companion to Romance: From Classical to Contemporary*, ed. Corinne Saunders (Malden, MA: Blackwell, 2004), 85–103.

15. On the Wife of Bath's rewriting of romance traditions in her tale, see Louise Fradenburg, "The Wife of Bath's Passing Fancy," *Studies in the Age of Chaucer* 8 (1986): 31–58.

16. For studies of Chaucer's debts to Boccaccio, see Piero Boitani, *Chaucer and Boccaccio* (Oxford: Society for the Study of Medieval Languages and Literature, 1977); David Wallace, *Chaucer and the Early Writings of Boccaccio* (Woodbridge: Brewer, 1985); Robert Edwards, *Chaucer and Boccaccio: Antiquity and Modernity* (New York: Palgrave Macmillan, 2002); and

bee postulates, "Every medieval poet who engages the classical tradition must . . . come to terms with the conflicting tendencies of the literary modes he seeks to align."[17] The glory of dying bravely in battle in classical epics brings honor to a warrior, yet such an ending cannot bring about the fecund expectations of generation of medieval romance. John Finlayson argues of Chaucer's generic debts: "To note that the Knight tells a romance is to fail to notice that the 'romance' he tells is unlike any other romance in English. . . . In addition, the *Teseida* is *not* a romance in the French, and derived English fashion, but is instead an attempt to transform a love story into something akin to epic."[18] Arcite's and Troilus's courtships do not conform to the typical parameters of medieval romance, for each man's quest to win his lady's love, when accomplished, is rewarded with death rather than communal adulation or a lifetime of erotic pleasure sanctioned in marriage. Within this hybrid genre of epic romance, a knight pursues his lady while exterior conflicts—the Theban campaigns with Athens, the Trojan War—complicate the knight's amatory affairs and his quest for erotic satisfaction.[19]

Before addressing the ways in which Arcite's and Troilus's desires for women become implicated with necrotic desires, it is helpful to consider Chaucer's most explicit statement concerning a desire for death: "Ne Deeth, allas, ne wol nat han my lyf" (6.727), laments the old man in the *Pardoner's Tale*, expressing his desire to end desire, which is also his desire to be desired by Death. Seeking to find eternal rest, the old man acknowledges the role of thanatos in his life's journey as he craves the maternal comforts of the grave. Furthermore, as Carl Phelpstead elucidates, the old man contaminates the young rioters with death, unveiling their latent mortal desire as camouflaged under their venality: "Their

---

Warren Ginsberg, *Chaucer's Italian Tradition* (Ann Arbor: University of Michigan Press, 2002).

17. Winthrop Wetherbee, "Romance and Epic in Chaucer's *Knight's Tale*," *Exemplaria* 2.1 (1990): 303–28, at 304.

18. John Finlayson, "*The Knight's Tale*: The Dialogue of Romance, Epic, and Philosophy," *Chaucer Review* 27.2 (1992): 126–49, at 128.

19. It should be noted that Lee Patterson disputes the classification of *Troilus and Criseyde* as a romance, arguing that "on the whole the term [of romance] was restricted to the narratives that fit the primary definition now offered by the *Middle English Dictionary*: 'A written narrative of the adventures of a knight, nobleman, king, or an important ecclesiastic; a chivalric romance'" (*Acts of Recognition: Essays on Medieval Culture* [Notre Dame, IN: Notre Dame University Press, 2010], 205). Yet similar to the anachronistic recasting of the Trojan War as fought by medieval knights, romance elements of courtly love are interspersed throughout *Troilus and Criseyde*, muddying any taxonomy that would strip it of its multiple significations.

encounter with the old man who is prepared for, and even desires death . . . fails to instill wisdom in them and he directs them to Death by indicating the way to treasure: their avarice leads them to murder one another, so that Death finds them."[20] Drawing on the longstanding analogy between the womb and tomb, the old man repeatedly refers to his grave with feminine imagery, calling the ground where he will be buried his "moodres gate" (6.729, cf. 6.731, 6.734). Chaucer constructs the old man's desire for death as a maternal longing, an urge to unite with the feminine at the moment when all desires—erotic or otherwise—cease, albeit one that, as Robert Sturges explains, is marked by an "image of impotence" in "the staff that cannot penetrate the female opening."[21] In this manner the *Pardoner's Tale* makes explicit what the *Knight's Tale* and *Troilus and Criseyde* camouflage under a veneer of eroticism: within a heteroerotic matrix of sexuality, a man's desire for death is entangled and in many ways inseparable from a desire for women, whether in the old man's quest for the maternal tomb or in Arcite's and Troilus's quests for erotic satisfaction.

Before necrotic desires enter the *Knight's Tale* and *Troilus and Criseyde*, erotic yearnings spark their plots, and in this regard in the romance tradition, to gaze at a beautiful woman is to be filled with love-longing. Medieval theories of sight accord varying degrees of agency to the viewer and the viewed, as Carolyn Collette summarizes: "the most influential late medieval thinking about optics assumed a degree of power in the object of vision itself. As a result, the subject one looked at was thought to be as important as the act of looking itself, and the act of looking always a dynamic interchange between viewer and viewed."[22] Such constructions of optical desire function narratologically to set the plot in motion—the

---

20. Carl Phelpstead, "'Th'ende is every tales strengthe': Contextualizing Chaucerian Perspectives on Death and Judgment," in *Chaucer and Religion*, ed. Helen Phillips and Helen Cooper (Cambridge: Brewer, 2010), 97–110, at 108–9.

21. Robert Sturges, *Chaucer's Pardoner and Gender Theory: Bodies of Discourse* (New York: St. Martin's, 2000), 99.

22. Carolyn Collette, *Species, Phantasms, and Images: Vision and Medieval Psychology in the* Canterbury Tales (Ann Arbor: University of Michigan Press, 2001), 14. For more on medieval sight and optics, see David Lindberg, *Theories of Vision from Al-kindi to Kepler* (Chicago: University of Chicago Press, 1976), as well as the following studies focusing on sight and optics in medieval literature: Sarah Stanbury, *Seeing the Gawain-Poet: Description and the Act of Perception* (Philadelphia: University of Pennsylvania Press, 1991), as well as her "The Voyeur and the Private Life in *Troilus and Criseyde*," *Studies in the Age of Chaucer* 13 (1991): 141–58; Emma Campbell and Robert Mills, eds., *Troubled Vision: Sexuality and Sight in Medieval Text and Image* (New York: Palgrave Macmillan, 2004); and Molly Martin, *Vision and Gender in Malory's* Morte D'Arthur (Cambridge: Brewer, 2010).

knight will prove his valor to win his beloved's affections—as they also establish the narrative within the purported purview of the erotic. Furthermore, these medieval theories of sight assign an important sense of agency to the female beloveds, who act and react simply by being seen by their lovers.

Jacques Lacan perceives such scenes of courtly desire as reflective of male narcissism, suggesting that "the element of idealizing exaltation that is expressly sought out in the ideology of courtly love . . . is fundamentally narcissistic in character,"[23] and in this regard, for Emily and Criseyde to function as appropriate narcissistic mirrors for Arcite and Troilus (and Palamon as well), they must be attractive. Chaucer stresses their radiant beauty in numerous lush passages, and such depictions of female beauty stand in stark contrast to the portrayal of the Loathly Lady in the *Wife of Bath's Tale*, in which much of its humor arises in her refusal to serve as a narcissistic mirror for the rapist knight, instead forcing him to lie in bed with a woman who is "so loothly, and so oold also" (3.1100). Emily and Criseyde, on the other hand, inhabit the role of the beautiful beloved unproblematically for their suitors. At the moments when Palamon, Arcite, and Troilus gaze upon them for the first time, the "love at first sight" trope that introduces these female beloveds reduces them to their bodies. Emily is "fairer . . . to sene / Than is the lylie upon his stalke grene" (1.1035–36), and Criseyde's matchless beauty elevates her above all other women: "Right as oure firste lettre is now an A, / In beaute first so stood she, makeles" (1.171–72). Furthermore, they are praised for the heavenly and divine nature of their beauty: Emily sings "as an aungel hevenysshly" (1.1055), and Criseyde is described as "aungelik" (1.102), as a "thing inmortal" (1.103), and as "an hevenyssh perfit creature" (1.104). Palamon wonders whether Emily is "womman or goddesse" (1.1101), and Troilus likewise muses whether Criseyde is a "goddesse or womman" (1.425). As Simon Gaunt notes of the interplay of spiritual and erotic discourses in the Middle Ages, "One consequence of taking religious imagery and language in medieval love literature seriously is that, taken at face value, they lend ethical seriousness to love, in that they impute to those subject to love a set of principles which determines right and wrong behavior and feelings, while offering concurrently a means of spiritual improvement and salvation."[24] Following the standard expectations of romance, Chaucer

---

23. Jacques Lacan, *The Ethics of Psychoanalysis, 1959–1960. The Seminar of Jacques Lacan, Book 7.* Ed. Jacques-Alain Miller. Trans. Dennis Porter (1986; New York: Norton, 1992), 151.

24. Simon Gaunt, *Love and Death in Medieval French and Occitan Courtly Literature: Martyrs to Love* (Oxford: Oxford University Press, 2006), 7.

eloquently expounds on Emily's and Criseyde's beauty to cement their status as embodiments of heteroerotic male desire that elevate earthly passions into matters of spiritual import.

Within an androcentric framework, the function of female beauty, its cultural work, however, is not limited to the purview of piquing the sexual interest of men, as it also stands in opposition to necrotic desires by encouraging men to live for and through their love. Freud, while admitting that "beauty has no obvious use," also claims that "civilization could not do without it."[25] As Lacan explains in his consideration of the death drive, beauty cannot negate thanatos, but it bears the power to neutralize it, at least momentarily:

> The true barrier that holds the subject back in front of the unspeakable field of radical desire that is the field of absolute destruction, of destruction beyond putrefaction, is properly speaking the aesthetic phenomenon where it is identified with the experience of beauty—beauty in all its shining radiance, beauty that has been called the splendor truth.[26]

Within the heteroerotic matrix of male desire that Lacan unpacks, in which a woman is conscripted to serve "as an object of desire," but one that "has nothing to do with her as a woman,"[27] her beauty allows her lover to transcend his mortality. To see this woman is to be inspired with the erotic and thus to suspend the necrotic, if only for the briefest of moments. Although one can never truly escape thanatos, much of the pleasure of medieval romance derives from the fantasy that loving a beautiful maiden allows a knight to accomplish this impossible feat. For Chaucer's narrators, however, the beauty of Emily and Criseyde does not circumvent the necrotic desires of men (as it cannot); rather, their attractiveness facilitates the knights' acceptance of death's inevitability.

Whether as objects of beauty or as purported means for forestalling the reemergence of thanatos, Emily and Criseyde frequently appear in the *Knight's Tale* and *Troilus and Criseyde* as reflections of male desire rather than as women in their own right, with the sharp irony that they are conscripted to serve as male fantasies despite their avowed preference for anti-eroticism. As Susan Crane argues, women in romance reflect male desire: "Intrinsic to masculine identity in romance is the concept of a fundamental difference between self and other. In the dominant paradigm of

---

25. Sigmund Freud, *Civilization and Its Discontents*, 33.
26. Jacques Lacan, *The Ethics of Psychoanalysis*, 216–17.
27. Ibid., 214.

courtship, women attest to their suitors' deeds and reflect back to them an image of their worth."[28] Crane's feminist readings of Chaucerian romance align with Lacan's psychoanalytic theories, as both point to the functionality of female characters for males. Indeed, although without the terms of feminist, queer, or psychoanalytic theory, medieval women's narcissistic functionality for men was recognized in much the same manner, as evident in the words of the wife in the *Book of the Knight of La Tour-Landry*, who, in debate with her husband, admonishes her daughters to beware men's fickle words. She castigates men for using women to enhance their reputations:

> "Lordes and felawes . . . saye that alle the honour and worshyppe whiche they gete and haue, is comynge to them by theyre peramours . . . but these wordes coste to them but lytell to say, for to gete the better and sooner the grace and good wylle of theyr peramours. For of suche wordes, and other moche merueyllous, many one vseth full ofte; but how be hit that they saye that 'for them and for theyr loue they done hit.' In good feyth they done it only for to enhaunce them self, and for to drawe vnto them the grace and vayne glory of the world."[29]

Lords and fellows exploit women to their narcissistic advantage, proving the instrumentality, more than the desirability, of women, at least from this fictional medieval woman's perspective. Lacan argues that narcissism and narcissistic desires are imaginary relations that obscure the identity of the beloved, for she merely mirrors what the man desires to see in himself: "At this point the object introduces itself only insofar as it is perpetually interchangeable with the love that the subject has for its own image."[30] Roughly 600 years prior to Lacan, the wife in the *Book of the Knight of La Tour-Landry* urges women not to heed men's empty words motivated more by narcissism than eroticism, for they erase the women supposedly at their core.

In the opening sequences of the *Knight's Tale* and *Troilus and Criseyde*, Palamon, Arcite, and Troilus perceive Emily and Criseyde not as women, in the sense of females granted autonomy of identity and agency, as much as they perceive them as fantasies of their male desires, stripped of any sig-

---

28. Susan Crane, *Gender and Romance in Chaucer's* Canterbury Tales, 13.
29. Thomas Wright, ed., *The Book of the Knight of La Tour-Landry* (London: Early English Text Society, 1906), 172; cited in Mary Wack, *Lovesickness in the Middle Ages: The Viaticum and Its Commentaries* (Philadelphia: University of Pennsylvania Press, 1990), 146–47.
30. Jacques Lacan, *The Ethics of Psychoanalysis*, 98.

nifying ability other than of male heteroeroticism. As Winthrop Wetherbee observes in regard to Criseyde, but which applies equally well to Emily: "The inability of the male figures in the poem to recognize Criseyde as a person in her own right . . . is symptomatic of the profound limitations of the chivalric view of life, limitations which it is one of the major projects of Chaucer's poetry to expose and criticize."[31] Emily and Criseyde are not allowed the freedom or agency to assert their amatory desires because both women live under the sufferance of their male patrons: as Hippolyta's sister, one who was likewise conquered when Theseus triumphed over "al the regne of Femenye" (1.866), Emily inhabits a marginal position in Athens, relying on the sufferance of her brother-in-law for her continued well-being. As Elizabeth Fowler dryly remarks, "Conquest is by definition supremely indifferent to consent," and in her reading of the tale's power dynamics, she asserts that "the *Knight's Tale* proves to be a consideration of conquest and its claims to dominion," as she also notes how the romance concludes with Emily's coerced marriage to Palamon mirroring Hippolyta's coerced marriage to Theseus.[32] In her reading of Emily as an "Amazon at the Gate," Karma Lochrie traces how "Emelye as Amazon is . . . disguised by her generic rendering as object of Palamon and Arcite's desire,"[33] for the focus of this epic romance is to reconstitute her as a courtly beloved despite her aversion to this role. Criseyde, whose residence in Troy is threatened due to her father's betrayal, depends on the mercy of Trojan men, particularly Hector, who permits her to "dwelleth with us, whil yow good list, in Troie" (1.119). Both women live in potentially

---

31. Winthrop Wetherbee, "Criseyde Alone," in *New Perspectives on Criseyde*, ed. Cindy Vitto and Marcia Smith Marzec (Asheville, NC: Pegasus, 2004), 299–332, at 318. See also Kate Koppelman, "The Dreams in Which I'm Dying: Sublimation and Unstable Masculinities in *Troilus and Criseyde*," in *Men and Masculinities in Chaucer's* Troilus and Criseyde, ed. Tison Pugh and Marcia Smith Marzec (Cambridge: Brewer, 2008), 97–114; and Holly Crocker, "How the Woman Makes the Man: Chaucer's Reciprocal Fictions in *Troilus and Criseyde*," *New Perspectives on Criseyde*, 139–64.

32. Elizabeth Fowler, "The Afterlife of the Civil Dead: Conquest in the *Knight's Tale*," in *Critical Essays on Geoffrey Chaucer*, ed. Thomas Stillinger (New York: Hall, 1998), 59–81, at 60.

33. Karma Lochrie, *Heterosyncrasies: Female Sexuality When Normal Wasn't* (Minneapolis: University of Minnesota Press, 2005), 127. Commenting on the ways in which a tension between absence and presence structures Chaucer's depictions of women and their desires, Susan Schibanoff similarly posits: "At the same time, Chaucer makes less more, in the sense that Emily has not only been a warrior but, also like a man, she wishes to control her own sexuality" ("Chaucer's Lesbians: Drawing Blanks?" *Medieval Feminist Newsletter* 13 [1992]: 11–14). Emily's dual perspectives on pursuits gendered masculine and feminine are sacrificed in her resignification as an object of heteroerotic desire.

hostile environments, necessitating that they adapt their erotic desires as circumstances dictate, and so they must sacrifice their avowed antieroticism as virgin and as widow in favor of the men who love them. As David Aers acknowledges of Criseyde and medieval women who share similar plights, "To survive in this society the isolated woman needs to make use of her sexuality and whatever courtly sexual conventions or fictions as may serve her."[34] Emily and Criseyde must act by reacting in this man's world. They never initiate a heteroerotic relationship based on their sense of their own desires; on the contrary, they are presented with lovers and must then confront the repercussions of being the object of a man's unsought affections. Thus, a fundamental irony arises in these romances, as Arcite and Troilus select erotic partners who, conscripted to love men for whom they share no interest, prefer to embody eroticism's death (or, at least, its dearth) rather than its flourishing.

In contrast to the many romance heroines who desire, or even toy with, a knightly protagonist's love, Emily and Criseyde reject heteroerotic desire, and their refusals align them in an adversarial position to their future lovers. Both Arcite and Troilus refer to their beloveds as their "swete fo[o]" (KT 1.2780, TC 1.874, 5.228), a phrasing that encapsulates the intersection of the erotic and the adversarial in their relationships. Aware of his sister-in-law's anti-erotic stance, Theseus laughs at Palamon and Arcite's violent conflict over her:

> "But this is yet the beste game of alle,
> That she for whom they han this jolitee
> Kan hem therfore as muche thank as me.
> She woot namoore of al this hoote fare,
> By God, than woot a cokkow or an hare!" (1.1806–10)

In one of the narrative's grand ironies, Emily has no knowledge of Palamon's and Arcite's affections for her, despite the many years they pursue her, and, more importantly, she expresses no desire to serve the role of the courtly beloved. Likewise, Criseyde's words to Pandarus, following his revelation that Troilus loves her, accentuate her anti-erotic stance:

> "What, is this al the joye and al the feste?
> Is this your reed? Is this my blisful cas?

---

34. David Aers, "Criseyde: Woman in Medieval Society," *Chaucer Review* 13.3 (1979): 177–200, at 181.

> Is this the verray mede of youre byheeste?
> Is al this paynted proces seyd—allas!—
> Right for this fyn? O lady myn, Pallas!
> Thow in this dredful cas for my purveye,
> For so astoned am I that I deye." (2.421–27)

Her string of rebuking rhetorical questions dismantles Pandarus's celebration of Trojan amorousness, as she pierces through the "paynted process" that grants her a lover when no love was sought. In the closing line of this passage, Criseyde ironically foresees her death resulting from a relationship with Troilus, not perceiving that, through erotic union with her, Troilus, too, will realize his necrotic desires.[35]

In light of their resistance to male desire, Emily and Criseyde must be conquered, and the texts unite in their depiction of the two women failing to withstand the onslaught of male desires as expressed through Palamon and Arcite's tournament for Emily's affections and through Pandarus's sly machinations to win Criseyde for Troilus. As Helen Cooper outlines of women's role in romance, "in the symbolic progression of the quest with its male hero, the dangers of sexuality will inevitably take the form of a female adversary, whether the point at issue is ultimately about the danger of women, the danger of his own unbridled sexuality, or . . . the danger of temptation at large."[36] In this passage Cooper writes particularly of such romance villainesses as Bertilak's wife in *Sir Gawain and the Green Knight*, those seductive temptresses who attempt to distract the knight from his morality and/or his mission. As much as Emily and Criseyde play the role of the female beloved, they are also female adversaries who must be subdued because of their erotic resistance to their suitors. These "sweet foes"

---

35. Despite the narrative's overarching focus on Troilus's death, Chaucer proleptically includes Criseyde's demise in the narrative's opening stanzas:

> Now herkneth with a good entencioun,
> For now wil I gon streght to my matere,
> In which ye may the double sorwes here
> Of Troilus in lovynge of Criseyde,
> And how that she forsook hym er she deyde. (1.52–56)

Criseyde's foretold death in *Troilus and Criseyde* and her literary afterlife, notably in Robert Henryson's *Testament of Cresseid* and Shakespeare's *Troilus and Cressida*, points to the instrumentality of women in male discourses of desire. For a brilliant discussion of Criseyde and her literary afterlives, see Gayle Margherita, "Criseyde's Remains: Romance and the Question of Justice," *Exemplaria* 12.2 (2000): 257–92.

36. Helen Cooper, *The English Romance in Time: Transforming Motifs from Geoffrey of Monmouth to the Death of Shakespeare* (Oxford: Oxford University Press, 2004), 78.

must be defeated as much as any knightly or otherworldly antagonists, even if such defeats are registered in the sexual consummation of amatory relationships rather than in their deaths.

Complementing their refusal of standard romance erotics in their rejection of male sexual desire, Emily and Criseyde also reject the future potential of motherhood in bearing children with Arcite and Troilus, and through these twin refusals, they disrupt the generative erotics of romance by spurning the necessity of reproductive futurism as symbolized in the figure of the Child. Although their respective cultures expect women to reproduce the social order by bearing children, these women resist the cultural imperative to procreate and thus are compelled to symbolize death within the romance's erotic imaginary. Lee Edelman perceives the cultural role of the Child in its work as the foundational tool of sexual policing: societies are based on "the ideological truism" that necessitates "our investment in the Child as the obligatory token of futurity."[37] Quite simply, cultures can only propagate themselves by producing children, regardless of the individual wishes of the women through whom this work must be borne. Building on Edelman's work, Noreen Giffney posits "the impossibility of exercising agency if one partakes of a system steeped in reproductive futurism which permeates all social, political, and cultural structures."[38] From this perspective, women living under patriarchal regimes, in snubbing their potential fecundity in favor of thanatos, have the power to tear the cultural fabric by refusing to stitch it whole through motherhood. By withholding their bodies and their generative capacity from the aegis of a masculinist ideology (and, in Emily's case, an overtly hostile one), Emily and Criseyde frustrate the generic expectations of medieval romance as much as they subvert the foundations of patriarchy. Patrilineal societies, despite their focus on the male's role in determining kinship relations, need women if they are to survive, but Emily and Criseyde resist reproducing the next generation of warriors to defend Athens and Troy, societies characterized by their hostile treatment of women through war, rape, and ravishment. In these amatory environments, where Emily and Criseyde cannot choose their lovers, they succeed in expressing an etiolated and queer sense of agency by rejecting childbirth. Men may love them despite their wishes to the contrary, yet men cannot compel

---

37. Lee Edelman, *No Future: Queer Theory and the Death Drive* (Durham, NC: Duke University Press, 2004), 12.

38. Noreen Giffney, "Queer Apocal(o)ptic/ism: The Death Drive and the Human," in *Queering the Non/Human*, ed. Noreen Giffney and Myra Hird (Aldershot, Hampshire: Ashgate, 2008), 55–78, at 63.

them either to love them in return or willingly to produce the babies they might wish for them to bear.

These queer edges to Emily and Criseyde are evident in their rebuffing of maternity, but also in their preference for homosocial environments. Emily would not reside in Athens if the Amazons had not been conquered, and, when readers first see Criseyde, she has ensconced herself among the homosocial company of her female reading group (2.81–84). Within Chaucer's necrotic romances, in which death awaits Arcite and Troilus, Emily and Criseyde repudiate children and childbirth in tandem with their refusal of male desire. In this light, Emily opposes reproduction in her prayer to Diana to be spared from marriage and childbirth, and as Robert Edwards notes, Chaucer reimagines Boccaccio's prayer sequences to allow her to speak: "Chaucer adds a description of Diana's temple to balance the descriptions of Mars's and Venus's temples in Boccaccio and to give a rare space for feminine subjectivity."[39] In this setting where female desires may be voiced, Emily aligns herself with anti-eroticism:

> "Chaste goddesse, wel wostow that I
> Desire to ben a mayden al my lyf,
> Ne nevere wol I be no love ne wyf.
> I am, thow woost, yet of thy compaignye,
> A mayde, and love huntynge and venerye,
> And for to walken in the wodes wilde,
> And noght to be a wyf and be with childe.
> Noght wol I knowe compaignye of man." (1.2304–11)

Choosing lifelong virginity, Emily denies any wifely or maternal desires, asserting for herself perpetual allegiance to the virginal Diana and life in the "wodes wilde." As William Woods proposes, "For Emelye, 'to ben a mayden al my lyf' is, in a psychological sense, to deny change and thus to be free forever. By contrast, the 'compaignye of man' may for her suggest eternal bondage."[40] Analyzing Chaucer's rewriting of this scene from Boccaccio's *Teseida*, Stephen Russell argues that Chaucer stresses Emily's preference for remaining a virgin rather than marrying, in direct contrast to the source text: "In the *Teseida*, Emilia's initial wish to remain in the company of Diana . . . seems largely *pro forma*. . . . Her real wish—to wind up with the one who loves her most—receives all the

---

39. Robert Edwards, *Chaucer and Boccaccio*, 32.
40. William Woods, "'My sweete foo': Emelye's Role in the *Knight's Tale*," *Studies in Philology* 88.3 (1991): 276–306, at 294.

rhetorical and narrative emphasis in the original. In Chaucer's version, however, Emily's prayer to remain a virgin is forceful, while her second choice . . . is a mere afterthought."[41] For Emily, a captive in Athens, reproduction would entail reproducing the society that has subjugated her, her sister, and her fellow Amazons. By striving to maintain her virginity through her allegiance to Diana, she refuses to propagate a social order that has literally captured her. Although she cannot pronounce a death sentence upon Athens and so destroy the commonweal, she can resignify her erotic conquest into an act of necrotic resistance. Furthermore, the troubling scene of childbirth depicted in Diana's temple—"A womman travaillynge was hire biforn; / But for hir child so longe was unborn, / Ful pitously Lucyna gan she calle / And seyde, 'Help, for thou mayst best of alle!'" (1.2083–86)—suggests that a woman's preference for virginity protects her from the mortal dangers of childbirth. In debasing fecundity and aligning herself with Diana, Emily may merely seek the simple anti-erotic pleasure of staying alive.[42]

In complementary contrast to Emily, Criseyde, as a widow, is no longer a virgin, but she appears similarly averse to reproduction. The narrator states obliquely, "But, wheither that she children hadde or noon, / I rede it naught, therfore I late it goon" (1.132–33), and through this elliptical passage, he refuses to take a definitive stance on the issue. Robert Levine proposes that "Chaucer may very well have refrained from making a categorical assertion of [Criseyde's] childlessness in the first book, to prevent a medieval reader from recognizing her immediately as an iconographical figure . . . of sterile love."[43] But if Chaucer were to depict Criseyde as a mother, and, in so doing, contradict Boccaccio's depiction of her in *Teseida*, she appears wholly unconcerned with her children, and no mention of any offspring is made when she leaves Troy to join the

---

41. Stephen Russell, "Dido, Emily, and Constance: Femininity and Subversion in the Mature Chaucer," *Medieval Perspectives* 1 (1986): 65–74, at 69.

42. For the intersection of Diana and Lucyna in classical and Chaucerian mythology, see Jane Chance, *The Mythographic Chaucer: The Fabulation of Sexual Politics* (Minneapolis: University of Minnesota Press, 1995), 207–9.

43. Robert Levine, "Restraining Ambiguities in Chaucer's *Troilus and Criseyde*," *Neuphilologische Mitteilungen* 87 (1986): 558–64, at 562. For additional studies of Criseyde's shifting character throughout classical and medieval texts, see Gretchen Mieszkowski, "The Reputation of Criseyde, 1155–1500," *Transactions of the Connecticut Academy of Arts and Sciences* 43 (1971): 71–153; and E. Talbot Donaldson, "Briseis, Briseida, Criseyde, Cresseid, Cressid: Progress of a Heroine," in *Chaucerian Problems and Perspectives*, ed. Edward Vasta, Zacharias Thundy, and Theodore Hesburgh (Notre Dame, IN: University of Notre Dame Press, 1979), 3–12.

Greeks. Instead, Criseyde's status as a widow guides her portraiture in the romance, with the narrator frequently emphasizing her black mourning weeds. She appears "in widewes habit large of samyt brown" (1.109) and "in widewes habit blak" (1.170). Her beauty shines through despite the darkness of her dress—"Nas nevere yet seyn thyng to ben preysed derre, / Nor under cloude blak so bright a sterre" (1.174–75)—and the narrator summarizes his view of her and her wardrobe succinctly: "She, this in blak" (1.309). In her black clothes symbolic of death, Criseyde not only enacts mourning but also personifies the necrotic end of all relationships. As her first husband died prior to fathering a child with her, so too will Troilus fail to generate life with a woman committed to the anti-erotic pleasures of widowhood.

Conscripted to serve as objects of heteroerotic male fantasy, Emily and Criseyde fail in staving off the advances of men in the patriarchal environs of medieval romance, but their grudging acquiescence to this role allows them, finally, freedom from Arcite and Troilus (if not from Palamon and Diomede). Slavoj Žižek sees subversive potential in a woman's position as male fantasy, declaring that the "ontological denigration of women as a mere 'symptom' of man . . . is, when it is openly admitted and fully accepted, far more subversive than the false direct assertion of feminine autonomy." He further suggests, "perhaps the ultimate feminist statement is to proclaim openly: 'I do not exist in myself, I am merely the Other's fantasy embodied.'"[44] Žižek identifies a radical power in feminine acquiescence to male power: forced to adapt themselves to Arcite's and Troilus's fantasies, compelled to cede resistance and accede to male sexual desire, they prepare Arcite and Troilus to succumb to the necrotic lure of their erotic desires. For, quite simply, Arcite and Troilus are virtually interchangeable with Palamon and Diomede, and if Emily and Criseyde cannot rid themselves of all lovers, Fortune and the generic structures of romance intervene to eradicate two of them: when two knights battle, typically only one survives, and such is true in the *Knight's Tale* and *Troilus and Criseyde* as Palamon and Diomede, the last men standing, assume their positions as the women's lovers.

In this manner, Emily and Criseyde, who affirm virginity and widowhood as their preferred cultural roles for the asexuality encoded in them, share their externally necrotic tendencies with their potential lovers. Freud suggests that one resists the death drive through the destruction of

---

44. Slavoj Žižek, *The Ticklish Subject: The Absent Centre of Political Ontology* (London: Verso, 1999), 306.

an entity exterior to the self: "It really seems as though it is necessary for us to destroy some other thing or person in order not to destroy ourselves, in order to guard against the impulse to self-destruction."[45] Emily and Criseyde do not appear to desire to destroy Arcite and Troilus in the sense of killing them; their goals are simply to live unmolested by heteroerotic desire, to preserve their asexuality in a homosocial environment, and to reject undesired amatory advances. Nor, it should be noted, do they desire to destroy children: Emily merely wishes not to bear any, and Criseyde has not done so despite her marriage. But the success of these anti-erotic goals hinges upon their eradication of male eroticism, for which they need only rely on male competition in love. The romance tradition frequently depicts amatory competitions resulting in at least one dead man, and the combative relationships both between Arcite and Palamon and between Troilus and Diomede follow this pattern, even if neither Palamon nor Diomede is directly responsible for his adversary's death. Readers may see Emily's and Criseyde's roles in Arcite's and Troilus's deaths as the necessary cost to preserve themselves, if only momentarily, as they queerly refract and recirculate male erotic desires through female anti-eroticism, anti-fecundity, and male competition. What else can a woman do, when a man loves her so passionately, despite her desire merely to be left alone?

CHAUCERIAN ROMANCE AND THE DEATH OF MEN

When medieval men say that they will die for love, readers should believe them, despite the exaggerations endemic to this discourse. As Mary Wack certifies in her magisterial *Lovesickness in the Middle Ages*, many medieval physicians and scholars viewed lovesickness as a physical malady, one with numerous causes, symptoms, and cures:

> The authority and pragmatism of the medical descriptions of lovesickness were able to assist the evolution of a cultural fantasy into social reality. "I'm dying of love" became both a cliché and a medical possibility, remote but dreadful. Once romantic ideology had become a social practice that the nobility had to reckon with, the medicalized vision of lovesickness enabled lovesick aristocrats to cope with their own erotic vulnerability.[46]

---

45. Sigmund Freud, "Anxiety and Instinctual Life," *Standard Edition*, 22.81–111, at 105; qtd. in Lee Edelman, *No Future*, 52.
46. Mary Wack, *Lovesickness in the Middle Ages*, 174.

Wack's scholarship showcases the circularity of medieval scientific thought and literary production, as romance depictions of love corroborated learned exegesis on the subject, and scientific accounts of lovesickness found their way into the literary record. As Donald Beecher and Massimo Ciavolella explain of medieval theories of lovesickness, "Because human love is fundamentally *amor concupiscentiae*, carnal desire, it is, by definition, capable of causing states of disease because, being a *passio*, it could alter the balance of elements within the body that constitutes health."[47] Within this medieval discourse, love bears somatic effects evident in the lover's behavior, such that the emotionality and physicality of love are intertwined in a shared enactment of love's pains. Although neither Arcite nor Troilus die of lovesickness—it is, after all, a horse accident and an enemy's superior might that kill them—the possibility that they will die for love percolates throughout the narratives, imbuing their stories with eroticism never devoid of its necrotic edges.

Chaucer describes Arcite's and Troilus's erotic suffering in detail, painting extended pictures of the lovers and the physical toll that love takes upon their bodies. Arcite's "loveris maladye" (1.1373) dramatically alters his appearance: "lene he wex and drye as is a shaft; / His eyen holwe and grisly to biholde, / His hewe falow and pale as asshen colde" (1.1362–64). Indeed, the plot of the *Knight's Tale* depends on the physical changes that lovesickness inflicts upon Arcite's body, for it is only due to the profound alterations in his appearance that he can return to Athens and assume his new identity as Emily's page Philostrate. In Troilus's case, lovesickness renders him prostrate for much of the romance's first two books. Pandarus diagnoses his lovesickness as a "disese" (2.1360) and a "maladie" (2.1515), and in an ironic passage indicative of her role in Troilus's illness, Criseyde affirms her ability to cure him: "Best koud I yet ben his leche" (2.1582), she muses to herself, as she earlier recognized that granting him her love would be "for his heele" (2.707). These passages underscore the physical effects that love bears on the male body, as it also foreshadows that such suffering typically ends in death. As Sealy Gilles observes of the interrelationship of love, gender, and disease in *Troilus and Criseyde*, "this redemptive function, the feminine body's efficacy in the reconstitution of the masculine whole, rests upon prior construction of that body as first pathogenic, then curative. The beloved infects, then cures, only to prove

---

47. Donald Beecher and Massimo Ciavolella, eds. and trans., *A Treatise on Love Sickness by Jacques Ferrand* (Syracuse, NY: Syracuse University Press, 1990), 75.

by her willful absence and fickleness that earthly salve is illusory."[48] But what happens when the woman refuses to share her curative powers with her afflicted lover?

In large measure, the converging discourses of lovesickness as an illness and as a cause of death explain the extraordinary focus on death in the *Knight's Tale* and *Troilus and Criseyde*, in which most of Arcite's and Troilus's laments focus on love and death but do not then metaphorically construct the beloved as death herself. When Arcite muses, "A man moot nedes love, maugree his heed; / He may nat fleen it, thogh he sholde be deed" (1.1169–70), he does not employ language that figures Emily as necrosis personified. In passages similar to this one, he suffers for his love and envisions himself dying but refrains from visualizing Emily as the allegorical embodiment of his imminent demise:

> . . . "Allas that day that I was born!
> Now is my prisoun worse than biforn;
> Now is me shape eternally to swelle
> Noght in purgatorie, but in helle." (1.1223–26)

In a similar manner, Troilus laments that love may kill him, yet he does not hold Criseyde accountable for his potential death. In an address to his spirit, he urges it to flee his body so that it may continue to follow Criseyde after his passing:

> "O wery goost, that errest to and fro,
> Why nyltow fleen out of the wofulleste
> Body that evere myghte on grounde go?
> O soule, lurkynge in this wo, unneste,
> Fle forth out of myn herte, and lat it breste,
> And folowe alwey Criseyde, thi lady dere.
> Thi righte place is now no lenger here." (4.302–8)

As with these lines, in the majority of instances in which Arcite and Troilus foresee their passing as consequences of their love, they do not see Emily and Criseyde as avatars of death. Love catalyzes lovesickness, and

---

48. Sealy Gilles, "Love and Disease in Chaucer's *Troilus and Criseyde*," *Studies in the Age of Chaucer* 25 (2003): 157–97, at 162. On the emphasis of death in *Troilus and Criseyde*, see also Karen Arthur, "A TACT Analysis of the Language of Death in *Troilus and Criseyde*," in *Computer-Based Chaucer Studies*, ed. Ian Lancashire and Patricia Eberle (Toronto: Centre for Computing in Humanities, 1993), 67–85.

lovesickness may kill, but that it does so does not entail that the lady herself is depicted as the embodiment of the knight's death drive, for the focus on death reveals the male lover's confusion of his own erotic and necrotic desires.

Despite the fact that Arcite and Troilus primarily vocalize their erotic desires for Emily and Criseyde as distinct from their willingness to die for love, it is striking just how briefly eroticism flowers in the *Knight's Tale* and *Troilus and Criseyde* before necrotic desires emerge, for to see the beloved is also to see a foreshadowing of one's death. In this regard, the collapse of the erotic as distinct from the necrotic, whose separation is the foundational fantasy of romance, obscures for the reader the cultural work of beauty. When Arcite first espies Emily, he is pained by her comeliness: "And with that sighte hir beautee hurte hym so" (1.1114), the narrator proclaims. The young knight then foresees his death arising due to her attractiveness: "The fresshe beautee sleeth me sodeynly / Of hire that rometh in the yonder place" (1.1118–19). He presciently avows, "I nam but deed; ther nis namoore to seye" (1.1122), and soon repeats himself almost verbatim: "I nam but deed; ther nys no remedye" (1.1274).[49] Troilus likewise responds visually to Criseyde—"'O mercy, God,' thoughte he, 'wher hastow woned, / That art so feyr and goodly to devise?'" (1.276–77)—and soon feels the grip of death clenching hold: "That sodeynly hym thoughte he felte dyen" (1.306). The beauty of Emily and Criseyde sparks the erotic plot of these romances, with Arcite pursuing Emily (as his cousin competes for her affections) and Troilus pursuing Criseyde (under Pandarus's able guidance), but these initial moments of desire also foretell the impossibility of separating necrotic desires from erotic ones. In a complementary fashion, both Arcite's and Troilus's desire for death can be read as their longing for the *petite mort* of orgasm, which imbues their

---

49. When Palamon first espies "fresshe Emelye" (1.1068), he likewise experiences the pains of love:

> "But I was hurt right now thurghout myn ye
> Into myn herte, that wol my bane be.
> The fairnesse of that lady that I see
> Yond in the gardyn romen to and fro
> Is cause of al my criyng and my wo." (1.1096–100)

In Palamon's stricken response, he denies himself the agency of a male lover, describing himself with passive phrasings ("I was hurt") that cast Emily as his conqueror (the "cause of al my criyng"). In contrast to Arcite, Palamon survives his encounter with Emily's deadly beauty, but his survival depends on Arcite's death, which allows him to preserve the romance fantasy that one's necrotic desires can be transcended through love.

amatory pursuits with an erotic optimism that camouflages their latent necrotics.

In many of their declarations of affection for Emily and Criseyde, Arcite and Troilus proclaim their willingness to die for love, linking their necrotic and erotic drives together as an expression of their own volition. Arcite proclaims not merely that he does not fear death but that he desires to die, if he can do so in Emily's presence: "Ne for the drede of deeth shal I nat spare / To se my lady, that I love and serve. / In hir presence I recche nat to sterve" (1.1396–98). It is certainly a strange mix of desires, such that, if the erotic drive merely to be in the lady's presence is sated, necrotic desires can be fully realized without regret. The narrator agrees with Arcite's assessment of his necrotic and erotic desires: "And shortly, outher he wolde lese his life / Or wynnen Emelye unto his wif" (1.1485–86). As Arcite realizes, death becomes his destiny simply because he loves:

> "Love hath his firy dart so brennyngly
> Ystiked thurgh my trewe, careful herte
> That shapen was my deeth erst than my sherte.
> Ye sleen me with youre eyen, Emelye!
> Ye been the cause wherfore that I dye." (1.1564–68)

Assuming a passive role in these lines, one who is pierced by love's dart and slain by his beloved's eyes, Arcite denies himself agency in love. He is capable of fighting Palamon for Emily's hand in marriage, but whether through passivity in love (such as when Emily slays him with her eyes) or activity (such as when he defeats Palamon but dies anyway), death can never be divorced from his motivations, for it is so frequently conjoined with his passion for her. Again, this desire for death alludes to orgasm, but the darkness of orgasm's metaphoric construction as a momentary death challenges a sustained optimistic view of the erotic.

In a striking passage describing the eroticism motivating Troilus to kill Greek soldiers, the narrator stresses that Troilus does so neither due to any enmity toward these foes of his homeland nor even due to any desire to save his people from the siege. On the contrary, death is a seductive tactic, one that enhances his desirability to Criseyde:

> But for non hate he to the Grekes hadde,
> Ne also for the rescous of the town,
> Ne made hym thus in armes for to madde,
> But only, lo, for this conclusioun:

To liken hire the bet for his renoun,
Fro day to day in armes so he spedde
That the Grekes as the deth him dredde. (1.477–83)

For the Greeks, Troilus personifies death. It is, of course, little surprise that the Greeks view him (or any other Trojan warrior) in this light, but it is critical to realize that Chaucer strips Troilus of any allegiance to the Trojan cause in his martial motivations. Internal erotics intersect with necrotics projected externally in this scene, as the Greeks' reaction to Troilus illuminates how his necrotic desires will shift into internal and self-directed ones.

Building on these corruptive links between eros and thanatos that denude the fantasy of their partition in romance, certain passages further erode the knights' fantasies of an eros uncorrupted by thanatos and bring to light that their "sweet foes" are inextricably linked to their imminent demises. In his death scene, Arcite couples his sense of his approaching demise with regret for losing Emily, uniting them into a joint expression of erotic and necrotic desire. In his cry "Allas, the deeth! Allas, myn Emelye" (1.2773), the two may be seen either as separate entities or as synonyms, and his words indicate simultaneously that he regrets that his death will deprive him of his beloved and that his beloved has caused his death. In his following words, he continues to merge love and death, describing Emily as the cause of his demise: "Allas, myn hertes queene! Allas, my wyf, / Myn hertes lady, endere of my lyf!" (1.2775–76). Arcite's subsequent lines further collapse any remaining distinction between Emily and death:

"What is this world? What asketh men to have?
Now with his love, now in his colde grave
Allone, withouten any compaignye.
Fare wel, my sweete foo, myn Emelye!" (1.2777–80)

It initially appears that the answer to Arcite's second rhetorical question is that a man desires to live with his love, but his attention then shifts away from such an erotic affirmation as he comments on the transience of life, observing that one is "Now with his love, now in his colde grave / Allone." The coupling of eros and thanatos in this passage tacitly paints them as equally desired, suggesting that Arcite has sought his death in equal measure to his love, for they both stand as the response to the question of what do men desire. As the guiding *demande d'amour* of the *Wife of Bath's*

Tale inquires what women most want and proposes its answer in women's sovereignty over men in their amatory decisions, Arcite's final musings on male desire point to the necessity of achieving equanimity between eros and thanatos, so that they are harmonized as one's life draws to a close. In these final words to Emily, who stands beside him as physical and emotional agony wracks his mind and body, Arcite reminds her that she is his enemy, his "sweete foo," who was long desired but never conquered. In defeat, he now seeks relief in the comforts of the grave.

In similarly striking passages, Troilus likewise reveals that his erotic desires are inseparable from his necrotic ones. Echoing Petrarch's "S' amor non è, che dunque è quel ch' io sento?," he questions in his first *Canticus Troili* how love could be united with suffering—"If love be good, from whennes cometh my woo?" (1.402)—but then confesses that their union results from his own volition: "O quike deth, O swete harm so queynte, / How may of the in me swich quantite, / But if that I consente that it be?" (1.411–13), as Petrarch wondered before him, "O viva morte, o dilettoso male, / come puoi tanto in me s' io nol consento?"[50] In these lines that explicitly link erotic and necrotic desires by describing death as a "swete harm so queynte," Chaucer unites thanatos with sexuality through the pun on *queynte* as female genitalia. In this love song, Troilus metaphorically constructs death and woman as consuming him from the inside, despite his inviting such suffering through his own free consent. One may reasonably counter that Troilus's sense of consent is meaningless: humans can no more consent to thanatos than they can consent to eros. Nonetheless, Troilus's sense of volition in this passage underscores that his attempts to negotiate eros merely camouflage his latent investment in realizing his death drive through Criseyde. The emergence of womb and tomb imagery in Troilus's song proleptically reminds readers of the young lover's fate, as it also points to the ways in which his expressions of desire confuse one's understanding of male desire, for the erotic merely enfolds the necrotic within it.

Arcite's and Troilus's quests for love are doomed attempts to free themselves from death, but love can never free a lover from death's snare. To stand as men and lovers, Arcite and Troilus need Emily and Criseyde, but doing so only proves the narcissistic necessity of women for men within the heteroerotic economy of medieval romance. When men desire undesiring women (not, it should be noted, undesirable women), the emptiness of

---

50. Petrarch, *The Canzoniere, or Rerum vulgarium fragmenta*, trans. Mark Musa (Bloomington: Indiana University Press, 1996), 216, for sonnet 132.

their eroticism comes to the fore, underscoring the futility of desires that are undesired in return yet that reveal the male's attempt at transcendence. Serge Leclaire intriguingly asserts that thanatos requires the sacrifice of the phallus that promises to generate signification:

> What has to be put to death are the constructions and phantasies claiming to account unambiguously for our filiation, or, more precisely, focusing on a single point the source of the forces moving us.... *What we must bring about so as to exist is our absolute separation from the phallus. At the same time, however, what we cannot erase in ourselves is the figure of that phallus.*[51]

With its first-person pronouns encoding the phallic order on all of his readers regardless of their sexes, Leclaire's analysis metaphorically reenacts the phallic impositions of discourse that he attempts to denude. Still, his theories of phallic separation highlight the tragedy of heteroerotic desire: if we can hypothesize that for a man to love a woman is to seek separation from the phallic order by embracing the feminine and the erotic, doing so requires the necessary impossibility of freeing himself from the phallic order that both privileges him in the social world yet ties him to the necrotic impossibility of severing himself from his penis. A man can only physically escape the symbolic signification of his penis through castration, but such a possibility does not arise within Chaucer's fictions (except possibly in the figure of the Pardoner). Indeed, as Jean-Joseph Goux explains, the threat of castration imbues the phallus with its symbolic meaning: "We may infer that the acceptance of castration affords access to the real, to realization."[52] Arcite and Troilus die with their penises rather than live with their loves, proving the virtual impossibility of transcending an erotic order that is coterminous with death.

Thus, the failure of erotic desires in the *Knight's Tale* and *Troilus and Criseyde* fractures the matrimonial and generative promises of the romance tradition, as Arcite and Troilus die without the women they love. Georges Bataille trenchantly observes, "Marriage is most often thought of as having little to do with eroticism,"[53] and such is the case with the *Knight's*

---

51. Serge Leclaire, *A Child Is Being Killed: On Primary Narcissism and the Death Drive*, trans. Marie-Claude Hays (Stanford, CA: Stanford University Press, 1998), 32–33; italics in original.

52. Jean-Joseph Goux, *Symbolic Economies: After Marx and Freud*, trans. Jennifer Gage (Ithaca, NY: Cornell University Press, 1990), 35.

53. Georges Bataille, *Erotism: Death and Sensuality*, trans. Mary Dalwood (1957; San Francisco: City Lights, 1986), 109.

Tale and *Troilus and Criseyde* as the texts rewrite the familiar trope of marriage(s) closing a romance. The *Knight's Tale* ends a mere ten lines after readers learn that Arcite's rival Palamon "hath . . . ywedded Emelye" (1.3098), and thus the abruptness of the conclusion abrogates any nascent eroticism in marriage beyond these skeletal outlines. In *Troilus and Criseyde*, the question of whether the two protagonists marry is perplexing: the narrator records that they "pleyinge entrechaungeden hire rynges, / Of which I kan nought tellen no scripture" (3.1368–69). Concerning the issue of Troilus and Criseyde's potential marriage, John Maguire demonstrates that clandestine marriages were a recognized social phenomenon in medieval England; however, the fact that the exchange of rings in *Troilus and Criseyde* is undertaken in a playful manner undercuts interpretations of their marriage, if it is one, as a serious affair.[54] In both cases, marriage (or quasi-marriage) harkens the end of eroticism, for the *Knight's Tale* concludes prior to the announcement of any childbearing with the curt pronouncement "Thus endeth Palamon and Emelye" (1.3107), and *Troilus and Criseyde* soon turns to Troilus's despair as Criseyde is traded to the Greeks for Antenor. Although Troilus's death is delayed, its inexorable approach imbues the final books with a dirgeful air, for the erotic climax of book 3 cannot halt the text's necrotic drive. Simon Gaunt posits that "the courtly lover speaks of death in order to live,"[55] but Arcite and Troilus prove that, in other instances, speaking of love only camouflages the knight's incessant pursuit of death.

Finally, despite the many similarities between Arcite's and Troilus's love affairs that end so disastrously, the reactions to their deaths contrast sharply. Arcite's death scene is long and drawn out, and, in scenes that feel emotionally contrived, Palamon and Emily grieve mightily for a man whom the former sought to kill and the latter sought to evade. Elizabeth Edwards reads Arcite's death and funeral scenes as indicative of the necessary cultural work of mourning to heal the loss of the loved one, as she also explores how this cultural production is coded as feminine: "That the excesses of mourning are figured as 'womanish' here, when the martial funeral and its games have been so markedly masculine, fits into the economy of loss of the entire textual genealogy, where, in Thebes or Athens, the work of mourning is woman's work, a different order of productivity."[56] In contrast, Troilus views his funeral from his new perspec-

---

54. John Maguire, "The Clandestine Marriage of Troilus and Criseyde," *Chaucer Review* 8 (1974): 262–78.

55. Simon Gaunt, *Love and Death in Medieval French and Occitan Courtly Literature*, 209.

56. Elizabeth Edwards, "Chaucer's *Knight's Tale* and the Work of Mourning," *Exemplaria*

tive in the afterlife and laughs at "hem that wepten for his deth" (5.1822). Alone yet newly aware of the trivial nature of erotic pursuits, Troilus perceives mourning as expressive of merely a transient desire that is ephemeral and benignly and forgivably risible: it represents the desire to call a lost loved one back from the grave, and thus it is the ultimate act of futility. From these divergent vantage points, of Arcite's survivors' grief and of Troilus's laughter, Chaucer limns the ways in which the cultural work of mourning must always and only commemorate that which has been lost, in women's tears on earth and in men's laughter in heaven, yet neither response alleviates the desire to find meaning in earthly suffering. Theseus's wan words on the subject—"Thanne is it wysdom, as it thynketh me, / To maken vertu of necessitee, / And take it weel that we may nat eschue" (1.3041–43)—encode the emptiness of signification through speech. As Aranye Fradenburg notes, "What is asked for is a boundless credence, a credence beyond the bounds of the law, which can only be produced through the arbitrariness of the law and the *jouissance* of the law's absurdity,"[57] and the impossibility of the law and its concomitant calls for its own transgressions ensnare Arcite and Troilus in necrotic pursuits camouflaged under the guise of eros. Beyond the obstacles of pursuing the imperious beloved of courtly romance, Arcite and Troilus must tackle the queer challenges of loving women aligned with female homosociality and anti-eroticism, never realizing that their eroticism blinds them to their own necrotic impulses.

CONCLUSION

In Shakespeare's *As You Like It,* Rosalind famously mocks men's necrotic impulses as expressed through their amorous pursuits, stating humorously, "men have died from time to time, and worms have eaten them, but not for love." In this same speech, she dismisses legendary depictions of Troilus's death, pointing out that, by dying in battle, he did not die for love: "Troilus had his brains dash'd out with a Grecian club, yet he did what he could to die before, and he is one of the patterns of love."[58] By laughing at

---

20.4 (2008): 361–84, at 371. On Arcite's death scene, see also Mark Infusino and Ynez O'Neill, "Arcite's Death and the New Surgery in the *Knight's Tale,*" *Studies in the Age of Chaucer* 1 (1984): 221–30.

57. Aranye Fradenburg, *Sacrifice Your Love: Psychoanalysis, Historicism, Chaucer* (Minneapolis: University of Minnesota Press, 2002), 173.

58. William Shakespeare, *As You Like It,* in *The Riverside Shakespeare,* ed. Blakemore

the possibility that lovesickness can kill, Rosalind in many ways personifies an inversion of desire as expressed in the *Knight's Tale* and *Troilus and Criseyde*; indeed, she tutors her beloved Orlando to live and to love her, and so here a woman desires, and succeeds in winning the object of her affections. Lovesickness, from this Renaissance woman's perspective, needs no deeper cure than female laughter at the excessive posturing of men in pursuit of their affections.

In contrast, both Arcite and Troilus die for love in the *Knight's Tale* and *Troilus and Criseyde*, believing that life without love is impossible. Arcite falls at Saturn's behest, and Troilus dies heroically in battle while defending his eponymous homeland in a scene startling for its brevity: "Despitously hym slough the fierse Achille" (5.1806). Even this slight glory in death, however, is predicated upon failure: Troy will fall as Troilus has fallen, and given Troy's dubious conduct in amatory affairs, with the rape of Helen and the exchange of Criseyde, it is by no means clear that Troy was worthy of the sacrifices mounted for its defense. Likewise, at the beginning of the *Knight's Tale*, Palamon and Arcite almost die in defense of Thebes, despite its vicious treatment of the bodies of enemy soldiers, thus again proving men's willingness to die for suspect causes that they pursue without regard to the questions of moral justice that should always be considered in martial conflicts. Although one might view war as an appropriate effort to channel the death drive into beneficial work on behalf of the commonweal, readers are given little reason to cheer the military causes of Troy, Thebes, and Athens. As Herbert Marcuse mordantly ponders, "Western civilization has always glorified the hero, the sacrifice of life for the city, the state, the nation; it has rarely asked the question of whether the city, state, nation were worth the sacrifice."[59]

In a similar manner, readers might well wonder whether women are worthy of the sacrifice of Arcite's and Troilus's lives: do Emily and Criseyde merit the men who fall to their affections for such beauty? They cannot merit this sacrifice from the perspective of male narcissism and its follies, for they were never women in these poems beyond necrotic reflections of male desire refracted through eroticism. Such an interpretation, it must be acknowledged, runs the risk of erasing women and female desire from these poems, but doing so within this framework alleviates Emily and Criseyde from the burden of male necrotic desires, ones that quite literally encrypt them as reflections of narcissistic desires that could never

---

Evans, 2nd ed. (Boston: Houghton Mifflin, 1997), 4.1.106–8 and 97–100.

59. Herbert Marcuse, *Eros and Civilization: A Philosophical Inquiry into Freud* (Boston: Beacon, 1966), xix.

bear fruit. But through their refusal to bear children with Arcite and Troilus, and further through Chaucer's refusal to depict their bearing children with Palamon and Diomede, the lovers from whom Fortune allows them no escape, Emily and Criseyde decline the generative erotics of courtship and marriage. Athens stands at the end of the *Knight's Tale*, whereas Troy's fall is imminent at the close of *Troilus and Criseyde*, but both polities suppress women's desires in the erotic realm to counterbalance the fantasies of anti-eroticism and childlessness that would be their ultimate undoing. In these instances, the reproductive logic of romance attempts to trap women in a downward spiral of perpetuating societies that celebrate women for their beauty while refusing to acknowledge that their deepest desires might well be to live their lives undesired and unmolested by men, in queer celebration of anti-eroticisms devoid of children and husbands but populated with pleasures left untold.

CHAPTER FIVE

QUEER FAMILIES IN THE *CANTERBURY TALES*

Fathers, Children, and Abusive Erotics

Surely D. S. Brewer is correct in his assertion, "Love of children is one of the orthodoxies of human nature which Chaucer takes for granted."[1] The evidence for his interpretation abounds: Griselda's multiple swoons upon reuniting with her lost children at the close of the *Clerk's Tale* illustrate the depth of a mother's love, and the "poure wydwe" of the *Prioress's Tale* likewise exemplifies maternal tenderness as she seeks her lost son with "moodres pitee in hir brest enclosed" (7.586, 593). The Parson frets that fathers may love their children so excessively that they will succumb to filial idolatry (10.860), and Chaucer's gentle dedication of his *A Treatise on the Astrolabe* to "Lyte Lowys my sone" (1) testifies to a father's affection for his son and concern for the boy's education. Such moments showcase parents' sincere feelings for their progeny, yet love is an ever protean, never stable emotion, and the loving concern that Chaucer expresses to his own child finds a surprising counterpart in the abuse, death, and torment meted out to many of the children depicted in his fictions.

In considering the psychological meaning of violence against children, Sigmund Freud notes the frequent appearance of an abusive fantasy—"It

---

1. D. S. Brewer, "Children in Chaucer," *Review of English Literature* 5.3 (1964): 52–60, at 52. Brewer also notes Chaucer's contradictory treatment of children, suggesting that "there is deep feeling in Chaucer about the death of children, yet his passing references are surprisingly flippant" (55).

is surprising how often people who seek analytic treatment for hysteria or an obsessional neurosis confess to having indulged in the phantasy: 'A child is being beaten'"[2]—and this commonplace psychological trope is repeatedly realized in depictions of violence against children throughout Chaucer's *Canterbury Tales*. The examples of parental affection cited above have their counterparts in such scenes as Walter's sequestering of his children from their mother for her psychological torment in the *Clerk's Tale*; the vicious execution of the "litel clergeon, seven yeer of age" in the *Prioress's Tale* (7.503); and the Parson's anxiety over parents who murder their offspring, whether these children are born or unborn, whether the parents act accidentally or purposefully (10.575–80). The narrative treatments of many other of Chaucer's child characters are equally violent: sexual assault (Maline in the *Reeve's Tale*), banishment (Mauricius's fate, alongside his mother's, in the *Man of Law's Tale*), death (Thomas's son in the *Summoner's Tale*), decapitation (Virginia in the *Physician's Tale*), severe wounding (Sophie in the *Tale of Melibee*), and starvation (Ugolino's children in the *Monk's Tale*). Children suffer in the tales of the Canterbury pilgrimage, providing a painful counterpoint to the eventual pleasure of the narrative's resolution. Freud argues that the fantasy of a beaten child stimulates erotic pleasure, that "at the climax of the imaginary situation there is almost invariably a masturbatory satisfaction,"[3] and so too do the beaten children of Chaucer's tales frequently engender narrative pleasure by serving as erotic surrogates in conflicts between adults (and mostly between men). By enduring the narrative pain that necessarily counterbalances the tales' resolutions, these children queerly reconceptualize the meaning of families predicated upon the fantasy of inviolate paternal authority.

Freud also observes that the fantasy of the beaten child is inherently variable in its effects and orientations, declaring that "it was impossible at first even to decide whether the pleasure attaching to the beating-phantasy was to be described as sadistic or masochistic."[4] As the valence of this

---

2. Sigmund Freud, "'A Child Is Being Beaten': A Contribution to the Study of the Origin of Sexual Perversions," in *The Standard Edition of the Complete Psychological Works of Sigmund Freud*, trans. and ed. James Strachey (London: Hogarth, 1953–74), 17.175–204, at 179. All quotations of Freud are taken from *The Standard Edition*.

3. Sigmund Freud, "A Child Is Being Beaten," 179. For the masturbatory pleasure implicit in reading, see Thomas Laqueur, *Solitary Sex: A Cultural History of Masturbation* (New York: Zone, 2003), in which he explores moralists' fears that "the fictional qualities of the characters in a novel or masturbatory fantasy made them more real, more compelling, more able to arouse sentiments than so-called real characters or real sexual partners" (322).

4. Sigmund Freud, "A Child Is Being Beaten," 181.

pleasure teeters between sadism and masochism, the beaten and eroticized child becomes interchangeable with the one fantasizing about this violence: "The child who is beaten has been changed into another one and is now invariably the child producing the phantasy. The phantasy is accompanied by a high degree of pleasure, and has now acquired a significant content.... Now, therefore, the wording runs: '*I am being beaten by my father.*' It is of an unmistakably masochistic character."[5] From this perspective, the father's role in the child's beating is critical. Although children's mothers can beat them as viciously as their fathers, Freud's account of this psychosexual fantasy underscores the ways in which paternal violence reveals paternal affection: "The idea of the father beating this hateful child is therefore an agreeable one, quite apart from whether he has actually been seen doing so. It means: 'My father does not love this other child, *he loves only me.*'"[6] For Chaucer's child characters as well as for his readers, the father becomes implicated with the pleasure of the abused child, for it is the father's desire that drives the narrative forward, as it is the ultimate regendering of the father that precipitates the narrative's queer resolution. This subversive narrative pleasure in the fantasy of beaten children paradoxically emerges when suffering children, if only through their passivity and suffering, counterbalance the patriarchal structures that claim to reward their pain with paternal love. Might not children queerly reimagine the contours of paternal masculinities that bolster their fathers' cultural privilege through their own torment and death?

One might hypothesize that the predominant desire surrounding beaten children is to rescue them, to save them from the minatory forces punishing them, but such a simplistic assessment of these violent fantasies ignores the multiplicity of desires circulating around the figure of the Child—often erotic, but also spiritual, familial, and economic—and the ways in which Chaucer depicts these desires to queer aspects of medieval masculinity. The following analysis proceeds in line with two of Chaucer's preferred literary modes—fabliau (*Reeve's Tale* and *Summoner's Tale*) and exemplary tales (*Clerk's Tale* and *Physician's Tale*). One might well assume that these genres share little in common: exempla are intended to illustrate important spiritual lessons, whereas fabliaux, despite the valedictory epigrams ironically positing moral meanings to narratives insistently divorced from didacticism, are intended for comic pleasure. Nonetheless, children are instrumental figures in many such tales, revealing fault lines

---

5. Ibid., 185.
6. Ibid., 187; italics in original.

of desire and erotic energy that circulate around them as the adult characters negotiate the wider world surrounding their offspring. These four tales showcase the ways in which fathers' relationships with their children, which are latently eroticized, illuminate the adult (and frequently homosocial) antagonisms at the core of their respective narratives.[7] As Eve Sedgwick's pioneering work in queer studies amply demonstrates, as has the work of her many followers, rivalries are often fought over the figure of a desired woman; so too may such aggressions be enacted through the figure of the desired, beaten, and/or dead child, for children frequently serve as apparently asexual surrogates in rivalries nonetheless fraught with eroticism. In her discussion of Chaucer's treatment of parent–child relationships, Jill Mann notes "the cruelty apparently inherent in the parent's right to exercise power over the child,"[8] and this analysis expands upon her and others' work to explore the ways in which misspent paternal authority bears the potential to queer the father wielding such power. If readers see the fantasy of the beaten child not as the child's masochistic ploy for the father's love but as a chink in the armor of his inviolate paternity, the potential sadism afforded to the father in the family drama becomes the means of his own undoing.

Before proceeding to the various Canterbury tales and their beaten children, the challenges of discussing medieval children and childhood must be considered. Like other markers of personal identity that are largely socially constructed, such as gender, sexuality, and race, children and childhood, as incarnated in the phantom ideal of the Child, are in many ways more reflective of cultural perceptions than of inherent truths, and so the Child shifts in the cultural meanings it produces within the various chronological frameworks it appears. Philippe Ariès famously proposed that the people of the Middle Ages did not perceive of childhood as a

---

7. It is beyond the scope of this chapter to address all of Chaucer's fictional children and the various roles they play in his narratives, and so I concentrate on his depictions of children in the *Canterbury Tales* in which a father's desires for his child(ren) become implicated in fantasies of eroticism, violence, and death. This strategy thus omits the child protagonist of the *Prioress's Tale,* whose father has died prior to the narrative's beginning. Due to the brevity of their portrayal, I also do not address Ugolino's starving children in the *Monk's Tale.* Other children, such as Mauricius in the *Man of Law's Tale,* do not interact sufficiently with their fathers to draw conclusions about the psychosexual paternal dynamics in the tale.

8. Jill Mann, "Parents and Children in the *Canterbury Tales,*" in *Literature in Fourteenth-Century England,* ed. Piero Boitani and Anna Torti (Tübingen: G. Narr, 1983), 165–83, at 165. See also Jane Cowgill, "Chaucer's Missing Children," *Essays in Medieval Studies* 12 (1996): 39–53; and Yvonne Truscott, "Chaucer's Children and the Medieval Idea of Childhood," *Children's Literature Association Quarterly* 23.1 (1998): 29–34.

sphere of life distinct from adulthood: "in the Middle Ages . . . children were mixed with adults as soon as they were considered capable of doing without their mothers or nannies, not long after a tardy weaning (in other words, at about the age of seven)."[9] His ideas, however, have been widely discredited by more-nuanced readings of source materials. In particular, Barbara Hanawalt succinctly puts forth her thesis—"The Middle Ages did recognize stages of life that corresponded to childhood and adolescence. These two life stages . . . appeared in learned medical and scientific texts, in literary works of the 'ages of man,' and in the folk terminology of the period"; she then demonstrates from a wide range of primary sources that medieval people considered childhood as a period of life with social, religious, and legal expectations that were notably distinct from those of adulthood.[10]

Pinpointing the exact parameters of childhood in the Middle Ages is difficult (as it remains difficult in modern times), but several recurrent themes assist in mapping out the terrain. Foremost the Christian Church recognized the concept of the age of reason, as recorded in such documents as Canon 21 of the Fourth Lateran Council: "Everyone who has attained the age of reason is bound to confess his sins at least once a year to his own parish priest . . . and to receive the Eucharist at least at Easter."[11] In his impressive overview of classical and medieval theories of childhood, Nicholas Orme summarizes the beliefs of such theorists as Aristotle, Isidore of Seville, and Giles of Rome. Aristotle argues that children should remain at home for their first years, observe education and exercise at the age of five, and then commence their schooling at seven (with their education lasting until the age of twenty-one). Isidore of Seville posits that the early years of life are divided into three stages (*infantia*, from birth to seven years, *pueritia*, from seven to fourteen years, and *adolescentia*, from fourteen to twenty-eight years). Giles of Rome proposes in his *On the Rule of Princes* that the first stage of life runs from birth to seven years, the next stage from seven to fourteen years, and the subsequent stage from fourteen to twenty-one, twenty-three, or twenty-seven

---

9. Philippe Ariès, *Centuries of Childhood*, trans. Robert Baldick (New York: Knopf, 1962), 411.

10. Barbara Hanawalt, *Growing Up in Medieval London: The Experience of Childhood in History* (New York: Oxford University Press, 1993), 5. See also Shulamith Shahar, *Childhood in the Middle Ages*, trans. Chaya Galai (London: Routledge, 1990).

11. H. J. Schroeder, ed., *Disciplinary Decrees of the General Councils* (St. Louis, MO: Herder, 1937), 259.

years.[12] The Middle English *Ratis Raving*, a conduct book for a son written in the voice of his father, divides the ages of life from birth to three, from three to seven, from seven to fifteen, from fifteen to thirty (at which age "perfeccioune / Of resone and discreccioune" is achieved), from thirty to fifty, from fifty to eighty, and from eighty to death.[13] These taxonomies of medieval life illustrate various views concerning the stages of a child's development, but it is also important to remember that a particular child's experience would in large part depend on numerous social and economic factors, as Charles Owen points out: "Adolescence was in some sense a privilege, explicitly denied to peasantry of both sexes . . . , accorded in variable terms to those destined for handicrafts, businesses, and professions, assured to men of gentle birth who aspired to knighthood."[14]

Chaucer's conception of childhood would thus likely be influenced by such considerations, and for the purposes of this analysis, I concentrate on children as defined both by their relative youth in comparison to their parents and other adult characters and by their dependency on their parents. For example, some may argue that Maline of the *Reeve's Tale* is no longer a child because she is twenty years old (1.3970). Nonetheless, her status as Symkyn's daughter determines her position in the narrative: she is unmarried, lives at home, and relies on her parents for her sustenance despite her somewhat advanced years. As this example demonstrates, childhood is often not defined by one's age as much as it is defined situationally with respect to a host of other factors. This matter is further complicated by Chaucer's frequent use of the word "childe" to refer to characters who appear no longer sufficiently young to be considered children, such as in his description of Absolon in the *Miller's Tale* as a "myrie child" (1.3325).[15] Notwithstanding the occasional semantic difficulties

---

12. Nicholas Orme, *From Childhood to Chivalry: The Education of the English Kings and Aristocracy, 1066–1530* (London: Methuen, 1984), 6. For additional discussion of the temporal parameters of childhood in the Middle Ages, see J. A. Burrow, *The Ages of Man* (Oxford: Clarendon, 1986); Shulamith Shahar, *Childhood in the Middle Ages*, 21–31; and Nicholas Orme, *Medieval Children* (New Haven, CT: Yale University Press, 2001), 305–41.

13. *Ratis Raving, and Other Moral and Religious Pieces, in Prose and Verse*, ed. Rawson Lumby (1870; London: Early English Text Society, 2002), 65, lines 2263–64.

14. Charles Owen, "'A certain nombre of conclusiouns': The Nature and Nurture of Children in Chaucer," *Chaucer Review* 16.1 (1982): 60–75, at 62.

15. The *Middle English Dictionary* offers as its primary definition of *child* a "young child, a baby," or a "boy or girl (usually to the age of puberty)." The term also refers to individuals typically considered older than children, such as in its meanings as "a young man; youth, lad" or "a youth in service"; "spiritual or moral descendant; follower, disciple, or devotee"; or a "child regarded as innocent or immature," "an immature, unwise, or foolish person."

in determining whether a particular character of the *Canterbury Tales* is a child, Chaucer's frequent depictions of suffering children showcase the tortuous and torturous routes to narrative pleasure as mediated through children's pain, as well as the ways in which the fathers' roles in their children's suffering redound to the undermining of their own gendered privilege.

Understanding medieval fatherhood presents challenges similar to understanding medieval children, and Derek Neal observes the historical record's relative silence concerning cultural expectations for medieval fathers: "Late medieval England may have been a patriarchal society, wherein fatherhood was a pervasive metaphor; ironically, however, from the historical record, we can know its men better as masters than as fathers."[16] Perspectives on medieval fatherhood can nonetheless be gleaned from boys' conduct books, which define cultural expectations for masculinity. Primarily imagined as the advice of fathers to their sons, such texts highlight the cultural expectations of masculinity for boys growing into adulthood and, presumably, fatherhood as well. Most of these volumes proffer standard advice on proper Christian masculinity, such as following the Ten Commandments,[17] privileging meekness and patience over pride and anger,[18] and avoiding taverns and gambling.[19] Such exhortations encourage boys to follow the proper path to culturally sanctioned masculinity and to respect their elders, but the early-fifteenth-century conduct book "Myne Awen Dere Sone" registers a father's latent fear that sons will avenge themselves upon their parents:

> For be thy chylder neuere so dere,
> And thou be put in thaire power,
> And thay thy gude in hande hafte hente,
> That wolde not rek if thou ware wente.[20]

---

16. Derek Neal, *The Masculine Self in Late Medieval England* (Chicago: University of Chicago Press, 2008), 84.

17. "How a Man Schal Lyue Parfytly," in *Minor Poems of the Vernon Manuscript*, ed. Carl Horstmann (London: Early English Text Society, 1892; Millwood, New York: Kraus, 1987), 1.221–51.

18. "Consail and Teiching at the Vys Man Gaif His Sone," in *Ratis Raving*, 90–103, at lines 3177–90.

19. "How the Goode Man Taght Hys Sone," in *The Trials and Joys of Marriage*, ed. Eve Salisbury (Kalamazoo, MI: Medieval Institute Publications, 2002), 233–45, at lines 58–64.

20. Tauno Mustanoja, ed., "Myne Awen Dere Sone," *Neuphilologische Mitteilungen* 49 (1948): 145–93, at 149–50, lines 17–20.

With this father (as narrator of the text) cautioning his son against the boy's children who are as yet unborn, he points to the limits of paternal masculinity. The violence occluded in this fantasy of the child taking revenge against his father reveals the tensions inherent in father–child relationships and the threat that it will erupt between the two. As a dominant metaphor of patriarchal power, fatherhood holds the male body as the incarnation of paternal beneficence and care, yet these words allow the possibility that children might seek their own advantage against their parents. After all, the fantasy of the beaten child is only a fantasy, one that Freud primarily assigned to masochists tormented by unresolved Oedipal complexes, but nothing prohibits a child within Chaucer's fictions—even a raped, beaten, or dead child—from beating back against their paternal tormentors and confronting these fathers with the queer limits of patriarchal privilege.

CHILDREN IN CHAUCERIAN FABLIAUX: *REEVE'S TALE* AND *SUMMONER'S TALE*

In concentrating on sexual farce among adults, Chaucer excludes children from most of his fabliaux altogether. John and Alison of the *Miller's Tale* are childless, and Perkyn Revelour of the *Cook's Tale*, although sufficiently young to serve as a "prentys . . . of a craft of vitailliers" (1.4365–66), is not typically viewed as a child both because his parents are absent from the story and because his narrative hints strongly of adult sexuality when he moves in with his friend whose wife "swyved for hir sustenance" (1.4422). Alison of Bath tells a romance in the tale-telling competition, yet the many bawdy elements in her portrait, in both the *General Prologue* and her *Prologue*, warrant her inclusion in discussions of Chaucer's fabliaux, and she too has borne no children, in blatant contradiction to her declared appreciation of God's command: "God bad us for to wexe and multiplye; / That gentil text kan I wel understonde" (3.28–29).[21] Despite January's desire for an heir, as expressed repeatedly in the *Merchant's Tale* (4.1267–76, 4.1433–40, and 4.1446–50), he and May are childless; discerning Chaucer's pointed irony, some critics suggest that Damian succeeds in impregnating May, due to these suggestive lines: "This Januarie, who is glad but he? / He kisseth hire and clippeth hire

---

21. For the many fabliau elements of Alison's depiction, see William Matthews, "The Wife of Bath and All Her Sect," *Viator* 5 (1974): 413–43.

ful ofte, / And on hire wombe he stroketh hire ful softe" (4.2412–14).[22] The merchant and his wife in the *Shipman's Tale* are also childless, but the narrator remarks that a "mayde child" (7.95) accompanies the merchant's wife on her garden rendezvous with the monk John. This child seems to be a young serving girl, not the merchant's daughter, and here again the situationality of childhood is suggested: should we see this minor character as a child or as a young woman learning her trade? She appears to straddle between childhood (as indicated by her youth) and nascent adulthood (as indicated by her domestic service in another's household).[23] Of Chaucer's fabliaux, only the *Reeve's Tale* and the *Summoner's Tale* include children and, through these portrayals, query their role in defining their fathers' masculinity.

If the fantasy of a beaten child reveals desires circulating in a narrative, in the *Reeve's Tale*, it ironically appears that Maline's father Symkyn no longer succumbs to eroticism. When John, jealous of Allen's sexual success with Maline, copulates with Symkyn's wife, readers learn that this miller does not exact payment of the marital debt with any frequency: "And on this goode wyf [John] leith on soore. / So myrie a fit ne hadde she nat ful yoore" (1.4229–30). These lines imply conflicting yet converging views of Symkyn's sexual prowess: he may be impotent, or lack interest in intercourse, or he may perform the sexual act with less erotic vigor than young John. Due to the presence of the "child that was of half yeer age" (1.3971), readers know that Symkyn impregnated his wife approximately fifteen months earlier, but little textual evidence attests to his continuing sexual attraction to her. The roughly nineteen years between the births of their children also points to Symkyn's reluctance to copulate with his wife (or conversely, although unlikely, a particularly effective form of medieval birth control).[24] A defining irony of the *Reeve's Tale* arises in its emphasis on erotic rivalries among men when its main character expresses little erotic desire.

---

22. For May's potential pregnancy, see Milton Miller, "The Heir in the *Merchant's Tale*," *Philological Quarterly* 29 (1950): 437–40; Emerson Brown, "Hortus Inconclusus: The Significance of Priapus and Pyramus and Thisbe in the *Merchant's Tale*," *Chaucer Review* 4 (1970): 31–40; and Peter Beidler, "The Climax in the *Merchant's Tale*," *Chaucer Review* 6 (1971): 38–43.

23. For the possibility that this "mayde child" is indeed the child of the merchant and his wife, see Peter Beidler, "Medieval Children Witness Their Mother's Indiscretions: The Maid Child in Chaucer's *Shipman's Tale*," *Chaucer Review* 44.2 (2009): 186–204.

24. Some readers propose that Symkyn and his wife's son may, in fact, be Maline's. The apparent anti-eroticism that characterizes their marriage supports this view; at the same time, Chaucer does not provide sufficient evidence to confirm such a supposition.

To point out that Symkyn does not sexually desire his wife is not to suggest that he does not desire, and in the opening lines of his tale, the Reeve introduces Symkyn and his family while focusing on this miller's social aspirations, which he hopes to achieve through his wife and daughter. As a narcissistic reflection of her husband's masculinity, Symkyn's wife registers the family's status within their community:

> A wyf he hadde, ycomen of noble kyn;
> The person of the toun hir fader was.
> . . . .
> For Symkyn wolde no wyf, as he sayde,
> But she were wel ynorissed and a mayde,
> To saven his estaat of yomanrye. (1.3942–43, 3947–49)

Chaucer includes numerous ironies in this passage, notably that Symkyn's father-in-law is the town's parson, and his wife's parentage enhances his social position and empty narcissism by preserving his "estaat of yomanrye." Within the terms of this depiction, he desires her in regard to his pecuniary and social ambitions, not in response to any erotic attractions, which appear to be readily sacrificed in favor of his non-erotic objectives. His ridiculous aspiration to the ranks of yeomanry—either in its sense as a retainer in a noble household or as a lower member of the landed gentry—highlights the follies of his desires while simultaneously establishing them as the focal point of a life mostly devoid of eroticism.[25]

To underscore Symkyn's predominantly asexual desires, the narrator pays little attention to Symkyn's wife's physical features, a narrative strategy standing in stark contrast to the lengthy portrait and mock blazon of Alison in the *Miller's Tale* that establishes her as the object of desire in John, Nicholas, and Absolon's erotic rivalry (1.3233–70). With the description of Symkyn's wife lacking, she registers not as a desirable woman in herself but more as a means for Symkyn to monitor other men's desires for her, despite the dearth of evidence that such attractions are simmering throughout their town. The Reeve details Symkyn's violent plan

---

25. In Douglas Gray's *Oxford Companion to Chaucer* (Oxford: Oxford University Press, 2003), "yeoman" is defined simply as "a servant ranking in a feudal household below a squire" (499). The *Middle English Dictionary* offers a secondary definition of "a member of the landholding class below the rank of squire; a man holding a small landed estate." It appears to be the latter definition of *yeomanry* to which Symkyn aspires, in contrast to such Chaucerian yeomen as the Knight's yeoman and the Canon's yeoman, who serve in secondary positions to their social superiors.

to quell any erotic interest in his wife—"Was noon so hardy that wente by the weye / That with hire dorste rage or ones pleye, / But if he wolde be slayn of Symkyn" (1.3957–59)—and equips this character with numerous phallic blades and weapons to paint him as an overbearing, intimidating, and aggressive man (1.3929–33).[26] The foundational structure of the erotic triangle guides the tale's opening and unfolding, yet ironically so, as Symkyn aggressively seeks to preserve for himself the woman for whom he expresses little erotic attraction, and without any suitors for her affections to spark the sexual competition at this tale's heart.

In contrast to the missing portrait of Symkyn's wife, the narrator's description of his daughter Maline focuses primarily on her physical appearance. The passage implies that, as her mother fails to attract her father sexually, she too is unlikely to spark erotic attractions from any potential suitors:

> The wenche thikke and wel ygrowen was,
> With kamus nose and eyen greye as glas,
> With buttokes brode and brestes rounde and hye.
> But right fair was hire heer; I wol nat lye. (1.3973–76)

The closing compliment to her hair damns Maline with faint praise, and one sees primarily a chubby young woman with a pug nose and dishwater eyes.[27] Because the majority of girls in the Middle Ages married while teens, her age of twenty years also points to her unattractiveness, or at least her difficulty in finding a mate. As Barbara Hanawalt observes, "Young women with wealthy parents still alive married even earlier [than sixteen]. Among the merchant class, marriage occurred for girls at age seventeen or younger," and Shulamith Shahar documents marriage for

---

26. W. W. Allman and Thomas Hanks, in "Rough Love: Notes toward an Erotics of the *Canterbury Tales*" (*Chaucer Review* 38.1 [2003]: 36–65), argue that these blades contribute to the aggressive valence of eroticism in the *Canterbury Tales* (43–45).

27. Several romance heroines have grey eyes, such as Guinevere in *The Awntyrs off Arthur* (in *Sir Gawain: Eleven Romances and Tales*, ed. Thomas Hahn [Kalamazoo, MI: Medieval Institute Publications, 1995], 169–226, at line 599), but Chaucer appears to parody this tradition in his depiction of Maline. The Prioress also has grey eyes ("Hir nose tretys, hir eyen greye as glas" [1.152]), but her overarching physical portrait, like Maline's, casts her as unattractive. By depicting Maline and the Prioress with grey eyes, Chaucer satirizes these female characters' fantasies of courtly love and romance. Also, in the *Romaunt of the Rose*, Chaucer's portraits of the morally suspect characters Idleness (546), Mirth (822), and Gladness (862) feature grey eyes.

girls taking place during their *adolescentia*.[28] Similar to Symkyn's antierotic treatment of Maline's mother, so too do no male suitors pursue Maline to sate their erotic desires; rather, her father and grandfather hope to satisfy their narcissistic desires for social aggrandizement through her: "His purpos was for to bistowe hire hye / Into som worthy blood of auncetrye" (1.3981–82). Both pandering his daughter to an appropriately wealthy suitor and restricting other men's access to her, Symkyn attempts to negotiate uxorial and filial eroticism to his advantage, while remaining unaware of its explosive force and its queer potential to undermine his performance of paternal masculinity. Indeed, the reference to Symkyn and his wife's infant son as "a propre page" (1.3972) further expresses his sense of the economic value of his children, foreseeing the child's rise in an aristocratic household as reflective of his own parental puissance.

Because Symkyn is less concerned with pursuing his amatory desires than in regulating his wife's and daughter's sexuality, he attempts to control the sexual instincts of any young men who might court them. And so as much as the *Reeve's Tale* focuses on Symkyn's humiliation when Allen and John respectively fornicate with his daughter and wife, thus depriving him of the commercial value of his daughter's hymen and cuckolding him, this sexual farce is complemented by the conflict between the generations that plays out over stolen grain. It is worth remembering that Allen and John do not initially embark on a sexual quest; instead, they are ensnared in an intergenerational battle between young and old that they resolve through their violent eroticism. Like Symkyn, then, Allen and John initially appear unconcerned with their erotic drives; they focus first on stopping Symkyn from stealing grain and only later on Allen's vengeful desire to copulate with Maline (to punish Symkyn) and on John's anxious desire to copulate with Symkyn's wife (lest Allen's sexual adventures shame him, once the story is shared within the homosocial environs of their Cambridge college). Numerous scholars have commented on the tale's depiction of men's traffic in women,[29] but I

---

28. Barbara Hanawalt, *Growing Up in Medieval London*, 206; Shulamith Shahar, *Childhood in the Middle Ages*, 224.

29. For representative voices of this discussion, see Ian Lancashire, "Sexual Innuendo in the *Reeve's Tale*," *Chaucer Review* 6 (1972): 159–70; John Plummer, "Hooly Chirches Blood: Simony and Patrimony in Chaucer's *Reeve's Tale*," *Chaucer Review* 18.1 (1983): 49–60; Heidi Breuer, "Being Intolerant: Rape Is Not Seduction (in the *Reeve's Tale* or Anywhere Else)," in *The Canterbury Tales Revisited: Twenty-First Century Interpretations*, ed. Kathleen Bishop and David Matthews (Newcastle upon Tyne, England: Cambridge Scholars, 2008), 1–15; and Nicole Nolan Sidhu, "'To late for to crie': Female Desire, Fabliau Politics, and Classical Legend in Chaucer's *Reeve's Tale*," *Exemplaria* 21.1 (2009): 3–23.

would add to this discussion that each man's initial objective is not erotic but rather simply to preserve the status quo of homosocial stasis: for Symkyn, not to lose his social position (ambiguous as it is), and for Allen and John, to remain within their university setting (from which they would not have departed without Symkyn's disruption of their food supply). These three men initially evince no desire for intercourse, nor any desire for women, but instead focus first on preserving and then on aggrandizing their standing among men through sexual acts, albeit sexual acts in which the desire to copulate with a female is secondary to the desire to defeat a male adversary.

For Symkyn, controlling other men entails establishing himself in a dominant position over them and thereby regulating their access to sexual pleasure, and his particular fantasy of masculine control revolves around his narcissistic belief that he can beat these young men, if not in the literal sense of a physical thrashing, then in the authoritarian sense of establishing his will over theirs. In these scenes Chaucer unites the intergenerational battle between old and young with the rivalry festering between town and gown. Despite Allen and John's superior education, Symkyn sees them as his intellectual inferiors, musing inwardly: "'The gretteste clerkes been noght wisest men,' / As whilom to the wolf thus spak the mare" (1.4054–55). Given this tale's treatment of animal sexuality (as discussed shortly), it is ironic that Symkyn casts himself in the feminized position of a mare in these lines; moreover, although recognizing Allen and John as predatory "wolves," he can protect neither his wife nor his daughter from their imminent sexual assault, nor himself from the subversion of his masculinity. Social-class strife emerges in these lines as well, with Symkyn chuckling over his ability to outwit two university students, but their mutual enmity is further predicated on their disparity in age and Symkyn's dismissive attitude toward young people. Complementary to this chapter's opening discussion of childhood and the stages of life, Susanna Greer Fein analyzes how the *Reeve's Tale* "borrows freely . . . from the iconography of the life cycle, placing the characters implicitly upon a wheel, where they vie for dominance at the topmost position," and Symkyn aims to best these young men through his devious tactics to ensure his continued dominance.[30] When he unties their horse so that he can steal their grain, he scorns Allen and John as

---

30. Susanna Greer Fein, "'Lat the children pleye': The Game betwixt the Ages in the *Reeve's Tale*," in *Rebels and Rivals: The Contestive Spirit in the* Canterbury Tales, ed. Susanna Greer Fein, David Raybin, and Peter Braeger (Kalamazoo, MI: Medieval Institute Publications, 1991), 73–104, at 75.

children: "Lo, wher he gooth! Ye, lat the children pleye. / They gete hym nat so lightly, by my croun" (1.4098–99). Because he believes Allen and John to be as manipulable as children—as manipulable as his daughter—Symkyn blinds himself to the men's and his daughter's erotic energies, a point Chaucer ironically underscores in the sexual adventures of Allen and John's horse. Horses often symbolize sexuality and lust,[31] and Allen and John's horse runs off, with an expressive "wehee," to where the "wilde mares renne" (1.4065–66). Symkyn's wife reiterates to the young men, "Allas! Youre hors goth to the fen / With wilde mares, as faste as he may go" (1.4080–81), and the insistent gendering of these wild mares (as female, obviously) hints at the animal lust, in the literal sense of the term, driving Allen and John's horse.[32] Symkyn manipulates bestial eroticism in his ploy to defeat Allen and John, yet he merely foreshadows that he will soon be hoisted on his own petard, as he unwittingly unleashes Allen and John's erotic energies on his daughter and wife.

Before Symkyn receives his narrative punishment, Allen rapes his daughter, and thus the miller's daughter becomes the surrogate who suffers for her father's transgressions. The fantasy of the beaten child, in this instance, represents the father's desire to preserve himself through the sacrifice of his daughter, sadistically scapegoating her to shield himself from retribution. The *Reeve's Tale* occludes the sexual violence inflicted upon Maline through its fabliau humor, but it is clear that she is assaulted:

And up he rist, and by the wenche he crepte.
This wenche lay uprighte and faste slepte,
Til he so ny was, er she myghte espie,
That it had been to late for to crie,

---

31. For a brief overview of the symbolism of horses, see Lucia Impelluso, *Nature and Its Symbols*, trans. Stephen Sartarelli (Los Angeles: Getty Museum, 2003), 257. A telling biblical example of the eroticism correlated with horses occurs in Jeremiah 5:8: "equi amatores et admissarii facti sunt, unusquisque ad uxorem proximi sui hinniebat" ("They are become as amorous horses and stallions: every one neighed after his neighbor's wife"). V. A. Kolve appraises Chaucer's equine imagery in his *Chaucer and the Imagery of Narrative: The First Five* Canterbury Tales (Stanford: Stanford University Press, 1984), 236–49. The Reeve appeals to this tradition when he describes himself as having a "coltes tooth" (1.3888) in regard to his untamed sexual appetite, despite his advanced years.

32. Based on her studies of medieval animal husbandry, Sandy Feinstein, in "*The Reeve's Tale*: About That Horse" (*Chaucer Review* 26.1 [1991]: 99–106), convincingly argues that the clerk's horse "is more than likely a gelding" (100). The fabliau, however, is not a genre constrained by realism, and Allen and John's horse appears sexually motivated, even if it is unlikely, given their socioeconomic status, that these university students would have access to a stallion.

And shortly for to seyn, they were aton.
Now pley, Aleyn, for I wol speke of John. (1.4193–98)

The narrator reports that, as Allen attacks Maline, "it had been to late for to crie." This line contrasts sharply with similar events narrated in the *Miller's Tale*, when Alison threatens Nicholas that she "wol crie 'out, harrow' and 'allas!'" (1.3286) before she then decides to copulate with him. Alison demonstrates agency in her erotic decision-making (even if such agency supports the male fantasy that attempting to rape women serves as a successful tactic in seducing them), but no such possibility of consent, however etiolated, is available to Maline. The violence against Maline excites much critical attention, as do the ways in which Chaucer deflects attention from rape's violence through Maline's mock aubade after her deflowering.[33] Troublingly, some critics do not see rape in this scene at all, but Heidi Breuer forcefully rebuts this view and declares that the "*Reeve's Tale* . . . suggest[s] rape/seduction is simply a male form of revenge against other men, reducing women's suffering to a mere side-effect of men's relationships to one another."[34] In a similar vein, Nicole Nolan Sidhu rightly notes the ways in which the *Reeve's Tale* "confronts the paradoxical status of women's desire in late-fourteenth-century English society, where Christian doctrine granting women's right of consent in matters of marriage and sex runs up against a lineage-based social system that renders women both the objects and the vessels of male power."[35] Holly Crocker cautions, however, that, as much as a man climbing into a woman's bed and copulating without her consent appears to be rape, the act depicted falls into a legal limbo: "Between Aleyn's stealth and Malyne's affection, neither the girl nor Symkyn has a legal claim to rape."[36] The sadistic and

---

33. On rape in medieval English literature, see Corinne Saunders, *Rape and Ravishment in the Literature of Medieval England* (Cambridge: Brewer, 2001); and Elizabeth Robertson and Christine Rose, eds., *Representing Rape in Medieval and Early Modern Literature* (New York: Palgrave, 2001).

34. Heidi Breuer, "Being Intolerant," 10. See also Daniel Pigg, "Performing the Perverse: The Abuse of Masculine Power in the *Reeve's Tale*," *Masculinities in Chaucer: Approaches to Maleness in the* Canterbury Tales *and* Troilus and Criseyde, ed. Peter Beidler (Cambridge: Brewer, 1998), 53–61, who concludes that "Chaucer . . . would have known the law regarding rape, and he encoded it into the incident" (58), as well as Pamela Barnett, "'And shortly for to seyn they were aton': Chaucer's Deflection of Rape in the *Reeve's* and *Franklin's Tales*," *Women's Studies* 22 (1993): 145–62.

35. Nicole Nolan Sidhu, "'To late for to crie,'" 4.

36. Holly Crocker, "Affective Politics in Chaucer's *Reeve's Tale*: 'Cherl' Masculinity after 1381," *Studies in the Age of Chaucer* 29 (2007): 225–58, at 246.

paternal fantasy of the *Reeve's Tale*, then, is that one can figuratively fuck the father by literally fucking the daughter, with the former remaining unscathed by the violence at hand and the latter suffering for his transgressions.

But can there be power, however tangential, however fleeting, in appropriating another's fantasy? Can Maline act as she is acted upon? Gilles Deleuze and Félix Guattari posit that children resist their tokenized status in the realm of adult sexuality through unexpected confluences of possibility and action: "Psychoanalysis has no feeling for unnatural participation, nor for the assemblages a child can mount in order to solve a problem from which all exits are barred him: a *plan(e)*, not a phantasy."[37] By reconfiguring the purported desires of the beaten child, Maline disavows her father's proprietary claims over her body, particularly her hymen, through her rape. Readers receive little insight into this child's fantasy life, but one can see the formulation of a plan, as she moves the narrative to another plane—from fabliau to romance, at least from her perspective. Symkyn perceives Maline as a pawn in his ambitions for social advancement, yet she queers her father by enjoying the violence that befalls her. The morning after their night together, Maline addresses her lover in a mock alba, one that registers her nascent, if limited, control of her erotic destiny:

> "Now, deere lemman," quod she, "go, far weel!
> But er thow go, o thyng I wol thee telle:
> What that thou wendest homward by the melle,
> Right at the entree of the dore bihynde
> Thou shalt a cake of half a busshel fynde
> That was ymaked of thyn owene mele,
> Which that I heelp my sire for to stele.
> And, good lemman, God thee save and kepe!"
> And with that word almoost she gan to wepe. (1.4240–48)

Albas, as Gale Sigal outlines, "tacitly criticize the stultifying gender roles and expectations that the love they create/portray seeks to transcend and that the characters in the alba heroically decry."[38] Although within the

---

37. Gilles Deleuze and Félix Guattari, *A Thousand Plateaus: Capitalism and Schizophrenia*, trans. Brian Massumi (Minneapolis: University of Minnesota Press, 1987), 259–60; italics in original.

38. Gale Sigal, *Erotic Dawn-Songs of the Middle Ages: Voicing the Lyric Lady* (Gainesville: University Press of Florida, 1996), 19; see also Jonathan Saville, *The Medieval Erotic Alba: Structure as Meaning* (New York: Columbia University Press, 1972).

parodic context of a fabliau, Maline's alba functions similarly, allowing her to speak to her lover and against her father, thereby undermining the gendered and familial roles that her father expects her to perform. As Tamarah Kohanski remarks, "Chaucer makes no clear statement about [Maline's] character or her complicity,"[39] and since Maline is indeed a cipher, readers must search through the gaps and silences of her actions to hypothesize her wishes. Still, Chaucer's primary sources for the *Reeve's Tale* do not depict the Maline character speaking after intercourse with her lover,[40] and, by giving Maline speech at this moment, the narrator allows her parting words to Allen to reveal her desire to act against her father by renouncing his petty crimes and freeing herself from association with him. In disclosing to Allen the location of the cake made out of the clerks' meal, she restores to its proper owner that which her father has taken.

So too does Maline, at least nominally, restore her body to herself through her alliance with Allen. After Allen rises from her bed, she vanishes from the fabliau's final scenes, and so she acts by not acting: unlike her mother, who assists Symkyn in the melee with the clerks, Maline witnesses but does not participate in defending either her lost hymen or her father's lost honor. As Jane Burns suggests of women in the Old French fabliau, "a variety of instances [in which] the female body [is] represented as a site of patriarchy's most reductive definitions of woman can also be a site for possible revision," one in which readers can "see the terms of a new female subjectivity emerge, a subjectivity in which the body makes a crucial difference."[41] With her agency occluded throughout the text, Maline's reconception of rape as romance, which she rapturously celebrates in her postcoital alba, and her return to passivity at the tale's climax are troubling visions of a woman's agency, yet as a child who sees no escape from her father's control, she inverts masculine fantasy by reas-

---

39. Tamarah Kohanski, "In Search of Malyne," *Chaucer Review* 27.3 (1993): 228–38, at 229. Sidhu similarly notes, "Why Malyne speaks romantically to the clerk and why she betrays her father for him remains a mystery since Malyne's eight-line aube is her only speech in the entire 400-line tale, and Chaucer gives us no additional insight into her motivations" ("'To late for to crie,'" 11).

40. Ribald tales of two men deceiving their host and sleeping with his wife and daughter are found in "Le meunier et les. II. clers: Text A" (MS 354 Bibliothèque de Berne, 1275–1300); "Le meunier et les. II. clers: Text B" (Hamilton MS, Berlin, 1275–1300); "Een bispel van .ij. clerken" (MS KB 15.589–623, Royal Library, Brussels "Hulthem Collection," 1350–75), and Boccaccio's *Decameron* (day 9, story 6); these sources are available in Robert Correale and Mary Hamel, eds., *Sources and Analogues of the* Canterbury Tales (Cambridge: Brewer, 2002), 1.23–73.

41. Jane Burns, *Bodytalk: When Women Speak in Old French Literature* (Philadelphia: University of Pennsylvania Press, 1993), 242.

sessing its prerogatives and acts by resignifying her narrative as romance while allowing her father's plotline to proceed to its fabliau climax. She finds a modicum of power through the eroticism that sparks her father's beating: she is first the beaten child, the surrogate suffering for her father's transgressions as a stranger in her home jumps upon her in the assumed sanctity of her bed, but she beats back against the paternal strictures that cast her as a prosthetic figure who preserves his masculine privilege by suffering in his place. She only inhabits her initial role as scapegoat for paternal fantasies of inviolate masculinity until this fantasy proves untenable, due to its conflict with her nascent erotic desires. Finally, as the tale establishes a punning parallel between the flour that Symkyn steals from Allen and John and the flower of Maline's maidenhead, she bestows upon Allen the "mele" that she helped steal. Without her father's approval of this gift, Maline further establishes that she will set the economic terms of her maidenhead and that she deems this trade mutually satisfying for herself and her lover, if not for the father who attempts to traffic in her sexuality.

For the Reeve, the beaten child reveals homosocial rivalries and queers the paternal masculinity of his protagonist, yet in many ways, his exploitation of children correlates with similar fault lines in his own gender. As is well established, the Reeve tells his tale to "quite" his fellow pilgrim the Miller by speaking "right in his cherles termes" (1.3916–17), and his tale therefore allegorizes the Miller as Symkyn, casting his enemy as the cuckolded protagonist of his story through the numerous parallels between them: their swords (1.558, cf. 1.3929–31), their piping (1.565, cf. 1.3927), and their thievery (1.562, cf. 1.3998). Beyond these similarities, Chaucer's protean irony creates additional parallels between Symkyn and the Reeve himself both in the description of the Reeve in the *General Prologue* and in the Reeve's self-description in his *Prologue;* undermining the allegory the Reeve attempts to establish against the Miller, Chaucer multiplies its satiric register through these additional congruencies. In terms of his sexual desires, the Reeve portrays himself as sexually voracious yet unhappily impotent—"for thogh oure myght be goon, / Oure wyl desireth folie evere in oon. / For whan we may nat doon, than wol we speke" (1.3879–81)— and these words of erotic longing align ironically with Symkyn's reluctance to copulate with his wife.[42] Likewise, as Symkyn believes himself

---

42. One may quibble that the Reeve describes old men's impotence, whereas the depiction of Symkyn does not evince impotence as much as a lack of sexual interest. Their mutual lack of erotic activity nonetheless links the teller of the tale with his character, in a manner ultimately derisive of his proclaimed masculinity. For the Reeve's metaphors of old

capable of manipulating Allen and John due to the folly he ascribes to their youth, so too does the Reeve take advantage of his young lord, and he has done so "syn that [he] was twenty yeer of age" (1.601). Chaucer as narrator reports how the Reeve deceives his inexperienced master: "His lord wel koude he plesen subtilly, / To yeve and lene hym of his owene good, / And have a thank, and yet a cote and hood" (1.610–12). Even Symkyn's many phallic knives, daggers, and swords find their counterpart in Oswald's "rusty blade" (1.618). These points of congruency between the Reeve and Symkyn do not overshadow the allegory between the Miller and Symkyn that the *Reeve's Tale* instantiates, yet they simultaneously highlight the inherent instability of allegory and the ways in which readers can uncover threads tying together disparate characters and themes that Chaucer's surface allegories otherwise obscure. As Symkyn learns in the *Reeve's Tale*, controlling his daughter and attempting to control the young men he sees as children cannot put the shine back on his rusty blade, and so too does the Reeve's performance of erotic desire and masculine puissance ring hollow, despite his apparent success in defrauding his immature lord, who is apparently unaware of the abuses that the old inflict upon the young.

As the *Reeve's Tale* exposes the frustration of paternal desire through the queering force of a raped child, the *Summoner's Tale* similarly undermines the authority of paternal masculinity through its treatment of Thomas's dead son. Beyond their mutual genre of fabliau, these tales share additional key features in regard to the erotic competitions at their heart, particularly in the ways in which the Reeve and Summoner tell their tales with the explicit purpose of humiliating their respective enemies, the Miller and the Friar, by depicting the sexual humiliations of their tales' protagonists. The unctuous friar of the *Summoner's Tale* parallels Symkyn in his humiliating narrative fate, yet the bedridden curmudgeon Thomas also aligns with Symkyn in regard to their mutual abasement through their children. With deft touches Chaucer hints that Thomas may not be the father of his deceased son (in much the same manner that May's potential pregnancy sparks doubts regarding January's paternity in the *Merchant's Tale*), and this possibility diffuses and multiplies the questions of paternal identity surrounding the narrative's dead child.

In a narrative moment akin to the Reeve's emphasis on Symkyn's impotence, the Summoner stresses Thomas's failures to satisfy his wife's

---

age and sexuality, see Carol Everest, "Sex and Old Age in Chaucer's *Reeve's Tale*," *Chaucer Review* 31.2 (1996): 99–114.

erotic desires, with the tale's anti-eroticism further subverting any image of masculine or paternal authority that Thomas might attempt to embody. John Fleming argues of Thomas's wife that "[she], like all of Chaucer's 'characters,' exists only to externalize certain intellectual propositions,"[43] and her function in this narrative is to undermine assumptions of conjugal fidelity and paternal prerogatives. She details her difficulties in exciting her husband's passion, exposing his amatory failings to his rival:

> "Chideth him weel, for seinte Trinitee!
> He is as angry as a pissemyre,
> Though that he have al that he kan desire;
> Though I hym wrye a-nyght and make hym warm,
> And ove hym leye my leg outher myn arm,
> He groneth lyk oure boor, lith in oure sty.
> Oother desport right noon of hym have I;
> I may nat plese hym in no maner cas." (3.1824–31)

Despite these amorous advances, as his wife writhes about him in their bed, Thomas evinces little interest in the conjugal pleasures of marriage. Such anti-erotic behavior would be more appropriate for the tale's friar, yet in this tale of misplaced and mismatched desires, the husband rejects what the friar seeks and evacuates the heterosexual eroticism presumably at the core of this triangulated affair.

In light of Thomas's anti-eroticism, the subsequent mention of his dead son is surprising, for it compels readers to hypothesize sexual activity in Thomas and his wife's bed, where it has been sketched as virtually unimaginable. Many readers therefore suspect that Thomas is not the child's father; in contrast, the friar's amorous embrace of Thomas's wife accentuates his erotic desires for her. The Summoner reports that, at Thomas's house, the friar "was wont to be / Refresshed moore than in an hundred placis" (3.1766–67), and Chaucer's frequent use of *refresshed* as a double entendre for sex (as evident in the *Wife of Bath's Prologue* 3.38 and 3.146) hints at the friar's enjoyment of sexual pastimes with her. Also, before she mentions her child's death, he flirts shamelessly with her:

> The frere ariseth up ful curteisly,
> And hire embraceth in his armes narwe,

---

43. John Fleming, "Anticlerical Satire as Theological Essay: Chaucer's *Summoner's Tale*," *Thalia* 6.1–2 (1983): 5–22, at 13.

> And kiste hire sweete, and chirketh as a sparwe
> With his lyppes: "Dame," quod he, "right weel,
> As he that is youre servant every deel,
> Thanked be God, that yow yaf soule and lyf!
> Yet saught I nat this day so fair a wyf
> In al the chirche, God so save me!" (3.1802–9)

With his compliments to her beauty, his courteous embrace of her, and his avowed dedication to perform as her servant, the friar assumes the role of the chivalric lover befitting a tale of courtly romance. Contrasted with the attention paid to Thomas's anti-eroticism, these lines imply that the friar may be the dead child's father, for his erotic and pecuniary drives propel his every action in the tale. By confusing the dead child's parentage, Chaucer muddies the trajectory of narrative vengeance set in motion: with the specter of this dead son haunting both men's assumptions of paternity, all fantasies of inviolate masculinity are undermined, for he, no matter who his father might be, ultimately symbolizes the failures of both men to negotiate their erotic drives to enhance their masculine identity.

Furthermore, by painting the friar as lascivious and Thomas as impotent, the Summoner establishes a tension between the two men that plays out in a submerged homoeroticism reflected in the friar's attempts to claim brotherhood with Thomas. As explored in chapter 3, sworn brotherhood between two men often carries a latent tinge of eroticism within otherwise normative homosocial bonds, and the friar relies on such language of brotherhood to win Thomas's trust. He declares to Thomas, "And by that lord that clepid is Seint Yve, / Nere thou oure brother, sholdestou nat thryve" (3.1944–45), and he concludes his lengthy exhortation with a similar appeal to brotherhood: "Now, Thomas, leeve brother, lef thyn ire" (3.2089). On the surface, the friar's words refer to monastic brotherhood and Thomas's position as a lay member of the order, but there is no need to circumscribe their connotations solely to the monastic, rather than the courtly, milieu. As John Bowers points out, "In the *Summoner's Tale* the wealthy and ailing Thomas is most aggressively solicited as 'oure brother' when the friar learns of the death of his infant child, his only male heir. The friar ushers the wife out of the sickroom and attempts to seduce the bed-ridden Thomas into a more generous compact of confraternity."[44] As the friar's flirtatious words to Thomas's wife expose his proclivity for

---

44. John Bowers, "Queering the Summoner: Same-Sex Union in Chaucer's *Canterbury Tales*," *Speaking Images: Essays in Honor of V. A. Kolve*, ed. Robert Yeager and Charlotte Morse (Asheville: Pegasus, 2001), 301–24, at 311.

rhetoric affiliated with chivalric romance, his appeals to brotherhood with Thomas similarly carry a valence beyond the monastic and into the romance realm of knightly brotherhood. This is not to suggest a specifically homoerotic cast to the simple yet repeated use of the word "brother" but to point to the ways in which masculine bonds are exploited in an attempt to deepen the men's relationship. Certainly, Thomas ironically responds in kind to the friar, asking him, "Ye sey me thus, how that I am youre brother?" (3.2125) and referring to him as "my deere brother" (3.2133) before exacting his flatulent revenge upon him.

Amid this triangulated wrangling appears the narrative's dead child, an unexpected yet telling signifier of the friar and Thomas's homosocial antagonism. Primarily, this dead child signifies a spectral eroticism in the tale—at some point, one of these men must have copulated with his mother—yet he also sparks these erotic tensions anew. Although Thomas's wife reminds the unctuous friar of her recent loss—"Now, sire . . . but o word er I go. / My child is deed withinne thise wykes two, / Soone after that ye wente out of this toun" (3.1851–53)—he continues his sexual pursuit of her and his pecuniary pursuit of her husband's riches without pause, despite his subsequent acknowledgment that the death of a child should curtail his effusive rhetoric. After recounting the story of Cambises's murder of his advisor's child, and thus concluding his litany of examples that condemn the sin of anger, the friar remarks upon the inappropriateness of speech following the devastating death of a beloved child: "His sone was slayn; ther is namoore to seye" (3.2073). Words are of little avail against the loss of a child, yet the friar's pursuit of Thomas's wife and riches leads him to continue speaking when he should remain silent; furthermore, the possibility that the friar should be grieving his own child magnifies the enormity of this social transgression. The story of Cambises and his advisor mirrors the narrative action of the *Summoner's Tale*, in which two men debate the relative merits of anger with a dead child marking their homosocial conflict. The death of the advisor's innocent son symbolizes his father's lack of power in his subservient position to Cambises, and the dead child of the *Summoner's Tale* similarly symbolizes both Thomas's lack of erotic control over his household and the friar's unrestrained sexuality that subverts his commitment to his fraternal order. In both instances, the children's deaths are central to their narrative meaning, for the image of their lifeless bodies proves their callous expendability within a social milieu predicated upon homosocial antagonisms between adult men.

As the two men battle for pecuniary advantage and paternal revenge, the fabliau climaxes as Thomas prepares his humiliation for the friar:

> "Now thanne, put in thyn hand doun by my bak,"
> Seyde this man, "and grope wel bihynde.
> Bynethe my buttok there shaltow fynde
> A thyng that I have hyd in pryvetee." (3.2140–43)

Ratcheting up the sexual farce of his source text "Li Dis de le vescie à prestre" ("The Tale of the Priest's Bladder"), in which a dying man bequeaths his bladder to greedy friars for them to store their pepper, the Summoner sends his unctuous friar to another man's anus.[45] Chaucer's polysemous humor arises in multiple levels in this moment of graphic fabliau humor: the grotesque physicality of the scene with its vulgar focus on anal excavations; the friar's privileging of physical, rather than spiritual, groping, despite that in his religious duties he should "grope tendrely a conscience" (3.1817); and the inversion of heterosexual romance (as presumably the friar achieved with Thomas's wife) in this tableau of antagonistic homoeroticism. Catherine Cox interprets this scene as a parody of anal intercourse: "The Friar's groping gesture therefore evokes a conventional satiric association of friars and sodomites, described by writers as diverse as Walter Mape and William Langland. . . . The fart is, in effect, shown to be the bastard fruit of unnatural coupling."[46] Furthermore, as Susan Signe Morrison notes, the fart functions homeopathically, in that the body's filth purges and punishes those who transgress.[47] The *Summoner's Tale* focuses on the friar in its closing scenes, as he seeks advice on the enigma of how to share the fart equally with members of his fraternal order, but one should not overlook the emptiness of Thomas's revenge: as the fecundity of his wife failed to create lasting life, so too does his fart highlight that his desires impotently dissolve into nothingness. Thomas failed to copulate with his wife and to sire living chil-

---

45. "Li Dis de le vescie à prestre" appears in *The Literary Contexts of Chaucer's Fabliaux*, ed. Larry Benson and Theodore Andersson (Indianapolis: Bobbs-Merrill, 1971), 345–59, and Robert Correale and Mary Hamel, *Sources and Analogues of the* Canterbury Tales, 2.462–77.

46. Catherine Cox, "'Grope wel bihynde': The Subversive Erotics of Chaucer's Summoner," *Exemplaria* 7 (1995): 145–77, at 165–66.

47. Susan Signe Morrison, *Excrement in the Middle Ages: Sacred Filth and Chaucer's Fecopoetics* (New York: Palgrave Macmillan, 2008), 113. See also Valerie Allen, *On Farting: Language and Laughter in the Middle Ages* (New York: Palgrave Macmillan, 2007), 74–76.

dren, and his simulated intercourse with the friar only produces a noxious explosion suggestive of the hollow eroticism behind paternal aggression.

Unlike Maline, the dead child of the *Summoner's Tale* cannot participate, even through inaction, in the tale's closing; the narrative nonetheless highlights, through the ingenuity of the squire Jankyn, the friar's final humiliation and the triumph of the Child as an imaginary construct. Jankyn, too, is one of Chaucer's innovations in this tale, for the humiliation of the greedy friars in "Li Dis de le vescie à prestre" occurs while town officials are watching but without the intervention of a child to resolve its spiritual conundrums. In solving the intricate riddle of "arsmetrike" (3.2222), Jankyn resignifies the tale's anal eroticism into a positive valence. The lord and his company first agree that Thomas behaved boorishly to the friar, with the lord wondering, "How hadde this cherl ymaginacioun / To shewe swich a probleme to the frere?" (3.2218–19), and his wife declaring, "I seye a cherl hath doon a cherles dede" (3.2206), thereby condemning Thomas's flatulent humor and registering their distaste for adult men fixated on anality. Jankyn's solution to the riddle of dividing a fart among thirteen friars, however, returns the friar to the anus, at least hypothetically, but instead of condemning the squire for this vulgar solution, as they condemned Thomas for his rudeness, the lord and his company now see the wisdom and justice of anal eroticism as a necessary solution to a complex problem. As Alan Levitan elucidates, Jankyn's directives parody Pentecost—"From the point at which Thomas bestows his gift upon Friar John, to the proposed solution of its division by Jankyn, what appears as a merely ribald anecdote is, in fact, a brilliant and satirical reversal of the descent of the Holy Ghost at Pentecost"—and thus the diffusion of the spirit that marks the evangelical beginnings of Christianity are inverted into the diffusion of the *flatus* that brings not merely the unctuous friar but all of his brotherhood into spiritual adulation of the anus.[48]

Other than his service as a squire in this lord's household, readers know little about Jankyn, but in this position, it is clear that he must be young, at

---

48. Alan Levitan, "The Parody of Pentecost in Chaucer's *Summoner's Tale*," *University of Toronto Quarterly* 40.3 (1971): 236–46, at 236; see also Penn Szittya, *The Antifraternal Tradition in Medieval Literature* (Princeton: Princeton University Press, 1986), who concludes that "Chaucer scatters Pentecostal allusions throughout the tale; and he repeatedly links Friar John to the apostles, not only to prepare for the pseudo-Pentecost at the end, but to parody the controversial claim of the historical fraternal orders to be imitators of the first apostles, reviving the spiritual purity of the primitive church" (245).

least in contrast to his elders.⁴⁹ A young man in the liminal space between childhood and adulthood, Jankyn incarnates the figure of the Child that the *Summoner's Tale* hides in its subconscious structures. Thomas's dead son barely registers in the tale's plot, for even the cause of his death is unexplained, yet as a symbol of corrupted and abusive erotics—whether the friar's bastard son from illicit coupling or Thomas's legitimate offspring in an anti-erotic marriage—he points to the paternal failures of both men to move beyond their homosocial conflicts as waged through the anus. With Jankyn as the dead boy's proxy, the figure of the Child triumphs against the text's adult figures, winning the award of the "gowne-clooth" (3.2247) by returning the friar to the anus from which he seeks to escape. Jankyn exposes the shallow fantasy of paternal puissance asserting itself through a discarded son, a vision that renders both the friar and Thomas queered through their anal fixations.

CHILDREN IN CHAUCERIAN EXEMPLA: *CLERK'S TALE* AND *PHYSICIAN'S TALE*

As Maline and Thomas's dead son register their fathers' failed masculinities in the humorous genre of fabliau, embodying the ways in which these men wage homosocial conflicts tainted by submerged eroticisms, Griselda and Walter's children in the *Clerk's Tale* and Virginia in the *Physician's Tale* likewise highlight the limitations of paternal authority in narratives that are, at least ostensibly, exemplary and allegorical in theme and genre.⁵⁰

---

49. The term *squire* is somewhat ambiguous in Middle English, as it can refer to servants or to boys training for knighthood. The physical location of the squire in the *Summoner's Tale*—"Now stood the lordes squier at the bord, / That karf his mete" (3.2243–44)—recalls the description of the Squire in the *General Prologue*: "Curteis he was, lowely, and servysable, / And carf biforn his fader at the table" (1.99–100). For accounts of the transition from squire to knighthood, see Maurice Keen, *Chivalry* (New Haven: Yale University Press, 1984); and Katie Stevenson, *Chivalry and Knighthood in Scotland, 1424–1513* (Suffolk: Boydell, 2006), 19–22.

50. Critical assessments of the *Clerk's Tale* and *Physician's Tale* often grapple with the tension between their exemplary and allegorical dynamics, as both tales can be allegorized into arguments for patiently suffering adversity only by overlooking the cruel fates endured by their protagonists. Charlotte Morse forcefully argues for reading the *Clerk's Tale* as an exemplary narrative in "The Exemplary Griselda" (*Studies in the Age of Chaucer* 7 [1985]: 51–86), and Linda Georgianna observes the tacit function of the tale's allegory for its readers, suggesting that, "as with other numinous religious narratives, our experience of the tale serves precisely as the Clerk says adversity does in God's scheme, 'as for oure excercise' (1156), so that by our pity we may at least come to know our own frailty" ("The Clerk's

The *Clerk's Tale* affirms its theme in an exhortation to suffer patiently ("every wight, in his degree, / Sholde be constant in adversitee" [4.1145–46]), and the *Physician's Tale* advises its readers to eschew sin: "Heere may men seen how synne hath his merite. / Beth war, for no man woot whom God wol smyte" (6.277–78). As numerous scholars observe in relation to both tales, any narrative expectation of a pat moral is undone by the tales' failures to signify themes proportionate to their protagonists' suffering. Elaine Tuttle Hansen argues of the *Clerk's Tale*, "whatever its specific significance, this poem appears to many to be bound up with its ambiguities and contradictions, the insolubility of its many problems,"[51] and Helen Cooper tartly observes of the *Physician's Tale*, given the disparities among Virginia's virtue, her fate, and the purportedly exemplary nature of the narrative, "If the tale as a whole is an *exemplum*, it is very hard to see what it exemplifies."[52] The hermeneutic cruxes that confront readers in the *Clerk's Tale* and the *Physician's Tale* hinder interpretive clarity, yet as Larry Scanlon observes, the failure of Chaucer's exemplary texts to deliver a moral paradoxically enables the texts' morals to cohere: "Chaucerian narrative resembles the exemplum in its striving after a moral authority which it implies, but which lies beyond it. It finds its own authority in precisely this striving; in what we can call its self-conscious acknowledgment of its own incompletion."[53] Such a sense of incompletion, in addition to its relevance to these narratives' unfolding, also inheres to the paternal masculinities on display. In the *Clerk's Tale* and *Physician's Tale*, the impossibility of depicting a just moral authority arises in large measure due to Walter's and Virginius's failures to protect their children. These fathers attempt to enhance their incomplete sense of masculinity through their children but doing so requires sacrificing their offspring to their narcissistic images.

Tale and the Grammar of Assent," *Speculum* 70 [1995]: 793–821, at 818). Anne Middleton categorizes the *Physician's Tale* as an exemplary narrative similar in theme and construction to Chaucer's *Legend of Good Women* ("The *Physician's Tale* and Love's Martyrs: 'Ensamples mo than ten' as a Method in the *Canterbury Tales*," *Chaucer Review* 8.1 [1973]: 9–32, at 10), and Howard Bloch affirms that "there is no denying that the *Physician's Tale* is an allegory" ("Chaucer's Maiden's Head: The *Physician's Tale* and the Poetics of Virginity," *Chaucer: Contemporary Critical Essays*, ed. Valerie Allen and Ares Axiotis [New York: St. Martin's, 1996], 145–56, at 146).

51. Elaine Tuttle Hansen, "The Power of Silence: The Case of the Clerk's Griselda," *Critical Essays on Geoffrey Chaucer*, ed. Thomas Stillinger (New York: Hall, 1998), 133–49, at 133.

52. Helen Cooper, *Oxford Guides to Chaucer*: The Canterbury Tales (Oxford: Oxford University Press, 1989), 249.

53. Larry Scanlon, *Narrative, Authority, and Power: The Medieval Exemplum and the Chaucerian Tradition* (Cambridge: Cambridge University Press, 1994), 22.

From the outset of this analysis of the *Clerk's Tale*, it must be acknowledged that no child is physically harmed in the narrative (except perhaps for any psychological scars inflicted on Walter and Griselda's daughter when she realizes how close she came to copulating with her father). At the same time, few tales—both Chaucer's *Clerk's Tale* and its immediate source, Petrarch's *Historia Griseldis*—ask readers to visualize so graphically the image of young children's bodies ravaged by wild animals.[54] The two children's murders are staged for their mother's torment, and these fantasies of dead children, along with Griselda's unfathomable yet always patient suffering, undermine Walter's performance of benevolent fatherhood with its immediate subversion. Freud's infamous formulation that "a child is being beaten" speaks to the prevalence of this fantasy, but as Lee Edelman observes, "the phrase strategically elides the agency by which this end is achieved."[55] When the desiring agent who envisions a beaten child is obscured beyond identification, this vision appears as a spectral fantasy, one present only as an image from a cruel imagination rather than as the physical embodiment of a suffering child, yet the horror of the *Clerk's Tale* arises because this abhorrent fantasy structures the narrative yet apparently does so to Walter's ultimate triumph. In contrast, Chaucer stresses Griselda's efforts to preserve her children's bodies, rendering their ready sacrifice even more troubling. She requests that the sergeant ostensibly dispatched to execute her daughter grant her body merely the dignity of a modest burial: "Burieth this litel body in som place / That beestes ne no bridges it torace" (4.571–72). She soon repeats this plea for her newborn son:

> Save this, she preyede hym that, if he myghte,
> Hir litel sone he wolde in erthe grave
> His tendre lymes, delicaat to sighte,
> Fro foweles and fro beestes for to save. (4.680–83)

This repeated image of a mauled infant functions metatextually—readers often react in horror to the *Clerk's Tale* due to its focus on Griselda's patient suffering through these emotional torments[56]—but it appears to

---

54. For the *Historia Griseldis*, see Robert Correale and Mary Hamel, ed., *Sources and Analogues of the* Canterbury Tales, 1.108–29.

55. Lee Edelman, *No Future: Queer Theory and the Death Drive* (Durham: Duke University Press, 2004), 41.

56. Thomas Van characterizes the *Clerk's Tale* as engendering "pleasurable exasperation" for its readers ("Walter at the Stake: A Reading of Chaucer's *Clerk's Tale*," *Chaucer*

have little effect on the narrative's affective register: Griselda patiently abides; Walter, with equal patience, continues testing her.

Throughout the *Clerk's Tale*, the narrator illustrates that the Child is a cultural construction bestowed on some young bodies (but not on others) to make them perpetuate their society; that is to say, the Child is a social fantasy that obscures the fact that young people are groomed to respond to their culture's ideological imperatives to reproduce the social order. As Lee Edelman observes of the Child's function, "The Child . . . marks the fetishistic fixation of heteronormativity: an erotically charged investment in the rigid sameness of identity that is central to the compulsory narrative of reproductive futurism."[57] Under such a paradigm, children are necessary not for their individuality within a family unit but for their instrumentality within their community, and Chaucer emphasizes the Child's social construction when Griselda's progeny arrive in Lombardy for her daughter's marriage to Walter. The narrator refers to them as children—"Abouten undren gan this erl alighte, / That with hym broghte thise noble children tweye" (4.981–82)—but despite this young girl's status as a child and her age of twelve years (4.736), the townspeople anticipate not a girl but a lady:

> Thus seyden sadde folk in that citee,
> Whan that the peple gazed up and doun,
> For they were glad, right for the noveltee,
> To han a newe lady of hir toun. (4.1002–5)

Marriage bears the potential to transform Griselda's daughter instantly from child to lady (as it can also elevate her in social status from her counterfeit position as an earl's daughter into a marquis's wife). To illustrate this point conversely, the Clerk returns her to the status of a child when she is released from her engagement to her father. In explaining his test to Griselda, Walter refers to their child(ren) as "thy doghter" (4.1065)

Review 22.3 [1988]: 214–24, at 214), but readers are generally troubled by the text, such that Anne Middleton views it as a "supreme test of its readers' interpretive power" ("The Clerk and His Tale: Some Literary Contexts," *Studies in the Age of Chaucer* 2 [1980]: 121–50, at 121).

57. Lee Edelman, *No Future*, 21. Edelman's study has greatly influenced my thoughts on children and their cultural construction, but whereas his analysis primarily focuses on how the figure of the Child regulates adult sexuality, I am interested here in the ways in which children are conscripted into the role of the Child to serve cultural ends dependent upon the destruction of the children employed in this position.

and "thy children tweye" (4.1071), and the narrator calls them "hire yonge children" (4.1081). Likewise Griselda apostrophizes them as "O tendre, o deere, o yonge children myne" (4.1093). These lines indicate that these children's very status as children is never assured but always variable in relation to the demands placed upon them to perform for their father and their community. When Walter needs a bride to test his wife, when the townspeople demand a new marchioness to breed an heir, a young girl's body is appropriated as a lady's, despite the transience of this vision by the tale's conclusion.

Whether compelling readers to imagine the desecrated bodies of murdered children or the incestuous vision of a young girl conscripted into matrimony with her father, Walter's perverse desires establish husbandly and paternal authority as sacrosanct within the *Clerk's Tale*, as his repeated fantasies of his children also reveal him to be the monster of the text. Freud observes that "a father is the prototype of the bogies that people see in anxiety-states,"[58] and in the *Clerk's Tale*, Walter's monstrous desires spark the anxieties of death that haunt Griselda.[59] Due to his apparent willingness to execute his children according to his whims, he fathers not only children but the corresponding images of their deaths, yet he must be rehabilitated from this horrific image to function simultaneously, if unconvincingly, as the benevolent *paterfamilias* of the tale's conclusion. As Mark Miller explains of this paradox,

> Like Job's love for God, Grisilde's love for Walter is supported only by her faith that he does in fact love her and will so reveal himself; and, as Paul puts it, such faith is "hope in things unseen," not a rational appraisal of the available evidence. But then, if Walter must show every sign of being unloving for Grisilde's patient love to confront the extremes that reveal its essential features, and if one of those features is that it refuses to count an unloving act as expressive of Walter's will, then patient love must involve a willingness not to count anything the beloved does as expressive of their will. And that is just what Grisilde does.[60]

---

58. Sigmund Freud, *From the History of an Infantile Neurosis*, 17.1–124, at 67.

59. For the Clerk's conceptions of death, see Kathy Lavezzo, "Chaucer and Everyday Death: The *Clerk's Tale*, Burial, and the Subject of Poverty," *Studies in the Age of Chaucer* 23 (2001): 255–87. Lavezzo articulates how the Clerk "emphasi[zes] death as the supreme leveler" (255), as well as how this vision of equality bears out in relation to Griselda's poverty.

60. Mark Miller, *Philosophical Chaucer: Love, Sex, and Agency in the* Canterbury Tales (Cambridge: Cambridge University Press, 2004), 242.

From Griselda's perspective, it is impossible to believe evil of Walter, and when his test of her ends, she continues viewing him as beneficent and encourages her children to view him in the same manner:

> "Youre woful mooder wende stedfastly
> That crueel houndes or som foul vermyne
> Hadde eten yow; but God of his mercy
> And your benyngne fader tendrely
> Hath doon yow kept." (4.1094–98)

What must Griselda's children think of their parents as this scene unfolds? Most critical commentary focuses on Griselda and her long-delayed emotional release, but her children learn in these lines that, while they were sequestered with their aunt for the entirety of their young lives, their mother believed them to be not only dead but consumed by wild animals. Confronted with the image of their defiled bodies—the foraged provender of "foul vermyne"—these children realize their callous expendability within their family unit at the same time they are expected to celebrate its reconstitution.

Chaucer's narrator refrains from allowing Griselda's children to voice any reaction to their parents: they condemn neither their father for employing them as tokens in his test nor their mother for sacrificing them to his whims. Through this silence, they tacitly enact their emotional alienation from the family that renders them instrumental yet also extraneous to the psychodrama between their mother and father. The narrator records in his description of their mother's embrace a scene of contrasting emotions:

> And in hire swowgh so sadly holdeth she
> Hire children two, whan she gan hem t'embrace,
> That with greet sleighte and greet difficultee
> The children from hire arm they gonne arace. (4.1100–103)

"Arace" is a powerful verb, and in its meanings of "to remove by force, pluck, pull, tear out or away; to snatch," it suggests that the children are wrenched away from their mother.[61] Readers are encouraged to be swept away in the cathartic release that this scene illustrates in its excessive emotionality, and subsequent lines depict such pleasure in the affective

---

61. These definitions are taken from the *Middle English Dictionary*. Secondary definitions of "aracen" include "to lacerate, to flay or skin (an animal), esp. by drawing the pelt off over the head" and "to erase or obliterate."

responses of Walter's many guests: "O many a teere on many a pitous face / Doun ran of hem that stooden hire bisyde; / Unnethe abouten hire myghte they abyde" (4.1104–6). Because these lines focus "on many a pitous face," not exclusively on the countenances of Griselda and her children, the narrator appears, in cinematic terms, to move his eye backward from a close-up of Griselda and her children to a long shot of the shocked wedding guests. The narrator subsequently adds, "And every wight hire joye and feeste maketh / Til she hath caught agayn hire contenaunce" (4.1109–10). Given the ambiguity of these lines in regard to these many "pitous faces" and the joy of "every wight," it is by no means certain that Griselda's children share in the guests' outburst commemorating their mother's steadfast rejection of them, as their violent pulling away from her suggests discomfort with their parents' views on child-raising and familial affection.

When Walter restores Griselda to her prior status as his wife, and concomitantly restores his daughter to her position as his child, he denies the possibility of incestuous desire for the girl. Erasing his dark fantasies from view, he cloaks his paternal deviance under the façade of a test of Griselda's womanly virtue:

> "And folk that ootherweys han seyd of me,
> I warne hem wel that I have doon this deede
> For no malice, ne for no crueltee,
> But for t'assaye in thee thy wommanheede,
> And nat to sleen my children—God forbeede!—
> But for to kepe hem pryvely and stille,
> Til I thy purpos knewe and al thy wille." (4.1072–78)

Walter rejects implications of malice or cruelty on his part, but he elides the possibility of incestuous desire for his daughter as a motivating factor in his test of his wife.[62] Because Griselda does not fail Walter's test of her, he does not marry and copulate with his daughter. This possibility nonetheless persists within the subconscious of the *Clerk's Tale*, disrupting

---

62. Tara Williams reads this passage as indicative of Chaucer's formulation of new ways of representing women and womanhood, in her "'T'assaye in thee thy wommanheede': Griselda Chosen, Translated, and Tried" (*Studies in the Age of Chaucer* 27 [2005]: 93–127). In terms of Walter's abuse of fatherhood, Williams posits that "silence about Griselda's motherhood allows Walter to fabricate the reaction of his people to his children" (121), which testifies further to his manipulation of paternity and childhood to prove his manhood in marriage.

the moral telos of the narrative: incest cannot be dismissed from Walter's desires, for it sparks an alternate and impossible ending that the tale's resolution forecloses but cannot fully overwrite. His daughter, as a figure of the Child, is an object of sexual instrumentality, for he would need to consummate his marriage with her if Griselda failed the test that their daughter's young body enables. Within the realm of reasonable speculation, his daughter would then be conscripted to bear him a son/grandson to serve as his heir. Because she must serve as the Child, rather than merely being a child, Walter's daughter represents the brute force of ideology to conscript the young into adult sexuality, no matter the repercussions for them, and for ensuing generations as well. This vision of Walter's incestuous child/grandchild, who cannot exist within this narrative yet who can neither be entirely removed from it, represents the depravities that adults inflict on children, in its straddling between such standard familial roles as child and grandchild and its eradication of the border between father and grandfather.

In this way, the disciplinary force of fatherhood guides the *Clerk's Tale* while camouflaging incestuous eroticism as a husband's test of his wife, but Walter's power to wrench his daughter into adult sexuality lies unchecked, as does this power for the culture at large. As monstrous a father as Walter may be, his actions concerning his daughter mirror his people's treatment of his own sexuality, in that he was compelled to shift his attentions from youthful pastimes and pleasures to sexual maturity when they demanded that he take a wife. He too illustrates the pains of being compelled to fill the role of the Child conscripted into adulthood and thus constructed for sexual utility beyond any immanent and interior desires. The tale's initial characterization of Walter concentrates on his youth, with the narrator describing him as "a fair persone, and strong, and yong of age" (4.73) and then reiterating that "Walter was this yonge lordes name" (4.77). His counselor describes him as blossoming in youth—"youre grene youthe floure as yet" (4.120)—but he must accede into manhood through matrimony: "That for to been a wedded man yow leste; / Thanne were youre peple in sovereyn hertes reste" (4.111–12). Although without the specter of incest, Walter's predicament at the narrative's beginning parallels those of Griselda and their daughter subsequently in the tale: marriage and marital sexuality are fates forced upon the young rather than internal and coherent erotic desires that children act upon through their own volition. Before the specters of dead children and incest haunt the narrative, heterosexuality emerges as the text's defining and queer trauma that Walter's subsequent cruelty reenacts. Freud notes the persistence of childhood perversions and the ways in which they are reenacted throughout adulthood—"A perversion in childhood, as is well known, may become the basis for the construction of a perversion having a similar sense and persisting throughout life, one which consumes the subject's whole sexual life"[63]—and Walter's destruction of his daughter's childhood merely reenacts the perverse destruction of his own youth, as a new generation is forcibly conscripted into premature eroticism.

Similar to Walter, Griselda evinces little desire for marital sexuality at the tale's beginning. She lives contentedly with her father, and this familial arrangement accentuates her youth and innocence, as well as her status as a child: "And ay she kepte hir fadres lyf on-lofte / With everich obeisaunce and diligence / That child may doon to fadres reverence" (4.229–31). The many descriptors stressing Griselda's youth—"this yonge mayden" (4.210), "thogh this mayde tendre were of age" (4.218), "Of so yong age" (4.241)—also encourage readers to see her as a child more than as a young woman. In contrast to brides who joyfully accept their suitor's proposal of marriage, Griselda visualizes and vocalizes a vision of death in response to Walter's request for her hand in matrimony:

> ... "Lord, undigne and unworthy
> Am I to thilke honour that ye me beede,
> But as ye wole youreself, right so wol I.
> And heere I swere that nevere willyngly,
> In werk ne thoght, I nyl yow disobeye,
> For to be deed, though me were looth to deye." (4.359–64)

The generative promise of marital erotics, although realized in the subsequent births of their children, are occluded through Griselda's premonitions of death at the very moment of her engagement. Griselda's age is unspecified yet clearly young, and this girl finds herself conscripted into marital service more to produce children than to serve Walter's erotic or amatory desires, let alone her personal wishes in this regard. The Child is sacrificed sexually and bodily to the culture that demands her fertility to perpetuate the social order.

For Walter's people do not really care about a wife as much as they are concerned with the necessity for him to produce an heir; thus, a female—any female—is merely a means to this greater end by which they hope to preserve their own future. Indeed, their shallow vacillations in response

---

63. Sigmund Freud, "A Child Is Being Beaten," 192.

to Griselda indicate that she is necessary only to fill the role of wife rather than to be appreciated as an individual for any benevolent qualities she might possess. They first believe "That she from hevene sent was, as men wende, / Peple to save and every wrong t'amende" (4.440–41), but they soon forget the salvific cast of Griselda's character and conclude of Walter's new fiancée: "For she is fairer, as they deemen alle, / Than is Grisilde, and moore tendre of age, / And fairer fruyt bitwene hem sholde falle" (4.988–90). Walter's people desire the Child as a means of ensuring the reproduction of their present into the future. In this manner, the narrative emphasizes Griselda's sexual instrumentality when her daughter is born: the people "had hire levere have born a knave child," but they realize that she "may unto a knave child atteyne" although "a mayde child coome al before" (4.444, 446–47). The *Clerk's Tale* reveals the torsions of individual identity and psychosexual agency necessary to reproduce the future: the grisly image of dead children transforms at the narrative's close into the image of a happy family, but in this family, all members must be ever ready to sacrifice themselves to a vision of the Child as reflective of a cultural desire to reproduce the social order, even when they are the Children to be so sacrificed.

Despite the strained happy ending of the *Clerk's Tale*, the fate of Walter and Griselda's children remains obscure, and if one envisions them as reliving the ideological constraints placed upon their parents, their futures look increasingly bleak. In detailing their prospects, the narrator assures his audience that these two young children grow and prosper into happy adulthood at the tale's conclusion. Readers learn that "richely his doghter maryed [Walter] / Unto a lord, oon of the worthieste / Of al Ytaille" (4.1130–32), and their son "succedeth in [Walter's] heritage / In reste and pees, after his fader day, / And fortunat was eek in mariage" (4.1135–37). These "happily ever after" endings for Walter and Griselda's children, however, merely mask the unknowability of their fate, and may suggest as well that they simply follow in their parents' unfortunate footsteps: just as Griselda married a worthy lord of Italy, and just as Walter succeeded into his father's lordship only to be compelled to pursue the fruits of marriage, readers have little reason to believe that these children escape the torturous fates of their parents, who married in response to societal desires about their reproductive futures, foreclosing their childhoods for adult sexuality in a mutually undesired marriage more striking for its fantasy of dead children than for its live ones.

Whereas the graphic image of dead children in the *Clerk's Tale* is proved untrue, the fantasy of the sacrificed child is rendered strikingly real within the fictions of the *Physican's Tale*, in which Virginia's decapitation provides its gruesome and ostensibly moral climax, despite the unimpeachable virtue that defines her as an illustrative daughter. In many ways the *Physician's Tale* and its classical source, Livy's *Ab urbe condita*, are less concerned about a specific child than with the Child's instrumentality in instigating governmental reforms.[64] The narrative focuses on her two roles that ultimately overlap—dutiful daughter and erotic prey—and to this end, the tale's opening stresses that Virginia is Virginius's lawful daughter: "This knyght a doghter hadde by his wyf" (6.5). Unlike the doubtful paternity issues in the *Summoner's Tale* and *Merchant's Tale*, Virginius's paternal claim to Virginia is certified by the narrator, but the strength of this bond affords her insufficient protection from him. She is sinless, blameless, and the epitome of maidenly virtue, yet the sexual innocence associated with her maidenly modesty is merely a façade. Although she appears ignorant of sexuality due to the narrative's focus on her virtue, the narrator reveals that she is aware—and wary of—amorous pursuits. Merely fourteen years old (6.30), Virginia retains her youthful modesty: "Shamefast she was in maydens shamefastnesse" (6.55). She avoids alcoholic drink to protect her virginity due to her awareness that "wyn and youthe dooth Venus encresse, / As men in fyr wol casten oille or greesse" (6.59–60). The narrator also mentions that "she floured in virginitee / With alle humylitee and abstinence" (6.44–45), but this pairing of humility and abstinence marks her virtuous chastity as both a central feature of her identity and as a performance on display for her fellow Romans to admire. To be humble about her abstinence, she must recognize that she has won the right to perform this virtue. Furthermore, Virginia is sufficiently cognizant of the licentious atmosphere at "feestes, revels, and . . . daunces" to avoid them because they are "occasions of daliaunces" (6.65–66). As murky as Virginia's knowledge of sexuality may be, she is aware that flirtations are illicit pastimes for her and other young girls to pursue because of the threats they pose to their chastity. Perhaps the most telling line in Virginia's description is that she acts so modestly due to "hir owene vertu, unconstreyned" (6.61), but that Virginia herself acts in accordance with cultural constructions of maidenly virtue merely hides that she has interiorized her society's sexual mores to the extent that she performs them without additional pressures. Lianna Farber sees Virginia as indoctrinated into a social order that convinces

---

64. For Livy's *Ab urbe condita*, see Robert Correale and Mary Hamel, ed., *Sources and Analogues of the* Canterbury Tales, 2.540–47. Chaucer's retelling of this legend is also influenced by Guillaume de Lorris and Jean de Meun's *Roman de la Rose*, lines 5589–658.

her to acquiesce to her death, in that she is sexually innocent insofar as she self-regulates in accordance with the ideological construction of her innocence.[65] She is thus the Child who has interiorized cultural projections of virtuous childhood, as yet unaware of the violence necessary to prop up this fantasy.

The cultural fantasy of the Child, as enacted upon young boys and girls, cannot be perpetuated forever as they grow into adulthood, and the narrator underscores that young girls' ignorance of sexuality must yield to sexual knowledge:

> Swich [dalliances] maken children for to be
> To soone rype and boold, as men may se,
> Which is ful perilous and hath been yore.
> For al to soone may she lerne loore
> Of booldnesse, whan she woxen is a wyf. (6.67–71)

Knowledge deemed illicit for children is appropriate for wives, but the Physician allows no indication of when young girls are to receive instruction in sexuality, other than on their wedding nights when their metamorphosis from child to woman (as they also transform from their father's daughter into their husband's wife) is complete. Such a transformation is lamented as occurring "al to soone," yet it is not clear within this cultural fantasy when sexual knowledge should be imparted to the young. Latent pedophilia lurks in these lines of the *Physician's Tale*, as men watch children ("men may se") for incipient signs of adult sexuality. At the same time that the narrator recoils at the possibility of pedophilia, exhorting that children should not be treated as sexual objects, he also highlights the contingency of the status of children. When sexual innocence in childhood is abrogated, as evident in Apius's desire to rape Virginia, children are compelled to become adults overnight.

The narrator's lengthy digression on child-rearing by nurses and parents (6.72–104) contains many paradoxes and thematic lapses, particularly because Virginia, as a model child, ostensibly needs little governance in pursuing her sound moral path. In this excursus, the Physician explores the utility both of chastity and of sexual transgression for nurses raising young children. Whether through sexual innocence or their past licentiousness, nurses are better able to preserve their young charges from sin, but this necessitates, at least for the unchaste nurses, that their own sexual inno-

---

65. Lianna Farber, "The Creation of Consent in the *Physician's Tale*," *Chaucer Review* 39.2 (2004): 151–64.

cence be sacrificed prior to their employment. The sexual knowledge from which nurses preserve young girls is thus ideologically functionable, for their transgressions of these mores establish them now as suitable guardians of other people's children:

> Outher for ye han kept youre honestee,
> Or elles ye han falle in freletee,
> And knowen wel ynough the olde daunce,
> And han forsaken fully swich meschaunce
> For everemo; therfore, for Cristes sake,
> To teche hem vertu looke that ye ne slake. (6.77–82)

It matters little whether these nurses sexually transgressed in their youth, for their knowledge is now deployed to preserve children. "Of alle tresons sovereyn pestilence / Is whan a wight bitrayseth innocence" (6.91–92), the Physician then declares, but this betrayal of children's innocence does not extend retrospectively in consideration of these nurses, only in the present and into the future to protect current children. The cultural signifier of the Innocent Child who must be preserved from sexual knowledge fluctuates in regard to its target: always a child but never the adults who were children before, who must now devote themselves to children so that children will not grow up to be adults like them. Furthermore, issues of social class circulate in this passage, for the lost sexual innocence of nurses and other servants can be lamented yet transformed into a benefit to the family and thus to society as well; for girls of higher status such as Virginia, no path to reformation allows them to be cleansed of the ostensible transgression of intercourse.

Virginia's reference to the biblical narrative of Jephthah and his daughter similarly registers the potential to reframe fallen female sexuality as beneficial to society, despite the paradoxes of this rhetorical move. Foremost, Jephthah, as described in the Book of Judges, is a "vir fortissimus atque pugnator filius meretricis" (11.1; "a most valiant man and warrior, the son of a woman that was a harlot"). In this biblical narrative, a sexually transgressive woman produces a heroic child, but Jephthah's heroism as a warrior is compromised by his rash vow that results in his daughter's execution. Virginia alludes to Jephthah's daughter to momentarily stay her father's hand when her own death approaches:

> "For, pardee, Jepte yaf his doghter grace
> For to compleyne, er he hir slow, allas!

> And, God it woot, no thyng was hir trespas,
> But for she ran hir fader first to see,
> To welcome hym with greet solempnitee." (6.240–44)

Numerous medieval Jewish and Christian commentators criticized Jephthah for adhering to his rash vow despite the price his daughter must pay,⁶⁶ but Virginia does not cite such textual authorities to plead for her life (in contrast to, for example, Dorigen in the *Franklin's Tale*, who convinces herself not to commit suicide despite the numerous examples of virtuous women who choose death over sexual dishonor). Both Jephthah and Virginius sacrifice their daughters to reflect their inherent honor, yet in neither story is such a sacrifice warranted within its theological logic. Within its erotic logics, however, in which a woman's virginity reflects positively on her father who has guarded this commodity, such a sacrifice is essential to the tales' androcentric resolutions.

The eroticism of the *Physician's Tale* is ultimately interconnected with the death drive, for it is based on the impossibility of stasis within childhood and virginity. Despite the assumed desirability of her sexual innocence, Virginia cannot remain a virginal child forever, but even the hypothetical possibility of endless childhood would render sexuality moribund. Within Chaucer's corpus, the inherent potential of the death drive intersecting with virginity is famously voiced by the Wife of Bath—"And certes, if ther were no seed ysowe, / Virginitee, thanne wherof sholde it growe?" (3.71–72)—and Virginia symbolizes a potential rejection of the social order through her very virtue that leads to her death. As Howard Bloch argues, "a certain inescapable logic of virginity, most evident in medieval hagiography, leads syllogistically to the conclusion that the only good virgin—that is, the only true virgin—is a dead virgin."⁶⁷ To describe Virginia as perpetuating an ideological system that requires her sacrificing her very self is troubling, as it reeks of misogynist discourses labeling victims of sexual violence as complicit in their suffering; however, such is the power of ideology to conscript subjects into acquiescence with their own sacrifice that Virginia agrees to her father's request to kill

---

66. For an overview of responses to the story of Jephthah's daughter, see Margaret Alexiou and Peter Dronke, "The Lament of Jephtha's Daughter: Themes, Traditions, Originality," *Studi Medievali* 12 (1971): 819–63; John Thompson, *Writing the Wrongs: Women of the Old Testament among Biblical Commentators from Philo through the Reformation* (Oxford: Oxford University Press, 2001), 100–78; and David Gunn, *Judges* (Malden, MA: Blackwell, 2005), 132–71.

67. Howard Bloch, "Chaucer's Maiden's Head," 150.

her. If readers believe that Virginia too readily cedes her life to paternal claims over her body and its social significations, by perpetually upholding her virginity in death, she sacrifices her fertility to the grave and thus her father's potential to perpetuate his bloodline. The fantasy of the beaten child again redounds to the detriment of the father in a public venue, in this instance when Virginius wages his battle with Apius. Michael Uebel argues that "Virginity seems always to be a matter of public rather than private affect,"[68] and so too is Virginius's performance of fatherhood publicly undone through his daughter's sacrifice of herself. Preserving her maidenhead entails losing her maiden's head, as Bloch affirms, yet in losing her head, she publicly reveals her father's privileging of the public over the private and destroys the possibility of propagating his bloodline. As the narrator affirms when proclaiming that Virginia is Virginius's lawful offspring, "No children hadde he mo in al his lyf" (6.6), and so her death registers, at least metaphorically, as his own.

The *Physician's Tale* is built on the myth of female passivity and pliancy, the fictions that daughters are molded to the pleasure of men for paternal self-aggrandizement. Anne Middleton sees Virginia as representing a "paradoxical mixture of active courage and passive forbearance,"[69] and Holly Crocker observes of the *Physician's Tale* that "the politically unifying fantasy of feminine passivity turns into a domestically divisive nightmare of masculine violence."[70] Virginius's actions, although horrific, acquire a logical equanimity: as his name makes apparent, he is the progenitor of Virginia but also her masculine counterpart. When Apius and Virginius jockey for control of Virginia, their homosocial struggle exposes Virginius's desire not merely to preserve his narcissistic image through his daughter but to assume Apius's authority within the social order. When he passes judgment on his daughter and condemns her to death, he mirrors Apius in his role of judge:

"O gemme of chastitee, in pacience
Take thou thy deeth, for this is my sentence.
For love, and nat for hate, thou most be deed;
My pitous hand moot smyten of thyn heed." (6.223–26)

---

68. Michael Uebel, "Public Fantasy and the Logic of Sacrifice in the *Physician's Tale*," ANQ 15.3 (2002): 30–33, at 31.
69. Anne Middleton, "The *Physician's Tale* and Love's Martyrs," 16.
70. Holly Crocker, *Chaucer's Visions of Manhood* (New York: Palgrave Macmillan, 2007), 64.

As Apius perverts the law in his corrupt pursuit of Virginia, Virginius similarly corrupts his paternal authority in sadistically executing his daughter. Gilles Deleuze points out that sadism resists reproduction—"The ultimate end of the sadist is to put an effective end to all procreation, since it competes with primary nature. . . . Sadism is in every sense an active negation of the mother and an exaltation of the father who is beyond all laws"[71]—and such are the results of Virginius's punishment of his daughter for sins she never committed. (Congruent to this logic, Virginia's mother is mostly absent from the text, as readers only see her when she accompanies her daughter to the temple where Apius's lust for her is inflamed.) Moreover, as Virginius asserts governmental authority over his fellow Romans after Apius's suicide, his arbitrary dispensation of justice and mercy—pardoning Claudius but executing the "remenant . . . / That were consentant of this cursednesse" (6.275–76)—exposes that the exercise of power takes precedence over his familial obligations. In assuming the position of the law, Virginius proves his fantasy of inviolate masculinity true, until his death, when it finally arrives, will ironically recall that he sacrificed his daughter's fecundity and coupled her virginity to his death drive. If readers recall the Physician's excursus on fallen nurses and the protections afforded by their illicitly gained knowledge, Virginia's final words—"Blissed be God that I shal dye a mayde! / Yif me my deeth, er that I have a shame" (6.248–49)—ironically indicate an alternative fate for her in a life of protecting children, and the children whom she might preserve from similar fates are themselves sacrificed to her father's fantasy of inviolate masculinity. As Harry Bailly concludes of Virginia, "Hire beautee was hire deth, I dar wel seyn" (6.297). In arousing Apius's erotic interests, Virginia inadvertently signs her death warrant, one that her father executes: to preserve the Child, he sacrifices his child. In the end, Virginia cannot access her sexuality except through the negative affect of perpetual virginity, a cycle that promises only additional sacrifices and never future fecundity.

CONCLUSION

In these queer families of the *Canterbury Tales*, the children of the *Reeve's Tale*, *Summoner's Tale*, *Clerk's Tale*, and *Physician's Tale* suffer through rape,

---

71. Gilles Deleuze, *Masochism* (New York: Zone, 1991), 60.

death, and their sexual instrumentality, but through the images of their suffering and/or their dead bodies, the hollow bravado and empty eroticism of their fathers' masculinities are made manifest for the world to see. In the *Reeve's Tale*, Symkyn faces humiliation at the hands of Allen and John, who rape his daughter and wife and then beat him as they escape, and the *Summoner's Tale* concludes with Thomas's invitation to another man to excavate his backside, with the friar facing further come-uppance due to the ingenuity of the young squire Jankyn. The dark fantasy of murdered children in the *Clerk's Tale* exposes Walter's tyrannical authority, as well as the limits of his powers during his youth when he was unable to pursue the asexual (and likely homosocial) pleasures of hunting and other such disports and was himself sacrificed to the demands of cultural reproduction. The *Physician's Tale* concludes with a vision of paternal masculinity so vicious that fatherhood is rendered morbidly unattractive and death emerges as Virginia's only weapon against her father, which denies him the possibility of furthering his bloodline. In grand ironies, in each of these tales the father confronts narrative fates as violent, humiliating, and/or despairing as his child(ren)'s. Gilles Deleuze reformulates Freud's formula that "a child is being beaten," positing instead a masochistic desire to reenact the father's abjection: "we have seen that what is beaten, humiliated and ridiculed in him is the image and the likeness of the father, and the possibility of the father's aggressive return. *It is not the child but a father that is being beaten.*"[72] To desire masochistically is to desire the pleasure of punishment, and so it is the father who must be disciplined in these tales, despite their attempted performances of their inviolate power. For to describe a fantasy of a beaten child is only to describe a desire, one that circulates destructively around the dreamer and the dreamed, and the intersecting desires between them.

To push this interpretation further, might these fathers represent the Father? The role of the Divine in each of these tales is occluded yet persistently present. Maline in the *Reeve's Tale* descends directly from "hoolly chirches blood" (1.3982), and in the *Summoner's Tale*, the possibility that Thomas's dead son was fathered by the friar likewise links the child to a religious bloodline. The *Clerk's Tale* finds an uneasy parallel in the biblical tale of Job—"Men speke of Job, and moost for his humblesse" (4.932), the narrator declares—but reading the *Clerk's Tale* as an allegory necessitates that Walter's role in the tale parallel God's role in the Book

---

72. Ibid., 66.

of Job, rendering Walter a callous incarnation of divine love.[73] Despite Virginius's clear paternal claims over Virginia, the narrator stresses as well her position as God's child when Nature describes herself as God's chief deputy—"For He that is the formere principal / Hath maked me his vicaire general" (6.19–20)—and then declares that she created Virginia for his pleasure: "I made hire to the worshipe of my lord" (6.26).[74] Furthermore, Virginia conflates her earthly and spiritual fathers in her final words to Virginius: "Dooth with youre childe youre wyl, a Goddes name!" (6.250). Chaucer conflates these children's fathers with the Father, and thus Christianity is implicated within an erotic system that undermines borders between the normative and the perverse, the just and the cruel. As these child characters of the *Canterbury Tales* suffer for an erotic pleasure suffused throughout their narratives, so too does Chaucer's conception of an erotic God subvert paradigms of gender and sexuality in an array of texts, as the next chapter explores.

---

73. The potential analogy between Walter and God has been explored in numerous nominalist studies of the tale, such as Elizabeth Kirk's poignant reading: "What the *Clerk's Tale* reflects especially is the predicament of a religious thinker in a world whose discourse is shaped by the assumption of nominalism: what desperate straits must be dared to affirm the goodness of God and the organic role of ethics in the fulfillment of the whole creature" ("Nominalism and the Dynamics of the *Clerk's Tale: Homo Viator* as Woman," *Chaucer's Religious Tales*, ed. C. David Benson and Elizabeth Robertson [Suffolk: Brewer, 1990], 11–20, at 118). See also Rodney Delasanta, "Nominalism and the *Clerk's Tale*," *Chaucer Review* 31 (1997): 209–31; Robert Stepsis, "*Potentia Absoluta* and the *Clerk's Tale*," *Chaucer Review* 10 (1975): 129–46; and David Steinmetz, "Late Medieval Nominalism and the *Clerk's Tale*," *Chaucer Review* 12 (1977): 38–54.

74. Barbara Newman addresses the relationship between the feminized deity Nature and the Christian God in her *God and the Goddesses: Vision, Poetry, and Belief in the Middle Ages* (Philadelphia: University of Pennsylvania Press, 2003), exploring how Nature represents the "goddess of biological life, and specifically of sexuality and reproduction." In this role she "remains God's daughter" while she "authorizes the scientific and philosophical study of 'nature,'" despite the confusion she engendered for some "medieval authors [who] disagreed as to how fully she is initiated into her Father's secrets" (53).

CHAPTER SIX

CHAUCER'S (ANTI-)EROTIC GOD

> *God precedes and transcends us, but first and above all in the fact that he loves us infinitely better than we love, and than we love him. God surpasses us as the best lover.*
> —Jean-Luc Marion, The Erotic Phenomenon[1]

The New Testament proclaims, "Deus caritas est et qui manet in caritate in Deo manet et Deus in eo" (I John 4:16; "God is charity: and he that abideth in charity, abideth in God, and God in him"), but defining, contemplating, and making God's *caritas* accessible through the written word exposes the impossibility of contemplating the Divine without subverting his perfection. Augustine pithily summarizes this conundrum of pondering divinity and urges his readers to strive for transcendence despite the limitations of human perception: "If you are not able now to comprehend what God is, comprehend at least what God is not; you will have made much progress, if you think of God as being not something other than He is."[2] In his analysis of medieval allegory and sexuality, Noah Guynn assesses this hermeneutic conundrum of discussing the Divine for classical and medieval rhetoricians, including Cicero, Donatus, Augustine, Isidore of Seville, and Hugh of St. Victor: "Yet there is almost always some degree of awareness, whether latent or fully articulated, that discursive, tropological meaning is internally and irremediably split, that signifiers are always 'other' with respect to an

---

1. Jean-Luc Marion, *The Erotic Phenomenon*, trans. Stephen Lewis (Chicago: University of Chicago Press, 2007), 222.
2. Augustine, *Lectures or Tractates on the Gospel According to St. John*, trans. John Gibb (Edinburgh: Clark, 1873), vol. 1, tractate 23.9, at 335.

essential, unvarying, and ineffable signified."³ The "essential, unvarying, and ineffable signified" that is the Divine creates these rhetorical traps, in that discussing his perfection through the imperfect medium of language inevitably corrupts the incorruptible. Humans can only approach the Divine through metaphor, allegory, and other such symbolic play with language that figures God within the limited terms of human comprehension, and due to these factors, amatory affection and eroticism—as understood, as they must be, through human experience—provide apt metaphors for considering the raptures of divine love.

Frequently in the Middle Ages, spiritual and metaphysical treatments of God assume a decidedly erotic cast, limning the Divine through a very human understanding of the body and sexual pleasure. For even if one embraces Augustine's suggestion to imagine God through what he is not, how is this possible except through the human terms that then constitute what the Divine is not? For example, Paul elliptically refers to the physicality of Divinity when he discusses the necessity of the Church approximating the Godhead:

> et ipse dedit quosdam quidem apostolos quosdam autem prophetas alios vero evangelistas alios autem pastores et doctores, ad consummationem sanctorum in opus ministerii, in aedificationem corporis Christi, donec occurramus omnes in unitatem fidei et agnitinois Filii Dei, in virum perfectum in mensuram aetatis plenitudinis Christi. (Ephesians 4:11–13)
>
> And he gave some apostles, and some prophets, and other some evangelists, and other some pastors and doctors. For the perfecting of the saints, for the work of the ministry, for the edifying of the body of Christ: Until we all meet into the unity of faith, and of the knowledge of the Son of God, unto a perfect man, unto the measure of the age of the fullness of Christ.

Paul's enigmatic image of the "virum perfectum in mensuram aetatis plenitudinis Christi" asks his followers to contemplate the Divine image, but it is unclear what they should then see as represented through his words. In his explications of Pauline thought, Augustine struggles with the issue of God's corporeality and its attendant physical form, such as when, in response to Paul's consideration of the "virum perfectum in mensuram

---

3. Noah Guynn, *Allegory and Sexual Ethics in the High Middle Ages* (New York: Palgrave Macmillan, 2007), 7.

aetatis plenitudinis Christi," Augustine euphemistically interprets Paul's metaphoric construction of the Body of Christ to necessitate "the union of head and body, which consists of all the members, and they will be completed in due time."[4] The euphemistic phrase referring to "all the members" tangentially adumbrates God's erotic nature in the inclusion of his humanly recognizable genitals. In his "Tome of Leo," Pope Leo the Great likewise addresses the issue of God's genitalia: "Thus there was born true God in the entire and perfect nature of true man, complete in his own properties, complete in ours."[5] The body of God, as a complete and perfect rendering of man's, tangentially raises a host of questions concerning God's erotic drives. Leo's precepts were adopted by the Ecumenical Council of Chalcedon in 451 C.E., which concludes:

> Therefore, following the holy fathers, we all with one accord teach men to acknowledge one and the same Son, our Lord Jesus Christ, at once complete in Godhead and complete in manhood, truly God and truly man, consisting also of a reasonable soul and body; of one substance with the Father as regards his Godhead, and at the same time of one substance with us regards his manhood; like us in all respects, apart from sin.[6]

This question of God's physical incarnation—whether he is equipped with a penis or not—is only one of numerous issues concerning God's erotic nature in the Middle Ages, including visual depictions of his circumcision and at times erect penis,[7] exegetical interpretations of vexing scriptural passages (such as Bernard of Clairvaux's detailed explications of the Song of Songs),[8] and mystical accounts of divine

---

4. Augustine, *City of God*, trans. Henry Bettenson (London: Penguin, 1984), 1058–59.

5. Henry Bettenson, ed., *Documents of the Christian Church* (New York: Oxford University Press, 1956), 70.

6. Ibid., 72.

7. As Leo Steinberg's provocative analysis of medieval and Renaissance art demonstrates, the issue of Jesus's penis and its symbolic representation of his humanity was a matter of prominent concern to numerous artists (*The Sexuality of Christ in Renaissance Art and in Modern Oblivion* [London: Faber & Faber, 1983]).

8. Studies of Bernard of Clairvaux that illuminate the sexual play in his allegorical reinterpretation of the Song of Songs include Ann Astell, *The Song of Songs in the Middle Ages* (Ithaca, NY: Cornell University Press, 1990); and E. Ann Matter, *The Voice of My Beloved: The Song of Songs in Western Medieval Christianity* (Philadelphia: University of Pennsylvania Press, 1990). Astell cites Pseudo-Richard of Victor's explication of erotic love and its spiritual import as depicted in the Song: "We learn from the words of this love; by the power of this love we burn in the love of Divinity. We must consider this repeatedly,

rapture.[9] Lara Farina notes that medieval religious writers employed language in the manner that they experienced it, despite its limitations: "the language with which [medieval religious writers] go about producing desire must not depart entirely from the desirable as it is already known, even if that means relying on imagery and rhetoric that are seemingly incongruous with Christian religious endeavor or its more ascetic doctrines."[10] While the issue of God's eroticism appears unthinkable within certain medieval discourses, Augustine's and Leo's careful euphemisms reveal that many medieval Christians could not refrain from pondering the eroticism of their Father, and other religious traditions, particularly those of mystics, thought of Divinity in insistently and graphically amorous terms.

When Chaucer includes depictions of God and God's love in his fictions, he too must confront the inherent paradox of describing divine perfection through the imperfect mediums of human language and thought. The impossibility of characterizing the ineffable, and particularly the impossibility of delineating the contours of spiritual love with terms of human physicality, coincides with overtly sensualized visions of the Divine in Chaucer's corpus. As Mark Miller suggests of Chaucer's play with sexuality in his fictions, "erotic energies trouble and cross presumptive borders between the normal and the perverse, even as in many ways they depend on the constitution of such borders,"[11] and such is the

---

however, lest when we hear the words of outward love, we remain with the superficial understanding" (28).

9. As Elizabeth Alvilda Petroff demonstrates, bodies and gender are inextricably connected to visionary writing: "Bodies—the visionary's own body and the body of Christ—are very important in women's visionary writings. . . . [I]n using the language of the body the medieval writer may be able to say unsayable or unthinkable things" (*Body and Soul: Essays on Medieval Women and Mysticism* [Oxford: Oxford University Press, 1994], 204). In a similar vein, Amy Hollywood notes: "many women were forced to seek access to the divine and to public voice by inscribing their bodies and souls with suffering, with wounds marking the presence of God and the limits of imagination" (*The Soul as Virgin Wife: Mechthild of Magdeburg, Marguerite Porete, and Meister Eckhart* [Notre Dame, IN: University of Notre Dame Press, 1995], 206). For an excellent study of the eroticism of mystical texts, including the *Ancrene Wisse* and the Wooing Group, see Lara Farina, *Erotic Discourse and Early English Religious Writing* (New York: Palgrave Macmillan, 2006), esp. 35–86; Farina also addresses Bernard of Clairvaux and the Song of Songs (6–12). For the mystical eroticism of Julian of Norwich and Margery Kempe, see Liz Herbert McAvoy, *Authority and the Female Body in the Writings of Julian of Norwich and Margery Kempe* (Cambridge: Brewer, 2004), esp. 152–53, 167–69 for Julian and 126–30 for Margery.

10. Lara Farina, *Erotic Discourse and Early English Religious Writing*, 6.

11. Mark Miller, *Philosophical Chaucer: Love, Sex, and Agency in the* Canterbury Tales (Cambridge: Cambridge University Press, 2004), 2.

case with Chaucer's divine eroticism, in which heavenly aspirations lead humans to contemplate the potential physicality of erotic union with the Divine, as well as hinting that the Divine responds to such spiritual carnality in a strikingly physical manner. Chaucer's conceptions of an erotic and eroticizing Christian God recall and parallel those of his forebears and contemporaries who similarly confront the sexual implications inherent in loving God, while the unique rhetorical situations of his narratives simultaneously position his vision of divine love as his own.

In theorizing the narrative effect of Chaucer's divine eroticisms, it should be noted that Chaucer's relationship to Christianity can only be hazily surmised through his fictions. Ruth Ames hypothesizes that Chaucer's theological perspective was that of "an enlightened fourteenth-century gentleman who held dogma without being dogmatic, of a moral artist whose milieu was ironic humor, of a Catholic who did not find the justification of faith easy, but who believed that God so loved the world that he gave his only son for its redemption."[12] Such interpretations, however, can only be built from the evidence of his polyphonic texts that ironically and humorously undercut one another. Certainly, Chaucer's knowledge of the Christian Bible was extensive, as evident from his many scriptural allusions.[13] In this chapter I do not explore Chaucer's religious beliefs or his relationship with Christianity but rather the narrative effects of his depictions of God's potential carnality, those that queer the meaning of divine love by positing it in insistently human terms that reimagine the teleological presumptions of Christian unity with the divine. Within Chaucer's fictions, these depictions of an erotic God trouble the border between the anagogical and the allegorical because, in many instances, the call to contemplate God's love becomes entangled with his narratives' various other themes and plotlines that veer away from issues of spirituality while simultaneously hypothesizing the possibility of God's sexual desire for the humans he has created. In *Legend of Good Women* and the *Parson's Tale*, two texts rarely analyzed in tandem, Chaucer hypothesizes the potential of a God unbound by his eroticism and sensuality. These texts are divergent in theme and structure—a dream vision *qua* apologia for antifeminism in *Legend of Good Women*, a moral treatise on penitence in the *Parson's Tale*—yet they unite in their reflections on the nature of

---

12. Ruth Ames, *God's Plenty: Chaucer's Christian Humanism* (Chicago: Loyola University Press, 1984), 2.

13. Chaucer's scriptural references are catalogued and explored in Lawrence Besserman's *Chaucer and the Bible* (New York: Garland, 1988) and *Chaucer's Biblical Poetics* (Norman: University of Oklahoma Press, 1998). See also David Jeffrey, ed., *Chaucer and Scriptural Tradition* (Ottawa: University of Ottawa Press, 1984).

God and his sensuality. In the fabliau humor of Chaucer's *Miller's Tale* and *Wife of Bath's Prologue*, the possibility of an erotic God enhances the sexual play of the narratives, positing the Divine as equally invested in sexuality (and sexual farce) as the narratives' earthly protagonists. In the *Second Nun's Tale*, readers witness Chaucer's allegorical yet frank depiction of human consummation with an erotic God, as the Transcendent physically ravishes Cecilia during her martyrdom for love. To conceive of one's love for God, whether in the Middle Ages or today, one must do so in human terms, for human terms are the only terms we have. Chaucer both exploits and obfuscates the queer narrative possibilities of loving a loving God, alternately reveling in and resisting the often graphic amorousness at play in pondering God and his bounteous eroticism.

LOVING GOD, LOVING TRANSGRESSION

As language can never fully illuminate the Divine, so too must any attempt at an experiential epistemology of the Divine falter due to the limits of human perception, and Chaucer addresses faith's inherent uncertainties in the opening lines of the *Legend of Good Women*. Pondering the foretold pleasures of heaven and pains of hell while introducing his surreal dream vision, Chaucer as narrator affirms religious belief while simultaneously contemplating the lack of empirical evidence to support its claims:

> A thousand tymes have I herd men telle
> That ther ys joy in hevene and peyne in helle,
> And I acorde wel that it ys so;
> But, natheles, yet wot I wel also
> That ther nis noon dwellyng in this contree
> That eyther hath in hevene or helle ybe,
> Ne may of hit noon other weyes witen
> But as he hath herd seyd or founde it writen;
> For by assay ther may no man it preve.
> But God forbede but men shulde leve
> Wel more thing then men han seen with ye!
> Men shal not wenen every thing a lye
> But yf himself yt seeth or elles dooth;
> For, God wot, thing is never the lasse sooth,
> Thogh every wight ne may it nat ysee.
> Bernard the monk ne saugh nat all, pardee! (*LGW* F.1–16)

These lines sketch the epistemological crisis inherent in faith, in that empirical evidence is lacking and so believers must rely on the authority of Scripture and the exegetical tradition to answer questions that are otherwise unanswerable. It is generally agreed that Chaucer's source for these lines is Jean Froissart's *Le Joli Buisson de jonece*, but whereas Froissart's lyric speaker ponders the unlikelihood of discovering the Fountain of Youth and then contrasts this chimerical vision with the truth of his Christian faith, Chaucer's narrator considers the impossibility of confirming religious doctrine.[14] As the tension between earnest and game defines Chaucer's *Canterbury Tales* (and as this tension disrupts interpretive efforts regarding the dynamics of the tale-telling contest), a similar tension between faith and experience invigorates Chaucer's attempts to depict the Divine in the *Legend of Good Women*, in that the narrator upholds the tenets of faith ("I acorde wel") while acknowledging the voices who demand experiential evidence. Chaucer begins four of these sixteen lines with the conjunction *but*, and this syndetic style signals opposing positions in the narrator's internal monologue in which he ponders the possibility of faith without evidence. Indeed, Chaucer's narrators raise similar points concerning the necessity of a divine epistemology in a variety of other narrative circumstances, such as when Antigone in *Troilus and Criseyde* muses, "Men moste axe at seyntes if it is / Aught fair in hevene (Why? For they kan telle), / And axen fendes is it foul in helle" (2.894–96). Sounding a similar note, the fiend in the *Friar's Tale* endorses the necessity of experiencing damnation in the afterlife to comprehend its mysteries:

"Come there thee nedeth nat of me to leere,
For thou shalt, by thyn owene experience,
Konne in a chayer rede of this sentence
Bet than Virgile, while he was on lyve,
Or Dant also." (3.1516–20)

---

14. The relevant lines from *Le Joli buisson de jonece* read: "Jai oy aparler souvent / De le fontainne de jouvent / Ossi de pieres invisibles / Mes ce sont coses impossibles / Car onques je ne vi cheli / Foy que doi a saint marcheli / Qui desist jai droit la este" ("Often I have heard men speak / Of the Fountain of Youth, / Also of invisible stones, / But these are impossibilities, / For never have I met anyone, / By the faith I owe Saint Marcellin, / Who said: 'I was actually there'" (Jean Froissart, *An Anthology of Narrative and Lyric Poetry*, ed. and trans. Kristen Figg, with R. Barton Palmer [New York: Routledge, 2001], 296–97, lines 786–91). After dismissing the wondrous but unconfirmed fantasy of a Fountain of Youth, Froissart's narrator "thanks God with folded hands" for imparting spiritual truths.

This is not to state that Chaucer suffers from a crisis of faith—it is the texts, not the author, who are under examination here—but that his narratives reveal the fault lines of faith and experience, in which texts teach of but cannot wholly portray the Divine.

This passage from *Legend of Good Women*, as well as the similar passages from *Troilus and Criseyde* and the *Friar's Tale*, suggests that to be human is to experience doubt, that the mysteries of the Divine must always remain mysteries, and such is the case with Chaucer's hazy depictions of God's erotic nature. Along with the impossibility of an experientially religious epistemology, Chaucer also highlights the ways in which religious tenets solicit their own erotic transgressions. When the Parson argues in his *Tale* that God rules over human sensuality, he exposes God's failure to govern human eroticism effectively. The Parson outlines a hierarchical relationship of lordship, in which God wields authority over humanity by placing his deputies of reason and sensuality in control of the unruly human body: "For it is sooth that God, and resoun, and sensualitee, and the body of man been so ordeyned that everich of thise foure thynges sholde have lordshipe over that oother, / as thus: God sholde have lordshipe over resoun, and resoun over sensualitee, and sensualitee over the body of man" (10.261–62). The Parson proceeds to observe that sensuality is the weak link in this chain of dominion. Although the Middle English word *sensualitee* refers primarily to the human senses and their ability to decode external stimuli, the word's secondary meanings as lust and passion bleed into its primary meaning,[15] and the Parson argues that the rebellious nature of *sensualitee* disrupts God's hierarchical dominion over the human body: "For sensualitee rebelleth thanne agayns resoun, and by that way leseth resoun the lordshipe over sensualitee and over the body" (10.265). The Parson then blames reason's failures to discipline sensuality for causing humanity's fall: "For right as resoun is rebel to God, right so is bothe sensualitee rebel to resoun and the body also" (10.266). Perpetually engaged in rebellion, sensuality subverts humanity's relationship to God, leading sinners to bodily pleasures rather than to spiritual truths.

At the same time, one might well wonder, why is reason derelict in its divinely ordained responsibilities? Reason's failure to discipline sensuality tacitly suggests God's failure to discipline reason, and in this man-

---

15. The *Middle English Dictionary* defines *sensualitee* as "(a) The natural capacity for receiving physical sensation understood as an inferior power of the soul concerned with the body; (b) physical desire or appetite, lust; a sinful, passionate emotion; also, lustful, sinful nature; (c) the body."

ner religion makes possible its subversion in that spiritual transgressions are called forth by the very religious prohibitions that forbid them. The logical, if unintended, extension of the Parson's argument is that God desires humanity to succumb to erotic transgressions from which he fails to protect them. For while the Parson's reasoning mirrors that of medieval theologians, it distorts such teachings by obscurely, if not incorrectly, reflecting their precepts. With words akin to the Parson's, Thomas Aquinas believes that "man's reason is right, in so far as it is ruled by the Divine Will, the first and supreme rule. Wherefore that which a man does by God's will and in obedience to this command, is not contrary to right reason, though it may seem contrary to the general order of reason."[16] However, in his discourse inspired by Aquinas yet derivative in its theology, the Parson allows the possibility, through its devaluation of divine authority into statements expressed in the subjunctive mood, that God loses control of reason and sensuality. If even God cannot control reason and sensuality, how can a Christian avoid sins of the flesh and other transgressions? Judith Butler argues that sin and guilt are preconditions of religious identity and experience: "This readiness to accept guilt to gain a purchase on identity is linked to a highly religious scenario of a nominating call that comes from God and that constitutes the subject by appealing to a need for the law, an original guilt that the law promises to assuage through the conferral of identity."[17] Slavoj Žižek sees in this dynamic the "perverse core of Christianity" and explains its function in his reading of Paul's first epistle to the Corinthians: "Paul basically says: 'obey the laws as if you are not obeying them,' [and] this means precisely that *we should suspend the obscene libidinal investment in the Law, the investment on account of which the Law generates/solicits its own transgression.*"[18] From Butler's and Žižek's readings of spiritual desire, transgression is the precondition to religious belief, the necessary intervention of the Law into the believer's sense of identity that creates the religious subject through and of this necessary repudiation of that which is to be believed, and, indeed, loved.

---

16. Thomas Aquinas, *The Summa Theologica of St. Thomas Aquinas, Second Part of the Second Part, QQ. CXLI–CLXX*, trans. Fathers of the English Dominican Province (New York: Benziger Brothers, 1921), 136.

17. Judith Butler, *The Psychic Life of Power: Theories in Subjection* (Stanford, CA: Stanford University Press, 1997), 109. In this analysis, Butler responds to Louis Althusser's theories of interpellation as explored in his "Ideology and Ideological State Apparatuses (Notes towards an Investigation)," in *Lenin and Philosophy and Other Essays*, trans. Ben Brewster (New York: Monthly Review, 1971), 127–88.

18. Slavoj Žižek, *The Puppet and the Dwarf: The Perverse Core of Christianity* (Cambridge, MA: MIT Press, 2003), 113; his italics.

For one to obtain a stake in religious identity, the law demands libidinal (and often blatantly eroticized) investments in its power, and the Parson's interpretation of sensuality constructs God as the Law generating concomitant transgressions, for any erotic transgression within this system must be queer, in that it subverts the very order that calls it forth from the precondition of sin. As Žižek further notes, "Pauline love is not the cancellation or destructive negation of the Law, but its accomplishment in the sense of 'sublation,' where the Law is retained through its very suspension, as a subordinate (potential) moment of a higher actual unity."[19] This dialectic double-crossing of desire—in which eroticism impels transgressions, yet transgressions facilitate the reconstruction and further maintenance of the Law—implicates God within an erotic system that can only function through a queer desire for transgression. Žižek's analysis responds to the following exhortation of Paul:

> unusquisque in quo vocatus est fratres in hoc maneat apud Deum. . . . hoc itaque dico fratres, tempus breve est, reliquum est ut qui habent uxores tamquam non habentes sint. Et qui flent tamquam non flentes, et qui gaudent tamquam non gaudentes, et qui emunt tamquam non possidentes. Et qui utuntur hoc mundo tamquam non utantur, praeterit enim figura huius mundi. (I Corinthians 7:24, 29–31)

> Brethren, let every man, where he was called, therein abide with God. . . . This therefore I say, brethren; the time is short; it remaineth that they also who have wives, be as if they had none; And they that weep, as though they wept not, and they that rejoice, as if they rejoiced not; and they that buy, as though they possessed not. And they that use this world, as if they used it not: for the fashion of this world passeth away.

As Dale Martin argues of this passage, "Paul does not speak of sexuality but of sexual actions and desires. And whenever the subject arises, Paul treats sex as potentially dangerous. If it cannot be completely avoided, it must be carefully controlled and regulated so as to avoid pollution and cosmic invasion."[20] In Paul's demand for those who have wives to live as though they had none, as well as in his subsequent calls for self-abnegation, he rejects conjugal coupling as a diversion from the Divine, as a tran-

---

19. Ibid., 112.
20. Dale Martin, *The Corinthian Body* (New Haven, CT: Yale University Press, 1995), 211; see also Craig Keener, *1–2 Corinthians* (Cambridge: Cambridge University Press, 2005), for contextualization of Paul's commentary on sex (61–72).

sient and earthly distraction from eternal bliss, yet this eroticism that must be sacrificed marks the very possibility of the potential sacrifice: one must have what must be lost. The Law calls for these investments of desires sexual and otherwise, engagements of the self through and of the body, yet by obtaining such purchase over the human sinner, religious belief encourages the transgressions that preclude its attainment. Furthermore, the latent eroticization inherent in virtually any hierarchy—in which the ruler and the ruled rally for power, all the while enjoying the power play as much as any pleasure to be derived—leaks out into the open when the top of the hierarchy transgresses its own dictates. While such an interpretation of the Parson's sermon may necessitate reading against the grain—surely the Parson, if one hypothesized his ability to do so, would disagree with Žižek's analysis of the law and its regulatory effects—other moments in the Chaucerian canon visualize not merely the pleasures of human sensuality but the Divine partaking in them.

From this perspective, it is not surprising to see that God does not rule over his own sensuality in Chaucer's fictions but instead seeks bodily transgressions with mortal lovers. Subsequent to the narrator's discussion of faith's epistemological crises at the beginning of the *Legend of Good Women*, God is presented as a potential lover to humanize in explicitly amorous terms the unknowable mysteries of the Divine. The description of God's libidinal reaction to Dido stresses the physicality animating divine amatory desires:

> This fresshe lady, of the cite queene,
> Stod in the temple in hire estat real,
> So rychely and ek so fayr withal,
> So yong, so lusty, with hire eyen glade,
> That, if that God, that hevene and erthe made,
> Wolde han a love, for beaute and goodnesse,
> And womanhod, and trouthe, and semelynesse,
> Whom shulde he loven but this lady swete?
> Ther nys no woman to hym half so mete. (*LGW* 1035–43)

The unabashed eroticism of this scene demands that readers reimagine the Christian God as one actively seeking human lovers. One could posit that Chaucer's use of the word *God* in this passage refers to Jupiter, or to the God of Love who figures so prominently in the *Legend of Good Women's* frame narrative, or to another classical deity; F. N. Robinson argues, however, that "the audacity of the comparison is not to be explained away on the ground that Jupiter was in Chaucer's mind or that Virgil compares Dido to Diana. Medieval taste differed from modern in speaking of sacred persons and things."[21] It should be noted as well that Chaucer phrases this passage in the subjunctive mood, describing not God's actual desires but his hypothetical yearning for Dido should he choose a human female as his divine consort. Speaking imaginatively of God's eroticism, Chaucer protects himself with the freedoms of the hypothetical, yet within this envisioning of God's erotic desires, Dido represents his ideal mate primarily due to her physical allure. Human *sensualitee*, which the Parson believes to be under the authority of reason and God, here rules God himself, with the passages focusing so intently on the visual pleasures afforded by Dido's beauty. Divine desire and libidinal transgression conflict yet cannot overrule each other: if the Divine sexually transgresses in this moment of attraction, it is his desires that stage the transgression and the law that creates the transgression. Dido's beauty fractures the law and its prohibitions, for she reveals the erotic core of the Divine that regulates human eroticism, but only to fall to similar temptation. The narrator's description of Dido—"That fayrer was than is the bryghte sonne" (1006)—is initially linked to the passion she incites in human lovers—"Of kynges and of lordes so desyred / That al the world hire beaute hadde yfyred, / She stod so wel in every wightes grace" (1012–14)—but human kings, the reader soon learns, are merely earthly symbols of the King of all who would succumb just as easily under the sway of her beauty.

Indeed, within the fictions of the *Legend of Good Women*, Chaucer reimagines the very meaning of hagiography, as the subtitle of his dream vision—*The Seintes Legende of Cupide*—links saintly suffering with women's amorous disappointments. The blending of classical mythology with Christianity is also apparent in the God of Love's description of his mother as "Seynt Venus" (F 388), in which the licentious passion of Venus is resignified as a Christian exemplar of divine eroticism. Many of the eponymous exemplary women, including Cleopatra, Thisbe, Dido, Hypsipyle, Medea, and Lucretia, are referred to as martyrs in the incipits of their legends,[22] and so the generic resignification of classical legend into amatory hagiography tacitly relocates at least some of these non-Christian women into the eternal pleasures of heaven, for where else do martyrs go upon their death, except to their perpetual reward for suffering such

---

21. F. N. Robinson, ed., *The Works of Geoffrey Chaucer*, 2nd ed. (Boston: Houghton Mifflin, 1961), 848 n; qtd. in Larry Benson, *Riverside Chaucer*, 1068 n.

22. Ariadne, Philomela, Phyllis, and Hypermnestra are not labeled as martyrs; instead, Chaucer refers to the legendary aspect of their narratives.

cruel torments? Whereas Ariadne is stellified into the astrological "signe of Taurus" (2223), suggesting that she remains in a pagan universe in her afterlife, Lucretia, although a pre-Christian woman, becomes a "seynt" with an accompanying feast day (1871). If God's response to Dido is any indication of his sexual interest in other human females, the beauty of these and other legendary women should be sufficient to catch his eyes (as his erotic attentions to Cecilia in the *Second Nun's Tale* likewise illustrate, as I address in the final section of this chapter).

In terms of their literary and aesthetic effect, in many instances Chaucer's project of highlighting God's eroticism drives his fictions to the teleological pleasure of a failed union with God, for any human effort to limn the Divine must end in failure to capture his fully resplendent glory. As Žižek argues, the mimetic failure that is constitutive of art and literature illuminates how desire creates unresolved aporias, which create a signifying chain predicated on failure that paradoxically leads one to the Divine:

> It is through this very failure to show its "true reference in reality" directly that a poem sublates its "pathological" idiosyncrasy, and generates its properly *universal* artistic impact. This shift, this sudden recognition of how the very obstacle preventing us from reaching the Thing Itself enables us to identify directly with it (with the deadlock at its heart), defines the properly *Christian* form of identification: it is ultimately *identification with a failure*—and, consequently, since the object of identification is God, God Himself must be shown to fail.[23]

For Žižek, literature's failure to achieve mimetic perfection, to create "real life" on the page, generates its artistic meaning, but this aestheticism is built upon absence and failure. As medieval exegetes realized the impossibility of discussing the Divine without tropological damage done to the idea of the ineffable, so too must any attempt to depict God end in failure. Thus, to identify with the failure of literature is to confront the failure of God but nonetheless to be brought to God: by contemplating the impossibility of knowing the Divine, readers are granted access to the Divine through the circuitous and queer pleasures of textual failures. And, indeed, most critics agree that the *Legend of Good Women* ends in failure, with the "Legend of Hypermnestra" concluding with the promise of a moral that never comes: "This tale is seyd for this conclusioun" (2723), the narrator proclaims, as the text then lapses into silence. As

---

23. Slavoj Žižek, *The Puppet and the Dwarf*, 89; his italics.

no moral is offered to Chaucer's stories of wronged women, their meaning can only be conjectured, which undoes the moral certitude expected in these hagiographies on the border between the secularly and spiritually erotic. Similarly, too, as Chaucer's depiction of God's desire for Dido calls forth the transgressions of desire that lead to God, Chaucer's narrator establishes himself as the font of earthly transgressions that would lead one to him as an earthly participant in erotic play. In his flirtatious close to the "Legend of Phyllis," he volunteers to solace women who have suffered betrayal: "Syn yit this day men may ensaumple se; / And trusteth, as in love, no man but me" (2560–61). As God's attraction to Dido models the eroticism inherent in Christian love, Chaucer establishes himself as an exemplar of its more earthly enactments, promising to provide sexual solace that could perhaps lay the foundation for a spiritual journey: once the body and sensuality transgress against reason and God, the return of reason and of God himself cannot be far behind.

CHAUCER'S FABLIAU HUMOR AND DIVINE EROTICS: GOD'S *PRYVETEE* AND PIMPING

All of Chaucer's fabliaux feature religious characters, themes, or subtexts. The *Miller's Tale* depicts dueling clerks who employ their knowledge of the Bible to advance their sexual agendas, and the *Reeve's Tale* satirizes the erotic transgressions of the priesthood in the parentage of Symkyn's wife. The *Summoner's Tale* and *Shipman's Tale* respectively feature a friar and a monk as their erotic antagonists, and the sexual rivalry at the heart of the *Merchant's Tale* reaches its narrative climax in a garden scene parodying the Fall of Adam and Eve. Chaucer's consistency in coupling religious themes with fabliau humor unites the sacred and profane, and in so doing, these tales humorously rail against the hypocrisies of the Church through their depictions of lascivious clerks and clergy. But as the clergy are God's representatives on earth, so too does God himself become a target of Chaucer's raunchy humor, as he questions the meaning of God's eroticism in the *Miller's Tale* and in some suggestive passages of the *Wife of Bath's Prologue*.

In its treatment of God's eroticism, the *Miller's Tale* embellishes the vulgar humor of Nicholas's earthly passion for Alison with crude spiritual import by repeatedly addressing the issue of God's *pryvetee*. In its surface significations, *pryvetee* refers simply to one's secrets and private affairs, but Chaucer frequently uses the word to refer to buttocks and genitalia. In the *Summoner's Tale*, Thomas whets the unctuous friar's pecuniary appetite by urging him to "grope wel bihynde / Byneth my buttok" so that he may find a "thyng ... hyd in pryvetee" (3.2143), and in the *Monk's Tale*, Julius Caesar modestly covers his genitals while dying: "His mantel over his hypes caste he, / For no man sholde seen his privetee" (7.2714–15). In his *Prologue*, the Miller similarly refers to *pryvetee*, but he obfuscates its referent by connecting it to the Divine:

> An housbonde shal nat been inquisityf
> Of Goddes pryvetee, nor of his wyf.
> So he may fynde Goddes foyson there,
> Of the remenant nedeth nat enquere. (1.3163–66)

Where, readers may wonder, precisely is the "there" that hides "Goddes foyson," his plenty? The male auditors to whom the Miller directs his words must discover the appropriate "there" to achieve their reward of God's bounty,[24] but they must simultaneously embrace ignorance regarding the meaning and the very possibility of knowledge necessary to bring them to rapture. Readers may reasonably conclude within the context of Chaucerian fabliaux that the Miller's "there" directs the male listener to pursue his pleasures in a woman's vagina, and this locus of pleasure surely stands as a site of "God's foyson" within the heteroerotic framework of the tale; nonetheless, the coupling of God's and women's *pryvetees* posits God's genitals as a site of mystery and pleasure as well, and it is likewise plausible within the crude humor of fabliau that one would find God's plenty through his divine yet unimaginable genitalia. God's genitals are linked to ignorance in these lines, limning the divinely erotic as a site beyond human knowledge yet instrumental for obtaining earthly pleasure.

This double entendre of *pryvetee* as a matter of secrecy and as a code word for genitalia continues throughout the *Miller's Tale*, as John the carpenter proclaims, in his paean to ignorance, "Men sholde nat knowe of Goddes pryvetee. / Ye, blessed be alwey a lewed man" (1.3454–55). Moreover, Nicholas, when admonishing John to prepare for the purported flood, also refers to God's *pryvetee*: "Axe nat why, for though thou aske me, / I wol nat tellen Goddes pryvetee" (1.3557–58). Much like the pun on *queynte* that signals Nicholas's groping lasciviousness for Allison, as

---

24. In referring to the Miller's male auditors, I acknowledge the fact that, except for the Wife of Bath, Prioress, and Second Nun, the Canterbury pilgrims are men. The erotics of the *Miller's Tale* are conceived within a paradigm of masculine pursuit and female conquest, even as this paradigm is subverted in the tale's resolution.

reduced to her vagina (1.3275–76), Chaucer's play on *pryvetee* illuminates and obscures his depiction of the Divine. Language fails in the gap between earthly and divine discourses because the word *pryvetee* cannot be cleansed of its erotic meanings. The inconceivable image of God's genitals thus circulates throughout the text, an invisible signifier of divine eroticism that remains virtually unimaginable yet that is explicitly linked both to Nicholas's quest for Alison's *queynte* and to questions concerning the proper purview of human knowledge. John and Nicholas agree that matters of *pryvetee* should be preserved from prying eyes—John in his professed and self-satisfied ignorance, and Nicholas in his manipulation of theological *pryvetee* for his sexual advantage. Despite the vast differences between the two men, their relationships to divine mysteries share a sense of their unplumbed depths, with Nicholas exploiting the mysteries of which John is proudly ignorant.

Several scholars, including Frederick Biggs, Laura Howes, Louise Bishop, and Karma Lochrie, address Chaucer's references to God's *pryvetee* and the intersection of the erotic and the Divine in the *Miller's Tale*. Biggs and Howes read *pryvetee* as "the limits to human knowledge, primarily of God but also of other humans," such that the term's confused references "both to human genitalia and to divine secrets" parodically allude to God's encounter with Moses on Mount Sinai, in which the thunder that greets Moses (Exodus 19:16) finds its Chaucerian echo in the flatulent "thonder-dent" (1.3807) that greets Absolon's nose.[25] Bishop examines the intersection of Alison's and God's *pryvetees*, positing that the "*Miller's Tale* gives its readers the mystery and power of unknowable woman: the mystery of her orifices, utterly confused even to the ostensibly initiated, and the mystery of her power, situated, unlike (or like) the divine's, in a triumphant 'Tehee.'"[26] Focusing on the ways in which the tale's erotic escapades merge with its concern over divine secrecy, Lochrie concludes that "both the Miller and Chaucer want to create the secret in order to reveal it and allay masculine fears that surround the feminized secret in medieval culture generally."[27] These perceptive readings of divine erotics in the *Miller's Tale* highlight the epistemological crises inherent in contemplating the Divine due to the many mysteries of faith,

---

25. Frederick Biggs and Laura Howes, "Theophany in the *Miller's Tale*," *Medium Aevum* 65.2 (1996): 269–79, at 269.

26. Louise Bishop, "'Of Goddes pryvetee nor of his wyf': Confusion of Orifices in Chaucer's *Miller's Tale*," *Texas Studies in Literature and Language* 44.3 (2002): 231–46, at 241.

27. Karma Lochrie, *Covert Operations: The Medieval Uses of Secrecy* (Philadelphia: University of Pennsylvania Press, 1999), 169.

especially given the thematic treatment of this issue in a fabliau ostensibly far removed from theological concerns. Because the Divine can only be perceived through that which he reveals, and because the Law instantiates itself through the required transgression that enables it, the *Miller's Tale* cannot reveal the Divine without tackling the mysteries of faith, even as it evinces little interest in pursuing them other than for their humorous potential within the realm of sexual farce. A fabliau requires some sort of transgression against cultural norms to build its humor, and, as Butler and Žižek outline, religious belief must likewise encode transgression into its foundations. From these twin perspectives, God's *pryvetee* in the *Miller's Tale* is virtually a prerequisite to the sexual farce unfolding, for it establishes the necessity of erotic transgression against a Law that, as the Parson makes clear, is itself always already transgressed.

As the *Miller's Tale* unfolds, God's eroticism, his *pryvetee*, becomes intimately connected with both human eroticism and human spirituality, as well as their confused interplay. Nicholas's and Absolon's pursuit of intercourse with Alison anagogically symbolizes what they should pursue in their vocation as clerks: transcendent union with the Divine. In pursuing the mysteries of women—a mystery that is inversely and graphically exposed to Nicholas when he "caughte [Alison] by the queynte" (1.3276)—Nicholas reveals his focus on sexual pleasures rather than spiritual mysteries. But it is surely telling that his knowledge of the Divine assists in his pursuit of Alison's genitalia, whether he distorts biblical authority (as in his rewriting of the story of Noah's Flood) or recites it accurately (as in his quotation of Ecclesiasticus).[28] Indeed, in his admonitions to John in preparation for the supposed flood, he regulates his landlord's sexual activity with Alison by usurping God's erotic authority over the sex lives of husband and wife:

"Be wel avysed on that ilke nyght
That we ben entred into shippes bord,
That noon of us ne speke nat a word,
Ne clepe, ne crie, but be in his preyere;
For it is Goddes owene heeste deere.

---

28. Nicholas cites Ecclesiasticus to convince John to obey his commands, declaring, "Werk al by conseil, and thou shalt nat rewe" (1.3530), which echoes the biblical injunction "sine consilio nihil facias et post factum non paeniteberis" (32:24; "do thou nothing without counsel, and thou shalt not repent when thou hast done"). Note that Nicholas attributes these words from Ecclesiasticus to Solomon, but this mistake was a rather learned one in the Middle Ages. For analysis of this biblical passage throughout Chaucer's corpus, see Curt Bühler, "Wirk alle thyng by conseil," *Speculum* 24 (1949): 410–12.

>   Thy wyf and thou moote hange fer atwynne;
>   For that bitwixe yow shal be no synne,
>   Namoore in lookyng than ther shal in deede.
>   This ordinance is seyd. Go, God thee speede!" (1.3584–92)

Nicholas refers in these lines to the traditional anti-erotic view that intercourse did not occur on Noah's ark, as expressed by such ministers as John Mirk: "And whan alle were browthe in, as God bad Noe, and hys thre sonnus gon into the schyppe be hemselfe, and Noes wyf and hys sones wyues be hemselfe, for encheson that in tyme of aflyxion men schuldon abstyne hem fro cowpul of wommen—so, whan thei were alle in, God closyd the dore aftur hem wythouteforth."[29] By alluding to this anti-erotic tradition, Nicholas prepares John to deny himself the pleasure of "God's plenty," employing biblical traditions and interpretations to coerce John into ceding sexual authority over his wife. Nicholas also encourages John to accept him within the parameters of his marriage when he declares, "And thanne shul we be lordes al oure lyf / Of al the world, as Noe and his wyf" (1.3581–82). Following the logic of these words, John must reconceptualize the parameters of traditional marriage to incorporate his rival within its postdeluvian bonds, granting Nicholas shared lordship with him and shared sexual pleasure with his wife. Citing God's prohibitions against sexual activity as a means to access sexual activity, Nicholas exploits the potential of religious doctrine to solicit its own transgressions. As Žižek argues, "the properly Christian Redemption is not simply the undoing of the Fall, but *stricto sensu* its repetition. . . . Adam's Fall (and the subsequent instauration of the Law) was a simple contingency—that is to say, that, if Adam had chosen obedience to God, there would have been no sin and no Law: *there would also have been no love.*"[30] For Nicholas, the reenactment of transgression guarantees the erotic pleasures he seeks, rendering and degrading the love created from Divinity into its most carnal and crude expression.

In contrast to Nicholas, who manipulates the Bible for erotic gain, John misunderstands the transgressive role of the Divine and thus cannot exploit biblical knowledge for sexual pleasure, as evident in his misreadings of biblical and biblically inspired texts. John's pronounced ignorance of religious teachings, such that he cannot discern the falsehood in Nicholas's prophecy of a flood (which contradicts God's promise in Genesis

---

29. John Mirk, *John Mirk's Festial: Edited from British Library MS Cotton Claudius A.II*, ed. Susan Powell (Oxford: Oxford University Press, 2009), 69.

30. Slavoj Žižek, *The Puppet and the Dwarf*, 81.

9:11), contrasts with his assumed air of wisdom through ignorance when he declares to Nicholas, "Ye, blessed be alwey a lewed man / That noght but oonly his bileve kan!" (1.3455–56). John must fail to preserve his wife's fidelity for the fabliau's humor to climax—that is, the narrative climax depends on his failure to climax with his wife—and his ignorance of the Divine contributes to his ensuing sexual punishment, despite that he models the very ignorance of God's *pryvetee* that the Miller thematically endorses. The *Miller's Tale* extols ignorance as the precondition to enjoying God's plenty, yet the character who epitomizes such ignorance fails to protect his erotic interests. In accord with Žižek's theorization of the ways in which the Law solicits its own transgressions, in the *Miller's Tale* Nicholas succeeds in bedding Alison while John loses sexual access to her inversely in accord with their propensity to transgress the Law. Within the carnivalesque world of Chaucerian fabliau, such an inversion is to be expected, but what is nonetheless surprising is that the Law functions so congruently with fabliau humor: the Law provides the foundation against which the carnivalesque humor of fabliau reacts, yet, once again, the Law depends on such transgressions not merely to reassert its authority but to reassert the transgressions that encode its power further.

As a parish clerk, Absolon should follow his vocational interest in the Bible, yet Chaucer stresses that this clerk, as part of his seductive repertoire, pursues avocational pastimes that merge his religious and erotic pursuits. The many gifts he sends to Alison—"pyment, meeth, and spiced ale, / And wafres, pipyng hoot out of the gleede" (1.3378–39)—allude to the wine and communion wafers of the Eucharist, thus substituting earthly pleasures for spiritual union with the Divine. Also, Absolon perceives his dramatic skills in mystery plays not as a means of sharing divine revelation with his audience but as a tactic for seducing John's wife:

> Somtyme, to shewe his lightnesse and maistrye,
> He pleyeth Herodes upon a scaffold hye.
> But what availleth hym as in this cas?
> She loveth so this hende Nicholas. (1.3383–86)

Absolon's dramatic skills fail to win him Alison's sexual interest, and his assumption of the role of Herod aligns him as the comic villain of the unfolding fabliau, one representing a petty, diminished avatar of one of Christianity's great antagonists. Stephen Knight suggests that many aspects of Absolon's characterization, including the erotic tone of the phrase "sensynge the wyves" (1.3341) in his initial portrait, reveal his tendency to exploit spirituality for sexual advantage.[31] In a similar vein, Absolon's plea to Alison at her window evokes imagery from the Song of Songs, which once again highlights his eagerness to exploit his faith for erotic pleasure:

> "What do ye, hony-comb, sweete Alisoun
> My faire bryd, my sweete cynamome?
> Awaketh, lemman myn, and speketh to me!
> Wel litel thynken ye upon my wo,
> That for youre love I swete ther I go.
> No wonder is thogh that I swelte and swete;
> I moorne as dooth a lamb after the tete.
> Ywis, lemman, I have swich love-longynge
> That lik a turtel trewe is my moornynge.
> I may nat ete na moore than a mayde." (1.3698–707)

Scholars including Nicolette Zeeman, R. E. Kaske, and Jesse Gellrich explore the allusions to the Song of Songs in this passage, particularly in its erotic lexicon of honeycombs, cinnamon, birds, and lambs.[32] The devolution of the sacred into the profane, while not surprising within the vulgar parameters of a Chaucerian fabliau, highlights the slipperiness of biblical erotics: because biblical erotics focus on bodily desire as they metaphorically stimulate spiritual desire, the body can never be dismissed from this allegorical consideration of physicality and instead depends upon the potential intermingling of bodies both heavenly and divine. This is not to hypothesize a crude one-to-one correspondence between Absolon and God through this fabliau reconfiguration of the Song of Songs, but because this biblical text and its allegorical interpretations focus so intensely on the physical, the devolution of this spiritual ideal to Chaucer's fabliau is not a particularly long journey: the fabliau is simply more candid about human sexuality than most exegetical attempts to tame the insistent eroticism of the Song of Songs.[33]

---

31. Stephen Knight, "'Toward the fen': Church and Churl in Chaucer's Fabliaux," in *Chaucer and Religion*, ed. Helen Phillips and Helen Cooper (Cambridge: Brewer, 2010), 41–51, at 44.

32. Honeycombs appear in Song of Songs 5:1, cinnamon in 4:14, birds in 5:12, and lambs in 6:6. See Nicolette Zeeman, "The Gender of Song in Chaucer," *Studies in the Age of Chaucer* 29 (2007): 141–82; Jesse Gellrich, "The Parody of Medieval Music in the *Miller's Tale*," *Studies in English and Germanic Philology* 73 (1974): 176–88; and R. E. Kaske, "The Canticum canticorum in the *Miller's Tale*," *Studies in Philology* 59 (1962): 479–500.

33. Taming the carnality of the Song of Songs challenged medieval exegetes because it exploits earthly eroticism to enlighten spiritual pursuits, and, from this perspective, even

In this fabliau anti-quest, in which the *pryvetees* of both God and a man's wife have been declared taboo knowledge, Nicholas succeeds in fornicating with Alison, yet he is simultaneously punished for his sexual transgressions. The *Miller's Tale* lacks thematic consistency in its ending, for its opening admonition not to inquire of God's *pryvetee* declares that, through ignorance of God's eroticism, one will find sexual pleasure. Following the logic of these lines, it appears that John's ignorance should protect him from the erotic onslaught of the two young clerks, yet the tale concludes with a commonplace religious exhortation—"God save al the rowte!" (1.3854)—that humorously posits the availability of spiritual salvation to both sinners and those sinned against. Indeed, numerous characters appeal for God's mercy and salvation as the tale reaches its climax: Absolon proclaims, "so God me save" (1.3795); Nicholas cries, "Help, for Goddes herte!" (1.3815); and Nicholas and Alison accuse John of insanity, blaming him for the debacle that has befallen him and declaring that "he preyed hem, for Goddes love, / To sitten in the roof" (1.3838–39). These various exclamations carry little religious import, yet they retain God's presence in the tale's conclusion, most obviously to highlight the contrast between religious principles and fabliau humor but also to recall the matter of God's *pryvetee* and its interrelationship with human sexual pursuits. The Law not only establishes the preconditions that necessitate its transgressions, but these transgressions emerge in tandem with an impossible vision both of God's genitalia and of his plans for human salvation that neither knowledge nor ignorance can discover.

In regard to Nicholas's, Absolon's, and John's quests for sexual transcendence with Alison, the concluding humor of the *Miller's Tale* ironically arises from what God refuses to save this fraternal company: the three men are respectively punished for their erotic transgressions, with John cuckolded, Nicholas anally branded, and Absolon flatulently humiliated.[34] The possibility remains for God to save these men in a transcen-

---

Bernard of Clairvaux's allegorical interpretations of it can never be divorced from unsanctioned interpretation. Stephen Moore reads Bernard's interpretation of the Song of Songs and pierces through the homoerotic play that Bernard stifles but cannot quell, declaring that "if the allegorical reading of the Song is an insubordinate (if sublimated) performance of sex, and hence of gender, the rules that are thereby being transgressed are precisely those that the expositors themselves (monks, priests, and prelates) have undertaken to make and maintain" (*God's Beauty Parlor and Other Queer Spaces in and around the Bible* [Stanford, CA: Stanford University Press, 2001], 72).

34. Despite Alison's characterization of John as "so ful of jalousie" that she fears he will murder her if her affair is exposed (1.3294–96), her husband never displays any violent tendencies, even when Absolon courts her at their window (1.3364–70). John resists the

dent sense, but the tale's conclusion also highlights the arbitrariness of divine justice, as Alison eludes punishment for her sexual escapades. At the same time, the *Miller's Tale* foretold that Alison, through her own pursuit of spiritual enlightenment, would escape retribution due to her narrative alignment with Christ: "Thanne fil it thus, that to the paryssh chirche, / Cristes owene werkes for to wirche, / This goode wyf went on an haliday" (1.3307–9). Within the poem's carnivalesque erotics, Alison has indeed performed "Christ's own work," for the *pryvetee* of her vagina, which was allegorized as the equivalent of God's *pryvetee*, has united the men in pursuit of spiritual and sexual mysteries beyond their ken. The poem's closing appeal to God's mercy tacitly proposes that all sinners are worthy of salvation, as it also points to the mysteries of salvation, which must remain as much a matter of divine *pryvetee* as the perplexing issue of God's genitalia, an image that can only be imagined in human terms and that surfaces repeatedly in the tale to contrast divine knowledge with the very earthly desire of many men to experience erotic pleasure through a woman's genitals.

Similar to the *Miller's Tale* as it repeatedly intersects God's *pryvetee* with Nicholas's and Absolon's insistent desires to fornicate with Alison, the *Wife of Bath's Prologue* exploits the amorous potential in divine eroticism. Alison of Bath encourages readers to laugh as she profanely reimagines the meanings of sacred texts, and the bulk of her argument reinterprets the Christian Bible to suit her sexual worldview, including her professed confusion over the moral of Jesus's conversation with the Samaritan woman (3.14–25), her delight in the bigamy recounted in the biblical stories of Solomon, Lamech, Abraham, and Jacob (3.35–58), and her passionate rebuttal of Paul's anti-erotic polemics (3.61–90). Alison mostly refrains from considering the issue of divine eroticism itself, but in perhaps her most blasphemous passage, she envisions Jesus as facilitating earthly intercourse:

> I nyl envye no virginitee.
> Lat hem be breed of pured whete-seed,
> And lat us wyves hoten barly-breed;
> And yet with barly-breed, Mark telle kan,
> Oure Lord Jhesu refresshed many a man. (3.142–46)

---

temptations of violence and sin, but in marrying a young woman, he casts himself as the *senex amans* who, in the world of fabliau, is punished for his inherent foolishness in marrying a young bride.

By portraying Jesus as virtually a pimp, one who oversees the "refreshment" of men, Alison resignifies the miracle of the loaves from its original denotation as physical hunger into the unbridled eroticism of sexually unsatisfied wives. The gospel accounts of this miracle depict the famished crowd's bodily need to symbolize their spiritual need: the loaves sate their desire for earthly sustenance, but this experience then catalyzes a deeper spiritual longing for God. Kevin Madigan records of the allegorical symbolism of the Miraculous Feeding of the 5,000 that "No later than Hilary of Poitiers, the pericope [of this miracle] was interpreted as an allegory of the multiplication of the letter of the Law (the five loaves being equated with the five books of the Pentateuch) into the heavenly food of the spiritual senses."[35]

In Alison's recasting of this miracle as sexual through her pun on *refresshed*—a word whose sexual connotations she exploits earlier in her celebration of Solomon's active sex life (4.35–38)—she corporealizes the human body into bread and expands her bawdy wordplay further. The bread that may become the Bread of Life through transubstantiation is the female body in its unchecked eroticism, but it is an eroticism that Jesus himself unleashes through the polysemous play of allusion and allegory when he proclaims, "ego sum panis vitae, qui veniet ad me non esuriet, et qui credit in me non sitiet umquam" (John 6:35; "I am the bread of life: he that cometh to me shall not hunger: and he that believeth in me shall never thirst"). As Alison demonstrates, the symbolism of bread can be readily resignified into the sordid erotics of prostitution and pimping, and, due to Jesus's metaphoric construction of himself as bread, Jesus himself symbolizes both the pimp and the female prostitute in Alison's refashioning of the gospels. In her call for sexual pleasure that is simultaneously earthly and divine, Alison dismantles the categories of body and spirit, uniting both in a shared transgression of the Law that the Law itself enables. Within this polyvalent sexual play, God's eroticism is implicated with Christian salvation, such that human copulation and eternal redemption are virtually interchangeable.

Chaucer's fabliau sensibility encourages readers to enjoy the humorous potential of God's *pryvetee* and Christ's pimping, yet the humor of these moments cannot be sterilized of their theological ramifications. Imagining divine *pryvetee* and pimping, as the Miller and Wife of Bath demand of their audiences, punctures the immaculate image of the Divine while

---

35. Kevin Madigan, *Olivi and the Interpretation of Matthew in the High Middle Ages* (Notre Dame, IN: University of Notre Dame Press, 2003), 124. The miracle of the loaves appears in each of the four gospels: Matthew 14:13–21, Mark 6:30–44, Luke 9:10–17, and John 6:1–14.

limning the power of transgression to bring readers to a new relationship with the Divine. Readers may dismiss such fabliau antics as crude illustrations of divine love, rendering grotesquely physical the image of Divine perfection, yet by inviting readers to confront the inherent transgression in conceiving any image of God within human terms, these transgressions spark reflection and contemplation that can reignite one's sense of communion with the Transcendent. As Augustine argues, one can only contemplate the Divine through that which he is not, and Chaucer's fabliau humor extends the logic of such claims to their most ridiculous, yet nonetheless illuminating, extreme. These fabliau portrayals of God's *pryvetee* imagine the earthly repercussions of unchecked eroticism, as does Chaucer's *Second Nun's Tale* in its depiction of Cecilia's earthly spiritual marriage to Valerian, which is symbolically yet graphically consummated only when God replaces her husband as her lover.

LOVING GOD IN THE *SECOND NUN'S TALE*

As Dido piques God's amatory interest in *Legend of Good Women*, Cecilia likewise stimulates God's erotic desires in the *Second Nun's Tale*, Chaucer's most extended depiction of divine courtship and sexual consummation. In the Prologue to her tale, the Second Nun tells the Canterbury pilgrims that she will faithfully retell St. Cecilia's legend from a translation, and on its surface, the *Second Nun's Tale* appears decidedly anti-erotic, most notably due to Cecilia's commitment to chastity. By sharing the story of a virgin martyr, the Second Nun aspires to lead her fellow pilgrims away from sin and to the Divine:

> And for to putte us fro swich ydelnesse,
> That cause is of so greet confusioun,
> I have heer doon my feithful bisynesse
> After the legende in translacioun
> Right of thy glorious lif and passioun,
> Thou with thy gerland wroght with rose and lilie—
> Thee meene I, mayde and martyr, Seint Cecilie. (8.22–28)

A virgin and a martyr, Cecilia is remembered for her diligent proselytizing of the Gospels and her conversion of countless Romans to Christianity. Both the rose and the lily are iconic representations of the Virgin

Mary, and as such they symbolize purity and chastity;[36] in this vein, the text's surface level of signification stresses the absence of sexuality within the narrative (notwithstanding the paradox of stressing an absence). The ensuing invocation to Mary (8.29–84) further grounds the Second Nun's symbolism in its Marian referents. St. Cecilia thus personifies maidenly chastity, despite the fact that the narrative's depiction of her as a virgin conflicts with its simultaneous portrayal of her as an object of much sexual desire—both human and divine.

Before the Second Nun addresses the erotic desires circulating around Cecilia, she considers the conflict and contrast between earthly and heavenly felicities. Her hagiography of Cecilia, which focuses on this virgin's renunciation of sexual congress in marriage, faces an internal contradiction in that its creation of narrative pleasure for its readers is predicated upon its dismissal of all earthly pleasures. This conflict emerges in the *Second Nun's Prologue* when she establishes her theme regarding the dangers of idleness, warning her audience that Satan deploys idleness as a tactic in his seductions: "Wel oghten we to doon al oure entente, / Lest that the feend thurgh ydelnesse us hente" (8.6–7). As Satan's potential prey, Christians must avoid idleness lest they succumb to illicit and predatory desires; rather, they must position themselves as objects of eternal salvation through a life actively devoted to their faith. In declaiming on this theme, the Second Nun introduces, by contrast and antithesis, a subtheme of pleasure into her text when she argues that "Ydelnesse" is the "porter of the gate . . . of delices" (8.2–3). As Gregory Sadlek explores in his *Idleness Working: The Discourse of Love's Labor from Ovid through Chaucer and Gower*, Idleness is often coupled with amatory pursuits in Ovidian verse and its medieval descendants, such as in Chaucer's *Romaunt of the Rose*, when Ydelnesse opens the gate for the dreamer: "In at the wiket went I tho, / That Ydelnesse hadde opened me, / Into that gardyn fair to see" (642–44, cf. *Knight's Tale* 1.1940).[37] Through his allusion to idleness, Chaucer both points

---

36. For an overview of the symbolism of roses and lilies, see Lucia Impelluso, *Nature and Its Symbols*, trans. Stephen Sartarelli (Los Angeles: Getty Museum, 2003), 85–89 and 118–27. As much as the lily and rose are complementary images in the Second Nun's depiction of Cecilia, these flowers and their colors symbolize a wide range of additional concepts. The lily is also associated with Juno, female fertility, and beauty, and the rose connotes death and Jesus's passion. The Second Nun also links the red of the rose and the white of the lily to Jesus when she refers to his blood and (presumably white) flesh: "That no desdeyn the Makere hadde of kynde / His Sone in blood and flessh to clothe and wynde" (8.41–42).

37. Sadlek also focuses on depictions of love as labor; see, in particular, Sadlek's "Love's Bysynesse in Chaucer's Amatory Fiction," in *Idleness Working: The Discourse of Love's Labor*

to the sexual nature hidden behind Ydelnesse's gate and underscores the Second Nun's interest in the sexual matters of which she attempts to cleanse her narrative. From her perspective, Idleness's door to pleasure, in her ensuing tale and likely in the *Romaunt of the Rose* as well, should remain shut, and the Second Nun posits that, by avoiding idleness, one consequently avoids untoward pleasures that would lead one away from God. At the very least, however, the Second Nun's allusion to the *Romaunt of the Rose* underscores that her reading habits do not accord with her spiritual exhortations to others, for the *Romaunt of the Rose* falls outside the hagiographical genre with which she chooses to instruct her audience in Christian morality. Hagiography is nonetheless a genre predicated upon pleasure, albeit a painful pleasure denied until the narrative reaches its conclusion and the saint unites with God. As Robert Mills outlines, the masochistic pleasures inherent in self-sacrifice and martyrdom illuminate the teleological drive of many hagiographies: "Martyrdom iconography . . . embodies this masochistic structure of suspense—it is, above all, an art of stillness and deferral, representing actions about to be fulfilled as much as things already carried out." In sum, hagiography celebrates the "aestheticization of pain . . . in the service of pleasure."[38] The dual edge of pleasure—as the sinful path to damnation and as the eternal joy of divine union—upsets the Second Nun's binary construction of idleness as sinful and activity as holy, for pleasure is revealed to be their shared and guiding telos, particularly when the tale climaxes with God's erotic union with Cecilia.

Somewhat surprisingly, given her conjoined themes of the sins of idleness and the dangers of pleasure, the Second Nun embodies the sin that she castigates, eschewing the diligence necessary to tell her tale expeditiously: "Yet preye I yow that reden that I write, / Foryeve me that I do no diligence / This ilke storie subtilly to endite" (8.78–80). Positioning her imperfect narration as a counterexample to Cecilia's active life, as she also requests forgiveness for her rhetorical failures, the Second Nun encodes the failure of her story as constitutive of its meaning. Her tale cannot succeed in capturing Cecilia's exemplary saintliness, as all attempts to capture the Divine through human speech must likewise fail (in congruence with Žižek's theorization of poetry's failure). In her prayer that her auditors "wole my werk amende" (8.84), the Second Nun thematizes failure into

---

from *Ovid through Chaucer and Gower* (Washington, DC: Catholic University of America Press, 2004), 208–58.

38. Robert Mills, "'Whatever you do is a delight to me!': Masculinity, Masochism, and Queer Play in Representations of Male Martyrdom," *Exemplaria* 13 (2001): 1–37, at 35.

the narrative, but this promise of failure is thus the precondition of her tale.

In this account of Cecilia's martyrdom, God's passion for women illuminates his quest for consummation with Cecilia, but it is therefore impossible for the Second Nun to tell the chaste story of a virgin martyr. The human body is stained with original sin—a sin of sexuality, in many exegetical interpretations[39]—and in her invocation to Mary, the Second Nun seeks divine assistance for purging herself of her sinfulness:

> And of thy light my soule in prison lighte,
> That troubled is by the contagioun
> Of my body, and also by the wighte
> Of erthely lust and fals affeccioun. (8.71–74)

The Second Nun's attention to her body, with its tendency toward earthly lust and false affection, puts the sinful human body thematically at the heart of the narrative. To diagnose her spiritual condition in the terms of Chaucer's Parson, her reason insufficiently governs her *sensualitee*, and thus her body contaminates her soul. By telling the exemplary story of St. Cecilia, the Second Nun attempts to cleanse her body and spirit of lust, but divine eroticism, evident in God's amorous interest in Cecilia, models the purging pleasures of sexual union with the Divine. The Second Nun desires what she cannot yet have—transcendent oneness with God—but the "contagioun" of her body foreshadows the eternal joys awaiting her, for this transgression is the precondition that the Law establishes for her eventual pleasure in heaven.

Following the Second Nun's anti-erotic efforts to erase traces of pleasure and sexuality from her Prologue, her tale initially focuses on the rejection of earthly sexual desire. Cecilia dedicates herself to God and promises her commitment to earthly chastity—"O Lord, my soule and eek my body gye / Unwemmed, lest that I confounded be" (8.136–37)—

---

39. The theological complexities of original sin are beyond the scope of this study, but it is worthwhile to note that many medieval exegetes derived their conceptions of it from Paul's declaration "sicut enim per inoboedientiam unius hominis peccatores constituti sunt multi, ita et per unius oboeditionem iusti constituenter multi" (Romans 5:19; cf. 1 Corinthians 15:22; "For as by the disobedience of one man, many were made sinners; so also by the obedience of one, many shall be made just"). In this typological interpretation, Adam introduces sin into the world, for which Jesus's sacrifice atones. For an overview of original sin, see Pierre Payer, *The Bridling of Desire: Views of Sex in the Later Middle Ages* (Toronto: University of Toronto Press, 1993), 42–60; and Linwood Urban, *A Short History of Christian Thought*, rev. ed. (New York: Oxford University Press, 1995), 125–55.

with these words foreshadowing her refusal to consummate her marriage to Valerian. As Dyan Elliot explains of spiritual and sexless marriages of the Middle Ages, the legend of St. Cecilia "possesses three irreducible elements that are common to most hagiographical depictions of virginal marriage: reluctance to marry, conversion of the spouse on the wedding night, and a secret resolve to preserve virginity."[40] Before God unites with Cecilia through her death, his amatory rival—Cecilia's husband Valerian—must be dismissed from the narrative, and in the triangulated desires among Cecilia, Valerian, and God, God's desires trump Valerian's, proving both the transience of human passion and the intransigence, as well as the ultimate physicality, of divine eroticism. Cecilia admonishes Valerian to quench his erotic desire for her:

> "And if that he may feelen, out of drede,
> That ye me touche, or love in vileynye,
> He right anon wol sle yow with the dede,
> And in youre yowthe thus ye shullen dye;
> And if that ye in clene love me gye,
> He wol yow loven as me, for youre clennesse,
> And shewen yow his joye and his brightnesse." (8.155–161)[41]

Cecilia's threat appears to strengthen the narrative's thematic treatment of anti-eroticism. If Valerian loves Cecilia "in vileynye"—a telling yet muddled reference to his spousal right to consummate their marriage—God's angel will intercede and enforce his prohibition against sexual activity by slaying Valerian. On the story's surface level, Cecilia's words are proved true as the narrative proceeds: no human copulates with her, and her virginity is thereby protected from earthly onslaughts.

When Cecilia threatens Valerian with his imminent demise should they consummate their marriage, the rejected groom sees himself as unwittingly ensnared in an erotic triangle, suspecting that his bride has taken a human lover and cuckolded him. Valerian, however, must learn that he himself is an object of divine desire as much as his wife. As Eve Sedgwick famously observes of triangulated desires and their latent homoeroticism, "there is a special relationship between male homoso-

---

40. Dyan Elliott, *Spiritual Marriage: Sexual Abstinence in Medieval Wedlock* (Princeton, NJ: Princeton University Press, 1993), 65.

41. It should be noted that Cecilia refers in these lines not to God but to "an aungel . . . that loveth me" (8.152). The angel, as God's proxy, preserves Cecilia from Valerian's eroticism, yet only then to deliver Cecilia in service to God's spiritual and erotic drives.

cial . . . desire and structures for maintaining and transmitting patriarchal power. . . . For historical reasons, this special relationship may take the form of ideological homophobia, ideological homosexuality, or some highly conflicted but intensively structured combination of the two."[42] With the Divine as one vertex in this erotic triangle, the homosociality inherent in the struggle between God and Valerian over Cecilia—brief as it is—transcends gender while remaining trapped within it. God's desires are genderless, so it seems, in that all Christians receive the bounties of his love, but God is insistently gendered male, and so the impossible act of contemplating the Divine's erotic drives requires one to contemplate a heavenly masculinity both unmoored from yet primarily conceivable within human terms of masculine sexuality, as understood within patriarchal paradigms of medieval thought.[43] The Second Nun herself models such a conflicted gendered space when she refers to herself as an "unworthy sone of Eve" (8.62), and Valerian must correspondingly learn to resignify the meanings of husbandly masculinity that no longer function when God disrupts his expectations of marital sexuality.

Within the homosocial competition between God and Valerian, Valerian exposes the latent violence of erotic triangles when women refuse to conform to their husband's desires. His attempts to monitor his bride's erotic life include his promise to murder her, should she prove untrue:

> Valerian, corrected as God wolde,
> Answerde again, "If I shal trusten thee,
> Lat me that aungel se and hym biholde;
> And if that it a verray angel bee,
> Thanne wol I doon as thou hast prayed me;
> And if thou love another man, for soothe
> Right with this swerd thanne wol I sle yow bothe." (8.162–68)

Still suspecting that Cecilia has taken a human lover, Valerian must realize that his earthly vision of a consummated marriage with Cecilia merely serves as a conduit to his as yet unconsummated relationship with God. John Hill points out that Cecilia is blessed with "a vision of luminous

---

42. Eve Sedgwick, *Between Men: English Literature and Male Homosocial Desire* (New York: Columbia University Press, 1985), 25.

43. As much scholarship has shown, medieval figurations of the Divine as male have their counterparts in maternal depictions of Jesus. Caroline Walker Bynum's *Jesus as Mother: Studies in the Spirituality of the High Middle Ages* (Berkeley: University of California Press, 1982) remains a definitive text in this field.

Truth," one that "awaits the chaste believer converted by [her] wisdom," and this vision of Truth "wins over her new husband, Valerian, who threatens wedding night violence" if he discovers that she is cuckolding him.[44] But divine Truth is also foreshadowed in Valerian's threat to penetrate Cecilia, either with his penis if he were to consummate their marriage or with a sword if he were to punish her suspected infidelity. This physical violence is postponed until the night of her gruesome martyrdom when the threat of the sword, in its crude phallic symbolism betokening hymenal penetration, is metaphorically realized, but also when God, metaphorically as well, penetrates her as his lover. Pope Urban's imagery of Jesus sowing seeds of chastity prefigures the narrative's conclusion, for at the same time that the Second Nun presents Cecilia as having escaped sexual penetration on her wedding night, the words of Pope Urban explain how Jesus has symbolically impregnated her:

"Almyghty Lord, O Jhesu Crist," quod he,
"Sower of chaast conseil, hierde of us alle,
The fruyt of thilke seed of chastitee
That thou has sowe in Cecile, taak to thee!
Lo, lyk a bisy bee, withouten gile,
Thee serveth ay thyn owene thral Cecile." (8.191–96)

Incarnating this paradoxical image of a spiritual sower of chastity, Jesus metaphorically consummates his relationship with Cecilia to procreate not newborn babies but newborn children of the faith, no matter their age. Perhaps surprisingly, given the contemporary equation of "the birds and the bees" as a euphemism for sexual knowledge, bees often connoted chastity in classical and medieval symbolism; as Lucia Impelluso documents, "based on the once-common belief that the insects [i.e., bees] reproduced by parthenogenesis, or the development of an unfertilized female gamete, bees were also used to connote chastity."[45] In contrast to Valerian, who was forbidden to sow the seed of a human child in his wife's womb, Jesus consummates his love for Cecilia through metaphorical intercourse that results in countless children of the faith, all of whom are presumed to be avatars of chastity themselves.

Because Valerian eroticized Cecilia as an object of human desire, he denied her the Christological relevance due to her as a proselytizing agent,

---

44. John Hill, *Chaucerian Belief: The Poetics of Reverence and Delight* (New Haven, CT: Yale University Press, 1991), 51.

45. Lucia Impelluso, *Nature and Its Symbols*, 334.

yet through his erotic confusion Valerian succeeds in finding God. As Jacqueline Rose observes of woman's role in signifying to and for men, "As negative to the man, woman becomes the total object of fantasy (or an object of total fantasy), elevated to the place of the Other and made to stand for its truth. Since the place of the Other is also the place of God, this is the ultimate form of mystification."[46] Valerian's mystification and objectification of his wife leads him to the Divine, and the Second Nun recounts the executions of Valerian and his brother Tiburce that bring the men to their heavenly reward: "With humble herte and sad devocioun, / And losten bothe hir hevedes in the place. / Hir soules wenten to the Kyng of grace" (8.397–99). By ceding his erotic claims to his wife's body, Valerian finds the salvation denied him when he focused on sexual pleasure in marriage. As the homosocial conflict between God and man is obscured in this encounter, so too is the eroticism at its heart, in which Valerian's purgation of sexual desire allows him to fulfill spiritual desires unrecognized until his wife refused to consummate their marriage; thus, he is able to be born into the faith as one of Jesus's "seeds of chastity" that has been impregnated in Cecilia.

Of particular consequence in the story of Cecilia's marriage to Valerian, and in line with the tale's anti-erotic façade, are Cecilia's attempts to preserve her virginity: she is defined morally by her intact hymen and its symbolic register within her community, primarily because her virginal status symbolizes the Church's purity as well. As Kathleen Kelly argues of early Christianity's investment in its martyrs, "Hagiography, in telling the story of the menaced virgin martyr, is really telling the story of a Church that reserved to itself the right to recognize, sanction, and reward virginity."[47] The wedding night violence with which Valerian threatens Cecilia, however, is merely delayed, not denied, and when Almachius orders Cecilia's execution, he stages her death to his desire, with his minions following his every command:

> . . . "In hire hous," quod he,
> "Brenne hire right in a bath of flambes rede."
> And as he bad, right so was doon the dede;
> For in a bath they gone hire faste shetten,
> And nyght and day greet fyr they under betten. (8.514–18)

---

46. Jacqueline Rose, *Sexuality in the Field of Vision* (London: Verso, 1986), 74.
47. Kathleen Kelly, *Performing Virginity and Testing Chastity in the Middle Ages* (London: Routledge, 2000), 62.

Unflinching passivity as inspired through her eroticized attachment to God motivates Cecilia's every action throughout her arduous execution. V. A. Kolve sees erotic tension in the traditional iconography of this scene, with the virgin's placement in a bath titillatingly suggesting her naked body surrounded by flames symbolizing sexual lust: "She is most commonly shown naked in a cauldron bath, with a fire blazing below and an executioner ready to strike at her neck with a sword. . . . This last image is heroic in both style and substance, but in respect to Cecilia's nakedness it is erotic too."[48] It should be noted that Chaucer does not specify Cecilia's nudity in his retelling of her story, and other visual depictions of Cecilia's martyrdom portray her fully clothed.[49] Nonetheless, the contrast between the burning flames and Cecilia's cool response to them—"She sat al cool and feelede no wo. / It make hire nat a drope for to sweete" (8.521–22)—points to the erotic energy of forbearance in her stance, one awaiting fulfillment in death. As she resisted Valerian's desire for her on their wedding night, she now proves herself impervious to all human desires to act upon her—whether such desire is to be enacted through sexual intercourse, decapitation, or immolation. The scene also inverts the famous Pauline admonition—"it is better to marry than to be burnt" (1 Corinthians 7:9)—and proves that burning for the faith in righteous chastity aligns one with the divine will. This scene also foreshadows the tale's recoding of the very meaning of marriage as Cecilia prepares herself for her role as God's bride.

A hint of human mercy appears in Chaucer's depiction of Cecilia's gruesome death scene when Almachius's servant, after cutting her throat with three strokes, refuses to strike her again due to a custom prohibiting excessive cruelty in punishments:

He myghte noght smyte al her nekke atwo;
And for ther was that tyme an ordinaunce
That no man sholde doon man swich penaunce
The ferthe strook to smyten, softe or soore. (8.528–31)

---

48. V. A. Kolve, "Chaucer's *Second Nun's Tale* and the Iconography of Saint Cecilia," in *New Perspectives in Chaucer Criticism*, ed. Donald Rose (Norman, OK: Pilgrim, 1981), 137–74, at 141, 143.

49. For an image of Cecilia in which she is executed while fully clothed (taken from Huntington Library MS H. M. 3027, fol. 161), see Robert Miller, ed., *Chaucer: Sources and Backgrounds* (New York: Oxford University Press, 1977), 114.

This legal injunction prohibits Cecilia's neck from being struck a fourth time, and the three strokes numerologically align her with the Trinity in a scene laden with erotic imagery. The cuts on her neck crudely register that the hacking of the phallic sword has successfully penetrated her body, and Cecilia's blood thus adumbrates not merely a physical wound but a spiritual deflowering. The rupturing of her hymen, a liminal event delayed from her wedding night, now metaphorically transpires as she ascends to her rightful place as God's eternal lover. Certainly, Cecilia's blood dominates the iconography of this scene:

> But half deed, with hir nekke ycorven there,
> He lefte hir lye, and on his wey he went.
> The Cristen folk, which that aboute hire were,
> With sheetes han the blood ful faire yhent. (8.533–36)

Death offers not merely the possibility of salvation but the consummation of divine intercourse, with the bloody sheets signifying the bleeding of Cecilia's hymen on her wedding night. True, readers see a bath instead of a bed in this erotic scene shared by God and Cecilia, but the focus on Cecilia's bloody sheets argues strongly for a metaphoric reconstruction of the bath as a scene of hymenal penetration.[50] Chaucer adapts these bloody sheets from his source "In festo Sancte Cecilie virginis et martyris" (Paris, Bibl. Nationale, ms. Latin 3278), but departs from its rather mundane depiction of the events—"cuius sanguinem omnes Christiani qui per eam crediderant bibleis linteaminibus extergebant" ("All the Christians she had converted came and wiped up her blood with cotton or linen cloths")—to paint a more lurid picture of Cecilia's bloody shifts, as she lies in a reclined position.[51]

---

50. On a lexical level, it does not appear likely that Chaucer's use of *sheets* to describe the cloths used to mop up Cecilia's blood refers merely to towels or cleaning fabrics. In every other instance Chaucer employs the word *sheets* he refers to bedsheets, such as in the scene when Troilus and Criseyde consummate their affections: "With that here heed down in the bed she leyde, / And with the sheete it wreigh, and sighte soore" (3.1055–56). Chaucer's other references to sheets include *Reeve's Tale* (1.4140), *Canon's Yeoman's Tale* (879), *Parson's Tale* (10.195–200), *Troilus and Criseyde* (3.1570), and "The Former Age" (45).

51. For the "In festo Sancte Cecilie virginis et martyris," see Robert Correale and Mary Hamel, eds., *Sources and Analogues of the Canterbury Tales* (Cambridge: Brewer, 2002), 1.516–27. Chaucer's other primary source for the *Second Nun's Tale* is Jacobus de Voragine's *Legenda Aurea*, which is available in Correale and Hamel, 1.505–17. The depiction of Cecilia's beheading in the *Legenda Aurea* does not depict bloody sheets or cloths, referring instead to the "cruentus carnifex" ("bloody executioner").

As Paul Strohm succinctly observes, "Bloody beds are rife in late medieval literature," and he cites the appearance of these overdetermined tropes of intercourse in the *Wife of Bath's Prologue,* Julian of Norwich's *Showings,* Beroul's *Tristan,* and Chrétien de Troyes' *Lancelot, ou le Chevalier de la charrete* to outline the persistence of this sexual symbolism in various highly charged erotic scenes.[52] In his reading of Chrétien's *Lancelot,* Jeffrey Jerome Cohen suggests that bloody beds disrupt gender to the point of incomprehensibility. When Lancelot fornicates with Guinevere after cutting his finger, the ensuing bloodstains reverse their genders such that masculinity and femininity no longer signify coherently:

> These bloody sheets are the wedding night topos, the display that announces consummation through feminine loss (the virgin's hymen), but here the male body has stained the sheets, and itself. Or, rather, the masculine body has become feminine. Or else masculine and feminine (along with lover/beloved, master/servant, vassal/lord, public/private) have temporarily lost their relational signifying power, each bifurcation blurring to the point at which it is no longer possible to contain them.[53]

Lancelot's blood in Guinevere's bed disrupts gender categories to the point of incomprehensibility, and, correspondingly, God's symbolic penetration of Cecilia's body disrupts the border between the spiritual and the physical, the heavenly and the earthly, and the very meaning of human eroticism when God pursues heavenly love in an earthly manner. At the same time, Cecilia proleptically demonstrates her understanding of such medieval thinkers as Alan de Lille, who encourages women to view themselves as forsaking earthly eroticism for the joys of an eternal bridegroom: "Si vis nubere terrestri marito propter divitias, considera quod terrenae divitiae fallaces sunt et transitoriae, quia aut in praesenti vita transeunt, aut saltem in morte recedunt. Nube ergo illi, apud quem thesauri sunt incomparabiles, et divitiae immutabiles; quas nec fur furatur, nec tinea demolitur" ("If you want to marry an earthly husband for riches, consider that earthly riches are deceptive and transitory, for they pass away either in the present life or at least in death. Therefore marry him whose treasures are incomparable, whose riches are immutable, where thief does not

---

52. Paul Strohm, *Theory and the Premodern Text* (Minneapolis: University of Minnesota Press, 2000), 202.

53. Jeffrey Jerome Cohen, *Medieval Identity Machines* (Minneapolis: University of Minnesota Press, 2003), 105.

steal, nor moth corrupt").⁵⁴ If one is to marry the Divine, the Second Nun suggests, one should be prepared for the heavenly erotic possibilities that an earthly anti-eroticism enables.

In its ostensible genre of hagiography, the *Second Nun's Tale* tells the predictable story of a virgin martyr who preserves her chastity as a sign of her purity and wins eternal joys in heaven for her forbearance; in its veiled yet insistent allusions to God's carnality, this hagiography troubles its genre by depicting God as a lover capable of and patiently pursuing physical consummation with his beloved. Cecilia's final acts are to bequeath her house to Pope Urban, thus establishing her maternal role within the early Church. With God as their spiritual father, Jesus as the impregnator of seeds of chastity, and Cecilia as their human mother, the children of the Church receive an earthly inheritance from their mother that foreshadows their heavenly reward. The generative erotics latent in the *Second Nun's Tale* reconfigure the human family as a spiritual hybrid of the earthly and the heavenly, but one that relies on the attenuated image of their heavenly father physically consummating his spiritual marriage to their mother, enacting the sexuality forbidden to earthly husbands and wives but readily available to sate the erotic yearnings of the Almighty.

Given the vast array of medieval conceptions of an erotic God in various allegorical, exegetical, and mystical texts and artworks, it would be remarkable if no vision of an erotic God entered Chaucer's expansive corpus. These queer hints and allusions to an erotic God, one unwilling to discipline himself to the same sexual standards established for his faithful, follow no set pattern, and indeed, in most instances one can refuse to see any visions of God's *pryvetee* because they are so occluded from view. Whether in a logical lapse in the *Parson's Tale* or in the sexual play of Chaucer's fabliaux, whether in response to a momentary vision of female beauty in *Legend of Good Women* or in a prolonged amatory rivalry in *Second Nun's Tale*, God loves in Chaucer's corpus, thereby upsetting the boundaries between the human and the Divine in provocative ways. As these themes mostly simmer beneath the surface of their narratives and do not cohere into a unified vision of divine love, one can see artistic failure in Chaucer's treatment of the Divine; if, however, Žižek is correct that poetry's failures lead to God, then perhaps Chaucer succeeds where he has failed, in a queer vision of the Divine who transgresses the anti-erotic regulations that his love demands.

---

54. Alan de Lille, *Summa de arte praedicatoria*, Patrologia Latina 210.195bc; the translation is by Barbara Newman, *From Virile Woman to WomanChrist: Studies in Medieval Religion and Literature* (Philadelphia: University of Pennsylvania Press, 1995), 32.

CHAPTER SEVEN

EPILOGUE

Chaucer's Avian Amorousness

As the previous chapters have explored, few of Chaucer's human characters succeed in the erotic sphere without vexed sacrifices of self and desire, and so it is intriguing to consider the implications behind the rooster Chauntecleer's depiction in the *Nun's Priest's Tale*, for he is painted as a creature capable of integrating sexual desire organically and pleasurably into his life. From the start it should be acknowledged that most medieval writers did not turn to roosters and hens for models of human sexual behavior. More typical is the viewpoint expressed by John Gower in the *Confessio amantis*, in which those with animalistic appetites corrupt the Church's efforts to extirpate incest:

> For of the lawe canonized
> The Pope hath bede to the men,
> That non schal wedden of his ken
> Ne the seconde ne the thridde.
> Bot thogh that holy cherche it bidde,
> So to restreigne Mariage,
> Ther ben yit upon loves Rage
> Full manye of suche nou aday
> That taken wher thei take may.
> For love, which is unbesein

Of alle reson, as men sein,
Thurgh sotie and thurgh nycete,
Of his voluptuosite
He spareth no condicion
Of ken ne yit religion,
Bot as a cock among the Hennes,
Or as a Stalon in the Fennes,
Which goth amonges al the Stod,
Riht so can he nomore good,
Bot takth what thing comth next to honde.[1]

Because love "is unbesein / Of alle reson," it bears the potential to strip humans of their humanity, depriving them of rationality and degrading them into lusty cocks and stallions. As male animals, both cocks and stallions suggest further the loss of masculine restraint in favor of sexual excess, thus tacitly adumbrating the potential for incest to emerge in humans who do not control their amorous desires.

Against such verse both anti-erotic and anti-avian, Chaucer's Chauntecleer models the proper masculinity both of a knight acting in deference to his courtly beloved and of the lusty lover reveling in unrestrained fabliau sexuality. From Chaucer's romances to his fabliaux, from his exempla to his hagiographies, from his dream visions to his moral treatises, the majority of his narratives do not depict a merry blend of conjugality and eroticism, yet in the *Nun's Priest's Tale*, Chauntecleer both sexually desires his wife and loves her as well. As is well established, the *Nun's Priest's Tale* parodies numerous genres, including romance, epic, dream vision, and beast fable, yet the tale's overarching parodic treatment of these genres does not preclude the possibility of obtaining erotic insight from their subversive deployments.[2] The Nun's Priest urges his fellow pilgrims to uncover a moral from his story, citing Paul's belief that pre-Christian texts enlighten Christian truths: "For Seint Paul seith that al that writen is, / To oure doctrine it is ywrite, ywis; / Taketh the fruyt, and lat the chaf be stille" (7.3441–43). Interpretations of the tale's "fruyt" abound, and often focus on Chauntecleer's sin of pride and the lesson he learns from his travails with the fox, although Stephen Manning cautions

---

1. John Gower, *The Complete Works of John Gower*, ed. G. C. Macaulay, vol. 3 (Oxford: Clarendon, 1901), 8.144–63.

2. For a thorough study of the *Nun's Priest's Tale* and its play with genres, see John Finlayson, "Reading Chaucer's *Nun's Priest's Tale*: Mixed Genres and Multi-layered Worlds of Illusion," *English Studies* 86.6 (2005): 493–510.

that, in the tale's moralizing, "Chaucer is poking fun at those who felt that a poem had to have some moral in order to justify its existence."³ Much of the pleasure of the *Nun's Priest's Tale* arises in its converging discourses of various genres, and Chaucer's parodic play with the erotics of romance encourages readings of this polyvalent tale that take seriously the humor of its avian amorousness.

The tale's opening description of Chauntecleer, with its mock blazon of his beauty and its praise of his royal bearing, establishes him as its courtly protagonist (7.2859–64), and the ensuing description of Pertelote—"Curteys she was, discreet, and debonaire, / And compaignable, and bar hyrself so faire" (7.2871–72)—likewise portrays her as the rooster's fair and imperious beloved. Within the courtly conventions of romance, Pertelote wins Chauntecleer's heart and amatory devotion: "That trewely she hath the herte in hoold / Of Chauntecleer, loken in every lith; / He loved hire so that wel was hym therwith" (7.2874–76). It is a simple description of a true love: with his beloved Pertelote by his side, Chauntecleer enjoys an erotic life of contentment and satisfaction. Furthermore, in accordance with the gendered parameters of romance, Pertelote must both narcissistically mirror Chauntecleer's attractiveness and challenge his worth as a courtly lover in her role as the imperious courtly lady. When Chauntecleer confesses his fears arising from his nightmare of bestial violence, Pertelote upbraids him, demanding that he affirm his role as a hero:

> "Allas," quod she, "for, by that God above,
> Now han ye lost myn herte and al my love!
> I kan nat love a coward, by my faith!
> . . . .
> Have ye no mannes herte, and han a berd?" (7.2909–11, 2920)

Due to her affronts to his masculinity and her veiled threats that he will lose erotic access to her, Chauntecleer must perform a sufficiently credible version of courtly and heroic masculinity to win back his beloved. As with many romance narratives, Chauntecleer must act valiantly to ensure his erotic desires are consummated, yet the tale then faces an inherent obstacle, for how can a rooster—a chicken—successfully perform the valor

---

3. Stephen Manning, "The Nun's Priest's Morality and the Medieval Attitude toward Fables," *Journal of English and Germanic Philology* 59 (1960): 403–16, at 416. On interpreting the *Nun's Priest's Tale*, see also Lesley Kordecki, "Let me 'telle yow what I mente': The Glossa Ordinaria and the *Nun's Priest's Tale*," *Exemplaria* 4.2 (1992): 365–85.

and violence requisite to defeat his (as yet chimerical) enemy? Indeed, it is impossible for such an ending to be effected: at the narrative's end, Chauntecleer succeeds in outwitting the fox that would devour him and thus achieves an important victory, but he does not defeat his adversary under the conditions of a martial combat, which serves as the preferred venue of masculine aggression in the romance tradition.

To win back his lady's affections, Chauntecleer must rely on his amatory intelligence as a courtly lover, and his lengthy disquisition on the prophetic nature of dreams establishes his rhetorical capabilities and argumentative skills as superior to Pertelote's. However, defeating her in debate appears to be an ineffectual amatory tactic, especially since she demands that he embody a courtly masculinity based on martial courage. And so, after their discussion of the meaning of dreams, Chauntecleer resolves any lingering disagreement with Pertelote by reminding her of their shared conjugal pleasures:

> "For al so siker as *In principio*,
> *Mulier est hominis confusio*—
> Madame, the sentence of this Latyn is,
> 'Womman is mannes joye and al his blis.'
> For whan I feele a-nyght your softe syde—
> Al be it that I may nat on yow ryde,
> For that oure perche is maad so narwe, allas—
> I am so ful of joye and of solas,
> That I diffye bothe sweven and dreem." (7.3163–71)

The prevailing interpretation of these lines is that Chauntecleer mistranslates the Latin phrases that he cites and thereby reveals the shaky foundations of his professed intellectualism. Nevertheless, if readers are willing to suspend their disbelief sufficiently to enjoy this story of chickens engaging in a philosophical discourse over dreams, they should also entertain the possibility that Chauntecleer deliberately misinterprets the Latin phrases and their misogynistic context so as to comfort his wife and thus to regain erotic access to her. As Peter Travis observes, "the most productive way of beginning to respond to this translation exercise is to read it as a heuristic parody of the very activity of translation itself, a parody whose reading regimen requires considerable patience as well as creativity to fully explore."[4] Chauntecleer's citation of *In principio* alludes to the first words

---

4. Peter Travis, *Disseminal Chaucer: Rereading the* Nun's Priest's Tale (Notre Dame, IN: Notre Dame University Press, 2010), 95.

of the Vulgate translation of Genesis, and thus puts the following adage, *Mulier est hominis confusio*, within a Christian context. Certainly, within the misogynist worldview that blames Eve for humanity's expulsion from Eden, women are indeed a destructive force in the lives of men. What is more important to Chauntecleer, however, than the Christian truth that his Bible reveals is his experiential belief in the earthly and erotic joys evident and abundant in wedlock. Thus, although Christian truth may denigrate women by linking its foundational narrative to misogyny, Chauntecleer realizes the limitations of this perspective, and, like the Wife of Bath, misreads the Bible so as to generate erotic pleasure on earth. Certainly, it seems safe to assume that the imperious Pertelote would not be amorously swayed by an accurate—and misogynist—translation of these Latin phrases, yet Chauntecleer's rewriting of the gendered traditions of Christian thought ensures sexual pleasure in his future by employing the biblical account of the Garden of Eden as a palimpsest upon which to revise earthly eroticism as newly freed from gendered discontents. In his reading of this passage, Joseph Dane posits that "What Chaucer has constructed here is a situation in which *any* foreign phrase, or for that matter, any English phrase would mean 'woman is man's joy and bliss'";[5] Chauntecleer's Latin words are eclipsed by his translation of them, as he rewrites the Vulgate to facilitate sexual conquest.

As much as Chaucer foretells Chauntecleer's and Pertelote's sexual pleasures in this passage, the rooster cannot consummate his affections for Pertelote because, at the moment he speaks these words, the close quarters of their perch prohibit intercourse. Chauntecleer nonetheless proclaims himself "ful of joye and of solas" as he revels in the pleasure of simply resting by her side. Of course, the fact that Chauntecleer enjoys his wife's company when they do not engage in intercourse does not preclude their indulging in sexual pastimes on subsequent occasions, and Chaucer describes the bestial lust that sparks Chauntecleer's immoderate pleasures:

> And with that word he fley doun fro the beem,
> For it was day, and eke his hennes alle,
> And with a chuk he gan hem for to calle,
> For he hadde founde a corn, lay in the yerd.
> Real he was, he was namoore aferd.
> He fethered Pertelote twenty tyme,

---

5. Joseph Dane, "'Mulier est hominis confusio': Note on Chaucer's *Nun's Priest's Tale*, Line 3164," *Notes and Queries* 39.3 (1992): 276–78.

And trad hire eke as ofte, er it was pryme.
He looketh as it were a grym leoun,
And on his toos he rometh up and doun;
Hym deigned nat to sette his foot to grounde.
He chukketh whan he hath a corn yfounde,
And to hym rennen thane his wyves alle. (7.3172–83)

The lines describing Chauntecleer as a "grym leoun" who "rometh" so energetically that his claws do not touch the ground are somewhat ambiguous, as they come between the passages detailing his energetic pursuit of intercourse with Pertelote and those detailing his search for grain. If one construes them as referring to his lovemaking, one visualizes Chauntecleer as a zealous copulator, frenetically pursuing pleasure after pleasure, yet one whose immediate task after passion is to find food for Pertelote and his other wives. By so closely linking Chauntecleer's erotic passions with his work to ensure a functioning civilization for them, in which the primary physical need of sating their hunger is fulfilled, Chaucer underscores that the rooster succeeds in building a sustainable culture, one remarkably free from the discontents that Freud locates in the disjunctions between personal desires and social regulations. For Freud, the conflict between civilization and the individual arises in the disjuncture between communal demands for maintaining the civic order and personal desires to pursue individual pleasures, as discussed in his *Civilization and Its Discontents*, and Chauntecleer models the possibility of integrating communal and personal desires into a coherent and unified life of pleasure in support of the commonweal. As the leader of the farmyard's civic order, he structures the foundations of his society as mediated through his sexual desires, as he also regulates patriarchal discourse in service of women's desire not to be construed as the foundational error of Western culture.

Against the backdrop of erotic tension throughout the *Canterbury Tales*, Chauntecleer's amatory exuberance and ready sexual pleasures stand in sharp contrast, yet it cannot be overlooked that Chauntecleer builds this social order not merely on a joyful eroticism in marriage but on incest and polyamory. He enjoys sexual congress with numerous hens in addition to Pertelote, as the opening description of his regal beauty details: "This gentil cok hadde in his governaunce / Sevene hennes for to doon al his plesaunce, / Which were his sustres and his paramours" (7.2865–67). In this regard, Chauntecleer flagrantly violates the incest taboo, which Freud believed to be the cornerstone of civilization: "The tendency on the part of civilization to restrict sexual life is no less clear than its other tendency to expand the cultural unit. Its first, totemic, phase already brings with it the prohibition against an incestuous choice of object, and this is perhaps the most drastic mutilation which man's erotic life has in all time experienced."[6] By curtailing the range of viable eroticisms, civilizations circumvent desires that potentially fracture their organic unity. Freud also notes, "The first form of a social organization came about with a *renunciation of instinct*, a recognition of mutual *obligations*, the introduction of definite *institutions*, pronounced inviolable (holy)—that is to say, the beginnings of morality and justice. Each individual renounced his ideal of acquiring his father's position for himself and of possessing his mother and sisters."[7] Chauntecleer's farmyard, based on the fantasy of a civilization liberated from the incest taboo, creates a realm free of masculine discontents in the possibility of multiple sexual partners without constraints on consanguinity or number.

Certainly, this vision of masculine sexuality untethered from the incest taboo is troubling: it subordinates women into a misogynist structure that Chauntecleer's excessive eroticism perpetuates, yet one from which his biblical exegesis ostensibly liberates them. Chauntecleer both cleanses his realm of Christian misogynist discourse that blames women for humanity's fall from grace and reinstitutes a pre-Christian culture that recognizes no taboos on male desire, for as the undisputed leader of the farmyard, he faces no threats to his masculine governance that might undermine his claim to his seven wives. If women are to find erotic satisfaction in Chauntecleer's world, they must do so as wives equal to one another yet jointly subservient to an erotic system predicated upon masculine authority and pleasure. Truly, then, Chauntecleer's world is one for the animals—unregulated in terms of the incest prohibitions necessary for a human civilization, yet one surprisingly enlightened in its rewriting of Christian misogyny through the shared joys of eroticism. And so, as the tension between seriousness and play circulates throughout the *Canterbury Tales*, the image of Chauntecleer's sexual pursuits illuminates a pleasureful vision of erotic exuberance yet one that can only be realized within an animal world freed from critical human taboos. As John Finlayson argues, "If Chauntecleer is more fully Man than in most fables, he

---

6. Sigmund Freud, *Civilization and Its Discontents*, ed. and trans. James Strachey (New York: Norton, 1961), 59.

7. Sigmund Freud, "Moses and Monotheism," in *The Standard Edition of the Complete Psychological Works of Sigmund Freud*, ed. and trans. James Strachey (London: Hogarth, 1953–74), 23.1–137, at 82; italics in original.

is also more exactly bird as well—and this ambivalence, which suggests many parallels and judgments on Man without reducing the story to mere didacticism, makes this beast-fable much more than an *exemplum*."[8] For his human readers, Chauntecleer can only model erotic wholeness if one is willing to sacrifice one's sense of the human as a constituent factor of human culture.

In many ways, then, the *Nun's Priest's Tale* asks readers to consider the meaning of the human–animal boundary and the ways in which animals model erotic possibilities for them. Susan Crane posits that "Chaucer's interest in animals encompasses his interest in how they are enmeshed in human culture,"[9] and this observation can be expanded to include the ways in which Chaucer ponders the meaning of the animal enmeshed in the human. After the Nun's Priest concludes his tale, Harry Bailly extols his fellow pilgrims, and the Nun's Priest in particular, to enjoy the possibility of following Chauntecleer's example of an erotically organic life:

> "This was a murie tale of Chauntecleer.
> But by my trouthe, if thou were seculer,
> Thou woldest ben a trede-foul aright.
> For if thou have corage as thou hast might,
> Thee were need of hennes, as I wene,
> Ya, moo than seven tymes seventeen.
> See, which braunes hath this gentil preest,
> So gret a nekke, and swich a large breest!
> He loketh as a sperhauk with his yen." (7.3449–57)

Surely, as with much of the humor of the *Canterbury Tales*, Harry's words are spoken with tongue firmly in cheek, yet in the perpetual tension between game and play, Harry speaks truth, perhaps unintentional truths, through his humorous words. His vision of the Nun's Priest as a *trede-foul*, a chicken-fucker, intriguingly posits the possibility of a human–animal hybrid capable of resolving the inherent tensions of erotic desire.

---

8. John Finlayson, "Reading Chaucer's *Nun's Priest's Tale*," 504. On Chauntecleer's human/animal hybridity, see also Paul Thomas, "'Have ye no mannes herte?' Chauntecleer as Cock-Man in the *Nun's Priest's Tale*," in *Masculinities in Chaucer: Approaches to Maleness in the* Canterbury Tales *and* Troilus and Criseyde, ed. Peter Beidler (Cambridge: Brewer, 1998), 187–202.

9. Susan Crane, "For the Birds," *Studies in the Age of Chaucer* 29 (2007): 23–41, at 27; see also her *Animal Encounters: Contacts and Concepts in Medieval Britain* (Philadelphia: University of Pennsylvania Press, 2013).

Harry further links the Nun's Priest with the avian amorousness featured in his tale by describing him as a sparrow hawk, and also by multiplying to 119 the number of female partners the Nun's Priest would need to sate his erotic desires. Harry's grotesquely comic vision of the Nun's Priest as excessively indulging in intercourse—whether with his own or another species—strips the Christian Church of its erotic authority, as the host resignifies a defender of the faith into a monstrous emblem of its sexual subversion.

Moreover, Harry's desire to see the Nun's Priest as a human–animal hybrid builds on his earlier call to the Monk, the "manly man" of the *General Prologue* (1.167), to see himself on the borders between the animal and the human. Harry believes that the Monk should be capable of successfully pursuing sexual pleasure unchained to the human condition:

> "I pray to God, yeve hym confusioun
> That first thee broghte unto religioun!
> Thou woldest han been a tredefowel aright.
> Haddestow as greet a leeve as thou hast myght
> To parfoune al thy lust in engendrure,
> Thou haddest bigeten ful many a creature." (7.1943–48)

Within Harry's erotic worldview, religion circumvents the Monk's and Nun's Priest's ability to metamorphose into avian sexuality, and thus to satisfy their erotic desires with abandon and without limit. As Chauntecleer reformulates the *In principio* of the Christian tradition to win back Pertelote's sexual favors, Harry Bailly also identifies prohibitions against unlimited sexual desires within Christian traditions and advocates to these representatives of the faith the necessity of energetically breaching its doctrines by aligning themselves with animals.

For the Monk and the Nun's Priest to do so, however, is, of course, impossible, for despite the sexual freedom embodied in the chimerical vision of a *trede-foul*, it remains merely a fantasy. Fantasies, however fleeting, are not without their psychological and cultural function, and in their critique of the Freudian master narrative of sexual maturation, in which one moves through the perversities of childhood into adulthood and adult sexuality, Gilles Deleuze and Félix Guattari posit the possibility of becoming pleasurably mired in perversion, of resisting the psychosexual wholeness that Freud offers as the telos of psychological development. Their view of becoming-animal, a state of fluctuating union with the animal world that allows an individual to escape the limitations of humanity, enlightens the potential meanings of what a *trede-foul* might become within Chaucer's imagination:

> What is real is the becoming itself, the block of becoming, not the supposedly fixed terms through which that which becomes passes. Becoming can and should be qualified as becoming-animal even in the absence of a term that would be the animal become. The becoming-animal of the human being is real, even if the animal the human being becomes is not; and the becoming-other of the animal is real, even if that something other it becomes is not. This is the point to clarify: that a becoming lacks a subject distinct from itself; but also that it has no term, since its term in turn exists only as taken up in another becoming of which it is the subject, and which coexists, forms a block, with the first.[10]

One cannot become a rooster, of course, but one can become roosterlike, freed from the limitations of desire that circumvent its formulation and fruition in the human realm, and, intriguingly, Chaucer may have encoded the possibility of his own becoming-animal in his *Nun's Priest's Tale*. His protagonist Chauntecleer is based on numerous avian forebears, including Marie de France's unnamed cock in *Del Cok e del Gupil* and Pierre de St. Cloud's Chantecler in Branch II of the *Roman de Renart*.[11] Chaucer's slight Anglicization of Chantecler to Chauntecleer need only reflect his pronunciation of the name, but the orthographic overlap between his and his rooster's names, which becomes complete as a *u* is added to Chantecler, links the two together, potentially painting the author as the foremost *trede-foul* of the pilgrimage.[12] To see Chaucer as a *trede-foul* in brotherhood with the Nun's Priest and Monk allows both a liberating vision of a human queerly unyoked from the human condition, and thus capable of pursuing eroticism freed from discontents, yet Chaucer sullies the utopic cast of this image as well, coupling it with a world bereft of the incest taboo that constrains certain desires but does so for the purpose of elevating the human above the animal. If Chauntecleer and

---

10. Gilles Deleuze and Félix Guattari, *A Thousand Plateaus: Capitalism and Schizophrenia*, trans. Brian Massumi (Minneapolis: University of Minnesota Press, 1987), 238. For a critique of Deleuze and Guattari's theory of becoming-animal, see Donna Haraway, *When Species Meet* (Minneapolis: University of Minnesota Press, 2008), 27–30.

11. For a brief review of Chauntecleer's literary forebears, see Jacqueline de Weever, *Chaucer Name Dictionary* (New York: Garland, 1996), 86.

12. On the potential allegorical significations of names in the *Nun's Priest's Tale*, see Dolores Warwick Frese, "The *Nun's Priest's Tale*: Chaucer's Identified Master Piece?" *Chaucer Review* 16.4 (1982): 330–43.

Chaucer as *trede-foul* emblematize queer freedoms in eroticism, untethered from the normative parameters of mate selection, they simultaneously acknowledge that all eroticisms are potentially corrupted with darker currents than pleasure acknowledges. Lesley Kordecki reminds readers that "Chaucer beguiles us by trying on the radical voices of animals, adjusting his sources, and playing with possibility in both genre and in apprehension of disparate perspectives,"[13] and this radical voicing and vision dismantles barriers between animality and humanity, incest and marriage, nature and civilization.

Deleuze and Guattari's concept of becoming-animal thus requires as a necessary corollary the concept of becoming-queer, in the open possibilities that merge in the quest for a sexual humanity in and beyond the Middle Ages. As apparent through this monograph, when eroticisms and their anti-erotic counterparts queerly circulate in Chaucer's corpus, his characters must endure the vagaries of gender and sexual identity inherent in pursuing their amatory passions, with their respective narratives foregrounding the negotiations of self and society necessary to consummate sexual desire. To experience a state of becoming-queer, to allow desires to surface only to confront the impossibility of their satisfaction, allows one to confront the erotic torsions inherent in human existence, as the previous chapters of this study have explored. In the *Franklin's Tale*, love necessitates that Arveragus and Dorigen push each other to the masochistic brink of utmost suffering, and the men who pledge brotherhood oaths to each other in the *House of Fame*, *Knight's Tale*, *Friar's Tale*, *Pardoner's Tale*, and *Shipman's Tale* find themselves debased by emulating rituals intended to elevate them, as latent eroticism colors their ostensibly chaste relationships with a tinge of homosexuality. Pursuing romantic love with women, Arcite in the *Knight's Tale* and Troilus in *Troilus and Criseyde* find themselves instead confronting the necrotic underbellies of their erotic desires; by compelling women to serve as the ideal beloved in their narcissistic fantasies, they confront the anti-erotic force of Emily's and Criseyde's rejection of romance and its potential repercussions to the social order. For Chaucer's child characters in the *Reeve's Tale*, *Summoner's Tale*, *Clerk's Tale*, and *Physician's Tale*, adult desires ensnare them in erotic plots that rob them of constitutive factors of their beings—their virginity, their parents, and often their lives—yet their apparent lack of erotic agency merely camouflages the power of passivity to subvert

---

13. Lesley Kordecki, *Ecofeminist Subjectivities: Chaucer's Talking Birds* (New York: Palgrave Macmillan, 2011), 106–7.

parental authority. Chaucer's God institutes regulations to govern human eroticism, only to be swept away by love's throes in the *Legend of Good Women* and the *Second Nun's Tale*, and his surprising surrender to human passions queerly subverts the very possibility of religious dogma. From these disparate moments of Chaucer's corpus, the queerness of eroticism surfaces in the tension between desire and social dictates, particularly from traditions endorsing anti-eroticism that must confront the necessity of their own transgressions. All desires spark becomings, and all those who desire find themselves confronted by its ever protean force in their visions of themselves and of their beloveds, and thus in their understanding of the unsteady and queer relations that are engendered through eroticism.

The annals of literature records the primacy of desires fulfilled and unfulfilled: the foundational narrative of Adam and Eve encapsulates the tribulations of eroticism, a story told, retold, reimagined, and reinvented throughout the centuries but with core consistencies: a snake in the garden destroying the bliss of an eternal love, and the snake, of course, symbolizing the very instrument necessary in many, but certainly not all, enactments of sexual desire. For Chaucer's queer eroticisms, so too is there often a snake—or perhaps a fox—in the garden of human sexuality, but there is also a rooster in a farmyard, guiding the ways to eroticisms united in a civilization free from discontents, while ironically modeling the necessity of erotic discontents if one is to become fully queer, and thus fully human.

WORKS CITED

Ackerman, Susan. *When Heroes Love: The Ambiguity of Eros in the Stories of Gilgamesh and David*. New York: Columbia University Press, 2005.

Aers, David. *Chaucer*. Atlantic Highlands, NJ: Humanities Press, 1986.

———. "Criseyde: Woman in Medieval Society." *Chaucer Review* 13.3 (1979): 177–200.

Ailes, M. J. "The Medieval Male Couple and the Language of Homosociality." In Hadley 214–37.

Alan de Lille. *Summa de arte praedicatoria*. Patrologia Latina 210.195bc

Alexiou, Margaret, and Peter Dronke. "The Lament of Jephtha's Daughter: Themes, Traditions, Originality." *Studi Medievali* 12 (1971): 819–63.

Allen, Valerie. *On Farting: Language and Laughter in the Middle Ages*. New York: Palgrave Macmillan, 2007.

Allman, W. W., and Thomas Hanks. "Rough Love: Notes toward an Erotics of the *Canterbury Tales*." *Chaucer Review* 38.1 (2003): 36–65.

Althusser, Louis. "Ideology and Ideological State Apparatuses (Notes towards an Investigation)." In *Lenin and Philosophy and Other Essays*, trans. Ben Brewster. New York: Monthly Review, 1971. 127–88.

Ames, Ruth. *God's Plenty: Chaucer's Christian Humanism*. Chicago: Loyola University Press, 1984.

Andreas Capellanus. *De Amore*. Ed. E. Trojel. Havniae: In Libraria Gadiana, 1892.

———. *The Art of Courtly Love*. Trans. John Jay Parry. New York: Columbia University Press, 1960.

Aquinas, Thomas. *The Summa Theologica of St. Thomas Aquinas, Second Part of the Second Part, QQ. CXLI–CLXX*. Trans. Fathers of the English Dominican Province. New York: Benziger Brothers, 1921.

Ariès, Philippe. *Centuries of Childhood*. Trans. Robert Baldick. New York: Knopf, 1962.

Arthur, Karen. "A TACT Analysis of the Language of Death in *Troilus and Criseyde*." In *Computer-Based Chaucer Studies*, ed. Ian Lancashire and Patricia Eberle. Toronto: Centre for Computing in Humanities, 1993. 67–85.

Astell, Ann. *The Song of Songs in the Middle Ages*. Ithaca, NY: Cornell University Press, 1990.

Auerbach, Erich. *Mimesis: The Representation of Reality in Western Literature*. Trans. Willard Trask. 1953. Princeton, NJ: Princeton University Press, 2003.

Augustine. *City of God*. Trans. Henry Bettenson. London: Penguin, 1984.

———. *Lectures or Tractates on the Gospel According to St. John*. Trans. John Gibb. Edinburgh: Clark, 1873.

———. *St. Augustine on Marriage and Sexuality*. Ed. Elizabeth Clark. Washington, DC: Catholic University of America Press, 1996.

Barnett, Pamela. "'And shortly for to seyn they were aton': Chaucer's Deflection of Rape in the *Reeve's* and *Franklin's Tales*." *Women's Studies* 22 (1993): 145–62.

Bataille, Georges. *Erotism: Death and Sensuality*. Trans. Mary Dalwood. 1957. San Francisco: City Lights, 1986.

Beecher, Donald, and Massimo Ciavolella, eds. and trans. *A Treatise on Love Sickness by Jacques Ferrand*. Syracuse, NY: Syracuse University Press, 1990.

Beidler, Peter. "The Climax in the *Merchant's Tale*." *Chaucer Review* 6 (1971): 38–43.

———, ed. *Men and Masculinities in Chaucer: Approaches to Maleness in the Canterbury Tales and Troilus and Criseyde*. Cambridge: Brewer, 1998.

———. "Medieval Children Witness Their Mother's Indiscretions: The Maid Child in Chaucer's *Shipman's Tale*." *Chaucer Review* 44.2 (2009): 186–204.

Benson, Larry, and Theodore Andersson, eds. *The Literary Context of Chaucer's Fabliaux*. Indianapolis, IN: Bobbs-Merrill, 1971.

Benson, Robert, and Susan Ridyard, eds. *New Readings of Chaucer's Poetry*. Cambridge: Brewer, 2003.

Bernard of Clairvaux. *Selected Works*. Trans. G. R. Evans. New York: Paulist Press, 1987.

Besserman, Lawrence. *Chaucer and the Bible*. New York: Garland, 1988.

———. *Chaucer's Biblical Poetics*. Norman: University of Oklahoma Press, 1998.

Bettenson, Henry, ed. *Documents of the Christian Church*. New York: Oxford University Press, 1956.

Biblia sacra iuxta vulgatam versionem. Stuttgart: Deutsche Bibelgesellschaft, 1994.

Biggs, Frederick, and Laura Howes. "Theophany in the *Miller's Tale*." *Medium Aevum* 65.2 (1996): 269–79.

Bishop, Louise. "'Of Goddes pryvetee nor of his wyf': Confusion of Orifices in Chaucer's *Miller's Tale*." *Texas Studies in Literature and Language* 44.3 (2002): 231–46.

Blamires, Alcuin. *Chaucer, Ethics, and Gender*. Oxford: Oxford University Press, 2006.

Bliss, Jane. *Naming and Namelessness in Medieval Romance*. Cambridge: Brewer, 2008.

Bloch, Howard. "Chaucer's Maiden's Head: The *Physician's Tale* and the Poetics of Virginity." In *Chaucer: Contemporary Critical Essays*, ed. Valerie Allen and Ares Axiotis. New York: St. Martin's, 1996. 145–56.

Boccaccio, Giovanni. *The Decameron*. Trans. G. H. McWilliam. Harmondsworth, UK: Penguin, 1972.

Boitani, Piero. *Chaucer and Boccaccio*. Oxford: Society for the Study of Medieval Languages and Literature, 1977.

Bond, Gerald. *The Loving Subject: Desire, Eloquence, and Power in Romanesque France*. Philadelphia: University of Pennsylvania Press, 1995.

Bossy, Michel-André. "The Elaboration of Female Narrative Functions in *Erec et Enide*." In *Courtly Literature: Culture and Context*, ed. Keith Busby and Erik Kooper. Amsterdam: Benjamins, 1990. 23–38.

Boswell, John. *Christianity, Social Tolerance, and Homosexuality: Gay People in Western Europe from the Beginning of the Christian Era to the Fourteenth Century*. Chicago: University of Chicago Press, 1981.

———. *Same-Sex Unions in Premodern Europe*. New York: Villard, 1994.

Bowers, John. "Queering the Summoner: Same-Sex Union in Chaucer's *Canterbury Tales*." In *Speaking Images: Essays in Honor of V. A. Kolve*, ed. Robert Yeager and Charlotte Morse. Asheville, NC: Pegasus, 2001. 301–24.

———. "Three Readings of the *Knight's Tale*: Sir John Clanvowe, Geoffrey Chaucer, and James I of Scotland." *Journal of Medieval and Early Modern Studies* 34 (2004): 279–307.

Bowman, Mary. "'Half as she were mad': Dorigen in the Male World of the *Franklin's Tale*." *Chaucer Review* 27.3 (1993): 239–51.

Bray, Alan. *The Friend*. Chicago: University of Chicago Press, 2003.

Breuer, Heidi. "Being Intolerant: Rape Is Not Seduction (in the *Reeve's Tale* or Anywhere Else)." In *The Canterbury Tales Revisited: Twenty-First Century Interpretations*, ed. Kathleen Bishop and David Matthews. Newcastle upon Tyne, England: Cambridge Scholars, 2008. 1–15.

Brewer, D. S. "Children in Chaucer." *Review of English Literature* 5.3 (1964): 52–60.

———. *The World of Chaucer*. Cambridge: Brewer, 2000.

Brooke, Christopher. *The Medieval Idea of Marriage*. Oxford: Oxford University Press, 1989.

Brooks, Peter. *Reading for the Plot*. New York: Vintage, 1984.

Brown, Emerson. "Hortus Inconclusus: The Significance of Priapus and Pyramus and Thisbe in the *Merchant's Tale*." *Chaucer Review* 4 (1970): 31–40.

Brozyna, Martha, ed. *Gender and Sexuality in the Middle Ages: A Medieval Source Documents Reader*. Jefferson, NC: McFarland, 2005.

Brundage, James. *Law, Sex, and Christian Society in Medieval Europe*. Chicago: University of Chicago Press, 1990.

Bühler, Curt. "Wirk alle thyng by conseil." *Speculum* 24 (1949): 410–12.

Bullough, Vern, and James Brundage, eds. *Handbook of Medieval Sexuality*. New York: Garland, 1996.

———. *Sexual Practices and the Medieval Church*. Buffalo, NY: Prometheus, 1982.

Burger, Glenn. *Chaucer's Queer Nation*. Minneapolis: University of Minnesota Press, 2003.

———. "Kissing the Pardoner." *PMLA* 107 (1992): 1143–56.

Burger, Glenn, and Steven Kruger, eds. *Queering the Middle Ages*. Minneapolis: University of Minnesota Press, 2001.

Burgwinkle, William. *Sodomy, Masculinity, and Law in Medieval Literature: France and England, 1050–1230*. Cambridge: Cambridge University Press, 2004.

Burke, Seán. *The Death and Return of the Author: Criticism and Subjectivity in Barthes, Foucault, and Derrida*. 2nd ed. Edinburgh: Edinburgh University Press, 1998.

Burns, Jane. *Bodytalk: When Women Speak in Old French Literature*. Philadelphia: University of Pennsylvania Press, 1993.

———. "Courtly Love: Who Needs It? Recent Feminist Work in the Medieval French Tradition." *Signs* 27.1 (2001): 23–57.

Burrow, John A. *The Ages of Man*. Oxford: Clarendon, 1986.

———. "Chaucer as Petitioner: Three Poems." *Chaucer Review* 45.3 (2011): 349–56.

Butler, Judith. *Gender Trouble: Feminism and the Subversion of Identity*. New York: Routledge, 1990.

———. *The Psychic Life of Power: Theories in Subjection*. Stanford, CA: Stanford University Press, 1997.

Bynum, Caroline Walker. *Fragmentation and Redemption: Essays on Gender and the Human Body in Medieval Religion*. New York: Zone, 1991.

———. *Jesus as Mother: Studies in the Spirituality of the High Middle Ages*. Berkeley: University of California Press, 1982.

Cadden, Joan. *Meanings of Sex Difference in the Middle Ages*. Cambridge: Cambridge University Press, 1993.

Calabrese, Michael. "Chaucer's Dorigen and Boccaccio's Female Voices." *Studies in the Age of Chaucer* 29 (2007): 259–92.

———. *Chaucer's Ovidian Arts of Love*. Gainesville: University Press of Florida, 1994.

Caldwell, James Ralston, ed. *Eger and Grime: A Parallel-Text Edition of the Percy and the Huntington-Laing Versions of the Romance, with an Introductory Study*. Cambridge, MA: Harvard University Press, 1933.

Campbell, Emma, and Robert Mills, eds. *Troubled Vision: Sexuality and Sight in Medieval Text and Image*. New York: Palgrave Macmillan, 2004.

Cañadas, Ivan. "The Shadow of Virgil and Augustus on Chaucer's *House of Fame*." *Medieval and Early Modern English Studies* 18.1 (2010): 57–79.

Cannon, Christopher. "Chaucer and Rape: Uncertainty's Certainties." *Studies in the Age of Chaucer* 22 (2000): 67–92.

———. "*Raptus* in the Chaumpaigne Release and a Newly Discovered Document Concerning the Life of Geoffrey Chaucer." *Speculum* 68 (1993): 79–94.

Carlson, Cindy, and Angela Jane Weisl, eds. *Constructions of Widowhood and Virginity in the Middle Ages*. New York: St. Martin's, 1999.

Chance, Jane. *The Mythographic Chaucer: The Fabulation of Sexual Politics*. Minneapolis: University of Minnesota Press, 1995.

Chaplais, Pierre. *Piers Gaveston: Edward II's Adoptive Brother*. Oxford: Clarendon, 1994.

Chaucer, Geoffrey. *The Riverside Chaucer*. Ed. Larry D. Benson. 3rd ed. Boston: Houghton Mifflin, 1987.

Chrétien de Troyes. *Arthurian Romances*. Trans. D. D. R. Owen. London: Everyman, 1993.

———. *Erec et Enide*. Ed. Jean-Marie Fritz. Livre de Poche, 1992.

———. *Erec and Enide*. Trans. Burton Raffel. New Haven, CT: Yale University Press, 1997.

Cicero. *De Senectute, De Amicitia, De Divinatione*. Ed. and trans. William Falconer. Cambridge, MA: Harvard University Press, 1979.

———. *On the Good Life*. Trans. Michael Grant. London, 1971.

Clark, David. *Between Medieval Men: Male Friendship and Desire in Early Medieval English Literature*. Oxford: Oxford University Press, 2009.

Cohen, Jeffrey Jerome. *Medieval Identity Machines*. Minneapolis: University of Minnesota Press, 2003.

Cole, Andrew, and Vance Smith, eds. *The Legitimacy of the Middle Ages: On the Unwritten History of Theory*. Durham, NC: Duke University Press, 2010.

Collette, Carolyn. *Species, Phantasms, and Images: Vision and Medieval Psychology in the Canterbury Tales*. Ann Arbor: University of Michigan Press, 2001.

Cooper, Helen. *The English Romance in Time: Transforming Motifs from Geoffrey of Monmouth to the Death of Shakespeare*. Oxford: Oxford University Press, 2004.

———. *Oxford Guides to Chaucer:* The Canterbury Tales. Oxford: Oxford University Press, 1989.

Correale, Robert, and Mary Hamel, eds. *Sources and Analogues of the* Canterbury Tales. 2 vols. Cambridge: Brewer, 2002.

Cowdrey, H. E. J., ed. and trans. *The Epistolae Vagantes of Pope Gregory VII*. Oxford: Clarendon, 1972.

Cowgill, Jane. "Chaucer's Missing Children." *Essays in Medieval Studies* 12 (1996): 39–53.

Cox, Catherine. *Gender and Language in Chaucer*. Gainesville: University Press of Florida, 1997.

———. "'Grope wel bihynde': The Subversive Erotics of Chaucer's Summoner." *Exemplaria* 7 (1995): 145–77.

Crane, Susan. *Animal Encounters: Contacts and Concepts in Medieval Britain*. Philadelphia: University of Pennsylvania Press, 2013.

———. "For the Birds." *Studies in the Age of Chaucer* 29 (2007): 23–41.

———. *Gender and Romance in Chaucer's* Canterbury Tales. Princeton, NJ: Princeton University Press, 1994.

Crocker, Holly. "Affective Politics in Chaucer's *Reeve's Tale:* 'Cherl' Masculinity after 1381." *Studies in the Age of Chaucer* 29 (2007): 225–58.

———. *Chaucer's Visions of Manhood*. New York: Palgrave Macmillan, 2007.

———. "Disfiguring Gender: Masculine Desire in the Old French Fabliau." *Exemplaria* 23.4 (2011): 342–67.

———. "How the Woman Makes the Man: Chaucer's Reciprocal Fictions in *Troilus and Criseyde*." In Vitto and Marzec 139–64.

———, ed. *Comic Provocations: Exposing the Corpus of Old French Fabliaux*. New York: Palgrave Macmillan, 2006.

Crow, Martin, and Clair Olson, eds. *Chaucer Life Records*. Austin: University of Texas Press, 1966.

Dane, Joseph. "'Mulier est hominis confusio': Note on Chaucer's *Nun's Priest's Tale*, Line 3164." *Notes and Queries* 39.3 (1992): 276–78.

Dante Alighieri. *De vulgari eloquentia*. Ed. and trans. Steven Botterill. Cambridge: Cambridge University Press, 1996.

———. *Il Convivio*. Trans. Richard Lansing. New York: Garland, 1990.

David, Alfred. "Literary Satire in *The House of Fame*." *PMLA* 75 (1960): 333–39.

Davies, R. T., ed. *Medieval English Lyrics: A Critical Anthology*. Evansville, IL: Northwestern University Press, 1964.

Davis, Craig. "A Perfect Marriage on the Rocks: Geoffrey and Philippa Chaucer, and the *Franklin's Tale*." *Chaucer Review* 37.2 (2002): 129–44.

D'Avray, D. L. *Medieval Marriage: Symbolism and Society*. Oxford: Oxford University Press, 2005.

Dean, Tim. *Beyond Sexuality*. Chicago: University of Chicago Press, 2000.

———. "Lacan and Queer Theory." In *The Cambridge Companion to Lacan*, ed. Jean-Michel Rabaté. Cambridge: Cambridge University Press, 2003. 238–52.

Delany, Sheila "A, A, and B: Coding Same-Sex Union in *Amis and Amiloun*." In *Pulp Fictions of Medieval England: Essays in Popular Romance*, ed. Nicola McDonald. Manchester: Manchester University Press, 2004. 63–81.

Delasanta, Rodney. "Nominalism and the *Clerk's Tale*." *Chaucer Review* 31 (1997): 209–31.

De Lauretis, Theresa. *Alice Doesn't: Feminism, Semiotics, Cinema*. Bloomington: Indiana University Press, 1984.

Deleuze, Gilles. *Masochism*. New York: Zone, 1991.

Deleuze, Gilles, and Félix Guattari. *A Thousand Plateaus: Capitalism and Schizophrenia*. Trans. Brian Massumi. Minneapolis: University of Minnesota Press, 1987.

De Rougemont, Denis. *Love in the Western World*. Trans. Montgomery Belgion. 1940. New York: Pantheon, 1956.

Desmond, Marilyn. *Ovid's Art and the Wife of Bath: The Ethics of Erotic Violence*. Ithaca, NY: Cornell University Press, 2006.

De Weever, Jacqueline. *Chaucer Name Dictionary*. New York: Garland, 1996.

Dinshaw, Carolyn. *Chaucer's Sexual Poetics*. Madison: University of Wisconsin Press, 1989.

———. *Getting Medieval: Sexualities and Communities, Pre- and Postmodern*. Durham, NC: Duke University Press, 1999.

———. "Rivalry, Rape, and Manhood: Gower and Chaucer." In *Violence against Women in Medieval Texts*, ed. Anna Roberts. Gainesville: University Press of Florida, 1998. 137–60.

Donaldson, E. Talbot. "Briseis, Briseida, Criseyde, Cresseid, Cressid: Progress of a Heroine." In *Chaucerian Problems and Perspectives*, ed. Edward Vasta, Zacharias Thundy, and Theodore Hesburgh. Notre Dame, IN: University of Notre Dame Press, 1979. 3–12.

Dull, S., A. Luttrell, and M. Keen. "Faithful unto Death: The Tombe Slab of Sir William Neville and Sir John Clanvowe." *Antiquaries Journal* 71 (1991): 183–84.

Edelman, Lee. *Homographesis*. New York: Routledge, 1994.

———. *No Future: Queer Theory and the Death Drive*. Durham, NC: Duke University Press, 2004.

Edwards, Elizabeth. "Chaucer's *Knight's Tale* and the Work of Mourning." *Exemplaria* 20.4 (2008): 361–84.

Edwards, Robert. *Chaucer and Boccaccio: Antiquity and Modernity*. New York: Palgrave Macmillan, 2002.

———. *The Flight from Desire: Augustine and Ovid to Chaucer*. New York: Palgrave Macmillan, 2006.

Edwards, Suzanne. "The Rhetoric of Rape and the Politics of Gender in the *Wife of Bath's Tale* and the 1382 Statute of Rapes." *Exemplaria* 23.1 (2011): 3–26.

Eliason, Norman. "Chaucer the Love Poet." In Mitchell and Provost 9–26.

Elliott, Dyan. *Spiritual Marriage: Sexual Abstinence in Medieval Wedlock*. Princeton, NJ: Princeton University Press, 1993.

Everest, Carol. "Sex and Old Age in Chaucer's *Reeve's Tale*." *Chaucer Review* 31.2 (1996): 99–114.

Farber, Lianna. "The Creation of Consent in the *Physician's Tale*." *Chaucer Review* 39.2 (2004): 151–64.

Farina, Lara. *Erotic Discourse and Early English Religious Writing*. New York: Palgrave Macmillan, 2006.

Fein, Susanna Greer. "'Lat the children pleye': The Game betwixt the Ages in the *Reeve's Tale*." In *Rebels and Rivals: The Contestive Spirit in the* Canterbury Tales, ed. Susanna Greer Fein, David Raybin, and Peter Braeger. Kalamazoo, MI: Medieval Institute Publications, 1991. 73–104.

Feinstein, Sandy. "*The Reeve's Tale*: About That Horse." *Chaucer Review* 26.1 (1991): 99–106.

Finlayson, John. "*The Knight's Tale:* The Dialogue of Romance, Epic, and Philosophy." *Chaucer Review* 27.2 (1992): 126–49.

———. "Reading Chaucer's *Nun's Priest's Tale*: Mixed Genres and Multi-layered Worlds of Illusion." *English Studies* 86.6 (2005): 493–510.

Flake, Timothy. "Love, *Trouthe*, and the Happy Ending of the *Franklin's Tale*." *English Studies* 77.3 (1996): 209–26.

Fleming, John. "Anticlerical Satire as Theological Essay: Chaucer's *Summoner's Tale*." *Thalia* 6.1–2 (1983): 5–22.

Ford, John. "Contrasting the Identical: Differentiation of the 'Indistinguishable' Characters of *Amis and Amiloun*." *Neophilologus* 86 (2002): 311–23.

Foucault, Michel. *The History of Sexuality*. Vol. 1, *An Introduction*. Trans. Robert Hurley. 1978. New York: Vintage, 1990.

———. *The History of Sexuality*. Vol. 2, *The Use of Pleasure*. Trans. Robert Hurley. 1985. New York: Vintage, 1990.

———. *The History of Sexuality*. Vol. 3, *The Care of the Self*. Trans. Robert Hurley. 1986. New York: Vintage, 1988.

Fowler, Elizabeth. "The Afterlife of the Civil Dead: Conquest in the *Knight's Tale*." In Stillinger 59–81.

Fradenburg, Aranye. *Sacrifice Your Love: Psychoanalysis, Historicism, Chaucer*. Minneapolis: University of Minnesota Press, 2002.

Fradenburg, Louise. "The Wife of Bath's Passing Fancy." *Studies in the Age of Chaucer* 8 (1986): 31–58.

Fradenburg, Louise, and Carla Freccero, eds. *Premodern Sexualities*. New York: Routledge, 1996.

Frantzen, Allen. *Before the Closet: Same-Sex Love from* Beowulf *to* Angels in America. Chicago: University of Chicago Press, 1998.

Frese, Dolores Warwick. "The *Nun's Priest's Tale*: Chaucer's Identified Master Piece?" *Chaucer Review* 16.4 (1982): 330–43.

Freud, Sigmund. *Civilization and Its Discontents*. Ed. and trans. James Strachey. New York: Norton, 1961.

———. *The Standard Edition of the Complete Psychological Works of Sigmund Freud*. Ed. and trans. James Strachey. London: Hogarth, 1953–74.

Friedman, John. "Dorigen's 'Grisly rokkes blake' Again." *Chaucer Review* 31.2 (1996): 133–44.

Fritz, Donald. "The Prioress's Avowal of Ineptitude." *Chaucer Review* 9.2 (1974): 166–81.

Froissart, Jean. *An Anthology of Narrative and Lyric Poetry*. Ed. and trans. Kristen Figg, with R. Barton Palmer. New York: Routledge, 2001.

Frye, Northrop. *Anatomy of Criticism*. Princeton, NJ: Princeton University Press, 1957.

Fyler, John. *Chaucer and Ovid*. New Haven, CT: Yale University Press, 1979.

Gantz, Jeffrey, trans. *The Mabinogion*. London: Penguin, 1976.

Ganze, Alison. "'My trouthe for to holde—allas, allas!': Dorigen and Honor in the *Franklin's Tale*." *Chaucer Review* 42.3 (2008): 312–29.

Gardner, John. *The Life and Times of Chaucer*. New York: Vintage, 1978.

Gaunt, Simon. *Love and Death in Medieval French and Occitan Courtly Literature: Martyrs to Love*. Oxford: Oxford University Press, 2006.

Gaylord, Alan. "Friendship in Chaucer's *Troilus*." *Chaucer Review* 3 (1969): 239–64.

Gellrich, Jesse. "The Parody of Medieval Music in the *Miller's Tale*." *Studies in English and Germanic Philology* 73 (1974): 176–88.

Georgianna, Linda. "The *Clerk's Tale* and the Grammar of Assent." *Speculum* 70 (1995): 793–821.

Giffney, Noreen. "Queer Apocal(o)ptic/ism: The Death Drive and the Human." In *Queering the Non/Human*, ed. Noreen Giffney and Myra Hird. Aldershot, Hampshire: Ashgate, 2008. 55–78.

Gilles, Sealy. "Love and Disease in Chaucer's *Troilus and Criseyde*." *Studies in the Age of Chaucer* 25 (2003): 157–97.

Ginsberg, Warren. *Chaucer's Italian Tradition*. Ann Arbor: University of Michigan Press, 2002.

———. "Dante's Dream of the Eagle and Jacob's Ladder." *Dante Studies* 100 (1982): 41–69.

Goodich, Michael. *The Unmentionable Vice: Homosexuality in the Later Medieval Period*. Santa Barbara, CA: ABC-Clio, 1979.

Goux, Jean-Joseph. *Symbolic Economies: After Marx and Freud*. Trans. Jennifer Gage. Ithaca, NY: Cornell University Press, 1990.

Gower, John. *The Complete Works of John Gower*. Ed. G. C. Macaulay. 4 vols. Oxford: Clarendon, 1901.

Gray, Douglas. *Oxford Companion to Chaucer*. Oxford: Oxford University Press, 2003.

Green, Donald. "Chaucer as Nuditarian: The Erotic as a Critical Problem." *Pacific Coast Philology* 18.1–2 (1983): 59–69.

Green, Richard Firth. "Cecily Champain v. Geoffrey Chaucer: A New Look at an Old Dispute." In *Law and Sovereignty in the Middle Ages and Renaissance*, ed. Robert Sturges. Turnhout: Brepols, 2011. 261–85.

———. *A Crisis of Truth: Literature and Law in Ricardian England*. Philadelphia: University of Pennsylvania Press, 1999.

———. "Further Evidence for Chaucer's Representation of the Pardoner as a Womanizer." *Medium Ævum* 71 (2002): 307–9.

———. "The Pardoner's Pants (and Why They Matter)." *Studies in the Age of Chaucer* 15 (1993): 131–45.

Gunn, David. *Judges*. Malden, MA: Blackwell, 2005.

Gust, Geoffrey. *Constructing Chaucer: Author and Autofiction in the Critical Tradition.* New York: Palgrave Macmillan, 2009.

Guynn, Noah. *Allegory and Sexual Ethics in the High Middle Ages.* New York: Palgrave Macmillan, 2007.

Hadley, D. M., ed. *Masculinity in Medieval Europe.* London: Longman, 1999.

Hahn, Thomas, ed. *Sir Gawain: Eleven Romances and Tales.* Kalamazoo, MI: Medieval Institute Publications, 1995.

Haines, Roy. *King Edward II.* Montreal: McGill-Queen's University Press, 2003.

Hanawalt, Barbara. *Growing Up in Medieval London: The Experience of Childhood in History.* New York: Oxford University Press, 1993.

———. *The Ties That Bound: Peasant Families in Medieval England.* New York: Oxford University Press, 1986.

Hanna, Ralph. *London Literature, 1300–1380.* Cambridge: Cambridge University Press, 2005.

Hanning, Robert. *Serious Play: Desire and Authority in the Poetry of Ovid, Chaucer, and Ariosto.* New York: Columbia University Press, 2010.

Hanrahan, Michael. "Seduction and Betrayal: Treason in the Prologue to the *Legend of Good Women*." *Chaucer Review* 30 (1996): 229–40.

Hansen, Elaine Tuttle. *Chaucer and the Fictions of Gender.* Berkeley: University of California Press, 1992.

———. "The Power of Silence: The Case of the Clerk's Griselda." In Stillinger 133–49.

Haraway, Donna. *When Species Meet.* Minneapolis: University of Minnesota Press, 2008.

Harper, April, and Caroline Proctor, eds. *Medieval Sexuality: A Casebook.* New York: Routledge, 2008.

Harwood, Britton, and Gillian Overing, eds. *Class and Gender in Early English Literature.* Bloomington: Indiana University Press, 1994.

Havely, N. R., ed. and trans. *Chaucer's Boccaccio: Sources of* Troilus *and the* Knight's *and* Franklin's *Tales.* Cambridge: Brewer, 1980.

Hermann, John. "Dismemberment, Dissemination, Discourse: Sign and Symbol in the *Shipman's Tale*." *Chaucer Review* 19 (1985): 302–37.

Heyworth, Gregory. *Desiring Bodies: Ovidian Romance and the Cult of Form.* Notre Dame, IN: University of Notre Dame Press, 2009.

Hill, John. "Aristocratic Friendship in *Troilus and Criseyde*: Pandarus, Courtly Love, and Ciceronian Brotherhood in Troy." In Benson and Ridyard 165–82.

———. *Chaucerian Belief: The Poetics of Reverence and Delight.* New Haven, CT: Yale University Press, 1991.

Hodges, Laura. *Chaucer and Clothing: Clerical and Academic Costume in the* General Prologue *to the* Canterbury Tales. Cambridge: Brewer, 2005.

Hoffman, Richard. *Ovid and the* Canterbury Tales. Philadelphia: University of Pennsylvania Press, 1966.

Hollywood, Amy. *The Soul as Virgin Wife: Mechthild of Magdeburg, Marguerite Porete, and Meister Eckhart.* Notre Dame, IN: University of Notre Dame Press, 1995.

Holsinger, Bruce. *The Premodern Condition: Medievalism and the Making of Theory.* Chicago: University of Chicago Press, 2005.

Holy Bible: Douay-Rheims Version. Charlotte, NC: Tan, 2009.

Horstmann, Carl, ed. "How a Man Schal Lyue Parfytly." In *Minor Poems of the Vernon Manuscript*. London: Early English Text Society, 1892. Millwood, New York: Kraus, 1987. 1.221–51.

Howard, Donald. *Chaucer: His Life, His Works, His World*. New York: Dutton, 1987.

Howie, Cary. *Claustrophilia: The Erotics of Enclosure in Medieval Literature*. New York: Palgrave Macmillan, 2007.

Hudson, Harriet, ed. *Sir Tryamour*. In *Four Middle English Romances*. Kalamazoo, MI: Medieval Institute Publications, 1996. 173–232.

Hume, Cathy. *Chaucer and the Cultures of Love and Marriage*. Cambridge: Brewer, 2012.

Hutcheson, Gregory, and Josiah Blackmore, eds. *Queer Iberia: Sexualities, Cultures, and Crossings from the Middle Ages to the Renaissance*. Durham, NC: Duke University Press, 1999.

Hyatte, Reginald. *The Arts of Friendship: The Idealization of Friendship in Medieval and Early Renaissance Literature*. Leiden; New York: Brill, 1994.

Impelluso, Lucia. *Nature and Its Symbols*. Trans. Stephen Sartarelli. Los Angeles: Getty Museum, 2003.

Infusino, Mark, and Ynez O'Neill. "Arcite's Death and the New Surgery in the *Knight's Tale*." *Studies in the Age of Chaucer* 1 (1984): 221–30.

Ingham, Patricia Clare. "Homosociality and Creative Masculinity in the *Knight's Tale*." In Beidler, *Masculinities* 23–35.

Jacobs, Kathryn. *Marriage Contracts from Chaucer to the Renaissance Stage*. Gainesville: University Press of Florida, 2001.

Jaeger, C. Stephen. *Ennobling Love: In Search of a Lost Sensibility*. Philadelphia: University of Pennsylvania Press, 1999.

Jeffrey, David, ed. *Chaucer and Scriptural Tradition*. Ottawa: University of Ottawa Press, 1984.

Jensen, Emily. "Male Competition as a Unifying Motif in Fragment A of the *Canterbury Tales*." *Chaucer Review* 24 (1990): 320–28.

Jones, Terry. *Chaucer's Knight: The Portrait of a Medieval Mercenary*. Baton Rouge: Louisiana State University Press, 1980.

Jones, Terry, Robert Yeager, Alan Fletcher, Juliette Dor, and Terry Dolan. *Who Murdered Chaucer? A Medieval Mystery*. New York: St. Martin's, 2003.

Jordan, Mark. *The Invention of Sodomy in Christian Theology*. Chicago: University of Chicago Press, 1997.

Jost, Jean. "Ambiguous Brotherhood in the *Friar's Tale* and the *Summoner's Tale*." In Beidler, *Masculinities* 77–90.

Karras, Ruth. *Sexuality in Medieval Europe: Doing unto Others*. New York: Routledge, 2005.

Kaske, R. E. "The Canticum canticorum in the *Miller's Tale*." *Studies in Philology* 59 (1962): 479–500.

Keen, Maurice. *Chivalry*. New Haven, CT: Yale University Press, 1984.

Keen, William. "Chaucer's Imaginable Audience and the Oaths of the *Shipman's Tale*." *Topic* 50 (2000): 91–103.

Keener, Craig. *1–2 Corinthians*. Cambridge: Cambridge University Press, 2005.

Kehew, Robert, ed. *The Lark in the Morning: The Verses of the Troubadours*. Chicago: University of Chicago Press, 2005.

Kelly, Kathleen. *Performing Virginity and Testing Chastity in the Middle Ages*. London: Routledge, 2000.

Kendrick, Laura. *Chaucerian Play: Comedy and Control in the* Canterbury Tales. Berkeley: University of California Press, 1988.

Kerr, John. "The Underworld of Chaucer's *House of Fame:* Virgil, Claudian, and Dante." In *Medieval and Renaissance Humanism: Rhetoric, Representation, and Form*, ed. Stephen Gersh and Bert Roest. Leiden: Brill, 2003. 185–202.

Kirk, Elizabeth. "Nominalism and the Dynamics of the *Clerk's Tale: Homo Viator* as Woman." In *Chaucer's Religious Tales*, ed. C. David Benson and Elizabeth Robertson. Suffolk: Brewer, 1990. 11–20.

Kittredge, G. L. "Chaucer's Discussion of Marriage." *Modern Philology* 9 (1912): 435–67.

Kline, Daniel. "'Myne by right': Oath Making and Intent in the *Friar's Tale*." *Philological Quarterly* 77 (1998): 271–93.

Klosowska, Anna. *Queer Love in the Middle Ages*. New York: Palgrave Macmillan, 2005.

Knight, Stephen. "'Toward the fen': Church and Churl in Chaucer's Fabliaux." In Phillips and Cooper 41–51.

Kohanski, Tamarah. "In Search of Malyne." *Chaucer Review* 27.3 (1993): 228–38.

Kolve, V. A. *Chaucer and the Imagery of Narrative: The First Five* Canterbury Tales. Stanford, CA: Stanford University Press, 1984.

———. "Chaucer's *Second Nun's Tale* and the Iconography of Saint Cecilia." In *New Perspectives in Chaucer Criticism*, ed. Donald Rose. Norman, OK: Pilgrim, 1981. 137–74.

Koppelman, Kate. "The Dreams in Which I'm Dying: Sublimation and Unstable Masculinities in *Troilus and Criseyde*." In Pugh and Marzec 97–114.

Kordecki, Lesley. *Ecofeminist Subjectivities: Chaucer's Talking Birds*. New York: Palgrave Macmillan, 2011.

———. "Let me 'telle yow what I mente': The Glossa Ordinaria and the *Nun's Priest's Tale*." *Exemplaria* 4.2 (1992): 365–85.

Kratins, Ojars. "The Middle English *Amis and Amiloun:* Chivalric Romance or Secular Hagiography?" *PMLA* 81 (1966): 347–54.

Kristeva, Julia. *Tales of Love*. Trans. Leon Roudiez. New York: Columbia University Press, 1987.

Kruger, Steven. "Claiming the Pardoner: Toward a Gay Reading of Chaucer's *Pardoner's Tale*." *Exemplaria* 6 (1994): 115–39.

Kuefler, Matthew, ed. *The Boswell Thesis: Essays on* Christianity, Social Tolerance, and Homosexuality. Chicago: University of Chicago Press, 2006.

Labbie, Erin Felicia. *Lacan's Medievalisms*. Minneapolis: University of Minnesota Press, 2006.

Lacan, Jacques. *The Ethics of Psychoanalysis, 1959–1960*. The Seminar of Jacques Lacan, Book 7. Ed. Jacques-Alain Miller. Trans. Dennis Porter. 1986. New York: Norton, 1992.

Lancashire, Ian. "Sexual Innuendo in the *Reeve's Tale*." *Chaucer Review* 6 (1972): 159–70.

Laqueur, Thomas. *Making Sex: Body and Gender from the Greeks to Freud*. Cambridge, MA: Harvard University Press, 1990.

———. *Solitary Sex: A Cultural History of Masturbation*. New York: Zone, 2003.

Laskaya, Anne. *Chaucer's Approach to Gender in the* Canterbury Tales. Cambridge: Brewer, 1995.

Lavezzo, Kathy. "Chaucer and Everyday Death: The *Clerk's Tale*, Burial, and the Subject of Poverty." *Studies in the Age of Chaucer* 23 (2001): 255–87.

Leach, MacEdward, ed. *Amis and Amiloun*. London: Early English Text Society, 1937.

Leclaire, Serge. *A Child Is Being Killed: On Primary Narcissism and the Death Drive*. Trans. Marie-Claude Hays. Stanford, CA: Stanford University Press, 1998.

Leech, Mary. "Dressing the Undressed: Clothing and Social Structure in Old French Fabliaux." In Crocker, *Comic Provocations* 83–96.

Levine, Robert. "Restraining Ambiguities in Chaucer's *Troilus and Criseyde*." *Neuphilologische Mitteilungen* 87 (1986): 558–64.

Levitan, Alan. "The Parody of Pentecost in Chaucer's *Summoner's Tale*." *University of Toronto Quarterly* 40 (1970–71): 236–46.

Lewis, C. S. *The Allegory of Love: A Study in Medieval Tradition*. Oxford: Oxford University Press, 1936.

Lewis, Celia. "Framing Fiction with Death: Chaucer's *Canterbury Tales* and the Plague." In Benson and Ridyard 139–64.

Lindahl, Carl. *Earnest Games: Folkloric Patterns in the* Canterbury Tales. Bloomington: Indiana University Press, 1987.

Lindberg, David. *Theories of Vision from Al-kindi to Kepler*. Chicago: University of Chicago Press, 1976.

Lindeboom, B. W. "Chaucer's 'Complaint to His Purse': Sounding a Subversive Note?" *Neophilologus* 92 (2008): 745–51.

Lipton, Emma. *Affections of the Mind: The Politics of Sacramental Marriage in Late Medieval English Literature*. Notre Dame, IN: University of Notre Dame Press, 2007.

Little, Katherine. "Chaucer's Parson and the Specter of Wycliffism." *Studies in the Age of Chaucer* 23 (2001): 225–53.

Lochrie, Karma. *Covert Operations: The Medieval Uses of Secrecy*. Philadelphia: University of Pennsylvania Press, 1999.

———. *Heterosyncrasies: Female Sexuality When Normal Wasn't*. Minneapolis: University of Minnesota Press, 2005.

Lochrie, Karma, Peggy McCracken, and James A. Schultz, eds. *Constructing Medieval Sexuality*. Minneapolis: University of Minnesota Press, 1997.

Loomis, Laura Hibbard. "Chaucer and the Auchinleck Manuscript: *Thopas* and *Guy of Warwick*." In *Essays and Studies in Honor of Carleton Brown*. 1940. Freeport, NY: Books for Libraries, 1969. 111–28.

———. "Chaucer and the Breton Lays of the Auchinleck Manuscript." *Studies in Philology* 38 (1941): 14–33.

Lucas, Angela. "The Presentation of Marriage and Love in Chaucer's *Franklin's Tale*." *English Studies* 72.6 (1991): 501–12.

Lumby, Rawson, ed. *Ratis Raving, and Other Moral and Religious Pieces, in Prose and Verse*. 1870. London: Early English Text Society, 2002.

Madigan, Kevin. *Olivi and the Interpretation of Matthew in the High Middle Ages*. Notre Dame, IN: University of Notre Dame Press, 2003.

Maguire, John. "The Clandestine Marriage of Troilus and Criseyde." *Chaucer Review* 8 (1974): 262–78.

Mandelbaum, Allen, trans. *The Metamorphoses of Ovid*. San Diego, CA: Harvest, 1993.

Mann, Jill. *Chaucer and Medieval Estates Satire: The Literature of Social Classes and the* General Prologue *to the* Canterbury Tales. Cambridge: Cambridge University Press, 1973.

———. *Feminizing Chaucer*. Cambridge: Brewer, 2002.

———. "Parents and Children in the *Canterbury Tales*." In *Literature in Fourteenth-Century England: The J. A. W. Bennett Memorial Lectures, Perugia, 1981 1982*, ed. Piero Boitani and Anna Torti. Tübingen: G. Narr, 1983. 165–83.

Manning, Stephen. "The Nun's Priest's Morality and the Medieval Attitude toward Fables." *Journal of English and Germanic Philology* 59 (1960): 403–16.

Marcuse, Herbert. *Eros and Civilization: A Philosophical Inquiry into Freud*. Boston: Beacon, 1966.

Margherita, Gayle. "Criseyde's Remains: Romance and the Question of Justice." *Exemplaria* 12.2 (2000): 257–92.

Marion, Jean-Luc. *The Erotic Phenomenon*. Trans. Stephen Lewis. Chicago: University of Chicago Press, 2007.

Martin, Dale. *The Corinthian Body*. New Haven, CT: Yale University Press, 1995.

Martin, Molly. *Vision and Gender in Malory's* Morte D'Arthur. Cambridge: Brewer, 2010.

Matter, E. Ann. *The Voice of My Beloved: The Song of Songs in Western Medieval Christianity*. Philadelphia: University of Pennsylvania Press, 1990.

Matthews, William. "The Wife of Bath and All Her Sect." *Viator* 5 (1974): 413–43.

McAlpine, Monica. "The Pardoner's Homosexuality and How It Matters." *PMLA* 95 (1980): 8–22.

McAvoy, Liz Herbert. *Authority and the Female Body in the Writings of Julian of Norwich and Margery Kempe*. Cambridge: Brewer, 2004.

McCarthy, Conor. "Love, Marriage, and Law: Three *Canterbury Tales*." *English Studies* 83.6 (2002): 504–18.

———. *Marriage in Medieval England: Law, Literature, and Practice*. Cambridge: Boydell, 2004.

McCormack, Frances. *Chaucer and the Culture of Dissent: The Lollard Context and Subtext of the Parson's Tale*. Dublin: Four Courts, 2007.

McEntire, Sandra. "Illusions and Interpretation in the *Franklin's Tale*." *Chaucer Review* 31 (1996): 145–63.

Meyer, Robert. *St. Athanasius: The Life of St. Antony*. New York: Newman, 1978.

Middle English Dictionary. Ed. Hans Kurath. Ann Arbor: University of Michigan, 1952–2001.

Middleton, Anne. "The Clerk and His Tale: Some Literary Contexts." *Studies in the Age of Chaucer* 2 (1980): 121–50.

———. "The *Physician's Tale* and Love's Martyrs: 'Ensamples mo than ten' as a Method in the *Canterbury Tales*." *Chaucer Review* 8.1 (1973): 9–32.

Mieszkowski, Gretchen. *Medieval Go-Betweens and Chaucer's Pandarus*. New York: Palgrave Macmillan, 2006.

———. "The Reputation of Criseyde, 1155–1500." *Transactions of the Connecticut Academy of Arts and Sciences* 43 (1971): 71–153.

Miller, Mark. *Philosophical Chaucer: Love, Sex, and Agency in the* Canterbury Tales. Cambridge: Cambridge University Press, 2004.

Miller, Milton. "The Heir in the *Merchant's Tale*." *Philological Quarterly* 29 (1950): 437–40.

Miller, Paul. "John Gower, Satiric Poet." In *Gower's Confessio Amantis: Responses and Reassessments*, ed. Alastair Minnis. Cambridge: Brewer, 1983. 79–105.

Miller, Robert, ed. *Chaucer: Sources and Backgrounds*. New York: Oxford University Press, 1977.

Mills, Laurens. *One Soul in Bodies Twain: Friendship in Tudor and Stuart Drama*. Bloomington, IN: Principia, 1937.

Mills, Robert. "'Whatever you do is a delight to me!': Masculinity, Masochism, and Queer Play in Representations of Male Martyrdom." *Exemplaria* 13 (2001): 1–37.

Minnis, A. J., with V. J. Scattergood and J. J. Smith. *Oxford Guides to Chaucer: The Shorter Poems*. Oxford: Oxford University Press, 1995.

Mirk, John. *John Mirk's Festial: Edited from British Library MS Cotton Claudius A.II*. Ed. Susan Powell. Oxford: Oxford University Press, 2009.

Mirrer, Louise, ed. *Upon My Husband's Death: Widows in the Literature and Histories of Medieval Europe*. Ann Arbor: University of Michigan Press, 1992.

Mitchell, Jerome, and William Provost, eds. *Chaucer the Love Poet*. Athens: University of Georgia Press, 1973.

Moore, Stephen. *God's Beauty Parlor and Other Queer Spaces in and around the Bible*. Stanford, CA: Stanford University Press, 2001.

Morrison, Susan Signe. *Excrement in the Middle Ages: Sacred Filth and Chaucer's Fecopoetics*. New York: Palgrave Macmillan, 2008.

Morse, Charlotte. "The Exemplary Griselda." *Studies in the Age of Chaucer* 7 (1985): 51–86.

Murray, Jacqueline, and Konrad Eisenbichler, eds. *Desire and Discipline: Sex and Sexuality in the Premodern West*. Toronto: University of Toronto Press, 1996.

Muscatine, Charles. *Chaucer and the French Tradition: A Study in Style and Meaning*. Berkeley: University of California Press, 1957.

Mustanoja, Tauno, ed. "Myne Awen Dere Sone." *Neuphilologische Mitteilungen* 49 (1948): 145–93.

Neal, Derek. *The Masculine Self in Late Medieval England*. Chicago: University of Chicago Press, 2008.

Newman, Barbara. *From Virile Woman to WomanChrist: Studies in Medieval Religion and Literature*. Philadelphia: University of Pennsylvania Press, 1995.

———. *God and the Goddesses: Vision, Poetry, and Belief in the Middle Ages*. Philadelphia: University of Pennsylvania Press, 2003.

Nightingale, Jeanne. "Erec in the Mirror: The Feminization of the Self and the Re-invention of the Chivalric Hero in Chrétien's First Romance." In *Arthurian Romance and Gender*, ed. Friedrich Wolfzettel. Amsterdam: Rodopi, 1995. 130–46.

O'Brien, Timothy. "Brother as Problem in the *Troilus*." *Philological Quarterly* 82 (2003): 125–48.

Olsen, Glenn W. *Of Sodomites, Effeminates, Hermaphrodites, and Androgynes: Sodomy in the Age of Peter Damian*. Toronto: Pontifical Institute of Mediaeval Studies, 2011.

Olson, Paul. *The* Canterbury Tales *and the Good Society*. Princeton, NJ: Princeton University Press, 1986.

Orme, Nicholas. *From Childhood to Chivalry: The Education of the English Kings and Aristocracy, 1066–1530*. London: Methuen, 1984.

———. *Medieval Children*. New Haven, CT: Yale University Press, 2001.

Ovid. *Le Metamorfosi*. Ed. Ferruccio Bernini. 2 vols. Bologna: Zanichelli, 1974.

———. *The Metamorphoses of Ovid*. Trans. Allen Mandelbaum. San Diego, CA: Harvest, 1993.

———. *Ovid's Metamorphoses, Books 1–5*. Ed. William Anderson. Norman: University of Oklahoma Press, 1997.

Owen, Charles. "'A certain nombre of conclusiouns': The Nature and Nurture of Children in Chaucer." *Chaucer Review* 16.1 (1982): 60–75.

Paglia, Camille. "Plighting Their Troth." Review of *Same-Sex Unions in Premodern Europe*, by John Boswell. *Washington Post*, 17 July 1994, wkb1.

Patrologia cursus completus, series Latina. Ed. J.-P Mighe. 221 vols. Paris, 1844–64.

Patterson, Lee. *Acts of Recognition: Essays on Medieval Culture*. Notre Dame, IN: University of Notre Dame Press, 2010.

———. "Chaucer's Pardoner on the Couch: Psyche and Clio in Medieval Literary Studies." *Speculum* 76 (2001): 638–80.

Paxson, James, and Cynthia Gravlee, eds. *Desiring Discourse: The Literature of Love, Ovid through Chaucer*. Selinsgrove, PA: Susquehanna University Press, 1998.

Payer, Pierre. *The Bridling of Desire: Views of Sex in the Later Middle Ages*. Toronto: University of Toronto Press, 1993.

Petrarch. *The Canzoniere, or Rerum vulgarium fragmenta*. Trans. Mark Musa. Bloomington: Indiana University Press, 1996.

Petroff, Elizabeth Avilda. *Body and Soul: Essays on Medieval Women and Mysticism*. Oxford: Oxford University Press, 1994.

Phelpstead, Carl. "'Th'ende is every tales strengthe': Contextualizing Chaucerian Perspectives on Death and Judgment." In Phillips and Cooper 97–110.

Phillips, Helen, and Helen Cooper, eds. *Chaucer and Religion*. Cambridge: Brewer, 2010.

Phillips, Seymour. *Edward II*. New Haven, CT: Yale University Press, 2010.

Pigg, Daniel. "Performing the Perverse: The Abuse of Masculine Power in the *Reeve's Tale*." In Beidler, *Masculinities* 53–61.

Pitard, Derrick. "Sowing Difficulty: The *Parson's Tale*, Vernacular Commentary, and the Nature of Chaucerian Dissent." *Studies in the Age of Chaucer* 26 (2004): 299–330.

Pitcher, John. *Chaucer's Feminine Subjects: Figures of Desire in the* Canterbury Tales. New York: Palgrave Macmillan, 2012.

Plummer, John. "Hooly Chirches Blood: Simony and Patrimony in Chaucer's *Reeve's Tale*." *Chaucer Review* 18.1 (1983): 49–60.

Pugh, Tison. *Queering Medieval Genres*. New York: Palgrave Macmillan, 2004.

———. *Sexuality and Its Queer Discontents in Middle English Literature*. New York: Palgrave Macmillan, 2008.

Pugh, Tison, and Marcia Smith Marzec, eds. *Men and Masculinities in Chaucer's* Troilus and Criseyde. Cambridge: Brewer, 2008.

Ramey, Lynn Tarte. "Representations of Women in Chrétien's *Erec et Enide*: Courtly Literature or Misogyny?" *Romanic Review* 84.4 (1993): 377–86.

Raybin, David. "'Wommen, of kynde, desiren libertee': Rereading Dorigen, Rereading Marriage." *Chaucer Review* 27.1 (1992): 65–86.

Robertson, D. W. "Why the Devil Wears Green." *Modern Language Notes* 69 (1954): 470–72.

Robertson, Elizabeth. "Marriage, Mutual Consent, and the Affirmation of the Female Subject in the *Knight's Tale*, the *Wife of Bath's Tale*, and the *Franklin's Tale*." In *Drama, Narrative, and Poetry in the* Canterbury Tales, ed. Wendy Harding. Toulouse: Presses Universitaires du Mirail, 2003. 175–93.

Robertson, Elizabeth, and Christine Rose, eds. *Representing Rape in Medieval and Early Modern Literature*. New York: Palgrave Macmillan, 2001.

Robinson, F. N., ed. *The Works of Geoffrey Chaucer*. 2nd ed. Boston: Houghton Mifflin, 1961.

Rock, Catherine. "Forsworn and Fordone: Arcite as Oath-Breaker in the *Knight's Tale*." *Chaucer Review* 40.4 (2006): 416–32.

Rocke, Michael. *Forbidden Friendships: Homosexuality and Male Culture in Renaissance Florence*. New York: Oxford University Press, 1996.

Rollo, David. *Kiss My Relics: Hermaphroditic Fictions of the Middle Ages*. Chicago: University of Chicago Press, 2011.

Roney, Lois. "Chaucer Subjectivizes the Oath: Depicting the Fall from Feudalism into Individualism in the *Canterbury Tales*." In *The Rusted Hauberk: Feudal Ideals of Order and Their Decline*, ed. Liam Purdon and Cindy Vitto. Gainesville: University of Florida Press, 1994. 269–98.

Rose, Christine. "Reading Chaucer, Reading Rape." In *Representing Rape in Medieval and Early Modern Literature*, ed. Elizabeth Robertson and Christine Rose. New York: Palgrave, 2001. 21–60.

Rose, Jacqueline. *Sexuality in the Field of Vision*. London: Verso, 1986.

Rossi-Reder, Andrea. "Male Movement and Female Fixity in the *Franklin's Tale* and *Il Filocolo*." In Beidler, *Masculinities* 106–16.

Rouse, Robert. "The Medieval Eroticism of Heat." In Rushton and Hopkins 71–81.

Rushton, Cory, and Amanda Hopkins, eds. *The Erotic in the Literature of Medieval Britain*. Cambridge: Brewer, 2007.

———. "Introduction: The Revel, the Melodye, and the Bisynesse of Solas." In Rushton and Hopkins 1–17.

Russell, Stephen. "Dido, Emily, and Constance: Femininity and Subversion in the Mature Chaucer." *Medieval Perspectives* 1 (1986): 65–74.

Sadlek, Gregory. *Idleness Working: The Discourse of Love's Labor from Ovid through Chaucer and Gower*. Washington, DC: Catholic University of America Press, 2004.

Salisbury, Eve, ed. "How the Goode Man Taght Hys Sone." In *The Trials and Joys of Marriage*. Kalamazoo, MI: Medieval Institute Publications, 2002. 233–45.

Sands, Donald, ed. *Havelok the Dane*. In *Middle English Verse Romances*. Exeter: University of Exeter Press, 1986. 55–129.

Saul, Nigel. *Richard II*. New Haven, CT: Yale University Press, 1997.

Saunders, Corinne. "Chaucer's Romances." In *A Companion to Romance: From Classical to Contemporary*, ed. Corinne Saunders. Malden, MA: Blackwell, 2004. 85–103.

———. *Rape and Ravishment in the Literature of Medieval England*. Cambridge: Brewer, 2001.

Saville, Jonathan. *The Medieval Erotic Alba: Structure as Meaning*. New York: Columbia University Press, 1972.

Scala, Elizabeth. *Absent Narratives, Manuscript Textuality, and Literary Structure in Late Medieval England*. New York: Palgrave Macmillan, 2002.

Scanlon, Larry. *Narrative, Authority, and Power: The Medieval Exemplum and the Chaucerian Tradition*. Cambridge: Cambridge University Press, 1994.

Schibanoff, Susan. "Chaucer's Lesbians: Drawing Blanks?" *Medieval Feminist Newsletter* 13 (1992): 11–14.

———. *Chaucer's Queer Poetics: Rereading the Dream Trio*. Toronto: University of Toronto Press, 2006.

Scholes, Robert. *Fabulation and Metafiction*. Urbana: University of Illinois Press, 1979.

Schroeder, H. J., ed. *Disciplinary Decrees of the General Councils*. St. Louis, MO: Herder, 1937.

Schultz, James A. *Courtly Love, the Love of Courtliness, and the History of Sexuality*. Chicago: University of Chicago Press, 2006.

Sedgwick, Eve. *Between Men: English Literature and Male Homosocial Desire*. New York: Columbia University Press, 1985.

———. *Epistemology of the Closet*. Berkeley: University of California Press, 1990.

Shahar, Shulamith. *Childhood in the Middle Ages*. Trans. Chaya Galai. London: Routledge, 1990.

Shakespeare, William. *As You Like It*. In *The Riverside Shakespeare*, ed. Blakemore Evans. 2nd ed. Boston: Houghton Mifflin, 1997.

Sidhu, Nicole Nolan. "'To late for to crie': Female Desire, Fabliau Politics, and Classical Legend in Chaucer's *Reeve's Tale*." *Exemplaria* 21.1 (2009): 3–23.

Sigal, Gale. *Erotic Dawn-Songs of the Middle Ages: Voicing the Lyric Lady*. Gainesville: University Press of Florida, 1996.

Slocum, Sally. "How Old Is Chaucer's Pandarus?" *Philological Quarterly* 58 (1979): 16–25.

Smith, Warren. "Dorigen's Lament and the Resolution of the *Franklin's Tale*." *Chaucer Review* 36.4 (2002): 374–90.

Stanbury, Sarah. *Seeing the Gawain-Poet: Description and the Act of Perception*. Philadelphia: University of Pennsylvania Press, 1991.

———. "The Voyeur and the Private Life in *Troilus and Criseyde*." *Studies in the Age of Chaucer* 13 (1991): 141–58.

Steadman, John. "Chaucer's Eagle: A Contemplative Symbol." *PMLA* 75.3 (1960): 153–59.

Stehling, Thomas. "To Love a Medieval Boy." *Journal of Homosexuality* 8 (1983): 151–70.

Steinberg, Glenn. "Chaucer in the Field of Cultural Production: Humanism, Dante, and the *House of Fame*." *Chaucer Review* 35.2 (2000): 182–203.

Steinberg, Leo. *The Sexuality of Christ in Renaissance Art and in Modern Oblivion*. London: Faber & Faber, 1983.

Steinmetz, David. "Late Medieval Nominalism and the *Clerk's Tale*." *Chaucer Review* 12 (1977): 38–54.

Stepsis, Robert. "*Potentia Absoluta* and the *Clerk's Tale*." *Chaucer Review* 10 (1975): 129–46.

Stevenson, Katie. *Chivalry and Knighthood in Scotland, 1424–1513*. Suffolk: Boydell, 2006.

Stevenson, Kenneth. *Nuptial Blessing: A Study of Christian Marriage Rites*. New York: Oxford University Press, 1983.

Stockton, Will. "Cynicism and the Anal Erotics of Chaucer's Pardoner." *Exemplaria* 20.2 (2008): 143–64.

Stillinger, Thomas, ed. *Critical Essays on Geoffrey Chaucer*. New York: Hall, 1998.

Stow, George Jr., ed. *Historia Vitae et Regni Ricardi Secundi*. Philadelphia: University of Pennsylvania Press, 1977.

Stretter, Robert. "Rewriting Perfect Friendship in Chaucer's *Knight's Tale* and Lydgate's *Fabula duorum mercatorum*." *Chaucer Review* 37 (2003): 234–52.

Strohm, Paul. *England's Empty Throne: Usurpation and the Language of Legitimation, 1399–1422*. New Haven, CT: Yale University Press, 1998.

———. "Saving the Appearances: Chaucer's *Purse* and the Fabrication of the Lancastrian Claim." In *Chaucer's England: Literature in Historical Context*, ed. Barbara Hanawalt. Minneapolis: University of Minnesota Press, 1992. 21–40.

———. *Social Chaucer*. Cambridge, MA: Harvard University Press, 1989.

———. *Theory and the Premodern Text*. Minneapolis: University of Minnesota Press, 2000.

Sturges, Robert. *Chaucer's Pardoner and Gender Theory: Bodies of Discourse*. New York: St. Martin's, 2000.

———. *Dialogue and Deviance: Male–Male Desire in the Dialogue Genre*. New York: Palgrave Macmillan, 2005.

———. "La(can)ncelot." *Arthurian Interpretations* 4.2 (1990): 12–23.

Sylvia, Daniel, Donald Howard, Beryl Rowland, E. Talbot Donaldson, and Florence Ridley. "Thwarted Sexuality in Chaucer's Works." *Florilegium* 3 (1981): 239–67.

Szittya, Penn. *The Antifraternal Tradition in Medieval Literature*. Princeton, NJ: Princeton University Press, 1986.

Tatlock, John, and Arthur Kennedy. *A Concordance to the Complete Works of Geoffrey Chaucer and to the Romaunt of the Rose*. Gloucester, MA: Peter Smith, 1963.

Taylor, Mark. "Servant and Lord / Lady and Wife: The *Franklin's Tale* and Traditions of Courtly and Conjugal Love." *Chaucer Review* 32.1 (1997): 64–81.

Taylor, Paul. *Chaucer's Chain of Love*. Madison, NJ: Fairleigh Dickinson University Press, 1996.

Tennyson, Alfred, Lord. *Idylls of the King*. Ed. J. M. Gray. London: Penguin, 1983.

Thomas, Calvin. "Straight with a Twist: Queer Theory and the Subject of Heterosexuality." In *Straight with a Twist: Queer Theory and the Subject of Heterosexuality*, ed. Calvin Thomas. Urbana: University of Illinois Press, 2000. 11–44.

Thomas, Paul. "'Have ye no mannes herte?' Chauntecleer as Cock-Man in the *Nun's Priest's Tale*." In Beidler, *Masculinities* 187–202.

Thompson, John. *Writing the Wrongs: Women of the Old Testament among Biblical Commentators from Philo through the Reformation*. Oxford: Oxford University Press, 2001.

Travis, Peter. *Disseminal Chaucer: Rereading the Nun's Priest's Tale*. Notre Dame, IN: Notre Dame University Press, 2010.

Tripp, Raymond. "The Franklin's Solution to the Marriage Debate." In *New Views on Chaucer: Essays in Generative Criticism*, ed. William Johnson and Loren Gruber. Denver: Society for New Language Study, 1973. 35–41.

Truscott, Yvonne. "Chaucer's Children and the Medieval Idea of Childhood." *Children's Literature Association Quarterly* 23.1 (1998): 29–34.

Uebel, Michael. "Public Fantasy and the Logic of Sacrifice in the *Physician's Tale*." *ANQ* 15.3 (2002): 30–33.

Urban, Linwood. *A Short History of Christian Thought*. Rev. ed. New York: Oxford University Press, 1995.

Van, Thomas. "Walter at the Stake: A Reading of Chaucer's *Clerk's Tale*." *Chaucer Review* 22.3 (1988): 214–24.

Van Duzee, Mabel. *A Medieval Romance of Friendship:* Eger and Grime. New York: Franklin, 1963.

Vitto, Cindy, and Marcia Smith Marzec, eds. *New Perspectives on Criseyde.* Asheville, NC: Pegasus, 2004.

Wack, Mary. *Lovesickness in the Middle Ages: The Viaticum and Its Commentaries.* Philadelphia: University of Pennsylvania Press, 1990.

Walker, Sue Sheridan, ed. *Wife and Widow in Medieval England.* Ann Arbor: University of Michigan Press, 1993.

Wallace, David. *Chaucer and the Early Writings of Boccaccio.* Woodbridge, Suffolk: Brewer, 1985.

———. *Chaucerian Polity: Absolutist Lineages and Associational Forms in England and Italy.* Stanford, CA: Stanford University Press, 1997.

Weisl, Angela Jane. *Conquering the Reign of Femeny: Gender and Genre in Chaucer's Romance.* Cambridge: Brewer, 1995.

Weissman, Ronald. *Ritual Brotherhood in Renaissance Florence.* New York: Academic, 1982.

West, Richard. *Chaucer, 1340–1400: The Life and Times of the First English Poet.* New York: Carroll & Graf, 2000.

Wetherbee, Winthrop. "Criseyde Alone." In Vitto and Marzec 299–332.

———. "Romance and Epic in Chaucer's *Knight's Tale*." *Exemplaria* 2.1 (1990): 303–28.

Wilder, Thornton. *Three Plays: Our Town, The Skin of Our Teeth, and The Matchmaker.* New York: Harper Perennial, 1985.

Williams, Tara. "'T'assaye in thee thy wommanheede': Griselda Chosen, Translated, and Tried." *Studies in the Age of Chaucer* 27 (2005): 93–127.

Winnett, Susan. "Coming Unstrung: Women, Men, Narrative, and Principles of Pleasure." *PMLA* 105.3 (1990): 505–18.

Woods, Constance. "Same-Sex Unions or Semantic Illusions?" *Communio* 22 (1995): 316–42.

Woods, William. "'My sweete foo': Emelye's Role in the *Knight's Tale*." *Studies in Philology* 88.3 (1991): 276–306.

Wright, Thomas, ed. *The Book of the Knight of La Tour-Landry.* London: Early English Text Society, 1906.

Yeager, R. F. "Chaucer's 'To His Purse': Begging, or Begging Off?" *Viator* 36 (2005): 373–414.

Zeeman, Nicolette. "The Gender of Song in Chaucer." *Studies in the Age of Chaucer* 29 (2007): 141–82.

Zeikowitz, Richard. *Homoeroticism and Chivalry: Discourses of Male Same-Sex Desire in the Fourteenth Century.* New York: Palgrave Macmillan, 2003.

———. "Silenced but Not Stifled: The Disruptive Queer Power of Chaucer's Pardoner." *Dalhousie Review* 82 (2002): 55–73.

Žižek, Slavoj. *Metastases of Enjoyment: Six Essays on Women and Causality.* London: Verso, 1994.

———. *The Puppet and the Dwarf: The Perverse Core of Christianity.* Cambridge, MA: MIT Press, 2003.

———. *The Ticklish Subject: The Absent Centre of Political Ontology.* London: Verso, 1999.

INDEX

Adam and Eve, 182, 186, 195, 215
Aers, David, 86n44, 109
Alan de Lille, 202–3
allegory, 18, 80, 82, 144–45, 151, 188, 189n33, 190, 191
Allman, W. W., 22–23
Althusser, Louis, 177n17
Amazons, 108, 112–13
Ames, Ruth, 173
Amis and Amiloun, 72–75
Andreas Capellanus, 9–12, 48
Anne of Bohemia, 82
anti-eroticisms. *See* eroticisms
Aquinas, Thomas, 8, 177
Ariès, Philippe, 130–31
Aristotle, 131
Astell, Ann, 171n8
As You Like It (Shakespeare), 124
aubade, 141
Auerbach, Erich, 98
Augustine, 7–8, 169–72, 192

Bataille, Georges, 122
Bernard of Clairvaux, 171, 172, 189n33

Biggs, Frederick, 184
Bishop, Louise, 184
Blackmore, Josiah, 3
Blamires, Alcuin, 58
blazon, 136, 206
Bloch, Howard, 164
Boccaccio, Giovanni, 11–12, 84, 94, 98, 102, 112, 113
Book of the Knight of La Tour-Landry, 107
Bossy, Michel-André, 42
Boswell, John, 5n10, 17, 69–70, 75
Bowers, John, 76n25, 86, 147
Breton lai, 102
Brewer, D. S., 127
brotherhood, 65–97, 147–48
Burger, Glenn, 16
Burns, Jane, 41, 143
Butler, Judith, 19, 39, 177, 185

Calabrese, Michael, 54–55
Chance, Jane, 18
Chaucer, Geoffrey: "Against Women Unconstant," 89; as Chauntecleer, 213; *Clerk's Tale*, 25, 127–28, 151–60, 166–67, 214; "The Complaint of Chaucer

237

238 • INDEX

to His Purse," 19–22; *Cook's Tale*, 134; erotic biography of, 13–15; *Franklin's Tale*, 15, 23–24, 31–32, 43–64, 78, 102, 214; *Friar's Tale*, 24, 87–91, 175, 214; as Ganymede figure, 18; *General Prologue*, 16, 60, 67, 89, 90, 134, 144, 212; Harry Bailly, 60, 61, 93, 166, 211, 212; *House of Fame*, 17–18, 24, 79–82, 214; *Knight's Tale*, 2–3, 23, 24–25, 53, 82–87, 98–126, 214; *Legend of Good Women*, 25–26, 82, 173, 179–82, 203, 215; "Lenvoy de Chaucer a Scogan," 14; as love poet, 1–2; *Man of Law's Tale*, 30, 102; *Manciple's Tale*, 30; as "medieval Ovid," 1–2; *Merchant's Tale*, 30, 78, 134–35; *Miller's Prologue and Tale*, 26, 78, 86–87, 132, 134, 144, 182–90; *Nun's Priest's Tale*, 26, 102, 204–15; *Pardoner's Prologue and Tale*, 24, 90–94, 214; *Parson's Tale*, 8, 26, 127–28, 173, 174–76, 203; *Physician's Tale*, 25, 151–52, 161–68, 214; *Prioress's Tale*, 127–28; as queer figure, 13–22; *Reeve's Tale*, 25, 132, 135–45, 166–67, 214; *Retraction*, 12; *Romaunt of the Rose*, 193–94; *Second Nun's Prologue and Tale*, 25–26, 30, 78, 192–203, 215; *Shipman's Tale*, 24, 94–97, 135, 214; *Sir Thopas*, 14n32, 101; *Squire's Tale*, 60, 101, 102; *Summoner's Tale*, 25, 145–51, 166–67, 214; *Tale of Melibee*, 31n2, 128; themes of game and play, 17, 60, 211; "To Rosemounde," 14; *A Treatise on the Astrolabe*, 127; *Troilus and Criseyde*, 24–25, 78, 88, 98–126, 175, 214; *Wife of Bath's Prologue and Tale*, 7, 26, 28, 30, 63, 102, 105, 120–21, 134, 146, 164, 174, 190–92, 202; "Womanly Noblesse," 14

chastity, 3–4, 6, 21, 161–62, 192–93, 195, 198–99, 200, 203

Chaumpaigne, Cecilia, 13–14

Chrétien de Troyes, 35–36, 41–42, 51, 202

childhood, medieval conceptions of, 132–33

children, 127–68

Cicero, 75, 84, 169

Clanvowe, John, 75–76

Cohen, Jeffrey Jerome, 3, 35, 36n15, 202

Collette, Carolyn, 104

conduct books, 132–34

Confessio amantis (John Gower), 204–5

Cooper, Helen, 110, 152

Corinthians (I and II), 6, 177, 178, 200

courtly love, 32–52 87, 105, 109, 123, 205–6

Crane, Susan, 106–7, 211

Crocker, Holly, 29, 94, 141, 165

cuckoldry, 13, 30, 59, 94–96, 138, 144, 189, 196, 198

Dane, Joseph, 208

Dante Alighieri, 9, 18, 79, 80n30

David and Jonathan, 70–72

Davis, Craig, 31

Dean, Tim, 27

Decameron (Boccaccio), 11, 94

Deleuze, Gilles, 19, 26, 27, 37, 45, 47, 50, 56, 57, 59, 142, 166, 167, 212, 214

demande d'amour, 62–63, 120

de Roet, Philippa, 13, 15

de Vere, Robert, 81–82

Diana, 112–13, 180

Dido, 25–26, 179–82

das Ding, 36

Dinshaw, Carolyn, 5n10, 14n31, 15n34

dream vision, 18, 68, 81, 96, 173–74, 180, 205

Ecumenical Council of Chalcedon, 171

Edelman, Lee, 27, 111, 153–54

Edward II, King, 75–77, 86

Edwards, Elizabeth, 123

Edwards, Robert, 9, 112

Eger and Grime, 72, 74–75, 100

Eliason, Norman, 1

Elliott, Dyan, 196
Ephesians, 170
Erec et Enide (Chrétien de Troyes), 41–43
eroticisms (and anti-eroticisms): in Christian thought, 7–9; and cultural norms, 6–7; as cultural transgression, 2–3; and desire, 19; of the Divine, 169–203; erotic identities, 6–7; versus carnality, 9–10; *see also* chastity; cuckoldry; femininity; gender; hermaphroditism; homosexuality; homosociality; hymen; impotence; incest; marriage; masculinity; masochism; narcissism; orgasm; queerness; sadomasochism; sexuality, history of; virginity; widowhood
erotic triangle, 53, 96, 137, 196–97
exemplum, 89, 90, 92, 96, 152, 211

fabliau, 12, 94, 96, 134–51, 182–92
Farina, Lara, 172
fatherhood, medieval conceptions of, 133–34
Fein, Susanna Greer, 139
femininity, 41, 50, 202
Il Filostrato (Boccaccio), 98, 102
Finlayson, John, 103, 210–11
Flake, Timothy, 50
Foucault, Michel, 5
Fourth Lateran Council, 131
Fowler, Elizabeth, 108
Fradenburg, Aranye, 124
Freud, Sigmund, 27, 39, 99, 100, 106, 114–15, 127–128, 129, 134, 153, 155, 158–59, 167, 209–210, 212
friendship (homosocial), 65, 67, 72, 74, 77, 78, 90–91, 93
Fritz, Donald, 61
Froissart, Jean, 175
Frye, Northrop, 100

Ganymede, 17–18, 21

Gaunt, Simon, 27, 28, 105, 123
Gaveston, Piers, 75–77, 86
gender, 15n34, 20, 39, 40, 41, 43, 56, 62, 129, 197
Giffney, Noreen, 111
Giles of Rome 131
Gilles, Sealy, 116
Goux, Jean-Joseph, 22
Gower, John, 204–5
Green, Richard Firth, 65n1
Gregory VII, Pope, 6–7
Guattari, Félix, 19, 26, 27, 142, 212, 214
Gust, Geoffrey, 16–17
Guynn, Noah, 169–70

hagiography, 164, 180, 193–94, 199, 203,
Hanawalt, Barbara, 131, 137
Hanks, Thomas, 22–23
Hanna, Ralph, 72n15
Hanrahan, Michael, 81
Hansen, Elaine Tuttle, 32n6, 152
Harper, April, 4
Havelok the Dane, 100
Henry IV, King, 19–21
Hermann, John, 94
hermaphroditism, 40–41, 46, 48, 58
Hermaphroditus, 40–41
Hill, John, 197–98
Historia Griseldis (Petrarch), 153
Hodges, Laura, 89
Hollywood, Amy, 172n9
homosexuality, 3–5, 67
homosociality, 74–75, 81, 85, 93, 124, 197
Hopkins, Amanda, 22
Horace, 68
horses (as erotic symbol), 140
Howes, Laura, 184
Hume, Cathy, 31
Hutcheson, Gregory, 3

hymen, 138, 142–43, 198, 199, 201–2

Idylls of the King (Tennyson), 41–42
impotence, 104, 135, 144, 145, 149
incest, 26, 148, 155, 157, 205, 209–10, 213–14
Ingham, Patricia Clare, 85
Isidore of Seville, 131, 169

Jaeger, C. Stephen, 10, 66–67
Jephthah, 163–64
Jesus, 92n54, 171, 190–91, 198, 203
John, Gospel of, 191
Le Joli Buisson de jonece, 175
Jones, Terry 21
Jost, Jean 77
jouissance, 124
Judges, Book of 163–64
Julian, St. 60
Julian of Norwich, 172n9, 202
Juvenal, 68

Karras, Ruth, 10
Kelly, Kathleen, 199
Kempe, Margery, 172n9
Kendrick, Laura, 16
Kittredge, G. L., 46n39
Knight, Stephen, 187
Kolve, V. A., 140n31, 200
Kordecki, Lesley, 214
Kristeva, Julia, 27, 101
Kruger, Steven, 92–93

Lacan, Jacques, 27–28, 34–36, 39, 105–7
Lancelot, ou Le Chevalier de la charette (Chrétien de Troyes), 35–36, 41, 202

Langland, William, 149
Lanval, 51
Laqueur, Thomas, 5n9, 128n3
Lavezzo, Kathy, 155n59
Leclaire, Serge, 122
Leech, Mary, 96
Leo the Great, Pope, 171
Levitan, Alan, 150
Lewis, Celia, 101
Livy, 161
Lochrie, Karma, 6, 108, 184

Mabinogion, 41–42
Madigan, Kevin, 191
Maguire, John, 123
maistrye, 46–47, 58
Mann, Jill, 46n39, 130
Manning, Stephen, 205–6
Marcuse, Herbert, 125
Marie de France, 51, 213
Marion, Jean-Luc, 169
marriage, 7, 13, 30, 44–50, 52, 70, 73, 123, 137, 154, 158, 160, 186, 196, 199
Mars, 112
Martin, Dale, 178
martyrs and martyrdom, 180, 192, 194–95, 198–201, 203
masculinity, 29, 34, 66, 94, 133, 144, 166, 197, 202, 206, 207
masochism, 32, 37–38, 42, 45, 47, 49, 51–58, 59, 129; see also sadomasochism
McEntire, Sandra, 61–62
Metamorphoses (Ovid), 40, 79, 80n30
Middleton, Anne, 152n50, 154n56, 165
Miller, Mark, 155, 172
Miller, Paul, 68
Mills, Robert, 194
Minnis, A. J., 80–81

Mirk, John, 186
Moore, Stephen, 189n33
Morrison, Susan Signe, 149
Morse, Charlotte, 151n50
Muscatine, Charles, 86n44
"Myne Awen Dere Sone," 133–34

names, thematic deployment of, 44n36
narcissism, 34, 37, 39, 42, 51–52, 55, 57, 60, 98, 105, 107, 121, 125, 136, 138–39, 165, 206, 214
Narcissus, 34
narrative theory, 2, 9, 62–63
Nature, 168
Neal, Derek, 133
Neville, William, 75–76
Newman, Barbara, 168n74
Nightingale, Jeanne, 42
norms and normativity, 3, 6, 23, 27, 34, 66, 67, 70, 94

oaths, 65–97
O'Brien, Timothy, 76
orgasm, 62, 101, 118–19
Orme, Nicholas, 131–32
Ovid, 1, 40–41, 79, 80n30, 193
Owen, Charles, 132

Patterson, Lee, 103n19
Paul, 6, 12, 170, 171, 177–78, 190, 195n39, 200, 205
Payer, Pierre, 4, 7
Petrarch, 121, 153
Petroff, Elizabeth Alvilda, 172n9
Phelpstead, Carl, 103–4
Proctor, Caroline, 4
pryvetee, 182–85, 189–92, 203

queer theory, 3–4, 9, 16, 27–28, 95
queerness, definition of, 3; as distinct from homosexuality, 3; of the Middle Ages, 2–13
queynte, 121, 183–84, 185

rape, 14, 18, 37–38, 40, 111, 125, 134, 140, 141–43, 145, 162, 166–67
Ratis Raving, 132, 133
Richard II, King, 20, 21n50, 81–82
Robinson, F. N. 179
romance, 42, 44, 51, 98–126, 206
Romans, 12, 195n39
Romeo and Juliet (Shakespeare), 101
Rouse, Robert, 19
Rushton, Cory, 52
Russell, Stephen, 112–13
Rypon, Robert, 90

Sadlek, Gregory, 193
sadomasochism, 37
Salmacis, 40–41
Samuel I and II, 70–72
satire, 66–69, 77–78, 87
Scala, Elizabeth, 63
Scanlon, Larry, 152
Schibanoff, Susan, 16, 18, 108n33
Scholes, Robert, 62
Schultz, James A., 70
Sedgwick, Eve, 130, 196–97
sensualitee, 176, 180, 195
sermon, 69, 90, 91, 96, 179
sexuality, history of, 4–5
Shahar, Shulamith, 137–38
Shakespeare, William, 124
Sidhu, Nicole Nolan, 141, 143n39
Sigal, Gale, 142
Sir Gawain and the Green Knight, 110

Sir Tryamour, 100
Smith, Warren, 57–58
squire, 136n25, 150, 151n49
Solomon, 184, 190, 191
Song of Songs, 171, 188
Stehling, Thomas, 43n35
Stretter, Robert, 85
Strohm, Paul, 21, 68, 202
Sturges, Robert, 20, 35n14, 104
sufferance, 47

Taylor, Mark, 48–49
Taylor, Paul, 22
Tennyson, Lord Alfred, 41–42
Teseida (Boccaccio), 84, 98, 102, 103, 112, 113
Thomas, Calvin, 3–4
Travis, Peter, 207
trede-foul, 211–14
Tripp, Raymond, 58
Troubadours, 33, 43

Uebel, Michael, 165

Venus, 112, 161, 180
virginity, 3, 7, 25, 98, 109, 112–14, 161–66, 190, 192, 196, 199, 200–1, 214

Wack, Mary, 115–16
Wallace, David, 89
Walsingham, Thomas, 81
Wetherbee, Winthrop, 102–3, 108
widowhood, 6, 25, 49n44, 98, 101, 109, 113–14
Wilder, Thornton, 30
Woods, Constance, 70
Woods, William, 112

yeomanry, 136
Yvain, ou Le Chevalier au Lion (Chrétien de Troyes), 35n14, 51

Zeikowitz, Richard, 67
Žižek, Slavoj, 27, 32–34, 37–40, 45, 114, 177–79, 181, 185–87, 194, 203

INTERVENTIONS: NEW STUDIES IN MEDIEVAL CULTURE
Ethan Knapp, Series Editor

Interventions: New Studies in Medieval Culture publishes theoretically informed work in medieval literary and cultural studies. We are interested both in studies of medieval culture and in work on the continuing importance of medieval tropes and topics in contemporary intellectual life.

Chaucer's (Anti-)Eroticisms and the Queer Middle Ages
TISON PUGH

Trading Tongues: Merchants, Multilingualism, and Medieval Literature
JONATHAN HSY

Translating Troy: Provincial Politics in Alliterative Romance
ALEX MUELLER

Fictions of Evidence: Witnessing, Literature, and Community in the Late Middle Ages
JAMIE K. TAYLOR

Answerable Style: The Idea of the Literary in Medieval England
EDITED BY FRANK GRADY AND ANDREW GALLOWAY

Scribal Authorship and the Writing of History in Medieval England
MATTHEW FISHER

Fashioning Change: The Trope of Clothing in High- and Late-Medieval England
ANDREA DENNY-BROWN

Form and Reform: Reading across the Fifteenth Century
EDITED BY SHANNON GAYK AND KATHLEEN TONRY

How to Make a Human: Animals and Violence in the Middle Ages
KARL STEEL

Revivalist Fantasy: Alliterative Verse and Nationalist Literary History
RANDY P. SCHIFF

Inventing Womanhood: Gender and Language in Later Middle English Writing
TARA WILLIAMS

Body Against Soul: Gender and Sowlehele *in Middle English Allegory*
MASHA RASKOLNIKOV

www.ingramcontent.com/pod-product-compliance
Lightning Source LLC
Chambersburg PA
CBHW021756230426
43669CB00006B/92